A MILTON ENCYCLOPEDIA

A MILTON ENCYCLOPEDIA

VOLUME 3 Ed–Hi

Edited by

William B. Hunter, Jr., *General Editor*

John T. Shawcross *and* John M. Steadman, *Co-Editors*

Purvis E. Boyette *and* Leonard Nathanson,
Associate Editors

Lewisburg
Bucknell University Press
London: Associated University Presses

© 1978 by Associated University Presses, Inc.

Associated University Presses, Inc.
Cranbury, New Jersey 08512

Associated University Presses
Magdalen House
136–148 Tooley Street
London SE1 2TT, England

A Milton encyclopedia.
Includes biblographical references.
1.   Milton, John, 1608–1674—Dictionaries, indexes, etc.
I. Hunter, William Bridges, 1915–
PR3580.M5   821'.4   75–21896
ISBN 0–8387–1836–1 (v. 3)

PRINTED IN THE UNITED STATES OF AMERICA

SYSTEM OF REFERENCES

Organization of the material in this Encyclopedia is alphabetical, with cross-referencing achieved in two ways. First, a subject may appear as an entry in the main alphabet, with citation of another entry under which that subject is treated. Second, subjects mentioned in an entry that are also discussed in other entries are marked with asterisks, with the exception of certain ones appearing too frequently for such treatment to be practical: the titles of all of Milton's works, each of which has a separate entry; the various named characters who appear in the works; and the names of Milton and his family, including his wife Mary Powell and her family, and his sister Anne Phillips and her family.

Titles of articles in serials have been removed, as have the places of publication of modern books. The titles of Milton's various works have been uniformly abbreviated in forms to be found in the front matter, as have references to the major modern editions and biographical works. All quotations of his writing are taken, unless otherwise indicated, from the complete edition published by the Columbia University Press (1931–1938).

SHORT FORMS USED
IN THIS ENCYCLOPEDIA

AdP	Ad Patrem
Animad	Animadversions upon the Remonstrant's Defense
Apol	An Apology
Arc	Arcades
Areop	Areopagitica
BrM	Bridgewater Manuscript
BN	Brief Notes upon a Late Sermon
Brit	The History of Britain
Bucer	The Judgement of Martin Bucer
CarEl	Carmina Elegiaca
Carrier 1, 2	On the University Carrier; Another on the Same
CB	Commonplace Book
CharLP	Character of the Long Parliament
Circum	Upon the Circumcision
CD	De Doctrina Christiana
CM	*The Works of John Milton* (New York : Columbia University Press, 1931–1938). 18 vols. The so-called Columbia Milton.
Colas	Colasterion
CivP	A Treatise of Civil Power
DDD	The Doctrine and Discipline of Divorce
1Def	Pro Populo Anglicano Defensio
2Def	Defensio Secunda
3Def	Pro Se Defensio
Educ	Of Education
Eff	In Effigiei ejus Sculptorem
Eikon	Eikonoklastes
El	Elegia
EpDam	Epitaphium Damonis
Epistol	Epistolarum Familiarium
EpWin	Epitaph on the Marchioness of Winchester
FInf	On the Death of a Fair Infant
French, *Life Records*	J. Milton French. *The Life Records of John Milton* (New Brunswick, N.J. : Rutgers University Press, 1949–1958). 5 vols.

Hire	Considerations Touching the Likeliest Means to Remove Hirelings from the Church
Hor	The Fifth Ode of Horace
Idea	De Idea Platonica
IlP	Il Penseroso
L'Al	L'Allegro
Literae	Literae Pseudo-Senatûs Anglicani Cromwellii
Lyc	Lycidas
Logic	Artis Logicae
Mask	A Mask (Comus)
Masson, *Life*	David Masson. *The Life of John Milton* (London, 1859–1880). 6 vols. plus Index.
May	Song : On May Morning
Mosc	A Brief History of Moscovia
Nat	On the Morning of Christ's Nativity
Naturam	Naturam non pati senium
NewF	On the New Forcers of Conscience
Parker, *Milton*	William Riley Parker. *Milton: A Biography* (Oxford : Clarendon Press, 1968). 2 vols.
Peace	Articles of Peace
PL	Paradise Lost
PR	Paradise Regained
PrelE	Of Prelatical Episcopacy
PresM	The Present Means
Prol	Prolusion
Ps	Psalm
QNov	In Quintum Novembris
RCG	Reason of Church Government
Ref	Of Reformation
Rous	Ad Ioannem Rousium
SA	Samson Agonistes
Shak	On Shakespeare
SolMus	At a Solemn Music
Sonn	Sonnet
StateP	State Papers
Tenure	The Tenure of Kings and Magistrates
Tetra	Tetrachordon
Time	Of Time
TM	Trinity Manuscript
TR	Of True Religion
Vac	At a Vacation Exercise
Variorum Commentary	*A Variorum Commentary on the Poems of John Milton.* 3 vols. to date (New York : Columbia University Press, 1970–).
Way	The Ready and Easy Way to Establish a Free Commonwealth
Yale *Prose*	*Complete Prose Works of John Milton.* 6 vols. to date. (New Haven, Conn. : Yale University Press, 1953–).

Wherever a reference is given by volume and page but without any other identification, *CM* (Columbia Milton) as given above is intended. Thus (11 : 21) refers to page 21 of volume 11 of that edition.

A MILTON ENCYCLOPEDIA

EDITIONS, POETRY. Most of Milton's poetry was published during his lifetime, and such printings establish the text with certain exceptions (*see* TEXTUAL PROBLEMS). Prior to the collected *Poems of Mr. John Milton, Both English and Latin, Compos'd at several times* (1645), a few individual items had appeared: *Shak* was printed in the Second Folio of Shakespeare's *Works* (1632) and in his *Poems* (1640); *Mask* received separate, anonymous publication in 1637 (probably early 1638); *Lyc* completed the English obsequies in *Justa Edovardo King naufrago* (1638); "Another on the same" [Hobson] was included in *A Banquet of Jests** (1640); and a private, limited printing of *EpDam* seems to be dated 1640. Apparently the Latin poems were also separately issued in 1645. The volume has been reproduced in facsimile a number of times. The second edition of the minor poems came out in 1673 as *Poems &c. Upon Several Occasions*; added to it was the second edition of *Educ*. Individual printings between these two editions include *Sonn* 13 in William and Henry Lawes's* *Choice Psalms Put Into Musick for Three Voices* (1648), "Another on the same" in *A Banquet of Jests* (1657), "On the University Carrier" and "Another on the same" in *Wit Restor'd* (1658), *Sonn* 17 in George Sykes's *The Life and Death of Sir Henry Vane* (1662); and *Shak* in Shakespeare's Third Folio (1664). The latter poem appeared also in the Fourth Folio of 1685. The only known minor poems not published in the 1673 collection are the two Latin fragments labeled "Carmina Elegiaca," found with *CB*, and four "political" sonnets, nos. 15, 16, 17, and 22, published in inaccurate versions by Edward Phillips in *Letters of State* (1694). The three major poems also appeared before Milton's death: *PL* in the ten-book version in 1667 (two issues), 1668 (two issues, the second of which added prefatorily the note on the Verse and the Arguments), and 1669 (two issues), and in the revised twelve-book version with arguments dispersed in 1674; *PR* and *SA* together in 1671.

The remaining years of the seventeenth century saw increased awareness of Milton's poetic work, including various editions, translations, and adaptations. Translations* include Latin renditions of *PL, PR, SA, Mask,* and *Lyc,* and German versions of *PL*. Adaptations* begin with operatic and rhymed renditions of *PL*. Such work continued in the ensuing years. The minor poems, given in revised order, were published by Jacob Tonson* in 1695; at times this volume is added to editions of the major poems, with a title page calling it *Poetical Works*. Five Latin poems were included in *Examen Poeticum Duplex,* 1698: "Elegia septima," pp. 194–98; "Elegia prima," pp. 199–203; "Elegia sexta," pp. 204–8; "Epitaphium Damonis," pp. 209–19; and "In Inventorem Bombardicam," p. 55 of the second pagination. The second edition of *PL* was reissued in 1675 (new title page only). The third edition came out in 1678; the very important fourth in 1688; the fifth in a publication by Richard Bentley* and Jacob Tonson in 1691 and in a reissue by Tonson alone in 1692; another "fourth" edition by R. E. for Jacob Tonson in 1693; and the sixth in 1695. The fourth edition of *PL* was sponsored by various important people, including John, Lord Somers, who is often credited as the main force behind the edition. This edition greatly improved Milton's reputation and aided in making his work, particularly his epic, the major influence in the eighteenth century that it became. There were three separate issues, two of which represent Tonson's first association with Milton's texts. The edition included Robert White's portrait*, drawn from William Faithorne's* work for the 1670 *Brit*, with John Dryden's* epigram engraved beneath, and John Baptista de Medina's* illustrations*. These were engraved by M. Burgess, except for that for Book 4, executed by B. Lens and engraved by P. P. Bouche. The text, portrait with epigram, and illustrations appear in many of the following editions of the earlier eighteenth century. At times this edition of *PL* is combined with the 1688 printing of *PR* and *SA*, which was republished from the second, often textually careless, edition of 1680. The so-called fourth edition of 1693 is a reissue of the fifth edition, first printing, of 1691. The 1695 edition of *PL* appears by itself, in combination with the 1688 edition of *PR* and *SA*, and in combination with a new 1695 edition of the latter poems, probably demanded when the earlier printing had finally been used up. Separated bindings of these two poems probably do not represent separate issues. The 1695 edition of *PL* at times includes a "Table" of descriptions, similes, and speeches, and "Annotations on Each Book" (called "Explanatory Notes" on the title page) by P[atrick] H[ume]*. Without evidence some people have assumed that Hume was also responsible for the Table. Some copies of the 1695 edition give neither of these items, some give one or the other or both. *Poetical Works*, 1695, combines all or some of the 1695 poetic volumes in varying arrangements. The sixth edition, however, was being prepared and was apparently ready by March 1692, for a note in Peter Motteux's *The Gentleman's Journal: or The Monthly Miscellany* for that date (1 : 9) has a

notice that can refer only to Hume's work : "*Milton's Paradise Lost* is Reprinting, with large Notes, to explain the less obvious and common Words, Phrases, and Passages of that most heavenly Poem." And to repeat, the further seventeenth-century editions of *PR* and *SA* are 1680, 1688, and 1695. Separate bindings of the two poems, despite their separate signatures, gatherings, and pagination, are apparently not original.

After 1700 Milton's poetic works were easily available in England in numerous editions and reissues as well as in the United States and in translations throughout the world. Glanced at here will be important or otherwise noteworthy editions.

Tonson's printing of *PL* continued in 1705, 1707, and 1711; these editions included Medina's illustrations. The tenth edition of 1719 reprinted Addison's* papers from *The Spectator* and was illustrated by George Vertue's engraving of the Faithorne portrait, with Dryden's epigram beneath, and drawings by Francis Hayman, and it included the index of descriptions, etc. This became the standard Tonson edition (although not all items, like *Spectator* papers, were always included), but certain ones, like Tickell's, Fenton's, Bentley's, and Newton's, did not follow this standard. Usually from 1720 on the epic and the remaining poems were published together (often in two volumes) as *Poetical Works* (e.g., in 1720, 1721, 1731, 1741, 1743, etc.). At times such volumes were also published separately as if they were separate editions of *PL* or of *PR* et al., individually produced. The illustrations were often reengraved by various hands. *PR, SA,* and the Minor Poems reappeared in 1707 as the fifth edition and in 1713 again as the fifth edition. The latter printing includes *Educ* and establishes the standard for most later editions. The 1713 volume gives the 1645 portrait and the Greek lines to its executor as frontispiece; there are nine illustrations (sometimes some are missing) probably engraved by Pigné, whose name appears on one of them. These depict Christ's Triumph over Satan, Christ's Baptism, Christ at the Temple, Christ and Satan in the Wilderness, The Son Administered by Angels; Samson Bringing down the Pillars; L'Allegro; Il Penseroso; Shakespeare. One copy at least omits the usual frontispiece, employs the illustration for Book 1 of *PR* as frontispiece, and a cancel and Medina's drawing for Book 1 of *PL* appears as replacement.

The 1720 *Poetical Works* in two volumes is known as Thomas Tickell's edition. It is elaborately produced and beautifully published. Volume 1 has Addison's papers and the Index to *PL*, Vertue's portrait as frontispiece, "Milton Inspired by the Muse" by Louis Chéron, engraved by G. van der Gucht, on the title page, and head and end pieces and a decorated initial for each book of *PL* by Sir James Thornhill, engraved by van der Gucht, or by Louis Chéron, engraved by C. du Bosc. Volume two includes *Educ* and the poem on Salmasius* in both Latin and English, a different engraving on the title page, and head and tail pieces and a decorated initial for each book of *PR* and for *Lyc*, first of the minor poems, executed by Thornhill, engraved by van der Gucht or Samuel Gribelin, Jr. Tonson's monopoly on Milton's texts was challenged from 1721 onward when the 1713 *PR* volume was reissued by W. Taylor, who still called it the fifth edition. There is a cancel of the 1713 title page, and separate title pages for the poems read 1713. In 1724 the Dublin publisher George Grierson brought out *PL* and *PR* (only); the volume has a prefatory note, separate title pages for the two poems, separate pagination but continuous signatures, and the (unpaged) Index to *PL*. The title page for *PL* lists it as the eleventh edition (correct), and that for *PR* lists it as the seventh edition (correct if the 1721 reissue is discounted). Other publishers continued to vie with the Tonsons for sales throughout the century.

Elijah Fenton's* edition of *PL* appeared in 1725, the twelfth edition, as the title page notes. The account of Milton's life, advertised on the title page, acts as a preface, followed by a postscript on textual changes between the first two editions. These items generally are reprinted in succeeding general (or standard) editions both from the Tonson press and from others. At times Fenton's "Life" is abbreviated or the source for a brief biographical (rather than critical) introduction. Richard Bentley's* notorious edition of the epic came out in January 1732 with its textual revisions indicated in margins and arguments for such revisions in the footnotes. A seven-page preface details his hypothesis that an editor intervened between Milton's text and its printed version, altering Milton's language, imagery, and prosody, and interpolating not only words but even passages. The main publisher was still Jacob Tonson.

Tonson's edition of *PL* in 1739 gives as a frontispiece an engraving of Milton's bust in Westminster Abbey by James Smith. Although a standard reprinting of *PL* by Tonson came out in 1741, W. Innys and D. Brown also produced an edition of the epic, but theirs included "A Verbal Index to Milton's *Paradise Lost*" by Thomas Coxeter. The first appearance of Thomas Osborne's often reprinted edition of *PL* and some of the prose was 1745. The minor poems were printed in Glasgow by Robert Foulis in 1747, and a revised text of *PL* by John Hawkey came out in Dublin in the same year (S. Powell, publisher). "The Most Remarkable Various Readings and Emendations" are given on pp. [395–400]. Grierson's reissue of the two epics in 1748 (Dublin) was accompanied by *SA, Lyc, L'Al, IlP, Arc, Mask*, and *Educ*. The signatures are made continuous with those of *PR*. A full collection of the poems without the major epic and including *Educ* finally was printed in Dublin in 1748 as the ninth edition, published for F. Risk, G. and A. Ewing, and W. Smith. Foulis published *PL* in Glasgow in 1752 as did Robert Urie, and a two-volume *Poetical Works* appeared in Edinburgh in the same year.

The major publication of the poetical texts in midcentury was that by Thomas Newton* (again through the Tonson firm), PL being given a two-volume folio production in 1749 and the remainder of the poems a corresponding one-volume printing in 1752. These are illustrated variorum editions with notes collected from published and manuscript sources as well as Newton's own commentaries. Addison's critique of PL, a postscript on William Lauder's* charges of plagiarism, the usual index, and the verbal index are included in the PL volumes, and the verses to Queen Christina*, plans and subjects from the TM, and a word index to the minor poems appear in the 1752 volume. The octavo two-volume editions of 1750 and 1753 respectively were frequently reissued with new title pages (thus, they were not truly new "editions"). The printings of the poems by John Baskerville, frequently sought by collectors, in two separate volumes in 1758, 1759, and 1760 (in Birmingham for Jacob and Richard Tonson) are all versions of one printing; these volumes (i.e., the 1758 PL, the 1758 PR, the 1759 PL, etc.) show reissues unto themselves (e.g., the first issue of the 1758 PL has six additional subscribers on p. [xxiv] and three cancels in two states [in T8, X6, Z5, or in T7, X7, Z6]; the second issue has seven additional subscribers and no cancels). Of great significance was "The Life of Milton" that Newton wrote for the first volume of PL. It uses all the previous lives, makes corrections, and at times errs in its inferences. It was reproduced in further editions of Newton's texts or was the source for some abbreviated versions. At times, however, Newton's texts are reproduced but the life is Fenton's or one drawn from Fenton's.

The first edition of the poetry in the United States (none being produced in the Colonies, which relied on imported English editions) was Paradise Lost. A Poem, in Twelve Books. The author John Milton. With the Life of Milton. By Thomas Newton, D.D. (Philadelphia: Robert Bell, 1777), but the title is misleading. It is a two-volume edition, printed as if they were separate volumes, with the usual listing of PR, SA, and Poems on Several Occasions on the second title page. But this is also misleading. Volume one includes Vertue's portrait with Dryden's epigram, Marvell's* poem, a very brief biographical essay (not Newton's "Life"), the arguments grouped before the poem and also dispersed throughout before their respective books, and only the first eleven books of PL. Volume two has Moseley's 1645 "Foreword," a title page for the poems, PL 12, the Index to PL, a form of Fenton's "Life," various English poems (but they are incomplete and oddly arranged), PR, SA, and Mask with Lawes's letter. PL with a life appeared also from Kilmarnock in 1785 and from Philadelphia in 1787 (two vols.), in 1788, and in 1791. PR and various minor poems or these plus PL in a two-volume set were also published in Philadelphia in 1791; there were three different editions, not always with the same minor poems. A similar edition came from Springfield, Massachusetts, in 1794, and from Boston in 1796.

Various other important editions of PL or the poetical works in the last half of the eighteenth century should be mentioned. Book 1 was edited by John Callander for Robert and Andrew Foulis in Glasgow, but his notes are plagiarized from Patrick Hume's 1695 annotations. John Marchant collected etymological, critical, classical, and explanatory notes, which he incorporated into a variorum edition of the epic in 1751. Here should be mentioned two collections of annotations that are little known to the twentieth century: James Paterson's A Complete Commentary, with Etymological, Explanatory, Critical and Classical Notes on Paradise Lost (1744) and William Dodd's A Familiar Explanation of the Poetical Works of Milton (1762), which is for the most part "Explanatory Notes on the Poetical Works of Milton, Alphabetically Digested." In a 1765 Dublin edition of PL, which also has a "Glossary, explaining the Antiquated and difficult Words used in this Work" [pp. 347–70], is printed the "Sonnet in a Church Window," written by Pope* and attributed to Milton as a hoax. An edition of *PL* in 1775, two volumes (the second includes *PR*), gives the "historical, philosophical, and explanatory notes. Translated from the French of the learned Raymond de St. Maur." The edition of Milton by Samuel Johnson* (vols. 3–5 of *The Works of the English Poets*) in 1779 brought forth the famous "Life" (Vol. 60 of the *Works*; Vol. 2 of the *Prefaces, Biographical and Critical*). Vols. 29–32 of John Bell's edition of *The Poets of Great Britain Complete From Chaucer to Churchill* (Edinburgh, 1779) reprint the poems of Milton. Noteworthy are engraved medallions in each volume : Vol. 1, Milton by Cook and Satan (with two lines of poetry) by Mortimer and engraved by Hall; Vol. 2, Eve (with one line of poetry) by Mortimer and engraved by Grignion; Vol. 3, Samson by Mortimer and engraved by Hall; Vol. 4, Milton being inspired (with one line of poetry) by Mortimer and engraved by Grignion. There was a two-volume English edition of *PL, PR, Lyc, L'Al*, and *IlP* in Paris in 1780.

A major work of scholarship and criticism is Thomas Warton's* edition of the *Poems Upon Several Occasions* in 1785. It offers Warton's important introductions and notes, and an Appendix to the Notes on *Mask*, consisting of "Corrections and Supplemental Observations," "Original Various Readings [from *TM*]," and "A List of Editions." The second edition in 1791 added the documents connected with Milton's nuncupative will* and Charles Burney's "Remarks on the Greek Verses of Milton," pp. 593–605. Indicative of the kind of treatment Milton's text underwent in the eighteenth century (and again in the twentieth) are Capel Lofft's editions of Book 1 (1792) and then Books 1 and 2 (1793) : *Paradise Lost. A Poem in Twelve Books. The Author John Milton. Printed from the First and Second Editions Collated. The Original System of Orthography Restored; the Punctuation Corrected and Extended. With Various Readings: and Notes;*

Chiefly Rhythmical (Bury St. Edmund's). John Gillies's edition of the epic (1793) is "Illustrated with Texts of Scripture" and also notes and allusions to Greek and Latin classics. William Hayley's* octavo edition of the *Poetical Works* came out in three volumes (1794, 1795, 1797) from W. Bulmer and Co., for John and Josiah Boydell, and George Nicol. Volume one prints George Romney's painting of Milton and his daughters, Hayley's "Life" (important for the Romantic period for its balance to Johnson's views and its emphasis on *PR*), and Books 1–6 of *PL*. Volume two gives Books 7–12 of *PL* and *PR;* volume three, *SA* and the remaining poems. The edition is illustrated. What appears to be a special printing of Hayley's edition as a large folio edition in eight volumes is found in the New York Public Library. Each volume, which is extra-illustrated, is dated 1794, but each was put together during the first thirty years or so of the nineteenth century, as the illustrations attest. The contents are: I, "Life," Part 1; II, "Life," Part 2; III, *PL* 1–4; IV, *PL* 5–8; V, *PL* 9–12; VI, *PR;* VII, *SA* and most English poems; VIII, *Mask, Lyc*, and the Latin poems. The illustrations include John Martin's for *PL* (1826) and portraits of historical or literary figures not necessarily associated with Milton and views of places and the like of biographical interest. A 1796 edition of *PL* in two volumes, with notes selected from Newton and gathered at the end, prints an abridged version of Johnson's "Life" and "Observations on Language and Versification" from Johnson's *Rambler* papers (Nos. 86 [January 12, 1751], 88 [January 19], 90 [January 26], and 94 [February 9]). And John Evans's edition of the epic (1799), which contains his own sketch of Milton's life and writings, also offers Johnson's criticism of the poem taken from his "Life of Milton."

L'Al and *IlP, Mask, PR*, and *SA* also enjoyed separate publications in the eighteenth century, and various poems appeared in poetic collections or scholarly volumes of various types. Robert Foulis of Glasgow published the companion poems in 1751, and George Friedrich Handel's settings were frequently printed, sometimes with just the words, sometimes just the music, sometimes with both (*see* ADAPTATIONS, MUSICAL). Perhaps because John Dalton's* version of *Comus*, for which Thomas Arne* wrote music, and later George Colman's* version of Dalton were so popular and so frequently published, Milton's original *Mask* was published in Glasgow again by Robert Foulis in 1747. No further printing of it occurred until Henry John Todd's* scholarly edition from Canterbury in 1798. This presents a discussion of Ludlow Castle, a discussion of the Bridgewater family*, remarks on Henry Lawes, a discussion of the sources of *Mask*, original readings from *TM*, the Ashbridge (i.e., Bridgewater) MS, and a list of editions of *Mask* (some of these were taken from Warton's edition of the minor poems). Another edition of the original masque appeared the next year from London; added to it are *L'Al* and *IlP* and the origin of the poem. It is illustrated and includes an account of Ludlow Castle (as in Todd's edition) and "General Opinions of Various Critics Concerning the Beauties and the Faults of 'Comus' " (pp. 91–104). *PR* was finally given separate publication in 1779 by Topkis and Burney (London). Prior to this, it had appeared only with *SA*, then with all or various poems other than *PL*, and then with *PL*. There had been, however, in 1771, a prose adaptation called *The Recovery of Man*, perhaps by George Graham. Further separate editions of the brief epic were one from Philadelphia in 1790, with an epigraph from Addison's "An Account of the Greatest English Poets," one from Alnwick in 1793, and the important scholarly edition by Charles Dunster* (1750–1816) in 1795. This has variorum notes, as well as some by Dunster and Robert Thyer (1709–1781), which had not been previously published. Separate editions of *SA*, apparently not generally known, occur in 1796 (with a reissue in 1797) and in 1797. It was "Printed for,

and Under the Direction of, George Cawthorn, British Library, Strand" (London, 1796), and gives Fenton's "Life," "The Character of *Samson Agonistes*," a frontispiece of Samson and Dalila (with two lines of poetry) by Thomas Stothard, engraved by Heath, and an illustration of Samson in chains (with two lines of poetry) by Graham, engraved by Audinet, facing p. 13. This was reissued in 1797 in vol. 34 of Bell's *British Theatre*. It was reprinted for Cawthorn's *British Library* in 1797.

Works included in poetic collections that should be mentioned (there are many more as well as selections in things like "Beauties from Milton *et al.*") are *Hor* in a collection of translations of the odes (and satires) by various hands in 1715 and again in 1730; *L'Al*, *IlP*, and *Lyc*, inserted by Fenton into John Dryden's *Miscellanies*, Ed. 4 (1716; there are further editions); the companion's poems in Oliver Goldsmith's *The Beauties of English Poetry* (1767; there are further editions); and "Lycidas" in *The Lady's Poetical Magazine, or Beauties of British Poetry* 2 (1781): 410–16, with an illustration by Thomas Stothard, engraved by Angus. Works included in representative other kinds of volumes (there are more examples) are:

1) *Idea*, in Gabriel John's [i.e., Thomas D'Urfey's] *An Essay Towards the Theory of the Intelligible World. Intuitively Considered. Printed in the year one thousand seven hunderd &c.* [London?, 1715?], pp. 17–18. There is no acknowledgment to Milton. This spoofing volume is listed under 1700 in Wing's *Short Title Catalogue*, but Warton in 1791, p. 516, lists the reprint of the poem as of 1715.

2) *Sonn* 13, printed in Fenton's edition of Edmund Waller's *Works* (1729; there are further editions), pp. lvi–lvii.

3) *May*, in *The Museum: or, The Literary and Historical Register* (London, 1746), no. 6, June 7, p. 217.

4) *Shak*, in David Garrick's *An Ode Upon Dedicating a Building, and Erecting a Statue, To Shakespeare, at Stratford upon Avon* (1769), pp. 20–21.

5) *L'Al* (pp. 261–66), *IlP* (pp. 266–71), *PL* 5. 153–208 (pp. 302–4), and *PL* 4. 32–113 (pp. 304–7), in William Enfield's *The Speaker,* to which is prefixed *An Essay on Elocution* (1774; there are further editions).

6) *Sonn* 13 and 20, in Sir John Hawkins's *A General History of the Science and Practice of Music* (1776), 1 : xxvii–xxviii. Included also are "Sweet Echo" from the Lawes MS (4 : 53–54) and the Morning Hymn, *PL* 5. 153–208 (5. 191–93).

7) *Sonn* 13, in *Psalmody for a Single Voice. By Henry Lawes* (York?, 1789), on verso preceding p. [i].

In addition a number of excerpts, primarily from *PL,* are found in various publications and even odd places.

The nineteenth and twentieth centuries have seen a great number of editions of Milton's poetry in various combinations and formats. Here will be cited only a few that exhibit special features for a study of Milton and his works. The variora editions of the poetical works by Todd* in 1801, 1809, 1826, and 1842, differ in contents, but each presents introductions and notes from prior editions and commentators. The edition of 1801 includes Todd's *Some Account of the Life of Milton,* also published separately, and that of 1809 adds a Verbal Index. William Cowper's* notes on *PL* (never completed) and translations of the foreign-language poems and tributes were published by William Hayley (Chichester, 1810). John Martin's *Twenty-four Copper Engravings of Paradise Lost* appeared in 1826 and were included in editions of the poem (or the works) from 1827 onward. *The Complete Poetical Works of John Milton, with Explanatory Notes and a Life of the Author, by the Rev. H. Stebbing* (1839; there are many further editions) also reprinted William Ellery Channing's* "Essay on the Poetical Genius of Milton," which raised the issue of Milton's alleged Arianism* and which refuted much of Dr. Johnson's criticism of the man and his work. Important because it contains new biographical

material such as state letters is John Mitford's *The Works of John Milton in Verse and Prose* (1841), eight vols., although the prose is not really complete. The edition was often reissued or reprinted, and became the source of a number of popular editions of the verse in England and the United States.

The Poetical Works of John Milton with a Memoir and Seven Embellishments by Fuseli, Westall, and Martin was printed in 1844 (and reissued); and Charles Dexter Cleveland's edition of the English poems (called, however, poetical works [Philadelphia, 1853]), includes introductions to the individual poems, notes critical and explanatory, an index to the subjects of *PL,* and the first version of his concordance to the poems. It has illustrations by R. Westall, J. M. W. Turner, and William Harvey. The notes are significant in Thomas Keightley's two-volume edition of the poems in 1859; and the notes by H. G. Bohn are found in a two-volume printing of the poetical works (1861) with a memoir and critical remarks by James Montgomery and 120 engravings from Harvey's drawings. R. C. Browne's annotations of the English poems first appeared from Oxford in 1866, and this edition was revised with etymological notes by Henry Bradley in 1894. Gustave Doré's well known illustrations of *PL* will be found in R. Vaughan's edition with a life and notes in 1866. Perhaps the various engravings by William Blake*, published in numerous editions in the nineteenth century, might best be referred to in the Nonesuch Press edition of *Poems in English by John Milton* (1926), two vols. In 1867 a reprinting of Sir Edward Brydges's popular edition of the poetical works, first published in 1835, has engravings based upon Martin's and Turner's work. Milton's biographer David Masson's* three-volume edition of 1874 (with many further printings) is still indispensable because of its notes and an essay on Milton's language and punctuation. The Cambridge Milton for Schools, edited by A. W.

Verity* in ten volumes, came out in 1891–1896, with revisions of *PL* up to 1910. Unfortunately, not all the poems are treated by Verity, whose introductions and notes should still be consulted by serious students of Milton. The popular Cambridge (Boston) edition of the poems by William Vaughan Moody first appeared in 1899; there are new translations of the foreign language poems and critical prefaces and notes to individual poems. William Aldis Wright's* facsimile of *TM* was also printed in 1899.

The first attempt to arrange the poems chronologically is H. J. C. Grierson's* two-volume 1925 edition, and this is followed by Merritt Y. Hughes's* edition of the poems other than *PL* in 1937 (his edition of the epic had appeared two years before) and his *Complete Poems and Major Prose* (1957), and by John T. Shawcross in 1963, revised 1971. Hughes's edition is a major contribution to a study of Milton because of the introductions and notes, and Shawcross's presents texts revised largely through a study of the manuscripts. Attempts to produce a text of the poems that more closely accords with Milton's alleged spelling (and pointing) practices are Helen Darbishire's* two-volume edition (Oxford, 1952–1955) and B. A. Wright's new Everyman's edition (1956). An edition of the *Poems of Mr. John Milton: The 1645 Edition with Essays in Analysis* (1951, 1957, 1968) by Cleanth Brooks and John E. Hardy has provocative original essays. The new Cambridge edition of the poetical works by Douglas Bush (1965) has new introductions and notes. And the summary and extension of scholarship on the poems found in Alastair Fowler's and John Carey's edition of 1969 is the best source for a survey of the most recent approaches to the poems (e.g., the structural, the numerological, the mythological, etc.).

Three indispensable research tools are the edition of the poems in *CM*, under the general editorship of Frank Allen Patterson (1931, two vols. in four, i.e., Vols. 1 and 2 of *The Works*); Harris F.

Fletcher's *John Milton's Complete Poetical Works, Reproduced in Photographic Facsimile* (1943–1948; four vols.); and the current Variorum Commentary (1969–). The Fletcher volumes do not include facsimiles of *CarEl* or of the Lawes MS of the songs for *Mask* or any of the incidental scribal versions found in miscellanies (e.g., *EpWin* in BM MS, Sloane 1446, ff. 37b–38). Published to date in the Variorum Commentary are Volume 1, covering the foreign-language poems, edited by Douglas Bush, J. E. Shaw, and A. Barlett Giamatti, and Volume 2 (in three parts), covering the minor English poems, edited by A. S. P. Woodhouse* and Douglas Bush. In addition Helen Darbishire's edition of *The Manuscript of Paradise Lost Book I* (Oxford, 1931) should be consulted for its introduction, although the manuscript is available in Fletcher's facsimile.

Among the number of editions of separate poems or selections may also be mentioned, first, Mark Pattison's *The Sonnets of John Milton* (1883), chronologically arranged and with translations of the Italian poems by John Langhorne and William Cowper; John S. Smart's* edition of the sonnets (Glasgow, 1921; rptd., Oxford, 1966), with its important biographical material; and E. A. J. Honigmann's volume (1966), which attempts a coverage of scholarship on the sonnets since Smart's edition. Next may be listed Walter MacKellar's edition of the Latin poems with introduction, notes, and new translations (New Haven, Conn., 1930); C. A. Patrides's *Milton's Lycidas: The Tradition and the Poem* (1961); with reprints of a number of twentieth-century articles on the poem, and Scott Elledge's *Milton's Lycidas: Edited to Serve as an Introduction to Criticism* (1966), with a retrospective reprinting of the pastoral* elegy and similar genres, materials pertinent to the period when the poem was written, and selected commentaries from the eighteenth through the twentieth centuries; and H. M. Percival's edition of *SA* (1890; 1916), with introduction, notes, and a study of the diction, and Ralph Hone's *John Milton's Samson Agonistes: The Poem and Materials for Analysis* (San Francisco, 1966), consisting of the text, sources, and selected criticism. And finally, important works on *Mask* may be cited : *Milton's Comus, Annotated with a Glossary and Notes Grammatical and Explanatory for the Use of Students, with Three Introductory Essays Upon the Masque Proper and upon the Origin and History of the Poem* (1878), ed. B. M. and F. D. Rankin; Sir Frederick Bridge's edition (1908) with Lawes's music as well as others'; an edition of the *BrM* in 1910 with a memoir by Lady Alex Egerton; E. H. Visiak's edition with Hubert J. Foss's "The Airs of Five Songs Reprinted from the Composer's Autograph Manuscript" appended (1937; also 1954, 1955); and John S. Diekhoff's reprinting of essays on the poem along with *BrM* and the Lawes songs (1968). [JTS]

EDITIONS, PROSE. Some of Milton's prose works have not reappeared in single editions since their original issue, and the relatively few collected editions have satisfied whatever demand there has been for the prose, with the obvious exceptions of *Educ* and *Areop.* The reissue of unsold copies of *Apol* and *RCG* together in 1654 and booksellers' catalogues listing other works for sale during the seventeenth century indicate that supply often outstripped demand. This article first cites editions of the prose after the original issue and during Milton's lifetime, then discusses works printed separately or at least not in collections, and finally considers important collected editions. Works enjoying more than one edition during Milton's lifetime were :

The Doctrine and Discipline of Divorce, augmented from 48 pages in 1643 to 88 pages (including a preface) in 1644, was republished in 1645 (Ed. 3) and pirated also in 1645 (Ed. 4). The infamy attached to "divorcers" during these years apparently accounts for these reprintings, although Milton's

three other divorce* tracts did not fare well in sales.

A second edition of *Of Education* was included in the second edition of the minor poems in 1673, setting a pattern for the eighteenth century.

The Tenure of Kings and Magistrates and *Eikonoklastes* were each republished with additions within a year. The additions are not really significant, clarifying statements here and there and, in the case of *Tenure*, appending corroborative opinion from a variety of "authorities." The volumes were tied to the political events of 1649–1650 and soon lost direct importance, although the highly charged attitudes toward Charles I's* execution and the controversies over *Eikon Basilike** kept *Eikon* before the public at least nominally. Because of the significant French relationships of the Royalist group, *Eikon* was ordered translated into French by the Council of State*. The translation of the second edition by John Dury* was published in London in 1652. Whether other continental translations were made (as is reported) is uncertain.

Defensio prima, because of its controversial nature, its defense of the Parliamentarian actions and government, and its importance for continental politics, was frequently republished both in England and on the Continent, often in pirated editions. There were eleven editions in 1651 (one issue bearing the date 1650), with three variant issues recorded for the first and two for the fourth, two editions in 1652 in the United Provinces, and an altered edition with an important personal postscript in London in 1658. One of the Dutch 1651 editions is a translation into Dutch. In addition, a reissue of the third edition was offered along with Salmasius's* *Defensio Regia, Pro Carolo I,* in Paris in 1651; it contains a preface. Some of these editions include the long index; some do not. This was certainly the most widely read of Milton's prose works during his lifetime, and it elicited the most contemporary comment and rebuttal of all his works.

John Phillips's *Responsio Ad Apologiam Anonymi** had four separate editions in the wake of the Salmasian controversy, the second, third, and fourth all being produced in 1652 in Amsterdam.

Defensio secunda carried on the infighting among adherents of the Cromwellian government and the Royalist factions, and thus a pirated edition appeared as if printed in London in 1654 from the press of Thomas Newcomb, the printer of the original edition. Probably, however, the printer was Adrian Vlacq* and the place of publication The Hague. There were three further pirated editions all by Vlacq from The Hague in 1654, the first of which has a preface to the reader by Vlacq. The last two of these pirated editions are added to Alexander More's* *Fides Publica* with a foreword by "Georgius Crantzius" along with Vlacq's preface.

Defensio pro Se, like the preceding *Defenses,* was immediately pirated for a continental audience, again by Vlacq at The Hague. The three *Defenses* and Phillips's *Responsio* were important during the early to middle 1650s, but, except briefly for *1Def* as noted later, they declined sharply in popularity as their immediate occasions for writing became history, even through the present day.

Milton's edition of *The Cabinet-Council** reappeared in 1661 as *Aphorisms of State,* without Milton's name on the title page and without his preface (since Milton was anathema for the early Restoration period).

The Ready and Easy Way To Establish a Free Commonwealth was immediately revised and augmented, and given a second edition within a month, changing from an 18-page printing in quarto to a 108-page printing in duodecimo. Though it had no influence on the Restoration settlement as it intended, it did bring forth a number of reactions and these may help account for Milton's immediate revision and republication of the tract.

Reflecting changed scholarly concerns and the discovery of Anglo-Saxon* records important to a knowledge of early British history, *The History of Britain* enjoyed reissue and further edition before and after Milton's death. In fact, Milton became for the end of the seventeenth century and the beginning of the eighteenth century an authority on early British history, even though he had not the advantage of the discoveries of early historical documents. The second issue of the first edition appeared a year after the first in 1671, and the second edition also appeared in two issues, the first in 1677, the second in 1678 (this latter advertising itself as "The second Edition"). These issues and editions all contain the Index.

Artis Logicae appeared in two issues, 1672 and 1673, perhaps because it had not sold well; the second issue has a totally new title page and advertises a new bookseller.

After Milton's death individual editions of the prose works (separate or in some kind of non-Miltonic collection) depends generally upon their significance for a contemporary controversy* (often with his work being abbreviated or paraphrased), upon contemporary concerns (such as British history, theories of education, censorship), and upon twentieth-century scholarly interests; in addition, of course, are those items published for the first time posthumously. *Ref* was given a scholarly edition with introduction and notes by Will T. Hale in 1916; a Japanese translation by Jun Harada, with introduction and notes, was published in 1972. A reprint of *Animad* appeared in 1919 from the press of Norman McLean, Cambridge. *DDD* has been translated into German by Franz von Holtzendorff (Berlin, 1855) and into Japanese by Tetsusaburo Nishiyama (Tokyo, 1961).

As indicated before, *Educ* was frequently before the eighteenth-century reading public in editions of *PR, SA,* and the minor poems, but there were also separate editions since educational theory had become so important and was to continue to be so important in the succeeding years. The tractate was added to a translation of Tannequi Lefevre's *A Compendious Way of Teaching Ancient and Modern Languages* (1723; frequently reprinted); it was published as *A Tractate of Education* by R. Urie and Co. (Glasgow, 1746), with "Four Papers, On the same Subject, From the Spectator"; it appears as *An Essay on Education* from the press of Charles Corbett in 1751; and it is included in R. Wynne's *Essays on Education by Milton, Locke, and the Authors of the Spectator* (1751). Parker notes an edition from 1753 but gives no other information; if it exists, it is not listed elsewhere. Francis Blackburne appended the pamphlet and *Areop* to his *Remarks on Johnson's Life of Milton* (1780). During the nineteenth and twentieth centuries publication has been quite frequent, but here might be mentioned a few important or at least historically important editions. *Milton's Treatise on Education. To Master Samuel Hartlib* was first published in the United States in Boston by the Directors of the Old South Work in 1800. *Milton's Plan of Education, in His Letter to Hartlib (Now Very Scarce), with the Plan of the Edinburgh Institution Founded Thereon,* by William Scott, was printed in Edinburgh in 1819 and reprinted in the (London) *Pamphleteer* 17 (1820): [121]–56. The often reprinted and influential Henry Barnard's discussion and text ("Milton's Views on Education") first appeared in *Barnard's American Journal of Education* in 1856. A scholarly edition, with some excerpts from other works, was produced by Oliver M. Ainsworth in 1928.

The tractate was translated into Dutch by Pieter le Clercq (published in George Savile's *New Year's Gift* [*Nieuwjaaregift aan de Jufferschap*], n.p., n.d.); into French as "Lettre de Milton où il propose une nouvelle manière d'élever la jeunesse d'Angleterre" by J. B. Le Blanc, in Claud de Nonney de Fontenai's *Lettres sur l'éducation des princes* (Edinburgh, 1746); into German by J. Zelle as "Remarks on and Translation of Milton's Treatise *Of Education*" in *Beilage zum Programm des Königl. und Stadt-Gymnasium* (1858), with a preface in English; again into German by Hermann Ullrich as "Uber Erziehung" in *Neue Jahrbücher für Philologie und Pädagogik,* 2 (1890): 81–105; and yet again into German by Joseph Reber, along with the English text, in *Beilage zum Programm der Löheren weiblichen Bildungs- anstalt zu Aschaffenburg* (1893); into French again by Paul Chauvel (Paris, 1909); into Spanish by Natalia Corsío (Madrid, 1919); and into Japanese by Jun Harada (Tokyo, 1972). John W. Good notes two German translations, apparently printed with German editions of the poetry in 1752 and 1781 (see *Studies in the Milton Tradition* [1915]), but he seems to be in error.

Although the twentieth century would like to think *Areop* a well-known and popular work, it was not so until the nineteenth century. There is an adaptation of part of the tract by Charles Blount in *A Just Vindication of Learning: Or, An Humble Address to the High Court of Parliament in Behalf of the Liberty of the Press* (1679), published as part of the opposition to governmental controls during the last quarter of the century. Blount's paraphrase is only eighteen pages long and its source is not indicated, although Milton is discussed in the preface. (Blount's use of *Areop* was noted, however, by Thomas Birch* in *A General Dictionary, Historical and Critical* [1735], ed. John Peter Bernard, Birch, and John Lockman; see 3 : 401n). *A Just Vindication* was reprinted in the *Harleian Miscellany* (Osborne edition), 6 (1745); (Dutton edition), 8 (1810); (White, Murray, and Hardy edition), 6 (1810). There was apparently no awareness that Blount was paraphrasing *Areop*. Blount also drew on the pamphlet for ideas and language in *Reasons Humbly Offered for the*

Liberty of Unlicens'd Printing (1693); both his tracts were reprinted in *The Miscellaneous Works of Charles Blount Esq.* (1695). Further, William Dunton also adapted *Areop* in *Jus Caesaris et Ecclesiae vere dictae* (1681), as "An Apology for the Liberty of the Press," added pages 1–[12]. A new edition of Milton's tract in 1738 presented an anonymous preface actually by James Thomson, and this was reprinted in full by Blackburne in *Remarks* (1780) along with *Educ*, as already noted. (Thomson's preface was also reprinted in *New Foundling Hospital for Wit . . . A New Edition, Corrected, and Considerably Enlarged* [1784; rptd. twice, 1786], 4 : 197–205). There were editions in 1772 (London), 1791 by James Losh (London), 1792 (Blamire), and 1793 by Robert Hall (London). Often republished in the nineteenth and twentieth centuries, the following can be cited for various historical reasons: Thomas Holt White edited the tract with prefatory remarks and copious notes, to which he added Mirabeau's* French adaptation in 1819; it remains one of the better editions of his work. *Milton's Prophecy of Essays and Reviews, and His Judgment on Prosecution of Them. Extracted from the "'Areopagitica,' . . ." To which is added An Extract from the Charge Delivered to his Clergy in 1861, by Walter Kerr, Bishop of Salisbury, on "Unity with the Bishop of Rome"* (1861) includes a few notes from White; Milton's tract is given on pp. 5–46. The edition by J. W. Hales* with introduction and notes first appeared in 1866, was revised in 1882, and was frequently reprinted thereafter. Edward Arber offered a reprint of the first edition in 1868 with illustrative documents, and this was reprinted three times. Blackburne's edition with Thomson's preface was reproduced by Sidney Humphries in 1911, 1912, and 1913; and the Noel Douglas Replicas published the original in facsimile in 1927.

Translations began with Count Mirabeau's *Sur la liberté de la presse, imité de l'Anglois, de Milton* (Londres [i.e., Paris], 1788), which was reprinted twice in 1789, again in 1792 at Paris, and called the second edition, and in 1826 from Paris as *De la Liberté de la presse et de la censure, traduit de Milton*. A German translation was made by Richard Koeppell in 1851, and another, entitled *Miltons Rede über Pressfreiheit*, in 1852 (anonymous). R. Ritter retranslated it into German in 1925; Oliver Lutaud retranslated it into French in 1956, and this is reprinted in a facing bilingual edition in 1969. S. Breglia did an Italian translation in 1933; A. C. Krebs, a Danish translation in 1936; José Carner, a Spanish translation in 1941; Kenji Ishida, Shungo Yoshida, and Seichi Neno, a Japanese translation in 1948; Sasibhushan Dasgupta, a Bengali translation in 1963; Balakrishna Rao, a Hindi translation in 1965; and Jun Harada, another Japanese translation in 1972.

Tenure was revamped anonymously to argue for William III's election to the kingship in the midst of the controversy after the Revolution of 1688; it appeared as *Pro Populo Adversus Tyranno: Or the Sovereign Right and Power of the People Over Tyrants, Clearly Stated, and Plainly Proved. With Som Reflections on the Late Posture of Affairs. By a True Protestant English-man, and Well-Wisher to Posterity* (1689). The first edition of 1649 was used as source. Milton's cogently argued work was again employed in a contemporary issue in 1784 in Dublin amidst political activity for the independence of Ireland; the text is slightly abbreviated and its few notes are directed to the contemporary Irish audience. A scholarly edition was produced by William Talbot Allison in 1911. A Japanese translation by Jun Harada was published in 1972.

After his death, Milton's *Eikon* became a focal point in two controversies over *Eikon Basilike** : whether Charles I* was indeed the author, and whether Pamela's prayer* was a Milton forgery inserted into *Eikon Basilike* to discredit Charles. The first edition of Milton's work was reprinted in 1690 in London (although the title page says Amsterdam), with a twelve-page preface discussing the authorship of "The King's Book." The point of view of the editor was that the tyranny and double-dealing of Charles I justified the people's election of William III as co-monarch with Mary. It was not until 1756, when Richard Baron reprinted Milton's tract, that the second edition was again before the public, since intervening collected editions had also used the first edition. A preface discusses "The Transcendent Excellency of Milton's Prose Works"; a second edition appeared in 1770. An extract from this preface was published as *The Immortal Milton's Opinion of the Bishops* [London?, 1820?]. No further separate editions have appeared, and no translations other than Dury's 1652 French version.

The three defenses have drawn only infrequent attention in the last three hundred years. *1Def* was translated into English by Joseph Washington in 1692 as *A Defence of the People of England, by John Milton . . . In Answer to Salmasius's Defence of the King* with a preface by the translator; it was reissued in 1695. However, it should be noted that sections of the tract were paraphrased by Samuel Johnson in *Julian the Apostate* (1682) and by Thomas Hunt in *Mr. Hunt's Argument for The Bishops Right: With the Postscript* (1682); these plagiaristic uses were first pointed out by Thomas Long in *A Vindication of the Primitive Christians* (1683). In 1789 J. B. Salaville adapted the tract into French as *Théorie de la royauté d'après la doctrine de Milton;* this includes "Sur Milton et ses ouvrages," probably by Mirabeau. A second edition came out in the same year; a third, in 1791; a fourth, in 1792 but without the essay and under the title *Défense du peuple anglais, sur le jugement et la condamnation de Charles Premier, Roi d'Angleterre* (Valence). There is also an abbreviated German translation, "Die Schutzrede von Johann Milton für des englische Volk," in *Fürst und Volk nach Buchanans und Miltons Lehre* (Aurau, 1821), pp. 81–141, by I. P. V. Troxler. "Sententiae" drawn from

the various works and "Animadversions" taken from *2Def* are given by Edmund Elys in *Joannis Miltoni Sententiae Potestati Regiae Adversarites Refutatio* (1699). A selection from *2Def*, with a separate Latin title page, in Latin on pp. 33–47 and, with another separate English title page, in English on pp. 115–29, is given by Francis Peck in *Memoirs of the Life and Actions of Oliver Cromwell* (1740). Francis Wrangham translated the full work into English and published it in *Sermons Practical and Occasional* (London, 1816), 3:1–199, reissuing it in *Scraps*, pp. 1–199, in the same year.

The Cabinet-Council was reprinted in 1662 as *The Arts of Empire,* this time with Milton's name on the title page and his preface included. It reappeared in 1697 as *The Secrets of Government* in two issues, one with Milton's name on the title page and the preface, and one without either. Thomas Birch* reprinted it in 1751 in his edition of Ralegh's* works (1 : 39–170), and it was still retained as Ralegh's in the 1829 edition of *Works* (8 : 35–150). *CivP* was reprinted with a dedication and Milton's name in full in 1790, and in two different editions of *Tracts for the People,* no. 1 (1839) and in *Buried Treasures,* part 2 (1851), edited with introduction and notes by Cyrus R. Edmonds. *Tracts for the People* also includes a part of *TR* and *Sonn* 16 and 17 (to Cromwell and Vane).

Because of its subject of tithing, *Hire* has occasionally re-emerged. *A Supplement to Dr. Du Moulin, Treating of the Likeliest Means to Remove Hirelings out of the Church of England* was published in 1680 and, with original title, it was reprinted in 1717 by S. Barker, in 1723, in 1736 (Edinburgh), and in 1743. The first publication of a Miltonic work in the Colonies was this tract under the title *An Old Looking-Glass for the Laity and Clergy . . . Being considerations touching the likeliest means to Remove Hirelings out of the Church of Christ* (Philadelphia, 1770). It also contains Elijah Fenton's* life and extracts from *Animad*, pp. 45–50; *Ref,* pp. 50–70; and *Apol,* pp. 71–74. The volume was reprinted in New Haven in 1774. Four separate editions appear in the nineteenth century: London, 1831; London: J. Cleave, 1834 (though undated); Aberdeen: Murdock, 1839; London, 1851, as part of *Buried Treasures*, part 2, pp. 29–68. An extract was printed as *An Address to the House of Commons, in the Year 1659, in favour of the Removal of Tithes* (London: James Low, 1817).

The second edition of *Way* was reprinted separately in 1744 and in 1791 (London: for J. Ridgway). It was also reprinted in Boston by the Directors of the Old South Work in 1895 and 1896. A scholarly edition was produced in 1915 by Evert M. Clark. Jun Harada has produced a Japanese translation (1972). The issues by the Directors of the Old South Work also contained *Brief Delineation of a Free Commonwealth* ("A Letter to General Monk"), i.e., *PresM*, on pp. 22–23, with an editorial note on pp. 23–24.

Brit was reprinted in 1695 in two separate issues, and although this is the third edition, it has usually been called the second edition. While it tries to follow the 1677 second edition closely, it is a totally new setting of type and thus constitutes a separate edition. The first 1695 issue was printed by R[ichard?] E[veringham?] for R. Scot, R. Chiswell, R. Bentley, and G. Sawbridge; it was sold by A. Swall and T. Child. The second issue of 1695 was printed for R. Chiswell and was to be sold by Nath. Roles. The Index is included in the third edition. The text of these early editions (rather than that in the 1698 *Collection*) is given by John Hughes in Vol. I of *A Complete History of England* (1706; 2nd ed., 1719), without the Index, on pp. 1–82. This collection of histories by various people is sometimes known as White Kennett's edition because he wrote Vol. 3. The only other separate editions of *Brit* have been in 1870 by the firm of A. Murray and Son, who gave a "Verbatim reprint from Kennet's England, ed. 1719," entitled *Britain under Trojan, Roman, Saxon Rule. By John Milton,*

with notes correcting Milton, and in 1878 by the firm of Ward, Locke and Co., who issued a stereotype reproduction of this edition. An excerpt is given in *Retrospective Review*, 6 (1882):87–100.

TR was republished in 1809, 1811, and 1826; *Occasional Essays on Various Subjects, Chiefly Political and Historical*, pp. 416–30; *Thoughts on True Religion, Heresy, Schism, and Toleration by John Milton . . . To Which Are Added Remarks on Essentials in Religion, Charitableness and Uncharitableness, Extracted from the Writings of Isaac Watts*, ed. B. Fowler; and *Protestant Union. A Treatise Of True Religion, Heresy, Schism, and Toleration. To which is affixed a preface on Milton's Religious Principles and Unimpeachable Sincerity. By T. Burgess.* An excerpt also is given in both editions of *Tracts for the People*, No. 1 (1839).

Milton's familiar letters were edited in translation by John Hall (1829) and Phyllis Tillyard (1932). A translation of the letter to Leonard Philaras*, September 28, 1654, by A. B. E., is found in *Monthly Magazine* 24 (1807):565–66. Mrs. Tillyard included her translation of the prolusions in the 1932 edition of the letters. Francis Peck gave both the Latin and an English translation of *Prol* 2 in *New Memoirs of the Life and Poetical Works of Mr. John Milton* (1740), and it was also translated by B. Smith in *Quarterly Journal of Speech* 14 (1928):392–95.

Literae Pseudo-Senatûs Anglicani, Cromwellii (1676) was reprinted or translated in whole or in part within the next twenty-five years; see the title entry. But other printings of some of the state papers also occurs from sources other than *Literae;* see PAPERS, STATE. A number of incidental printings of a few state letters also are found in a variety of works from the seventeenth through the twentieth century, but no full bibliographic study of the letters has been made to date and no complete listing is currently in print.

CharLP, at times reinserted in *Brit,* was reprinted by itself three times in the

Harleian Miscellany, 5 : 540–43, in 1745; 5`: 576–79, in 1810 (for John White et al.); 5 : 37–41, in 1810 (for Robert Dalton). Francis Maseres called it "Reflections on the Civil War in England" and published it in *Select Tracts Relating to the Civil Wars in England in the Reign of King Charles the First* (1815), 2 : 805–15. An edition of *Mosc* with an important introduction came from Prince D. S. Mirsky in 1929, and Robert R. Cawley provided a full, scholarly treatment in his *Milton's Literary Craftsmanship: A Study of a Brief History of Moscovia, with an Edition of the Text* (1941; rptd. 1965). A Russian translation by Iu. v. Tolstoi was published by the Imperial Society of Russian History and Antiquities at the Moscow University (Moscow, 1875; rptd., 1907).

CD was published in 1825, two years after its discovery, in Latin and in English by Charles R. Sumner. The translation was immediately reprinted in two volumes in Boston. The Latin text was reprinted by E. Fleischer in Brunswick, Germany, in 1827. A number of selected versions also exist : *John Milton's Last Thoughts on the Trinity* (London, 1828); a reprint of this at Boston in 1847; another reprint at London in 1859; and *Milton On the Son of God and the Holy Spirit* (London, 1908; rptd., 1908).

Collected editions of most of the works or of selected works, however, must also be remembered when one attempts to determine the knowledge of Milton's prose and the extent that they were read at any specific time. Perhaps in an effort to get an edition of the prose of Milton before the public, to reap rewards from the renewed interest in Milton that the 1688 edition of *PL* caused, someone produced *The Works of Mr. John Milton* in 1697. There seems to be no connection between this volume and the registry of rights by Awnsham Churchill for various prose works on January 30, 1689. It may have been a hurried affair to get into print before *A Complete Collection*, which apparently was begun in 1694. *The Works* includes *DDD, Tetra, Colast,*

Bucer, Ref, RCG, CivP, Hire, PrelE, Animad, Apol, Way, Areop, Tenure (2d ed.), *Brief Notes, TR, E:kon* (1st ed.), and *Observations.* It thus omits all Latin prose works, all posthumous works, and *Educ, Grammar, Brit,* and *Declaration.* Most items have simulated title pages usually dated 1697. The very next year the very important *A Complete Collection Of The Historical, Political, and Miscellaneous Works of John Milton, Both English and Latin. With som Papers never before Publish'd* appeared in three volumes. It was published in London, although the title page says Amsterdam. The first volume contains the Life of Milton (dated 1698) by John Toland*, and thus this publication has erroneously been called Toland's edition. Some of the individual title pages are dated as early as 1694. Some sets are bound in two volumes; the Latin third volume is often found without the other two. Pagination is erratic, and separate for each volume. It includes all the prose works published to date except *CharLP*; John Phillips's *Responsio,* Joseph Washington's translation of *1Def,* and Edward Phillips's translation of the *Letters of State* are likewise given; and the new papers never before published are *A Letter to a Friend* and *The Present Means.* In addition a slightly revised and augmented *Brit* is printed, and this became the text of all future editions except for those of John Hughes, John Mitford, and *CM.* The last prints separately the changes, which are said in 1698 to be "from a Copy corrected by the Author himself." The Index is also included in the 1698 edition. The texts of *Tenure* and *Eikon* are both first editions.

A Complete Collection, with the same leading title, was re-edited by Thomas Birch*, with a new biographical introduction, in two volumes in 1738. He inserted *CharLP* into *Brit* and omitted the Index; added to the canon is *Scriptum dom. Protectoris*, in Latin and in English translation. This edition was in turn revised by Richard Baron in 1753, but its contents are the same. These editions sufficed the reading public until 1806, when Charles Symmons published a seven-volume *Prose Works,* to which he prefaced his Life of Milton. New translations by Robert Fellowes are given, including the first full English translation of *2Def* and the first translation of *Epistol.* In 1809, George Burnett edited the *Prose Works,* given, though it was not so complete, with new translations by himself, and including the first English translations of Phillips's *Responsio* and *3Def.*

A brief collection by Francis Maseres, entitled *The History of Britain* (1818) includes *Tenure* with the 1650 additions in quotation marks, *Way* (2d. ed.), *A Letter to a Friend, The Present Means, Brief Notes,* and *Brit* with the Index, the first time since 1698. Maseres also printed Phillips's Life of Milton. Another selection appeared in 1820, this time of the four divorce tracts, "With a Preface Referring to Events of Deep and Powerful Interest at the Present Crisis; Inscribed to the Earl of Liverpool. By a Civilian." Oddly enough, the not very long *Colas* is given in somewhat abridged form. The nineteenth century also saw a number of further complete or near-complete editions of the prose works, and these were frequently reprinted: Robert Fletcher's edition first appeared in 1833, and the Index was added to *Brit* with the William Bell printing in 1838; Rufus W. Griswold's edition came out of Philadelphia in 1845; James A. St. John's frequently inaccurate but "standard" edition in six volumes (the Bohn Library edition) was first published between 1848 and 1881, and it included a revision by Sumner of his translation of *CD;* and John Mitford produced *The Works* (including the poetry) in eight volumes in 1851. This last added some state papers, but lacks *CD* and some other items. Other editions during the nineteenth century are drawn from the aforementioned, but a two-volumes-in-one edition of the prose and poetry in Paris in 1836 should be mentioned, because it at least made some prose works available on the Continent

through texts derived from Fletcher's edition. And a few translations should be cited here that present two or more items. French translations of *Areop* and *Educ* are found in *Bibliothèque étrangère, par M.* [Etienne] *Aignan,* 2 (Paris, 1823); and German translations of the anti-prelatical tracts ("John Milton's prosaiche Schriften über Kirche") in *Historisches Taschenbuch,* 3, nos. 3 and 4 (Leipzig, 1852–53), ed. F. von Raumer, and reprinted in *Geschichte des Reformations-Zeitalters* (Leipzig, 1874), pp. 398–616, ed. Georg Weber. *John Miltons Politische Hauptschriften* (Berlin and Leipzig, 1874), 3 vols., trans. Wilhelm Bernhard, was reprinted in 1876 and 1879; and *Milton's pädagogische Schriften und Ausserungen* (Langensalza, 1890), ed. Jürgen Bona Meyer, includes *Educ,* four letters, and parts from *Areop* and the church pamphlets.

The most significant edition in the twentieth century has been *The Works,* ed. Frank A. Patterson et al., known as the Columbia Milton or Columbia Edition, eighteen volumes in twenty-one (1931–1938). It prints all known materials, including "Proposalls of certaine expedients," certain state papers and similar items, and "A Postscript" never before included in collections of Milton's works, in original languages and in translations. It has not been superseded and there seems no likelihood that it will be in the near future. However, it is sometimes inaccurate; its translations are frequently faulty; and it gives no indication of the original format and paging of the prose works. In addition there are no explanatory notes. Attempting to remedy the faulty texts and translations of *CM* and to provide explanatory notes is the *Complete Prose Works,* ed. Don M. Wolfe et al.; six of a projected eight volumes have appeared. No foreign languages are given; but all texts in foreign languages are presented in new translations. Original paging is indicated. An important edition of selections is that by Merritt Y. Hughes because of the introductions and annotations; a separate volume appeared in 1947 and a combined volume of poetry and prose in 1957. Another selection with new translations and annotations, *The Prose of John Milton* (1967), ed. J. Max Patrick et al., includes some items not yet annotated in the Yale *Prose*. [JTS]

EDITORS. During the seventeenth century what editorial work was done on contemporary texts usually involved format, illustrations, and extratextual items like forewords and indexes. Often such work was accomplished by the printer* and/or publisher*. Deliberate revision of a text by an editor seems impossible to determine and such eighteenth-century editorial practices as notes and critical introductions seem to appear only late and seldom. John George Pritius acted as editor for *Literae nomine Senatus Anglicani* (Leipzig and Franckfort, (1690), writing a preface (pp. ix–xvi) to this first German publication of the 1676 State Papers. In a sense Patrick Hume*, who produced the first annotations for *PL*, the first such explicatory notes for a contemporary poem, was functioning as an editor. In the more usual editorial function, however, Jacob Tonson*, the publisher of this 1695 printing, would be considered the editor. The printer-publisher-editor for the 1697 collection of prose *Works*, with its simulated title pages, is unidentified; it would be most important to know who was so enterprising as to create such a collection at this time. Part of the impetus was probably Milton's rising poetic popularity and surely the impending publication of *A Complete Collection*, which came out in 1698. Erroneously John Toland* has been called the editor of this edition because his "Life of Milton" was printed in the first volume. But though there seems to have been a close connection between Toland and the publisher-editor, there is no evidence that he served any function other than author of the "Life" and channel for the two previously in-edited pieces, *A letter to a Friend* and *PresM*, and the revisions for *Brit*. Spec-

ulations as to the publisher-editor have not proved fruitful; however, John Darby, Jr. (d. 1733), entered the "Life" in the Stationers' Register on December 15, 1698, and published it in 1699. Darby thus remains a possibility. Another editor whose name would be significant to know produced *Oliver Cromwell's Letters* in 1700, published by John Nutt. Nineteen state letters are given in English translations, not in chronological order, and an appendix is printed on pp. 40–45, in which the anonymous writer discusses Milton's function as Secretary and the value of his work on the letters. His conclusions are that Milton was only functionary; Milton was of *"Romish* stamp" but "(to give the Devil his due)" he translated "admirably well."

The kinds of editorial practices that have become standard for the twentieth century appear early in the eighteenth-century publications of Milton's works. The tenth edition of *PL*, published by Tonson in 1719, reprints Addison's* papers as an appendix, as well as the index of topics, similes, etc., which had first appeared in the 1695 *PL*. In 1720 an edition, ordinarily called Thomas Tickell's, not only reprinted the *Spectator* papers and the index, but also included the verses from the prose and the poem on Salmasius* (in Latin and in English). The edition is well illustrated and beautifully printed. Revised texts, with a statement about textual changes in the first two editions, begin with Elijah Fenton's* edition of *PL* in 1725, in which his account of Milton's life was first published. This "Life" is noteworthy because it attempts critical evaluations and thus acts as an introductory commentary on the work reprinted. The first use of footnotes to the text aiming at clarity of meaning and sources appears in the French translation published in 1729. This is the second edition of Raymond de Saint-Maur's translation, revised by C. J. Chéron de Boismorand, in three volumes. The first English edition to offer such notes is Thomas Newton's* two-volume variorum edition of *PL* in 1749. Some few notes appear in Thomas Birch's* edition of the prose in 1738 and textual notes in Richard Bentley's* edition of the epic in 1732, but Newton's are the first aiming at clarity of meaning and sources. Major notes in this edition serve as introductions to individual poems or evaluations of them. One other matter should be mentioned here, the editor of *A Complete History of England* (1706; rptd. 1719, with notes by John Strype), in which *Brit* reappeared as the first item in Volume 1. The histories reprinted in the first two volumes were collected and edited by John Hughes, not by White Kennet, as has sometimes been said. Kennet wrote (and in that sense only edited) Volume 3, which covers seventeenth-century British history.

Important editors of Milton's works, who are discussed in separate entries in this encyclopedia, are Richard Baron, Richard Bentley, Thomas Birch, Charles Dunster, Elijah Fenton, William Hayley, David Masson, Thomas Newton, Henry John Todd, and Thomas Warton. Among the editors of the poetry whose work should be consulted for texts, notes, or other general significance are the following, cited under EDITIONS, POETRY : H. G. Bohn, R. C. Browne, Douglas Bush, Charles Dexter Cleveland, Helen Darbishire*, John Evans, Harris F. Fletcher, Alastair Fowler and John Carey, John Gillies, George Grierson, H. J. C. Grierson*, Merritt Y. Hughes*, Thomas Keightley, Capel Lofft, Walter Mac-Kellar, John Marchant, John Mitford, William Vaughan Moody, Frank Allen Patterson, John T. Shawcross, John S. Smart*, Henry Stebbing, A. W. Verity*, and B. A. Wright. See also Jacques Blondell under TRANSLATIONS, POETIC. Among editors of the prose whose work should be consulted are the following, cited under EDITIONS, PROSE : Oliver M. Ainsworth, William Talbot Allison, Francis Blackburne, George Burnett, Robert R. Cawley, Evert M. Clark, Robert Fletcher, Rufus W. Griswold, Will T. Hale, J. W. Hales*, Jun Harada, Merritt Y. Hughes*, J. B. Le

Blanc, Oliver Lutaud, Francis Maseres, Count Mirabeau*, Prince D. S. Mirsky, John Mitford, J. Max Patrick, Frank Allen Patterson et al., James St. John, Charles R. Sumner, Charles Symmons, James Thomson, Thomas Holt White, and Don M. Wolfe et al. [JTS]

EDUCATION, MILTON'S: *see* St. PAUL'S SCHOOL; CHRIST'S COLLEGE, CAMBRIDGE; TUTORS, MILTON'S; and LEARNING, MILTON'S.

EDWARDS, THOMAS. Presbyterian divine, Thomas Edwards (1599–1648) was educated at Queens' College, Cambridge, and took both the B.A. and M.A. degrees at Cambridge, where he was University Preacher. His *Gangraena; Or a Catalog and Discovery of Many Errors, Heresies, Blasphemies, and Pernicious Practices of the Sectaries of This Time Vented and Acted in England in These Last Four Years,* appeared in February 1646. Sixteen sorts of sectaries were enumerated, 180 errors or heresies, and 28 alleged malpractices. The book concludes with an outcry against toleration*, which nearly exhausted the language of abuse. A second and third edition of the book appeared in answer to attacks on it by John Lilburne*, John Saltmarsh, William Walwyn*, and John Goodwin*. Milton's *DDD* was error number 154 in the first part of *Gangraena*, and Milton refers to Edwards in *NewF* as a result. [NH]

EGERTON FAMILY. The Egertons were famous in Milton's day both in public life and as literary patrons. Milton wrote *Arc* and *Mask* to celebrate two of its members, but there is no firm evidence that he was ever known personally to any of them or was ever a visitor in their homes. His connection seems to have been founded on his friendship with Henry Lawes*, who taught music to some of the children during the early 1630s. The following is an abbreviated family tree. Numbers in it refer to subsequent paragraphs.

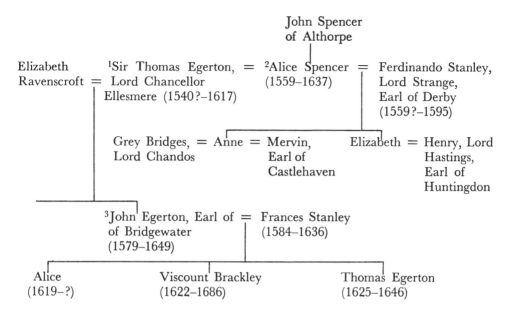

John Spencer
of Althorpe

Elizabeth   ¹Sir Thomas Egerton, =   ²Alice Spencer =   Ferdinando Stanley,
Ravenscroft = Lord Chancellor   (1559–1637)   Lord Strange,
          Ellesmere (1540?–1617)   Earl of Derby
                                                                    (1559?–1595)

Grey Bridges, = Anne = Mervin,   Elizabeth = Henry, Lord
Lord Chandos   Earl of   Hastings,
                           Castlehaven   Earl of
                                                               Huntingdon

³John Egerton, Earl of = Frances Stanley
of Bridgewater   (1584–1636)
(1579–1649)

Alice   Viscount Brackley   Thomas Egerton
(1619–?)   (1622–1686)   (1625–1646)

1. Sir Thomas Egerton, a successful lawyer, became very popular with Queen Elizabeth, who named him her Keeper of the Great Seal. His success at court continued under James*, who created him Lord Chancellor and later Viscount Brackley. The family residence was at Harefield*, where *Arc* was to be performed. He was well known and widely admired as a patron of writers; Jonson* and Daniel, for instance, wrote poems in his honor. For a while Donne was a member of his household, and he assisted Bacon* in various ways. He married three times—first to Elizabeth Ravenscroft and, after a childless second marriage, in 1600 to Alice Spencer, the widowed Duchess of Derby. Among the issue of the marriage to Elizabeth was John Egerton.

2. Alice Spencer was one of the daughters of John Spencer of Althorpe, with whom Edmund Spenser* claimed kinship. She married first Ferdinando Stanley, Lord Strange, the fifth Earl of Derby, who was a literary patron, particularly of the company of players known as Lord Strange's, later the Lord Chamberlain's. She had several children by him. The oldest daughter, Anne, after the death of her first husband, Lord Chandos, married in 1624 the widowed Earl of Castlehaven Within a few years, after a scandalous public trial, he was executed in 1631 for a variety of sexual perversions to which he subjected his Lady and others. It has been suggested by Barbara Brested (*Milton Studies* 2) that *Mask*, written for the family by Milton in 1634, exhibits in its stress upon chastity* an attempt to expiate this family horror.

The second daughter, Frances, married the Earl of Bridgewater, and the youngest daughter, Elizabeth, married the Earl of Huntingdon. She was a friend of Donne, who addressed two verse letters to her.

The connection of Lady Alice with writers is, aside from that of royalty, probably the most remarkable in English literary history. As has been noticed, Spenser claimed kinship. He also dedicated his *Teares of the Muses* to her and she is probably the "Amaryllis" of his *Colin Clouts Come Home Againe,* lines 432ff., with "Amyntas" being her husband, Lord Strange. Because of his patronage of an important theatrical group she must have associated with actors and dramatists; several, like Nashe, wrote adulatory poetry to her. Her second husband, Sir Thomas, and her daughter Elizabeth surely made her acquainted with Donne. Marston wrote a masque to be presented in her honor, a line of which appears in the collection of epigraphs to T. S. Eliot's "Burbank with a Baedeker": "so the countess passed on until she came through the little park, where Niobe presented her with a cabinet, and so departed." She may well be the "Countess of Derby" who danced in several of Jonson's masques; in any case Jonson addressed several poems to her husband as Lord Chancellor. Finally, Milton wrote *Arc* in her honor, performed at Harefield, the family residence. It has been argued (*English Language Notes* 11:47-7) that the presentation was in honor of her seventy-fifth birthday, which occurred on May 4, 1634. As is clear from the family tree, Alice was both stepmother and mother-in-law to the Earl of Bridgewater.

3. John Egerton was created Earl of Bridgewater in 1617, shortly after his father's death. He supported James and then Charles* in a variety of offices. He had fought with Essex in Ireland in 1599 and would fight for Charles after 1642. In 1631 Charles named him Lord President of Wales, but he did not take up residence in the official mansion, Ludlow Castle, until late summer 1634. *Mask* was performed for the occasion, with three of the Earl's children in leading parts. Alice, youngest of eight surviving daughters, aged 15, played the Lady. The parts of the two brothers were taken by the Earl's two sons, Viscount Brackley, aged 11, and Thomas, aged 9. All three children had participated in the great court masque *Coelum Britannicum* the previous February, its music, like that of *Mask,* having been written by their teacher Henry Lawes. Viscount Brackley later was active in the royalist cause and was favorably recognized in the Court after the Restoration. His copy of *1Def* survives; on its title page the mature Cavalier wrote in Latin that the book deserved to be burnt. His sister, Lady Alice, married Richard Vaughan, Earl Carbery, about 1653. After the Restoration he was named President of Wales and moved with his wife to the castle at Ludlow where she had performed as the Lady a generation earlier. Their secretary was Samuel But-

ler, who, tradition has it, composed *Hudibras* there. [WBH]

EIDOLON. In the *Sophist* (266b–c) Plato* defines *eidolon* as a product of divine and human activity. As "the off-spring . . . of divine workmanship," all natural things, living and nonliving, are "attended by images [*eidola*] which are not the actual thing, and which also owe their existence to divine contrivance" (*Plato's Theory of Knowledge,* trans. F. M. Cornford [1935], pp. 326–27). *Eidola* of the divine creation comprise dream images, "semblances which we call 'shadow,' " and images reflected in a mirror or in water (ibid., p. 327). In the productions of human art the builder produces an actual thing (a house), and the painter makes an image of it—"a house of a different sort, as it were a man-made dream for waking eyes" (ibid., p. 328). Earlier in the *Sophist* (235d–36b) Plato distinguishes between the art of making likenesses or replicas of things (*eikastiké*—the art of the builder) and the art of making semblances or fictitious likenesses (*phantastiké*—the art of the painter) (ibid., p. 197). *Phantastiké* depends on the use of *phantasia*, the combination of perception and judgment that "imposes on us false judgments by means of the senses . . ." (ibid., p. 321). The fine arts are rife with the semblances (*phantasmata*) of *phantasia* (ibid.).

John M. Steadman in *Journal of English and Germanic Philology* 59: 640–54, traces the technical meaning of the word *idol,* as Milton uses it to characterize Satan in the phrase "idol of Majesty Divine" (*PL* 6.101), back to Plato; he says: "In affecting divine honors and heroic leadership, Satan represented the sort of *eidolon* that Phavorinus and Suidas had defined as a fictitious likeness, that Francis Bacon* had described as a false appearance, and that Plato had classified as *phantasma* (or appearance), as distinguished from *eikon* (or likeness)" (p. 651). In *PL* the various *eidola* or *phantasmata* are directly connected with Satan's activities in Hell* and on earth; they include the false speeches and opinions of the devils debating in Pandaemonium*, Sin and Death, the dream intruded into Eve's imagination, the delusive fruit eaten by the devils, and the various idolatries of the devil-deities who pollute the earth in the heathen era. These are the main elements of illusion that constitute the negative side of the epistemological conflict between "reality and appearance, revelation and illusion, right reason and fallacy" (p. 654).

One should also consider the ontological significance of the *eidolon*. According to Cornford, Plato in the *Sophist* (239c–40c) defines *eidolon* as an image of something that is neither wholly real nor utterly nonexistent (pp. 210–12). It occupies an intermediate realm of existence; consequently, as Cornford says, it "has a less degree of reality, as the reflections and pictures instanced by Theaetetus are thought to be less real than the actual things they image" (p. 212). Sin and Death are the best examples of *eidola* occupying an intermediate realm, an allegoric* realm, in Milton. The "double-form'd" (2. 741) monster Sin, and "that Phantasm" (2. 743) Death, whose "substance" is scarcely distinguishable from "shadow" "for each seem'd either" (2. 669–70), owe their existence to Satan's inner corruption, the corruption of Satan's angelic being through the "gross imaginations" of Pride and Envy (*see* IDOLATRY). The "propensity to sin" is rooted in the imaginations of the thoughts of the heart—"Gen. vi. 5. 'God saw that every imagination of the thoughts of his heart was only evil continually' " (*CD* 15 : 195). Sin and Death are conceived, begotten, through Satan's spiritual fornication with his own image. As distorted reflections of Satan, their existence is contingent upon the perpetual existence of corruption—corruption is their food. Thus Sin and Death actually feed on Satan and the corruption he brings into being through the Fall of Man*. Satan's self-idolatry causes a vitiation of his angelic being, and with the Fall, Adam and Eve experience an internal vitiation that corresponds to the external vitiation of Nature. The Father says of Sin and Death to the Son* : "I call'd and drew them thither / My Hell-hounds, to lick up the draff and filth / Which man's polluting Sin with taint hath shed / On what was pure" (10. 629–32).

With respect to Sin and Death, Milton's ontology is strongly colored by Augustinian psychology. For St. Augustine*, in *The City of God*, when man turns away from God, his being becomes "more contracted than it was when he clung to Him who supremely is. Accordingly, to exist in himself, that is to be his own satisfaction after abandoning God, is not quite to become a nonentity, but to approximate to that" (*The Basic Writings of St. Augustine,* trans. Marcus Dod [1948], 2 : 258). In *On the Trinity* St. Augustine sees the soul turning aside from the Image of God because it is "delighted by corporeal forms and motions . . . , and because it is wrapped up in their images, which it has fixed in the memory, and is foully polluted by fornication of the phantasy . . ." (ibid., trans. A. W. Haddan, rev. W. G. T. Shedd, p. 817). The antithesis between phantasies and diabolic agency on the one hand and truth and Christ on the other is a major theme in all of St. Augustine's works. In *The Confessions* the phantasms of phantasy (the faculty of imagination) adulterate the real and the substantial which are associated with Christ. To escape this predicament of sin, the reasoning faculty must raise "itself up to its own intelligence . . . , withdrawing itself from the crowds of contradictory phantasms, that so it might find out that light by which it was besprinkled, when, without all doubting, it cried out, that the unchangeable was to be preferred before the changeable . . ." (ibid., trans. J. G. Pilkington, 1 : 105). For Milton it is the "sovran Reason" (*PL* 9. 1130) regenerated that frees man from the *eidola* or *phantasmata* of this world. [TAB]

EIKON BASILIKE: *The True Portraiture of His Sacred Majesty in His Solitudes and Sufferings* (i.e., "The King's Book"), purportedly Charles I's* meditations in prison during his trial and while awaiting sentence. It appeared soon after his execution on January 30, 1649, and by February 9. Since Charles was buried on February 8, it has been speculated that publication was made to coincide. The substance of the book is a sentimental account of well-known actions by the king for his people, an indictment of the unprovoked changes in loyalty toward him, and a narrative of recent, misunderstood events leading up to his imprisonment. But the form is one of a kind of personal reminiscence for Charles's eyes alone, a spiritual autobiography of a maligned and misunderstood, benevolent leader of men. It was very frequently reprinted, and was even put into rhyme by Thomas Stanley (1625–1678) and translated into Latin by John Earle, Bishop of Salisbury (1601?–1665), in 1649.

The author was John Gauden* the king's chaplain, who acknowledged his authorship in a letter to Edward Hyde, Earl of Clarendon* and Lord Chancellor, on January 21, 1661. (There are five other related letters.) The letter was printed in Thomas Wagstaffe's *A Vindication of King Charles the Martyr* (1697), pp. 20–22. However, a debate over authorship immediately arose and raged throughout the seventeenth century, was not totally stilled in the next, was revived in the early nineteenth, and has sometimes been reprised in the twentieth. Adherents of Charles have argued, on the one hand, that the book was his and charged Gauden with self-aggrandizement, and on the other, that it was not his because of certain statements and the prayers that later appear in it. Opponents of Charles have also been of two kinds, some removing it from his hand to deflate public opinion and others keeping it as his to charge him with deceit and dishonesty. *The Princely Pellican. Royal Resolves presented in sundry choice Observations, extracted from His Majesties Divine Mediations*, published around July 2, 1649, defended Charles's authorship. (It was reprinted in *Memoirs of the Two Last Years of the Reign of That Unparallell'd Prince, of ever Blessed Memory, King Charles I* [1702], pp. 241–99.) An anonymous refutation *Eikon Alethine, The Pourtraicture of Truths most sacred Majesty* was published by August 16, 1649, and *The Constant Man's Character* (1650) classified it as a fraud, pp. 53–62. *Eikon Alethine* evoked an anonymous answer, *Eikon Episte. Or, the Faithfull Pourtraicture of a Loyall Subject, in Vindication of Eikon Basilike* (September 11, 1649). Various other tracts like Richard Perrinchief's *The Royal Martyr: Or, the Life and Death of King Charles I* (1676), pp. 209–10, between 1650 and 1690 defended Charles and assumed his authorship.

Milton's assignment in writing *Eikon* (1649) was to discredit Charles and the sympathy that "The King's Book" had created for him. He thus had to assume Charles's authorship although he implies that he recognized the legitimacy of the rumors about it. The main attack on Charles throughout the book was to discredit his honesty and sincerity in it. In 1690 a new edition of *Eikon* (supposedly published in Amsterdam but actually in London) discussed the controversy in a twelve-page preface; it was reprinted to advance argument for the succession settlement. Some copies included an advertisement of a memorandum by Arthur Annesley*, Earl of Anglesey, stating that Gauden had written the work. Edward Millington, a bookseller and friend of Milton, had found the note when he auctioned off Annesley's books in 1686. Immediately followed reactions and counteractions, for example, among others, Richard Hollingworth's *A Second Defense of Charles I* (1690); *Restitution to the Royal Author or a Vindication of King Charls the Martyr's most Excellent Book* (1691), which reprints the note on p. 3; Anthony Walker's *A True Account of the Author of a Book entituled Eikon Basilike*

(1692), which identified Gauden as author and Brian Duppa, Bishop of Salisbury and Winchester, as a contributor; *Vindiciae Carolinae: or, A Defense of Eikon Basilike . . . In Reply to a Book Intituled Eikonoklastes, Written By Mr. Milton, and Lately Re-Printed at Amsterdam* (1692), assigned to Hollingworth or to John Wilson; *A Letter from General Ludlow to Dr. Hollingworth* (Amsterdam [?], 1692), by "Edmund Ludlow" (a pseudonym); *Ludlow no Lyar* (Amsterdam [?], 1692), by Joseph Wilson (a pseudonym?) or Slingsby Bethel (?); Hollingworth's *The Character of King Charles I* (1692) and *The Death of King Charles I* (1693); Thomas Long's *Dr. Walker's True, Modest and Faithful Account of the Author of Eikon Basilike* (1693), a rebuttal of Walker; *Truth Brought To Light: Or the Gross Forgeries of Dr. Hollingworth* (1693), with the substance of Gauden's letter on p. 37; and Wagstaffe's *Vindication* (1st ed. 1693). These various tracts often discussed Milton and *Eikon*, and *Ludlow no Lyar* plagiarized from Milton's work, especially in the prefatory letter. In the eighteenth century the question is continued in such volumes as John Burton's *The Genuineness of Ld Clarendon's History of the Rebellion Printed at Oxford Vindicated* (1744), pp. 114–19, 149–73; and William Harris's scholarly *An Historical and Critical Account of the Life and Writings of Charles I. King of Great Britain* (1772; frequently rptd.), pp. 106–8, 110–11, and 115–16. In 1824 Christopher Wordsworth published *"Who Wrote Eikon Basilike?" Considered and Answered. In Two Letters, Advanced to His Grace the Archbishop of Canterbury*. Wordsworth's answer "Charles" was disputed by Henry John Todd's* *A Letter to His Grace the Archbishop of Canterbury Concerning the Authorship of Eikon Basilike* (1825), to which Wordsworth replied with *Documentary Supplement to "Who Wrote Eikon Basilike?"* (1825). William Grant Broughton, among others, got into the controversy with *A Letter to a Friend touching the Question, "Who was the Author of Eikon Basilike?"* (1826),

and in rebuttal came *King Charles the First, the Author of the Icon Basilike further proved* (1828) by Wordsworth. Todd's surrejoinder was *Bishop Gauden the Author of Icon Basilike* (1829) and Broughton's, *Additional Reasons In Confirmation of the Opinion that Dr. Gauden, and Not King Charles the First was the Author of Eikon Basilike* (1829). Today the book is assigned to Gauden with help from Duppa, and no one seriously raises the question of Charles's authorship.

Another controversy over *Eikon Basilike* is the authenticity of the prayers, specifically of Pamela's prayer taken from Sir Philip Sidney's* *Arcadia,* found in editions from around March 15. The manuscript of *Eikon Basilike,* which was not written during the trial, was ready for publication around December 24, 1648; none of the alleged king's prayers were included. This manuscript was published around February 1649 and reprinted. The manuscript had been brought to Richard Royston, the publisher, by Edward Simmons, a servant of the king. On February 23, 1649, John Playford (1623–1686?), a musician and bookseller, was licensed by James Cranford to print the prayers, which were apparently in a separate, additional manuscript. Simmons in the meantime delivered a different manuscript with the additional material integrated into the text to William Dugard*, later a printer for the Council of State*. Dugard published the work around March 15, 1649, and was promptly arrested on the next day. Because Cranford had licensed the prayers he was removed from office and Dugard was set free. Matthew Simmons*, printer for the Council of State, entered the work as a blocking action, under the license of Joseph Caryl, on March 16, the day of Dugard's arrest. (See Francis F. Madan, *A New Bibliography of the Eikon Basilike of King Charles the First* [1950], for a full listing of the various editions and versions of this volume.) Milton, recognizing the plagiarism of Pamela's prayer, made much of it in *Eikon* to discredit Charles, the nominal author. In the heat of controversy in the early 1690s the prayer became a focus for praise or dispraise of Milton or Charles. *Restitution to the Royal Author* (1691) discussed it on pp. 7–8, and *A Letter from Major General Ludlow to Sir E[dward] S[eymour]* (Amsterdam, 1691), reprinted Charles's alleged prayer and Pamela's prayer in parallel columns in "A Postscript," pp. 29–30, to insure that the reader could not overlook the full extent of the plagiarism. Wagstaffe argued in *Vindication* (1693) that Milton must have forged the meditation into *Eikon Basilike* because of his position and the connection with Dugard. The second edition of this work in 1697 offered further evidence for the charge derived from the former Parliamentarian printer Henry Hills (d. 1691), on pp. 50–51. (An edition in 1711 adds some ancillary material.) According to Wagstaffe, Thomas Gill and Francis Bernard, physicians to Charles, reported the story of the plagiarism to Hills, who informed him. In proof Wagstake published a letter from Gill to Charles Hatton, dated May 1, 1694, and a testimonial statement from Bernard, dated May 10, 1694. The story that Gill says he heard was that John Bradshaw* and Milton contrived the deception and that Milton had Dugard insert this particular prayer. Bernard alleges that Hills heard Bradshaw and Milton laugh at this deception that they had perpetrated. *Truth Brought To Light* (1693) commented upon the matter favorably for Milton, p. 34.

The controversy reappeared in 1699 and the years following when the heretical beliefs of John Toland*, expressed in his "Life of Milton" (1698 in *A Complete Collection,* and separately published in 1699), evoked Offspring Blackall's *Remarks on the Life of Mr. Milton, As Publish'd by J. T. With a Character of the Author and His Party* (1699). Toland's answer became involved in the controversy over the prayer: *Amyntor: or, A Defense of Milton's Life, Containing . . . A Complete History of the Book, Entitul'd Icon Basilike, Proving Dr. Gauden, and not King Charles the First, to be the Author of it: With an Answer to All the Facts Alleg'd by Mr. Wagstaf to the Contrary* (1699). Toland quotes from Wagstaffe to rebut him and prints the prayer from its two "sources" in parallel columns. He also cites Gauden's letters and Hyde's replies on the authorship both in the "Life" and in *Amyntor.* He received answers from Blackall (*Mr. Blackalls Reasons for Not Replying to a Book Lately Published, Entituled, Amyntor,* 1699) and Wagstaffe (*A Defense of the Vindication of King Charles the Martyr . . . In Answer to a Late Pamphlet, Intituled, Amyntor,* 1699). Biographical dictionaries of the eighteenth century refer to the controversy, usually under "Wagstaffe," and Thomas Birch* was taken in by the accusation against Milton in his introduction to his edition of the prose in 1738. However, Richard Baron's revision of this edition in 1753 rejects Milton's alleged forgery. In his attempt to mitigate his own forgery, William Lauder* revived the matter in *King Charles I. Vindicated from the Charge of Plagiarism Brought Against Him by Milton, and Milton Himself Convicted of Forgery, and a Gross Imposition on the Publick* (1754). See also Harris's life of Charles, pp. 102–6.

Like Samuel Johnson* (see *Life of Milton* [1781 ed.], 1 : 157–58), some twentieth-century antagonists of Milton— S. B. Liljegren, Paul Phelps-Morand, William Empson among them—have repeated the charges. The allegations have been refuted often, but see particularly Merritt Y. Hughes, *Review of English Studies,* 3 : 130–40. [JTS]

EIKONOKLASTES ("The Image-Breaker"), written to counter the effect of *Eikon Basilike** ("The King's Book"), purportedly Charles I's* meditations in prison during his trial and while awaiting sentence. *Eikon Basilike* appeared by February 9, 1649, and immediately began to build sympathy for the king, who had been executed on January 30. Nonofficial rebuttals to the sentimental King's Book appeared, but the Council of State* first urged John Selden* to produce it. He declined, but by June 11 *The Metropolitan Nuncio, No.* 3, reported that an answer was being prepared. Milton became Secretary for Foreign Tongues* around March 15, and in *Eikon,* pp. [vi–vii], he says, "I take it on me as a work assign'd rather then by one chos'n or affected." The tract may have appeared around October 6, the date given by George Thomason*, but this may be in error. *A Briefe Relation of Some Affairs,* no. 9 (November 13–20, 1649), p. 96, a semi-official newspaper printed by Matthew Simmons* as was *Eikon,* notes that the tract was "published the last weeke." This volume was the source of the text after 1650 and until 1756. The printing is not careful, and a second edition, slightly longer through clarifying revisions and brief additions, was called for in 1650. This edition was printed by Thomas Newcomb; there are two issues; one lists Newcomb only, the other says the volume was to be sold by Tho[mas] Brewster and G[regory] Moule. The second edition was published after June 19, 1650, when news of Anthony Ascham's murder in Madrid, alluded to on p. 208, reached London. An official translation into French was executed by John Dury*, using the second edition, published by November 1652 in London. The report of a Latin translation by Lewis Du Moulin, younger brother of Milton's later antagonist, Peter Du Moulin*, has not been substantiated. A new edition of the 1649 tract in 1690 contributed greatly to the development of controversies over *Eikon Basilike.* In 1756 Richard Baron reprinted the second edition (rptd., 1770).

Like the anonymous *Eikon Alethine* (1649), which contains a dedicatory epistle to the Council of State, *Eikon* is a chapter-by-chapter refutation of *Eikon Basilike.* Its aim was to nullify the sympathy that *Eikon Basilike* was building for Charles and thus the antagonism against the new government. To the people Charles was a martyr, and an equation with Christ was pushed by his adherents. Milton, even though comments in the work indicate that he knew better, had to write under the assumption that Charles was the author of the King's Book in order to discredit his honesty and sincerity. Yet the effect of the sentimentality of *Eikon Basilike* and of the concept of royal infallibility was not really overcome. Milton's work attempts to show that Charles's allegations of his actions and intents are false and dishonest, that his adherents in the Presbyterian* camp who supported him had started by opposing him, and that the style and part of the content are derivative. Milton's version of historical events, his discovery of one of Charles's prayers as that of Pamela in Sir Philip Sidney's* *Arcadia,* his quotation and interpretation of Scripture against the king's employment of biblical references and citation of the Psalms as if they were written by him all logically destroy *Eikon Basilike* as a truthful and moral work in all but the public's eye. His major source of factual governmental information comes from the *History of Parliament* by Thomas May*, an official record. *Eikon* is for a modern audience tedious, long, and repetitive, problems inherent in its method of chapter-by-chapter refutation of a long and repetitive work. In this pamphlet Milton defends regicide and justice and denounces tyranny again. His own idealism comes through as well as his contempt for the common man, which is seen elsewhere, as in the *Ode to Rouse* (1647). (For discussion of its authorship and the use of Pamela's prayer, *see* EIKON BASILIKE.)

Reactions to *Eikon* include two specific tracts and many favorable and adverse comments in England and on the Continent, depending on prejudice for or against the king, for or against the Cromwellian government, or (on the Continent) for or against Catholicism or Protestantism. If Milton was not well known before the appearance of this tract, he certainly was thereafter. However, not all knew that "J. M." was Milton until after *1Def* in 1651, despite an identification in *Mercurius Pragmaticus,* a Royalist newspaper. Along with *1Def* this tract was primary in establishing an infamous reputation as a regicide for Milton during the seventeenth and eighteenth centuries, countered and overcome finally by his poetic reputation. In a proclamation dated August 13, 1660, one of his first, Charles II* suppressed *Eikon* and *1Def,* and notices of book-burning appeared in the news sheets. A number of years later on June 21, 1683, Oxford University passed a decree again suppressing both volumes as two of the "Pernicious Books and Damnable Doctrines Destructive to the Sacred Persons of Princes, Their State and Government, and of All Humane Society."

The first printed answer to *Eikon* was Joseph Jane's *Eikon Aklastos. The Image Unbroaken. A Perspective of the Impudence, Falshood, Vanitie, and Prophannes, Published in a Libell Entitled Eikonoklastes* ([London], 1651), reissued in 1660 as *Salmasius His Dissection and Confutation of the Diabolical Rebel Milton.* It was written before December 4, 1650, but was not published until about April 1651. Jane, who may have died in 1660, does not cite Milton, obviously not knowing that he was the author. Like *Eikon* itself, *Eikon Aklastos* is a point-by-point answer, but its substance is largely indignation and abuse. Jane has little to say other than praise for the king and dispraise for the anonymous author. The second tract directed against *Eikon* was *Carolus I., Britanniarum Rex. A Securi et Calamo Miltonii Vindicatus,* written in Latin and published supposedly in Dublin in 1652. Its author has been identified as Claude Barthelemy Morisot, and the book seems to have been printed in Dijon. The author attempts to answer Milton's arguments and not to stoop to mere insults, but the book seems to have been little known and to have had little effect. Some of Morisot's material comes from George Bate's defense of the king in *Elenchus Motuum Nuperorum in Anglia* (1650), in which Milton is not mentioned although he is in the second (and successive editions) in 1661 (pp. 237–38). Bate (1608–1669) was a court physician. [JTS]

ELEGIES, MILTON'S LATIN. Milton's Latin elegies apparently were written between 1626 and 1630 when he was sixteen to twenty-one; they are followed by an elegiac epilogue, a "retraction," dating perhaps as early as 1630 or as late as 1645. The elegies and the epilogue were published in 1645 in an edition that divided the Latin poems into two groups, *Elegiarum Liber (Book of Elegies)* and *Sylvarum Liber (Book of Sketches*—a standard seventeenth-century definition of "sylva" was "a work made up in haste"). *Elegiarum Liber* includes not only the seven elegies and the epilogue but also nine epigrams on various subjects in elegiac meter. *Sylvarum Liber* contains poems in a variety of meters, including three in dactylic hexameter.

That Milton should have written twenty-nine poems in Latin is not surprising for a Renaissance poet. George Buchanan's* Latin poetry fills two folio volumes; Thomas Campion, Abraham Cowley*, Richard Crashaw, George Herbert, and Andrew Marvell* were excellent poets in Latin as well as in English. Milton's early poetry is chiefly in Latin: of the 1703 extant lines of poetry that he wrote before he was twenty-two, 1,178 were in Latin, 445 in English, and 80 in Italian. The decision to abandon Latin verse for English, which he writes of (in Latin) in *EpDam* (168–78), clearly is one he thought out deliberately and with some self-conscious regret. Milton's career as a Latin poet began with elegies deeply influenced by Ovid* (a chief example in the schools), but he moved from Ovid toward Virgil*, and then toward a style of his own. As Bradner says, "Although no reader would wish the elegies unwritten, it is certain that Milton found the Latin hexameters a much more suitable medium for his use. In the short sentences required by couplets his great gift for the expansive poetic paragraphs was allowed no room for development." Yet E. K. Rand found that the early Latin elegiacs "breathe a spirit of Horace* and Ovid; they might be proudly claimed by either of those vinous souls and polished poets."

The term *elegia* as Milton uses it refers to the verse form, the elegiac distich or couplet, and not to the subjects of the poems, which are varied—friendship, love, death, the shortcomings of Cambridge University. The elegiac distich is a form employing a series of paired lines, the first in dactylic hexameter, the second another hexameter with two half-feet missing, making it a kind of pentameter. A typical pair of lines might have this pattern :

$$-\cup\cup \mid -\cup\cup \mid -\cup\cup \mid -\cup\cup \mid -\cup\cup \mid -\underset{\smile}{\vee}$$
$$-\cup\cup \mid -\cup\cup \mid -\wedge \mid -\cup\cup \mid -\cup\cup \mid -\wedge$$

(The mark ∧ indicates the missing half-foot.) Coleridge, imitating Schiller, constructed an English example :

In the hexameter rises the fountain's silvery column;
In the pentameter, aye, falling in melody back.

Greek elegies dealt with almost any subject—war, politics, love, etc. The Romans, especially Propertius, Tibullus, and Ovid, borrowed from the Greeks, and Ovid's elegies are perhaps the best Latin poems in the form.

El 1 was probably written in the spring of 1626. It takes the form of a verse letter to Milton's close friend Charles Diodati*. The occasion seems to have been Milton's "rustication*" (temporary suspension) from Cambridge University because of some quarrel with his tutor, William Chappell*. It cannot have been a very serious matter because Milton returned to Cambridge by mid-April.

Overtly *El* 1 is an explanation to Diodati of how Milton is spending his time in London—reading, enjoying both comedy and tragedy, and delighting in the beautiful girls of London, the most beautiful girls in the world, he says. He rejoices in being free of the ugliness of the Cambridge countryside and the indignities of the University. In many ways this aspect of the poem is a preparation for *L'Al* and *IlP*; it collects and recites

with enthusiasm the books and the scenes he is enjoying in London.

Like most of Milton's poems it also revels in echoes and paraphrases of Greek and Roman poetry—here, echoes of Ovid in particular. But the poem also makes very clever use of its recollections of Ovid and of the similarities of Milton's own position at the moment to Ovid's: Milton has been exiled from Cambridge to London; Ovid was exiled from Rome to Tomis, a village on the Black Sea, in 8 A.D. by Augustus Caesar for reasons that are still not completely clear.

But *El* 1 is adroitly fashioned from the idea that Milton's and Ovid's positions are alike only superficially; in reality they are reversed. Milton is as happy in exile from Cambridge as Ovid was in residence in Rome; Milton's residence at Cambridge was as miserable as Ovid's exile at Tomis. Since every seventeenth-century schoolboy knew of Ovid's unhappy exile and had read at least a few of his poems written to friends in Rome, pleading for his exile to be ended, Milton's poem is not merely a friendly note on London life, but also a clever, pungent insult to Cambridge University.

Milton manages this not only by open reference to Ovid—

O utinam vates nunquam graviora tulisset
    Ille Tomitano flebilis exul agro;
Non tunc Jonio quicquam cessisset Homero
    Neve foret victo laus tibi prima Maro.
(lines 21–24)

(Ah! Would that the bard who was a pitiful exile in the land of Tomis had never had to bear anything worse! Then he would have yielded nothing to Ionian Homer and you, O Maro, would have been conquered and stripped of your prime honors.—Trans. M. Y. Hughes)— but also by allusion to Ovid's complaints against Tomis (*Tristia*, 1. 1. 47–48) concerning the hardships of his exile, while Milton makes the point that his place of exile nourishes the poet. On the other hand, Milton laments, even the landscape of Cambridge discourages poetry (14–15), which lines reverberate with Ovid's repeated despair in the barren plains, and the fields without trees or grapes, to which he was banished at Tomis. London, on the other hand, to which Milton has been exiled, has shady lanes (49–50), leisure for study (25–26), the richness of the theater (27–46), and above all, the beautiful English girls (63–64, 71–72). But, he concludes, it has been decided that he must go back to the reedy fens of the Cam and to the noisy school.

Critical evaluation of the poem has been mixed. Lord Monboddo* (1714–1799), Samuel Johnson's* friend, thought it equal to anything by Ovid or Tibullus. Hanford calls it "a less mature and more personal 'L'Allegro' and 'Il Penseroso' in one." Parker says it is "a funny, pathetic, normal effort for an adolescent boy, rich in unintended humor."

El 2 was probably written in November 1626, not long before Milton's eighteenth birthday and perhaps six months after *El* 1. The occasion was the death of Richard Ridding* of St. John's College, who had been Senior Esquire Bedell (Beadle) of Cambridge University. The poem is in the main a conventional expression of regret at the death of Ridding who, though his hair was white, was "dignus tamen Haemonio juvenescere succo" ("worthy to have your youth restored by the drugs of Haemonia" [a land of magic mentioned by Ovid]). Milton protests the fact that Death should have taken Ridding rather than the useless rabble of the earth and then concludes with an exhortation to the University to grieve for this good man. *El* 2, like much neo-Latin verse, is crammed with classical allusions: Jove, Athene, Apollo, Leda, the land of Haemonia, Medea, Aeson, Aesculapius, the Styx, Mercury, Troy, Priam Eurybates, Agamemnon, Achilles, and Avernus are all so crowded into a poem of only twenty-four lines that there is hardly room for the man being eulogized. In fact, there is so little of Ridding in the poem that, without Milton's headnote giving his own age as seventeen, we should be unable to discover who is being commemorated. Rid-

ding was probably in his early fifties when he died; he had served as beadle for thirty years, but had resigned on September 16, 1626, apparently shortly before his death. None of these facts appear in the poem. Milton enlivens it with a mild conceit on Ridding's duties as beadle, or marshall of the University's academic processions (34). Leigh Hunt considered one phrase, *magna sepulchrorum regina* ("great queen of sepulchers," line 17), worthy of Dante* or of Milton's mature poetry. But there is no sense of personal loss anywhere in the piece.

El 3, on the death of Lancelot Andrewes*, Bishop of Winchester, was also written in the autumn of 1626; Andrewes, who had died on September 25, had been Master of Pembroke Hall, Cambridge (1589–1605), and was one of the translators of the King James version of the Bible and a great preacher, but there is no evidence that Milton knew him. This poem and another written at the same time, "In Obitum Praesulis Eliensis" ("On the Death of the Bishop of Ely"), which is not in the elegiac meter, are of interest partly because of Milton's later attacks on episcopacy. But it would be a mistake to take these statements of a seventeen-year-old as serious expressions of an ecclesiastical position, especially when the occasion is the death of the two bishops and when epicedia of this sort were the normal convention. One should note, however, that Milton included them in the 1645 edition of his poems, at the height of the ecclesiastical controversies over episcopacy, and printed them again in the 1673 edition.

El 3 begins with fourteen lines of generalized grief at the ravages of Libitina, the goddess of death (at least one-sixth of the population of London had died in the plague of 1625), and particularly grief at the death of "clarique ducis, fratrisque verendi" ("that glorious duke and his brother"). There is some disagreement as to who these two were; it has been customary to identify them as Count Ernest of Mansfeld and Duke Christian of Brunswick-Wolfenbüttel. But

Bush makes a strong case for their being King James I*, who had died eighteen months before, and Maurice, Prince of Orange, who had died in April 1625. It is indicative of the immaturity of Milton's poem that their identification matters not the least in the poem as a poem.

Milton then (lines 15–36) turns to Andrewes and to Death itself; he complains that Death should be satisfied with its dominion over the lower forms of life—the lilies, the oak, birds, and animals. Why must Death fling its darts at the spirit half divine? Then night comes (lines 31–65) and weariness lulls the poet to sleep, whereupon he has a vision of the surpassing beauty of Heaven; and there the company of saints greets Andrewes, its new companion, and the reverend old man joins their numbers. They embrace him, promising him eternal rest. Milton awakens (lines 66–68) in tears and prays for frequent dreams like this. The last line, however, is oddly incongruous: "Talia contingant somnia saepe mihi" ("May dreams like these often befall me") adapts an erotic line from Ovid's *Amores* having to do with a day spent in bed with Corinna. Perhaps Milton's unexpected use of the line is intended to carry satiric import.

El 3 is an interesting step in Milton's development; it is one of eight poems commemorative of a death (six, if we exclude the two jocular poems on the death of Hobson*) that Milton wrote before he was twenty-three. Of these, in many ways *El* 3 most foreshadows his two great epicedia, *Lyc* and *EpDam*, although it falls far short of them. Like them, it begins in grief, protests the injustice of death, and finds ultimate justification in the poet's vision of the dead man in Heaven in the company of the saints. In all three the beatific vision is of course Christian, but with pagan and classical overtones. Maclean points out that "in Elegy III Christian images supersede the classical vision, but do not banish the images of the classical story. . . . The Christian victory, so to speak,

contains or even (for its fullest effect) depends upon the continued presence of the classical elements, which imaginatively take their place in the eternal scheme" (see *ELH: A Journal of English Literary History* 24 : 296–305). *El* 3 has received little critical attention, apparently because most critics have found it, as Daiches suggests, an exercise in which Milton is flexing his poetic muscles.

There is some uncertainty over the date of *El* 4, but most editors place it in 1627, a few months after *El* 2 and *El* 3. It is a verse letter, like *El* 1, but this time addressed to Thomas Young* (1587?–1655), a Scottish minister then chaplain to the English merchants in Hamburg, who had been Milton's tutor* probably from 1618 until perhaps the autumn of 1620. Their friendship was close, as evidenced not only by this poem but by two letters, one dated March 26, 1625 (perhaps a misdating for 1627) and one on July 21, 1628.

The first fifty lines of *El* 4 are addressed not to Young but to the letter itself, urging it across the sea to Hamburg. Then it addresses Young, delivering no news whatsoever but apologizing for its lateness and expressing concern for Young's safety, since the Protestants under Christian IV of Denmark had been defeated and Hamburg was in danger. The letter expresses indignation that Britons like Young must seek their livings abroad; it assures him that he is still under God's protection and that he will return to England to better times.

Like *El* 2, this poem, particularly in its opening lines, is so laden with learned allusions that it almost sinks : Aeolus, Doris and her nymphs, Medea, Jason, and Triptolemus all crowd into the first twelve lines. Alcibiades, Telamon, Socrates, Alexander the Great, Aristotle*, the Phoenix, Chiron, and Achilles and his Myrmidons clutter the next fifteen lines. But then, almost as if he had finished reciting his lessons, Milton relaxes and lets his concern for the welfare of his teacher break through. It develops from the filial worry of an eighteen-year-old for his forty-year-old teacher to something that is almost paternal anxiety. The onomatopoeia (reminiscent of Virgil) with which he describes God's protection against the enemy is worthy of Milton in his maturity:

Cornea pulveream dum verberat ungula campum,
Currus arenosam dum quatit actus humum.
(119–20)

(When the loud trumpet sounded in the empty air, and the horny hoof beat the dusty plain, and the hard-driven chariot shook the sandy earth.)

El 5, "In Adventum Veris" ("On the Coming of Spring"), was written in the spring of 1629 and follows the long tradition of spring poems that date from Horace, the *Pervigilium Veneris,* and such Renaissance Latin poems as George Buchanan's "Maiæ Calendæ." Structurally the poem divides into two major sections: (1) lines 1–24 (or 28), in which Milton speaks of the return of spring, his excitement, his "sacer furor" ("sacred ecstasy"), and his song of inspiration; and (2) lines 25 (or 29) to the end (140), which are the song itself. He joins the nightingale in celebrating the honors of spring; he describes in sexual terms the female Earth baring herself and begging for the love of Phoebus, the returning sun god. She offers not only herself but the bribes of the cool grass, the morning breeze, and a couch of humid roses to soothe their bodies. Men follow the example of Earth in their passion, and even the gods of Olympus, the Dryads, and the Nymphs join in. The poem closes with a prayer for eternal spring, or at least a long, slow season before winter brings back the long nights.

In a close analysis of the poem Woodhouse (*University of Toronto Quarterly* 13:66–101) sees it, not as a casual first impression might suggest, as an exuberant, formless outpouring, but as shaped by a comprehensive and coherent development. He divides the poem into eight sections "controlled by a closely knit pattern": (1) lines 1–4, "the first mark of spring is seen in the good green earth"; (2) 5–24, the poetic impulse revives; (3) 25–28, "poet and nightingale are respectively civic and sylvan heralds of the spring"; (4) 29–54, the poet sings of spring in the heavens and the retreat of Night; (5) 55–94, the Earth woos the sun god; (6) 95–112, humans rejoice under the sway of Venus, Cupid, and Hymen; (7) 113–36, climatically, through the shepherds of Arcady and the deities of the forest and field, the poet proceeds to the gods of Olympus, who desert the sky for the fertile joys of earth; (8) 137–40, the poet prays for the days of spring to pass slowly, postponing the return of winter and night.

Milton's poem thus unites itself around its frank acceptance, fusion, and celebration of creative power in both the physical and the aesthetic sense with spring and sexual love. *El* 5 resolves no conflicts, justifies no ways of God; it is an enthusiastic paean of praise to things as they are at the return of spring. It never even raises the morality of "carpe diem"; it directly and unreservedly pours out Milton's vigorous joy. But it avoids amorphous burbling by its integrated development from the opening lines on the greeting of the earth, through the song of the sexual union of earth and sun, to the joyful excitement of humans under the spell of the season, the erotic pleasures of the gods, and the prayer that the season might last forever.

Critical opinion of *El* 5 has been generally very favorable, although there is disagreement as to how original or imitative the poem is. E. K. Rand says, "It is Pagan from beginning to end, joyous in spirit, sensuous in flavor, perfect in form. Really if Milton had written it on musty parchment and had somebody discover it, the Classical pundits of his day would have proved beyond question by all the tests of scholarship that a lost work of Ovid had come to light" (*Studies in Philology* 19:109–35). Harding says it is a splendid tour de force but "the poem is all Ovid; there is little in it of Milton at all" (*The Club of Hercules* [1962)]. Daiches says of it, "Though Ovidian in style almost to the point of parody, this rapturous welcome to spring nevertheless pulses with genuine feeling." But Fletcher unequivocally calls it "Milton's finest poem in Latin" (*The Intellectual Development of John Milton,* 2 [1961]), and Woodhouse says it is "the peak of Milton's earlier Latin poetry," and stresses its originality. One cannot, he observes, "point to any single model in Ovid and his fellows, or (save in the most general terms) in the Renaissance. Even in Tibullus nature plays a small part; and, despite the invitation in much classical myth and popular custom, the theme of love and spring-time rarely come together in Roman poetry save in one or two of Horace's odes and the late *Pervigilium Veneris.*"

El 6, like *El* 1, is a verse letter to Charles Diodati. Milton dated it December 1629, at the same time as, or immediately after, his composition of *Nat.*

El 6 begins playfully: Diodati had written Milton a verse letter (not now extant) in Latin or Greek on December 13, 1629. In it he apologized for the poor quality of the verse on the grounds that his reception by his friends had been too lavish. Milton mockingly laments his own empty stomach but commends Diodati for his pleasant holiday, then very un-Puritanically expands on the pleasures of wine, revelry, and poetry for twenty-eight lines (9–36) and for another twelve dwells on music and love as sources of poetic inspiration. These joys are appropriate to the elegiac poet, Milton says, but the epic poet must lead an ascetic life, let herbs furnish his innocent diet, and have purest water stand beside him in a bowl. Homer*, Milton points out, was a spare eater and a drinker of water. As for himself, he adds, he is singing the Heaven-descended King, the infant cries of our God in the manger. He concludes with a promise to present his new verses (*Nat*) to Diodati.

El 6 has been read in two contrasting lights. By some it has been taken as a major turning point in Milton's poetic career, and by others as a pleasant per-

sonal poem to a friend who asked what he was doing. Hanford sees it as the first fruit of Milton's dedication of his life to "something higher and more serious than amatory lyrics" and connects the description of the ascetic life (55–78), as opposed to the self-indulgence of the elegiac poet, with Milton's statement thirteen years later in 1642 (*Apol*) that "he who would not be frustrate of his hope to write well hereafter in laudable things, ought himself to be a true poem, that is a composition and pattern of the best and honorablest things." Woodhouse agrees in seeing *El* 6 as "a rejection of the type of erotic emotion found in the elegies."

Parker finds such a reading "quite unwarranted," pointing out that Milton devotes more of the poem to the pleasures of wine and love than he does to the virtues of asceticism. "To argue that Milton must be speaking of himself, confiding his own plans, in the section on the ascetic life, yet merely bantering in the section on the festive life, is equivalent to arguing that Milton is really Il Penseroso and only exercising his wrist in [L'Allegro]."

The closing couplet is also the subject of some scholarly disagreement. The last four lines of the poem are as follows:

Dona quidem dedimus Christi natalibus illa,
　Illa sub auroram lux mihi prima tulit.
Te quoque pressa manent patriis meditata cicutis,
　Tu mihi, cui recitem, judicis instar eris.
　　　　　　　　　　　　　(87–90)

(These are my gifts for the birthday of Christ—gifts which the first light of its dawn brought to me. For you these simple strains that have been meditated on my native pipes are waiting; and you, when I recite them to you, shall be my judge.— Trans. Hughes. Charles Knapp's translation, in *CM*, differs in important respects.) The first pair of these lines is unquestionably a continuation of Milton's statement to Diodati that he is writing *Nat.* Most critics have taken the last two lines as a conclusion of this reference to the ode.

But Bateson and Fletcher have argued

that "quoque" ("also") in line 89 makes the last two lines refer to some poem in addition to the ode ("for you other strains too are waiting," in Knapp's translation). Further, "cicutis" ("pipes," line 89), Bateson and Fletcher maintain, is a term used only to refer to pastoralism*, of which there is little in the ode. Therefore, they argue, the allusion in these last two lines must be to Milton's only pastoral poems of this period, *L'Al* and *IlP*, whose dates have for other reasons been the subject of considerable speculation. Bateson and Fletcher's reading of these two lines in *El* 6 would thus put *L'Al* and *IlP* two years earlier than the generally accepted date of 1631.

Other scholars (Bush, Leishman, and Martz) reject this reading and take the final twelve lines as referring only to *Nat*. Leishman argues that by "cicutis" Milton meant "not any particular kind of poetry, but any kind of poetry composed in his native tongue." Further, "the Nativity Ode, with its shepherds, might be more (though still not very) appropriately described as a pastoral than either *L'Allegro* or *Il Penseroso*." Martz says that the "quoque" of line 89, rather than referring to the writing of some other poem, "modifies *te*; or rather it is pleonastic and is best omitted." And Leishman admits that in this passage Milton's Latin has "a certain harshness and inelegance." In any case it would have been awkward and cramped of Milton to introduce a fourth type of poem into the last two lines; he has discussed elegies and epics, and for at least ten of the last twelve lines he has expanded on his poem on Christ's birth. Now to conclude with a two-line digression on a hitherto-unmentioned pastoral poem, or poems, would be a kind of structural excrescence; and by the time Milton was twenty-one, in 1629, he would seem to have outgrown such faults.

The date of *El* 7 is uncertain; Milton wrote it, he says, in the spring, "anno aetatis undevigesimo" ("in the nineteenth year of [his] age"), which can be taken to mean 1627. But Milton usually dates his early poems "anno aetatis" meaning "at the age of . . . ," which here would mean 1628. It should also be noted that, as best one can tell, the previous six elegies are numbered in the order they were written; if Milton were eighteen or nineteen when he wrote *El* 7, it should have preceded *El* 5 and perhaps even *El* 4. But if *El* 7 follows *El* 6 chronologically, as *El* 6 seems to follow *El* 5, then Milton was twenty-one when he wrote it; Parker therefore argues that "undevigesimo" misprints Milton's "uno et vigesimo" ("twenty-one"), dating the poem in May 1630.

The argument is further complicated by the ten-line epilogue that follows it, beginning

Haec ego mente olim laeva, studioque supino
  Nequitiae posui vana trophaea meae.
                                    (103–4)

(These are the monuments to my wantonness that with a perverse spirit and a trifling purpose I once erected.) Does Milton mean the epilogue to apply to all the elegies or only to *El* 7? Only *El* 5, *El* 7, and part of *El* 1 can be called erotic. One may therefore argue that since Milton wanted the epilogue as a conclusion to the series of elegies, and since it was inapplicable to *El* 6, the last to be written, therefore he shifted *El* 7 from its proper chronological position to one more appropriate to this concluding "retraction." In any case we must not ignore the fact that Milton printed both the epilogue and whichever elegies it professes to retract in both the 1645 and the 1673 editions of his poems.

El 7 is the most personally erotic of Milton's poems; he begins telling of the contempt he had felt for Cupid, and the rest of the poem is taken up with Cupid's revenge. The poem ends with Cupid's victory: Milton never again saw the girl with whom Cupid had assailed him, and he begs for release from his madness; or rather, since the pain of love is a pleasure, he pleads that the next time his love be reciprocated.

Like the praise of self-indulgence in

El 6, Milton's confession of an over-whelming, instantaneous, but unrequited love for an unknown girl contradicts the stereotype of Milton as an ascetic, self-disciplined, totally God-fearing poet. The eroticism of *El* 7 as well as the wry self-deprecation—he got the punishment from Cupid his arrogance deserved—represents a side of Milton's personality that rarely emerges in the great poems of his maturity. The Ovidian theme of Cupid's revenge, however, is conventional and there is no evidence as to whether the incident is autobiographical* or fictional. In any case it is a pleasant poem; the poet's ironic overstatement of his feelings is deftly managed. Here the classical allusions, which all but crushed some of the early elegies, give an attractively comic air to his fleeting glimpse of the pretty girl. Milton's promises to appease Cupid are sardonically mock-epic, and his con-clusion is appropriately anti-sentimental.

The date of the epilogue is unknown. The most obvious choices are about 1630, after the last of the elegies had been written, or 1645, just prior to their pub-lication. It has been argued from the phrases "olim" ("formerly") and "indocil-isque aetas" ("undisciplined youth"), and the past tenses of most of the verbs in the epilogue, that it must postdate the elegies by some time; but Keightley raises the point that the phrasing of the last four lines is odd for Milton to have written in 1645, for they would have been written within three years of his court-ship and marriage to Mary Powell, and whatever the facts of Milton's wooing, these lines do not seem to fit. It is safest to say that the epilogue might have been written in any year between 1630 and 1645. [RC]

ELIOT, GEORGE: *see* INFLUENCE ON THE LITERATURE OF NINETEENTH-CENTURY ENGLAND, MILTON'S.

ELIOT, T(HOMAS) S(TERNS) (1888–1965), poet and critic. Although he published well under fifty pages of crit-icism of Milton (and referred in *The*

Waste Land only once to *PL,* line 98n), Eliot must rank as one of his chief twentieth-century interpreters in view of the immense influence carried by his pronouncements, which encouraged others to a redefinition of Milton as a poet, which caused a reappraisal of the "organ voice," and which elicited spirited responses from such critics as C. S. Lewis* and Douglas Bush.

It is not surprising that as a royalist and high-church Anglican Eliot was antagonistic to the Independent* defender of the Commonwealth, admitting his con-tinuing "antipathy towards Milton the man." But the real force of his censure was directed against the supposed damage that Milton had inflicted upon poetic diction by dissociating it sharply from ordinary language. As early as his essay on Dryden (1922), Eliot had argued that "in the seventeenth century a dissociation of sensibility set in, from which we have never recovered." This dissociation is owing primarily to Milton and Dryden*. Narrowing his focus to Milton alone, he amplified this judgment in the famous "Note on the Verse of John Milton," in *Essays and Studies by Members of the English Association* 21 : 32–40, where he asserts that "there is more of Milton's influence in the badness of the bad verse of the eighteenth century than of any-body's else." Indeed, he fulminates, "Mil-ton's poetry could *only* be an influence for the worse, upon any poet whatsoever." The reasoning back of this judgment is significant : unlike Shakespeare*, Milton turned away from the living language of speech to construct an artificial one of his own in his poetry. It is the acceptance of such artifice that has led other poets to bad writing; the appraisal is addressed to them rather than to Milton.

Eliot himself did not reprint the essay, but twenty years later, in "Milton," *Proceedings of the British Academy* 33: 61–80, his judgment remained essentially unchanged, though he admitted that his earlier strictures upon Milton had been unfair. Such dissociation of sensibility as produced Milton's poetry was probably inherent in society and in any case Milton was not responsible for the bad verse of his followers. But Eliot still finds that "in Milton there is always the maximal, never the minimal, alteration of ordinary language," even though now he does not find such deviation to be reprehensible. He concludes that poets now "are sufficiently removed from Milton . . . to approach the study of his work without danger." The two essays are salutary in calling attention to important matters of diction*, but they have no significant insights as to the content of the poetry.

It is not certain how much significance attaches to Eliot's imitation of Milton's title and work in *Sweeny Agonistes. See also* INFLUENCE ON TWENTIETH-CENTURY LITERATURE, MILTON'S. [WBH]

ELLWOOD, THOMAS (1639–1713), young Quaker* friend of Milton who left an important contemporary biographical statement of the poet's life after the Restoration. Following a youth that he later regarded as dissipated, Ellwood at the age of twenty met Isaac Pennington the younger, a recent convert to the Society of Friends; shortly thereafter he himself joined this new minority sect. Deciding that he needed a better education, in 1662 he arranged to meet the former teacher Milton through a mutual friend, Dr. Paget*. In exchange for reading to the blind poet he was instructed in Latin and records that Milton spoke that language with Italian pronunciation instead of English. Despite being jailed several times for his faith, he continued on friendly terms with the poet. In June 1665 he found a residence* for him at Chalfont St. Giles, where Milton lived during the year of the great plague.

Probably in the late summer of 1665 Milton loaned Ellwood a manuscript of *PL*. According to the account of the latter, when he returned it Ellwood "pleasantly said to him, 'Thou hast said much here of Paradise Lost, but what hast thou to say of Paradise Found?'"

Milton, he says, "sat some time in a muse" and then changed the subject. By the next summer Milton had returned to London, where he sometime thereafter showed the young man a second manuscript, *PR*, and added "This is owing to you; for you put it into my head by the question you put to me at Chalfont." Because Ellwood did not clearly state the date of Milton's later remark, it does not finally establish the date of composition of *PR*. Biographers* tend to play down the importance as a motivation for Milton that the statement suggests.

The Quaker remained familiar with the poet until the latter's death. It has been suggested by Shawcross that he may indeed have written the receipt of payment from Samuel Simmons* for the publication of *PL* (*see* E. T. McLaughlin, "Milton and Thomas Ellwood," *Milton Newsletter* 1 : 17–28). Sometime after Milton's death he wrote a highly adulatory epitaph in riming tetrameters that dwells particularly on the polemics against King Charles* and Salmasius* and that praises Milton's "Measures without Rime" in which the poet forsook "The common road." It survives in the Friends Library, London, and has been reprinted in facsimile and transcription by McLaughlin.

The rest of Ellwood's life does not concern Milton. He became a leader in the growing movement of the Friends. In 1678 and later he attacked tithing but does not seem to have known *Hire*. He wrote voluminously : pamphlets on contemporary religious issues, biblical interpretation, some poetry including a long work *Davideis* (begun before 1688 and completed before he had read Cowley's* poem with the same title), and especially *The History of the Life of Thomas Ellwood* (1714), a major document in Quaker history and the source of his recollection of Milton. In 1743 John Nickolls* published *Original Letters and Papers of State, Addressed to Oliver Cromwell*, claiming their authenticity from Cromwell* to Milton to Ellwood to the latter's friend Joseph Wyeth, and finally through the latter's widow to the editor himself. Whether or not the story is true, it indicates the respect shown Ellwood as Milton's friend in the eighteenth century. [WBH]

ELZEVIR PRESS, THE. The press of Abraham Elzevir (1592–1652) in Leyden continued by Ludovic, and that of Daniel in Amsterdam, frequently figure in the publication of Milton's works before and after his death. *1Def* was published in two editions by Ludovic Elzevir; one, Madan No. 6, came out in March 1651 in duodecimo with the index, and the other, Madan No. 7, came out shortly thereafter in 1651, also in duodecimo but without the index. According to a letter from Nicolaas Heinsius* to Isaac Vossius*, dated May 8/18, 1651, Elzevir spoke of Milton's high birth and great wealth, obviously as a result of exaggerated rumor that had reached him. Vossius probably received his copy of *1Def* from Elzevir. Dirk Graswinckel (1600–1666), a lawyer, announced in May his intention of writing a reply to Milton according to letters from Heinsius to Vossius, dated May 14/24, 1651, and from Vossius to Heinsius, dated June 1/11 and 8/18. Heinsius told Johann Friedrich Gronovius* in a letter dated June 18/28 that Graswinckel wanted his book published by the Elzevir Press. Graswinckel was dissuaded from his intentions by the Dutch government. John Phillips's *Responsio** was also reprinted by Elzevir in 1652, in an effort to capitalize upon the controversy that had developed over the English government, Salmasius*, Milton, and Rowland, whom Phillips was answering. It is a duodecimo easily distinguished from other pirated editions by the spelling of the author's first name, "IOANNUS." One of John Thurloe's* correspondents from the Hague reported that in an effort to suppress *2Def* Alexander More* bought up the 500 copies that the Elzevir Press had obtained; see *A Collection of the State Papers of John Thurloe* (1742), 2: 452, the letter being dated July 24, 1654. Daniel Elzevir's *Catalogus Librorum*

(Amsterdam, 1674) advertised Milton's 1645 *Poems*, *1Def* (an Amsterdam duodecimo and the London quarto), *3Def* (the London octavo and the Hague duodecimo), and *2Def* (the London octavo and the Hague duodecimo), p. 121. During 1676–1677, and apparently during the previous year, Elzevir was involved in negotiations with Daniel Skinner* to publish the state papers. But the difficulties he encountered with the English government through its embassy in the Hague forced him to forgo this venture and he remarked that he would have nothing to do with Milton's works. The eventual publication of *Literae Pseudo-Senatûs* in 1676 was by Pieter and Jan Blaeu and immediately after that in a pirated edition by E. Fricx of Brussels. Parker's guess of Elzevir's connection with the publication is without foundation. Apparently what happened is that Skinner negotiated with Elzevir for publication of the state papers around 1675, leaving the manuscript with him; this manuscript is now known as the Skinner MS* in the Public Record Office, SP 9/194. Another copy of the letters had been bought by the London bookseller Moses Pitt*, who had them published in Holland, after Skinner was unable to effect publication with Elzevir as Pitt had requested (see Skinner's deposition dated October 18, 1676). The possible publication of *CD* was also involved. Elzevir wrote to Sir Joseph Williamson, Secretary of State, on November 10/20, 1676, about the matter (Dutch archives; Holland 203; Foreign Entry Books, London, No. 66), and Skinner's father wrote to Elzevir on February 2, 1677 (the letter is not extant), thanking him for return of the manuscripts. Two replies by Elzevir to Skinner, Sr., are extant, one dated February 9/19, 1677, the other dated March 10/20, 1677 (both in the Dutch archives: Holland 204; Foreign Entry Books, London, No. 66). The manuscripts were deposited in the Public Record Office, apparently by Williamson, where they remained until 1823. [JTS]

EMERSON AND MILTON. Ralph Waldo Emerson (1803–1882), the leading exponent of American transcendentalism, provides a clearly documented record of John Milton's influence in nineteenth-century life and writing. In an 1815 letter to his brother William, Emerson records that he "began Milton"; thereafter, references to the English poet continue virtually unabated through sixty-nine years of journals, notebooks, sermons, lectures, essays, and correspondence. Emerson attained his respect for Milton's works while under the powerful Puritan influence of his mother, Ruth Haskins, and his aunt, Mary Moody Emerson; this respect continued through his Unitarian training (1825–1826), his break with the Unitarian Church (1832), and his progressive enthusiasm from about 1829 with English writers of a quite different period and persuasion—Wordsworth*, Coleridge*, and Carlyle.

In the New England educational system of the 1820s Milton was ranged as a giant in English literature. One reason appears in a long peroration about the Puritans recorded in Emerson's *Journals and Miscellaneous Notebooks* on New Year's Day, 1824: "The Puritans had done their duty to literature when they bequeathed it the Paradise Lost & Comus" (2 : 197). Milton's Puritanism undoubtedly reinforced his importance in other areas upon the young Emerson's mind. In his copy of Milton's *Prose Works* (Boston, 1826), nearly every passage about the mission and function of the poet is underlined. This close attention to seventeenth-century poetics is evidenced in Emerson's poetry of the 1830s, which is formally closer to the poetry of Milton, Herbert, and Vaughan than to the less remote English Romantics. One important poem, "Uriel" (*Works,* 9 : 13–15), important for its autobiographical currents, derives its title directly from Milton's Archangel. Emerson's term of praise for the classical form found in the best works of art, which necessarily display energy and symmetry, was *architectural*—derived from Emerson's extended exposure to the cathedrals of Europe during his 1832–33 trip abroad. In its architectural form Milton's work ranked with that of Michelangelo, Dante, Swedenborg, Pythagoras, and Paracelsus (*JMN,* 8 : 252). The full explanation of the "marble beauty" of *Lyc,* he contended, would be "criticism for the gods" (*JMN,* 4 : 111); indeed, Emerson knew this poem so well that during a long storm at sea, amid "anticipations of going to the bottom," he comforted himself by remembering "nearly the whole of Lycidas, clause by clause" (*JMN,* 4 : 103).

Emerson's admiration for Milton did not put him above the biases of his own developing thought. Thus, in 1834, during a period of deep immersion in the English Romantics, he wrote that "Milton was too learned, though I hate to say it. It wrecked his originality. . . . Wordsworth is a more original poet than he" (*JMN,* 4 : 312). But later, in "Self-Reliance" (1841), the "highest merit" of Milton is that he "set at naught books and traditions" (*Works,* 2 : 45). Such remarks, however, are outweighed by scores of references attesting to Milton's supreme place in Western letters. Thus, in 1838: "If you would know the power of character, see how much you would impoverish the world if you could take clean out of history the lives of Milton, Shakespeare, and Plato" (*Works,* 1 : 161). And, in 1870: "The human mind would be a gainer if all the secondary writers were lost,—say, in England, all but Shakspeare, Milton and Bacon,—through the profounder study so drawn to those wonderful minds" (*Works,* 7 : 194).

Emerson's "Milton," first published in the *North American Review* (1838) and now available in Emerson's *Early Lectures* (1 : 144–63), derives from the text of his 1835 lecture on Milton, one of six biographical lectures Emerson delivered in a series at the Masonic Temple in Boston. This series represents the earliest version of Emerson's use of exemplary historical figures as a way of defining generic Man. The mature version is found in *Representative Men* (1850), from which, however, Milton was omitted. The 1835 lecture was worked up from Emerson's knowledge of Milton's *Prose Works*, a recent biography by Ivimey, and Johnson's* *Lives of the Poets*; and stimulated in part by the recent discovery of Milton's *CD*. Influenced perhaps by Channing*, Emerson stressed Milton's inspirational quality: "The idea of a purer existence than any he saw around him, to be realized in the life and conversation of men, inspired every act and every writing of John Milton" (*EL*, 1 : 150). In Milton's prose writings, however, Emerson felt that "the whole is sacrificed to the particular . . . he has never *integrated* the parts of the argument in his mind" (*EL*, 1 : 146)—an ironically sensitive remark beside Emerson's confession to Carlyle that his own style was "fragmentary . . . each sentence an infinitely repellant particle." Emerson's primary response to Milton centered on his character—seen always from the perspective of Emersonian self-reliance. Thus Milton was compounded of "antique heroism," "Christian sanctity," and "perfect humility"; he was truly "an apostle of freedom" (*EL*, 1 : 156, 159). The full extent of Milton's profound influence on Emerson has yet to be charted, although William M. Wynkoop's *Three Children of the Universe: Emerson's View of Shakespeare, Bacon, and Milton* (The Hague, 1966) makes a good beginning; a few earlier studies of Milton and Emerson are listed in *EL*, 1 : 145. [BW]

ENCHIRIDION LINGUAE LATINAE: *see* CANON.

ENCOMIUM EMMAE REGINAE. Written for Emma herself by a Flemish monk about 1040–1042, "The Praise of Queen Emma" was intended to glorify her role in reconciling Danish and Saxon factions for a united England. Daughter of Richard I of Normandy, she married King Ethelred of England in 1002, bearing him the ill-fated Alfred* and Edward the Confessor. With the Danish invasion in 1013, she took them to Normandy until four years later, when King Canute

called her back to marry him, promising that the sons of their union would have precedence over their other children. This provision led to thirty years of bloody intrigue and to her second exile (1037–1040), until finally the success of her son Harthaemut restored her to the comfort commemorated by the *Encomium*, which she enjoyed till her death in 1052. Milton used the *Encomium* for the sixth chapter of *Brit*, tempering its propaganda while valuing its treatment of the political crises attending the Danish dynasty in England. *See also* DuCHESNE, ANDRÉ. [PMZ]

ENOCH, BOOK OF: *see* HEBRAISM.

ENTHUSIASM: *see* RELIGIOUS SECTS.

ENVY. "Envy" denotes sorrow at another's prosperity and joy at his adversity. Christian moralists were indebted to Aristotle* not only for the basic concept but also for an analysis of the causes, conditions, and effects of envy (*Rhetoric* 2. 10). Milton follows the Aristotelian concept in *CD*, adding as examples of this vice such figures as Satan, Cain, Esau, Joseph's brethren, and the laborers in the vineyard (17 : 267–69). In *PL* he continues to be guided by this concept but also draws upon a literary tradition stemming from Ovid*. The story of Aglauros in the *Metamorphoses* (2. 709–832) exerted a pervasive influence on medieval and Renaissance depictions of envy. The allegorization of Ovid—exemplified in the seventeenth century by George Sandys in his *Ovids Metamorphosis* (1632, 1640)—is reflected in much of the imagery used by Milton.

In the Satan of *PL*, envy, traditionally one of the seven deadly sins, grows out of pride and directs itself toward both the Son* and man. When Satan beholds the exaltation of the Son, his pride does not permit him to bear that sight and he becomes fraught "with envie against the Son of God" (5. 661–65). This envy manifests itself during the night that follows. Satan awakens his companion Beelzebub and, while ordering him to assemble forces in the north, indulges in covert slander against the Son (5. 673–93). Beelzebub does as he is bidden, and mingles with his orders "ambiguous words and jealousies" cast forth to "sound / Or taint integritie" (5. 702–4). This episode recalls previous accounts of a victim infected by a figure of envy, for example, of Cain by Medusa (alternately called Envy) in Peyton's *The Glasse of Time in the Second Age* (stanzas 65–66), of Saul by Envy in Cowley's* *Davideis* (1. 303–12), and—the ultimate source for all such depictions—of Aglauros by Envy in Ovid's *Metamorphoses* (2. 797–832). When Satan addresses his forces, he begins with innuendo and then gradually shifts to open and direct verbal attacks (5. 772–802), a progression that corresponds closely to the analysis of envy made by Aquinas* (*Summa Theologica*, 2–2, q. 36, a. 4). Satan's words have their effect: as the Son approaches the next day, the rebel angels, "grieving to see his Glorie, at the sight / Took envie" (6. 792–93). And the Son tells the loyal angels that it is "not you but mee they have despis'd, / Yet envied; against mee is all thir rage" (6. 812–13).

With the creation of man, Satan has a new object for his envy. At the outset of *PL,* we are informed that the infernal serpent deceived the Mother of Mankind because he was "stird up with Envy and Revenge" (1. 35). This envy begins to develop in the infernal council when the devils consider rumors of a new creature, man. Beelzebub expresses resentment at the favored position of this new creature, but this resentment turns to joy at the prospect of turning man against his Creator. Beelzebub is speaking on behalf of Satan, who first devised and in part proposed this plot of such deep malice. The other devils accept this plan, and joy sparkles in their eyes as they vote assent (2. 370–89). Hence envy spreads from Satan to Beelzebub and ultimately to the rest of the fallen angels.

When Satan directly confronts man, his envy takes the form of grief or joy depending upon the circumstances. He observes "with grief" Adam and Eve enjoying happiness in the garden (4. 358–92). He turns away "for envie" and looks with "jealous leer maligne" when the pair embrace; his eyeing this scene "askance" is in keeping with the Ovidian tradition of describing the envious (4. 502–4). That night he assumes the form of a toad—a traditional symbol of envy—and inspires in Eve a dream*. Like the episode of Satan infecting Beelzebub, this dream, as Eve recounts it the next day (5. 28–93), alludes to Ovid's description of the personified Envy corrupting Aglauros and to the similar descriptions by Peyton and Cowley. But Satan's initial grief reverses itself after Adam and Eve have fallen, and accordingly he returns to hell "with joy" (10. 345–51).

Envy on the human level is exemplified by Cain in the first of the visions that Michael presents to Adam (11. 429–60). Michael explains the significance of this scene: "th' unjust the just hath slain, / For envie that his Brothers Offering found / From Heav'n acceptance" (11. 455–57). Adam then laments both the deed and the "cause" (11. 461). Genesis gives no explanation as to the motivation of Cain, but Christian exegetes recognized the incident as an embodiment of the Aristotelian concept of envy. St. Augustine* made such an interpretation in *The City of God* (15. 5. 7), and Dante* cited Cain as the biblical example of envy, paralleling that of Aglauros from the classical tradition (*Purgatorio* 14. 130–38). Milton himself in *CD* twice refers to Cain in his discussion of envy, once as an example of the vice itself and again as an example of how envy leads to other crimes (17 : 267). Hence, with respect to envy, Cain on the human level is the counterpart to Satan on the diabolical. [RF]

EPIC, PARADISE LOST AND THE CLASSICAL. Perhaps the most important thing about Milton's relation to the epic tradition is that he turned away from the predominantly allegorical* mode of the Renaissance, with its schematic representation of human virtues* and vices, to the more realistic mode of classical epic, with its rich and organic delineation of character. In *PL* Milton recaptures the psychological depth and complexity and all-roundness that one finds in the major characters of Homer* and Virgil*. Thus, despite all his debts to "sage and serious Spenser*," whom he found "a better teacher than Aquinas*," the great classical epics remained his strongest literary influence. His frequent and emphatic rejection of the traditional themes of classical epic as "tedious and fabled havoc" may keep us from seeing how pervasive their influence is—and how decisive.

Milton's realistic psychological mode, which focuses on the inward man, is the necessary concomitant of his radical Christian conception of human freedom and responsibility. Obviously the concept has its sources in the Bible, but it is also central to the *Odyssey,* as Milton reminds us in *CD*. Milton's man is intensely individualistic. He is represented again and again throughout the poetry and prose as being alone with his conscience. Except for Adam and Eve before the Fall, the Deity appears to man only through this inner light. Thus Abdiel, whose "fortitude . . . maintained his singularity of virtue against the scorn of multitudes," in Dr. Johnson's* felicitous phrase, is Milton's norm. With not even a Palmer to guide and counsel him, he endures the taunts and hatred of his fellows to be rewarded only with a hearty "well-done" and the discomfiture of seeing his side apparently defeated in battle. Ultimately, the Miltonic hero is a lonely figure, like Christian in *Pilgrim's Progress;* it is in their conceptions of characters pursuing their solitary ways "with dangers and with darkness compassed round" that the two great Puritan writers are closest to each other. At the end of *PL* the wayfaring Adam and Eve thus "hand in hand, with wandering steps and slow / Through Eden take thir solitary way." *Solitary* certainly has the force of "alone together," but who can doubt, after all the evidence

of antagonism and mutual miscomprehension in the scenes leading up to and following the Fall*, that it will also apply to each of them separately?

The characters of Adam and Eve owe more to those of Hector and Andromache, Helen and Paris, Odysseus and Nausicaa, Aeneas and Dido, than they do to all the characters of Renaissance epic and romance, English and continental. Milton's preoccupation with allegory in *Mask* had its counterpart in his later poems, however, but not in terms of the schematization of the psychomachia, however subtle, as in Dante and Spenser, but in what Chapman had called (speaking of the theme of the *Odyssey*) "the Mind's inward, constant and unconquered Empire, unbroken, unaltered with any most insolent and tyrannous infliction." Chapman was not there proclaiming a perfect and unmovable Odysseus, but one in whom, in the long run, external forces and temptations must yield to inner resources, with the help of Heaven. It follows that in his major works in poetry and prose (as well as in many of his shorter poems) Milton's one grand theme is the attainment of freedom through a single-handed combat with temptation, and the result is what looks to many of our contemporaries like a paradox —the inseparableness of freedom and obedience.

Although Milton abandoned his earlier schemes for a heroic drama on a national theme in favor of the narrative mode of epic and a Christian theme, his long preoccupation with the concentration and intensity of certain kinds of dramatic agons helped to determine the character of the conflicts he developed in *PL* and *PR*. The conflicts represented in these epics are, essentially, debates*. Only two characters really participate, even when, as in the debates in Pandemonium, others are present. The critical encounters always have two adversaries: Adam and Eve, Eve and Satan, Abdiel and Satan, the Son and Satan. Here *SA* is illuminating because, despite the size of the dramatis personae, we never have Samson encountering more than one adversary at a time. What Milton did, in effect, in terms of Greek drama*, was to return to the earlier two-character Aeschylean tragedy, rather than to the models of Sophocles or Euripides in which a third character was added. Despite its striking resemblances to *Oedipus at Colonus,* in which a formerly mighty hero, now blinded, impoverished, and humiliated, combats a succession of tempters and aggressors, *SA* as a dramatic conception is far closer to Aeschylus's *Prometheus Bound* with its immobilized hero than to any play of Sophocles or Euripides. The influence of this Aeschylean drama upon Milton's imagination is indicated by the fact that twenty-four allusions to it are listed in the index to *CM* as compared with a total of twelve for the *Agamemnon, Eumenides, Persians, Seven against Thebes,* and *Suppliants.* From this it follows that Milton's heroes, like Prometheus, tend to be physically passive. They are not doers of mighty and spectacular deeds, on the whole, although Samson's final feat of strength, which, of course, is only reported, outdoes all other ancient warriors in violence. The Lady in *Mask,* Adam, Eve, the Son in *PR,* or secondary figures such as the Brothers, Abdiel, Michael, and Raphael, are not heroic by dint of heroic force or guile but by virtue of possessing or attaining "the mind's inward, constant and unconquered Empire, unbroken, unaltered with any most insolent and tyrannous infliction." Their heroism is of the mind and spirit, and it leads, as Louis Martz has shown, to the Paradise within, and to "calm of mind, all passion spent."

In *PL* heroic feats of arms and guile are performed by Satan. In rousing and marshaling his fallen warriors, in conducting the great debate, in confronting Sin and Death at the gates of Hell, in floundering and struggling through Chaos, and in the War in Heaven, he is a paramount actor and outdoes all previous epic heroes in the magnitude of his feats. In destroying the citadel of mankind and thereby confounding in one root the entire human race, he outdoes those archetypal city-wreckers, Achilles and Odysseus. He

is an actor in other senses, too, as we are reminded by the Greek word from which *hypocrite* is derived. Our earliest insight into the ineradicable division between these two senses of the word occurs at his first appearance in the poem, when, after his rousing speech to his comrades on the burning lake, Milton describes him as "vaunting aloud, though wrack'd with deep despair." Satan asserts repeatedly the firmness of his resolution "never to submit or yield," but his soliloquies and Milton's comments show him the victim of a never-ending flux of painful thoughts and feelings, of "ire, envy, and despair." Enthralled to himself, he discovers despite his boast that "the mind is its own place, and in itself / Can make a Heav'n of Hell, a Hell of Heav'n," that even a flight through interstellar space from the Abyss to Paradise is insufficient to escape the horror of his inner self:

Me miserable! which way shal I flie
Infinite wrauth, and infinite despaire?
Which way I flie is Hell; my self am Hell;
And in the lowest deep a lower deep
Still threatning to devour me opens wide,
To which the Hell I suffer seems a Heav'n.
(4. 73–78)

The grim pilgrimage of Satan's ego is a plumbing of lower deeps beyond successive lowest deeps, as Pope's* parodic "Anti-Christ of Wit" shows:

Swearing and supperless the Hero sate,
Blasphem'd his Gods, the Dice, and damn'd his Fate.
Then gnaw'd his pen, then dash'd it on the ground,
Sinking from thought to thought, a vast profound!
Plung'd for his sense, but found no bottom there,
Yet wrote and flounder'd on, in mere despair.
(*Dunciad* [1742], 1. 115–20)

Pope recognized Milton's conception of wickedness as being essentially folly or unreason as well as malignity, a synthesis also to be found in the indictment, at the beginning of the *Odyssey,* of human *atasthalia,* "criminal folly." Waldock, Empson, and others, instead of seeing the innate consistency of this conception, charge Milton with "degrading" Satan, but such is not the case. By a principle of moral gravity Satan must degrade himself as long as he rebels against his Creator, and his malignity must, as the Creator says, "redound / Upon his own rebellious head." The moral world of *PL,* even though it permits evils, is in perfect balance. Every moral force is articulated, and Divinity, instead of being reduced to eavesdropping or impulsively intervening in the affairs of men, as Homer's and Virgil's gods appear to do much of the time, has allowed man a breadth of knowledge about himself and his universe and a moral autonomy that are breathtaking. The spatial polarities, which seize our imaginations in *PL,* symbolize moral and spiritual polarities, heroically conceived as mighty opposites of good and evil, love and hatred, obedience* and rebelliousness, and so forth. Spatially, as in his use of light and darkness, Milton is closer to Dante than to other epic poets. His world is dynamically three-dimensional, while that of Homer or Virgil or Spenser or Tasso* is predominantly planar. The descents from heaven or the descents into hell, which interrupt this general planar conception, become, as Thomas Greene suggests, the main narrative armature of *PL.* No one has written of space so imaginatively as Milton, thus demonstrating the illimitable resources of a blind man's imagination. "Presented with a Universal blanc / Of Nature's works to me expung'd and ras'd," he implores his "Celestial Light" to

Shine inward, and the mind through all her
    powers
Irradiate, there plant eyes, all mist from
    thence
Purge and disperse, that I may see and tell
Of things invisible to mortal sight.
                                    (3. 52–55)

The strenuousness of Satan's enterprise is excelled by the energy of Milton's long contemplation. Casting aside the classical precedent of authorial anonymity and impersonality, Milton, turning to the example of Dante, wrote himself into the fundamental narrative movement of the poem, making himself, in his imagination,

a companion of Omniscience and Omnipresence as he sings of "things invisible to mortal sight."

With Satan assuming the traditional heroic occupations of warrior, orator, and voyager that in former epics were pursued by such as Achilles, Odysseus, Aeneas, or Turnus, and with the central roles devolving upon the human pair, the question naturally arises as to whether *PL* has a hero, and if so, who he (or she) is. The Son* is presented as the natural counterpart of Satan : his voluntary submission to incarnation* and death in order to redeem man clearly counterpoints Satan's ruinous mission, while exceeding it immeasurably in grandeur and true greatness. But the poem only forecasts this mission. Within the narrative itself the Son's chief role is as a deputized Creator, who repairs the ruins the Satanic rebellion has caused by creating the World and all living things within it. Omnipotence and Omniscience would disqualify the Son as a hero in the traditional sense. He lacks the indispensable qualification of mortality, though, of course, he will assume it long after the Fall of Man, which is the main subject of the poem.

This brings us to a consideration of Adam, or Adam and Eve, or Eve as hero. How can a person who fails in his only responsibility qualify as an epic hero? Can falling or failing be a heroic act? Dryden* thought not :

> Spenser had a better plea for his *Fairy Queen,* had his action been finished, or had been one. And Milton, if the devil had not been his hero instead of Adam, if the giant had not foiled the knight, and driven him out of his stronghold, to wander through the world with his lady-errant. (*Works,* 14 : 144)

Charging Dryden with petulance, Johnson proclaimed, as he cited the example of Lucan's Cato, that "there is no reason why the hero should not be unfortunate except established practice, since success and virtue do not go necessarily together" (*Lives of the Poets,* Hill ed., 1 : 176).

In view of Milton's anti-heroic conception of the epic and his emphatic rejection of "Wars, hitherto the only Argument / Heroic deem'd," we must expect drastic alterations in the characteristics and values of the hero. Where goodness supersedes heroic greatness, charity and humility supersede those virtues which traditionally find expression in mighty deeds. Thus Milton approaches the *sublimitas-humilitas* paradox of the New Testament that Dante wrote into the *Divine Comedy*. Some such notion of the hero as sufferer seems to lie behind Landor's* indignant rejection of Satan as hero and his assertion that "it is Adam who suffers most, and on whom the consequences have most influence. This constitutes him the main character" (*Imaginary Conversations,* 4 : 201).

If, as Douglas Bush says, the *Odyssey* was Milton's favorite poem, we find many clues to Milton's conceptions of true heroism* in that poem. The adjective *polutlas,* "much-enduring," occurs thirty-seven times in the *Odyssey* and is applied only to Odysseus; in its five appearances in the *Iliad* it is also reserved as an epithet for him. Although scholars have often pointed to the Odyssean traits of Milton's Satan, such as his guile and resourcefulness, they have tended to overlook the more acceptable virtues of endurance and patience that are also a part of the Odyssean character. While Odysseus the sacker of cities is obviously a prototype for Satan, Odysseus the much-enduring provides a standard by which Satan is judged and found wanting. This aspect of Odysseus is incorporated in other ways into *PL,* most of all, perhaps, in the character of the epic poet whose "personal touches . . . remind us, intimately, that this poem is an action of thoughts within a central, controlling intelligence that moves with inward eyes toward a recovery of Paradise" (Martz, *The Paradise Within,* p. 106). This interior journey of the poet is the implicit or subliminal action of the poem, most clearly seen in the invocation to "holy Light" that opens Book 3. Having escaped the dark abyss, Milton revisits the realms of light, like Odysseus in the Nekuia, or like Aeneas emerging from the underworld in *Aeneid* 7.

Since Man is the focal point of *PL* and since his virtues and weaknesses are distributed among various characters, it may be that the poem lacks a hero, or that the role of the hero is shared among various characters. Surely Adam is the central figure, as Landor says, but in an important sense the Poet, singing his adventurous song and pursuing his strenuous course of contemplation under the inspiration of divine Wisdom, is a new Odysseus, struggling homeward through dangers and darkness, guided by a new Athene. Milton, the Poet in the poem, is a surrogate for Man. He is heroic in this representative sense, as his famous invocation to light suggests :

Thee I re-visit now with bolder wing,
Escap't the *Stygian* Pool, though long detain'd
In that obscure sojourn, while in my flight
Through utter and through middle darkness
    borne
With other notes than to th' *Orphean* Lyre
I sung of *Chaos* and *Eternal Night,*
Taught by the heav'nly Muse to venture down
The dark descent, and up to reascend,
Though hard and rare. . . .
(3. 13–21)

Adam's last words to Michael in Book 12 end with a similar emphasis on endurance, patience, and suffering :

    that suffering for Truths sake
Is fortitude to highest victorie,
And to the faithful Death the Gate of Life;
Taught this by his example whom I now
Acknowledge my Redeemer ever blest.
(569–73)

This final view of fallen but redeemable man, with its emphasis upon what Milton calls elsewhere "the better fortitude" of patience, obedience, and love*, is of course, primarily Christian. But

just as Milton synthesized the accounts of creation in Genesis and various hexaemeral books with that in the *Metamorphoses,* as Davis Harding has shown, so did he fuse Christian precepts with the highest virtues of Homeric and Virgilian epic.

The enunciation of man's moral freedom and responsibility that God delivers in Book 3 of *PL* serves a function comparable to that of Zeus in the Olympian conclave in Book 1 of the *Odyssey*, which Milton cites at a central point in *CD*. Milton's rejection of Calvinistic predestination*, though linked to Arminianism*, also reanimates the principle of moral freedom at the center of Homer's poem. In effect Milton rejects the tragic view of life exemplified by the career of Achilles. What, then, does *PL* owe to the *Iliad*? Certainly the indomitable, rebellious, and wrathful hero who, by his defection, involves his associates and co-partners in destruction, is Achillean. Satan's pride and egotism are Achillean. But the two characters diverge at a crucial point. When Odysseus encounters Achilles in the underworld in *Odyssey* 11, he renounces the tragic heroism by which he had lived and died :

Better, I say, to break sod as a farm hand
for some poor country man, on iron rations,
than lord it over all the exhausted dead.
(489–91)

Here is the epitaph for the old code of heroic glory. On the same question Satan in Book 1 obstinately affirms the old standard of pride and egotism, underscoring his intransigence :

Here we may reign secure, and in my choyce
To reign is worth ambition though in Hell :
Better to reign in Hell, than serve in Heav'n.
(261–63)

Perhaps no episode in *PL* has received more unfavorable critical attention than the War in Heaven*. Dr. Johnson found there a "confusion of spirit and matter" which resulted in "incongruity." Arnold Stein, acknowledging the incongruity, sees it as "a scherzo, like some of Beethoven's—with more than human laughter, too elevated, and comprehensive, and reverberating not to be terribly funny" (*Answerable Style*, p. 20). Incongruity and absurdity are indeed there, but, to be fully understood, the episode should be read against its Homeric

model. The *Iliad* has its share of incongruous and absurd episodes that produce similar scherzo effects. The deception of Zeus by Hera in Book 14 is one, which Milton alludes to, surprisingly, in his touching description of Adam and Eve:

So spake our general Mother, and with eyes
Of conjugal attraction unreprov'd,
And meek surrender, half imbracing leand
On our first Father, half her swelling Breast
Naked met his under the flowing Gold
Of her loose tresses hid : he in delight
Both of her Beauty and submissive Charms
Smil'd with superior Love, as *Jupiter*
On *Juno* smiles, when he impregns the
        Clouds
That shed *May* flowers. . . .
            (4. 492–501)

The allusion here to Zeus at his most besotted and uxorious gives an ominous undertone to the description and anticipates Adam's weakness just as Eve's Narcissus-like preoccupation with her own image anticipates her weakness, although, as Tillyard argues, these are not moral flaws in characters that are perfect, but mere inclinations.

One of the other sources of comedy in the *Iliad* arises from the warfare of the gods, sometimes with other gods and sometimes with mortals. The absurdity stems from the inconclusiveness of the combats (they settle nothing) and from the simple fact of the god's being immortal. For immortals to engage in mortal conflict is inherently ridiculous. As Bowra has written, "the heroic standards of honour were so high that they revealed the weaknesses of theologies older than themselves, and the natural result was that the gods were made figures of fun" (*Tradition and Design in the "Iliad,"* p. 239). The two days of inconclusive combat in Heaven (*PL* 6) heighten the absurdity of the Homeric theomachies. Since no mortals are involved, the conflict is inherently pointless, and therein lies its point : the power of the combatants on both sides, enormous and outrageous as it is, is limited by God, who explains his position to the Son thus:

sore hath been thir fight,
As likeliest was, when two such Foes met
  arm'd;
For to themselves I left them, and thou
  know'st,
Equal in thir Creation they were form'd,
Save what sin hath impaird, which yet hath
  wrought
Insensibly, for I suspend thir doom;
Whence in perpetual fight they needs must
  last
Endless, and no solution will be found:
War wearied hath perform'd what Warr can
  do. . . .

(6. 687–95)

Milton has caught the innate futility of Homeric theomachies and has allowed God to interrupt what would otherwise have been a perpetual comic-strip series of gigantic deeds of destruction interspersed with pratfalls. Yet in one respect he fails to achieve the high seriousness that often informs Homer's heroic farces. The reason is that no mortals are involved in these combats, while in Homer what is play to the gods is death and wounds to men. The incongruity that Johnson complained of in the "confusion of spirit and matter" is entirely functional in revealing the inferiority of physical force to spiritual power. In John Steadman's phrase, the War in Heaven is a "critique of fortitude."

A neglected instance of Milton's use of Homeric theomachies is the encounter of Gabriel and Moloch,

furious King, who him defi'd
And at his Chariot wheeles to drag him
  bound
Threatn'd, nor from the Holie One of Heav'n
Refrain'd his tongue blasphemous. . . .
(6. 357–60)

His blasphemies and boasts are soon transformed: "anon / Down clov'n to the waste, with shatter'd Arms / And uncouth paine [he] fled bellowing" (360–62). Here Milton is alluding to the wounding of Ares, another "furious King," by Diomedes and Athene in *Iliad* 5 :

After him Diomedes of the great war cry
  drove forward
with the bronze spear; and Pallas Athene,
  leaning on it,

drove it into the depth of the belly where the
  war belt girt him.
Picking this place she stabbed and driving it
  deep in the fair flesh
wrenched the spear out again. Then Ares the
  brazen bellowed
with a sound as great as nine thousand men
  make, or ten thousand. . . .
(855–60)

Ares' flight to Olympus and self-pitying plea to father Zeus is a model for Stein's "gigantic scherzo." There, despite his distaste for Ares, Zeus reluctantly acknowledges his paternal responsibilities and tells Paieon to heal him. Then "Hebe washed him clean and put delicate clothing upon him. / And rejoicing in his strength he sat down beside Kronion," exactly as though nothing at all had happened. Milton must also have had this heroic absurdity in mind when he described Abdiel's wounding of Satan with the invincible sword of Michael :

it met
The sword of *Satan* with steep force to smite
Descending, and in half cut sheer, nor staid,
But with swift wheele reverse, deep entring
  shear'd
All his right side; then *Satan* first knew pain,
And writh'd him to and fro convolv'd; so sore
The griding sword with discontinuous wound
Pass'd through him, but th' Ethereal substance clos'd
Not long divisible. . . .

(6. 323–31)

Rescued from the battle by fellow warriors, Satan lies

Gnashing for anguish and despite and shame
To find himself not matchless, and his pride
Humbl'd by such rebuke, so far beneath
His confidence to equal God in power,
Yet soon he heal'd; for Spirits that live
  throughout
Vital in every part, not as frail man
In Entrails, Heart or Head, Liver or Reines,
Cannot but by annihilating die. . . .
(6. 340–47)

By assimilating Homer's most hateful god to Moloch and Satan, Milton underscores their deep malice and rage and also their ultimate futility.

There is another aspect of the War in

Heaven that deserves comment, and that is the discomfiture of the good angels*. If Homer treated his gods at times with disrespect, it was usually limited to those gods who disgraced themselves, such as Ares and Aphrodite and Hera and, possibly, Hephaistos (who was hurled from Heaven like Satan, and fell for three days, Milton reminds us). In the *Iliad* there are other gods who escape such disrespectful treatment, among them Apollo, Athene, and Poseidon. In *PL,* however, even the good angels are subjected to indignities in the War in Heaven, when, clad in cumbersome armor, they are bowled over by the devil's artillery :

> down they fell
> By thousands, Angel on Arch-Angel rowl'd;
> The sooner for thir Arms; unarm'd they might
> Have easily as Spirits evaded swift
> By quick contraction or remove; but now
> 'Foul dissipation follow'd and forc't rout;
> Nor serv'd it to relax thir serried files.
> What should they do? if on they rusht repulse
> Repeated, and indecent overthrow
> Doubl'd, would render them yet more
> despis'd,
> And to thir foes a laughter; for in view
> Stood rankt of Seraphim another row
> In posture to displode thir second tire
> Of Thunder : back defeated to return
> They worse abhorr'd. *Satan* beheld thir plight,
> And to his Mates thus in derision call'd.
>   (6. 593–608)

Having suffered already a barrage of execrable puns in addition to physical assault, the good angels are now assailed with outrageous Satanic sarcasms. In view of Plato's* famous objections to Homer's treatment of the gods, one wonders how he would have felt about Milton's treatment of the angels. Perhaps with Plato in mind Addison* execrated the speech of Satan that follows the passage just quoted "as being nothing else but a String of Punns, and those too very indifferent" (*Spectator,* no. 279). In a recent article on the War in Heaven Stella Revard has argued that these first two days of dubious battle are a trial of the obedience of the good angels. Abdiel had identified right with might and expected victory :

> nor is it aught but just,
> That he who in debate of Truth hath won,
> Should win in Arms, in both disputes alike
> Victor, though brutish that contest and foul,
> When Reason hath to deal with force, yet so
> Most reason is that Reason overcome.
>   (6. 121–26)

God defeats this expectation by permitting the temporary humiliation of his angels, thus showing, as he does with the forbidden fruit, that He will not always provide reasons for obeying Him.

The War in Heaven culminates in the Son's rout of the rebels and their fall into the Abyss. Book 6 ends just where the action of Book 1 begins. What is given as direct narration in the opening Books is completed by the delegated narrative of Raphael in Books 5 and 6. The education of Adam is half completed at this point, and the second half will be continued in Books 7 and 8, where the Creation*, which balances the Rebellion, will be narrated by Raphael. *PL* thus pivots on these central books of Destruction and New Creation. It has often been observed that such a structure is modeled on the *Aeneid,* where Aeneas assimilates his past in Books 1–6 (the Odyssean half, according to Brooks Otis) and assumes his future in Books 7–12 (the Iliadic half). Milton also divided his poem into Iliadic and Odyssean halves, but reversed the Virgilian order. The Achillean wrath and rebellion of Satan dominate the first half, while the second half, despite the central episode of the Fall of Man, is dominated by the Odyssean motif of return and reconciliation. But even within this Odyssean half of *PL,* as Martin Mueller argues (*Comparative Literature Studies* 6 : 292–316) Milton has assimilated the climactic episode of the *Iliad.* He sees the reconciliation of Adam and Eve in Book 10 as modeled on the reconciliation of Achilles and Priam in Book 24. "The abrupt and discordant end of the *Aeneid,*" he says, "contrasts significantly with the quiet conclusions of the *Iliad* and of *PL.*"

One should add that the actions of the two Homeric poems are even more intricately interwoven in Milton's poem, since Odysseus's heroic voyage is adumbrated in Satan's voyage in Books 2, 3, and 4. In addition, Milton's structure resembles the *Odyssey* in that the first half of the poem is primarily retrospective, while the second half deals with time* present and future.

To the extent that *PL* follows the movement of the *Iliad,* beginning with wrath and ending with reconciliation, its climax lies in the resolution of conflict between Adam and Eve and their acceptance of their lot. Like Achilles they assume their destinies. As Mueller observes :

> The action of the *Aeneid* determined later notions of a proper heroic poem. Its subject had to be some great enterprise of prosperous design. So Camoens* chose the circumnavigation of Africa, and Tasso* the liberation of Jerusalem. Milton chose differently. In his epic the event that corresponds to the destruction of Troy is the eventual defeat of Satan by Christ. But this final victory is no more the subject of *Paradise Lost* than the Achaean triumph over the Trojans is the subject of the *Iliad.* The wrath of Achilles and the disobedience of Adam are both apparent setbacks in the larger struggle, but paradoxically they make the final victory all the more certain. The main concern of both poets was not with the splendor of that triumph but with the bitterness of that disastrous event that impeded, and by impeding, necessitated, the final success. (p. 295)

In his detailed treatment of the Fall, Mueller shows how close, in terms of Aristotelian *philia,* the relationship of Adam and Eve is to that of Achilles and Patroclus, and he shows how Adam's failure to protect Eve from the encounter with Satan resembles Achilles' neglect of his responsibilities to Patroclus by letting him go alone into battle. The *pathos* in *PL* and the *Iliad* is more effective than the impact of Pallas's death on Aeneas, he continues, because Homer and Milton apostrophize Patroclus and Eve in a way that makes the reader identify with them. Virgil fails to do this in the case of Pallas.

Mueller's chief point is that while the reconciliation of Achilles and Priam is assimilated to that of Adam and Eve, Milton reverses the tragic conclusion. "Thus, the real crisis of the work is not the illusion of tragic necessity but the gradual resolution of what appeared to be an irrevocable tragic situation" (p. 304). This argument is very persuasive and again shows how brilliantly and sensitively Milton could make use of his classical models. In general it may be said that the relationship of *PL* to the Homeric poems is much more vital and intricate than Milton's explicit belittlement of heroic themes, like the following, would indicate :

>   I now must change
> Those Notes to Tragic; foul distrust, and breach
> Disloyal on the part of Man, revolt,
> And disobedience: On the part of Heav'n
> Now alienated, distance and distaste,
> Anger and just rebuke, and judgment giv'n,
> That brought into this World a world of woe,
> Sinne and her shadow Death, and Miserie
> Deaths Harbinger: Sad task, yet argument
> Not less but more Heroic than the wrath
> Of stern *Achilles* on his Foe pursu'd
> Thrice Fugitive about *Troy* Wall; or rage
> Of *Turnus* for *Lavinia* disespous'd,
> Or *Neptune's* ire or *Juno's,* that so long
> Perplex'd the *Greek* and *Cytherea's* Son. . . .
>   (9. 5–19)

Milton engaged Homeric themes and motifs in a variety of ways, from more or less explicit imitation to the subtlest allusions. The net effect is part of the firm but exquisite modulations of meaning that make *PL* so profound and sensitive. No seventeenth-century Englishman was a more perceptive student of Homer, and so, being aware of Homer's own sensitivity and profundity, Milton was a long way from a blanket dismissal of the Homeric epics. The tenderness, remorse, compassion, and devotion of Achilles are rendered in the fallen Adam, just as the wrath, egotism, and fierce pride of Achilles are rendered in Satan. The endurance, persistence, and patience of Odysseus contribute to Milton's conception of the repentant and hopeful Adam, just as the adventurousness, guile, and deceitfulness of Odysseus contribute to the Enemy of Mankind.

Milton's debt to the *Aeneid* is almost as vast as his debt to Homer. In some ways the influence of the *Aeneid* is more pervasive than that of the *Iliad* and the *Odyssey*. They contribute chiefly to the narrative structure and the characters, while the *Aeneid,* although not negligible as an influence on structure and character, has everywhere influenced the style. Milton's rhetoric* and diction* are a sort of English equivalent for the rhetoric and diction of the *Aeneid*. The influence of the *Aeneid,* both local and general, has been succinctly described by K. W. Grandsen :

> There are two kinds of classicism in *Paradise Lost.* There is first the omnipresence in structure, language and syntax of the *Aeneid,* providing a ground-bass through the poem : or (better) a palimpsest in which the teleological epic of Christian heroism supersedes, while leaving traces of, the epic of Roman heroism. And for this procedure Virgil himself is the exemplar, since the *Aeneid* is the first moral and teleological epic and is itself constructed on the palimpsest of the Homeric epics. (*Essays in Criticism* [1967], p. 281)

As Davis Harding shows, the exordium of the *Aeneid* is modeled on those of the *Iliad* and the *Odyssey,* and the character of *PL* as palimpsest is revealed by its brilliant recapitulation in the Virgilian mode of all three epics, especially in the use of the insinuated comparison :

> There is, first of all, the apparently innocent phrase at the end of the third line, "and all our woe." Most readers will perceive at once the rhythmical and accentual emphasis Milton has given it, but only a reader familiar with the classical epic will apprehend the reason for that emphasis. The phrase is, in fact, exceedingly guileful; it is a clear reminiscence of a kindred expression occurring in the exordia of all three classical epics. Thus, in the *Iliad,* the wrath of Achilles is responsible for the "woes innumerable" (*muri . . . alge*) of the Greeks. In the *Odyssey,* we learn that the hero will be afflicted by "many woes" (*polla . . . algea*) on his long journey home to Ithaca. Likewise, Aeneas is to undergo "many woes" (*tot . . . casus*) before he can accomplish his divine mission. But, Milton reminds us, Adam's sin of disobedience is the root of *all* our woe. Contrasted with the woes of which he will write—which are those not of a single man or of a single people struggling to be born, but of Man himself—the sufferings described by Homer and Virgil are made to seem relatively petty and unimportant. This is Milton's way of asserting one aspect in which his subject is superior to the epic subjects of the past. (*The Club of Hercules* [1962], p. 35)

Even this long quotation gives only a small part of Harding's exegesis of the exordium and its relation to Homeric and Virgilian prototypes. Of great importance is his discussion of the way in which Milton adapts the prophetic mode of his predecessors (and especially Virgil's "dum conderet urbem") in his anticipation of the Redemption : "till one greater Man / Restore us, and regain the blissful Seat." The *Aeneid* may end, as Mueller says, abruptly and discordantly (as Bentley* thought *PL* did), but its exordium, in pointing to an eventual triumph beyond the life of the present hero, served as an indispensable model for Milton.

Harding also shows in detail how *PL* is permeated with the *Aeneid*. Satan's first words to his companions on the burning lake are a version of Aeneas's exhortation to his shipmates in the opening storm; the building of Pandemonium is modeled on the building of Carthage, so that Satan's imperial ambitions are even more threatening than those of Rome's inveterate enemy; Christ is identified with Julius Caesar, and Satan with Turnus; Satan flees from Gabriel at the end of Book 4 in lines that echo the death of Turnus; and so forth. There is no doubt that the *Aeneid* is "omnipresent," as Grandsen says, in structure, language, and syntax. Roman discipline, celebrated by Virgil, obviously informs Milton's treatment of military formations and vast assemblies, especially in Hell. And, in a more general way, the discipline of obedience and *pietas,* which pervades Milton's poem, is to a large extent derived from the *Aeneid.*

Yet *PL* diverges from the *Aeneid* in a fundamental way. Virgil's *pietas* involves a kind of self-abnegation totally foreign to Milton. Aeneas's stoical subjugation of his personal desires and wishes to the demands of empire and his sacrifice of the self, which leaves him almost without personal identity at the end of the poem, is far from Milton's notions of obedience and freedom. Virgilian obedience means loss of freedom; Miltonic obedience is the basis of freedom. So here we find another of the many ways in which Milton departs from Virgilian stoicism. A kindred departure is Milton's rejection of the collectivist outlook of Virgil. In peace and war alike the Virgilian individual submerges his identity in some corporate institution. Those who do not, like Dido, Nisus and Euryalus, Turnus, or Mezentius, are seen as misguided virtuosos. It is customary to relate this collectivistic emphasis in Virgil to his grave moral and social purposes, but the fact remains that we do not find it in Milton. The spirit of Christ's self-sacrifice is one of love, not one of self-abnegation. The spirit of Aeneas's enormous self-denial is mainly ascetic. The Miltonic emphasis on individualism and freedom means that in *PL* we are much closer to the Homeric celebration of vital personal experience than we are to the *Aeneid's* celebration of the individual's immolation on the altars of empire. Against the cruel privations of the Dido episode let us place the Miltonic celebration of sexual love :

Hail wedded Love, mysterious Law, true source
Of human offspring, sole proprietie
In Paradise of all things common else. . . .
These lulld by Nightingales imbracing slept,
And on their naked limbs the flowrie roof
Showrd Roses; which the Morn repair'd.
  Sleep on
Blest pair; and O yet happiest if ye seek
No happier state, and know to know no more.
(4. 750–52; 771–75)

The formative influences from the classical epic that inspired Milton's conception of Adam and Eve are not to be found in Virgil, ultimately, but in Homer. The wedded love Homer celebrates in Hektor, Andromache, Nausicaa, Penelope, and Odysseus helped to form Milton's conception of "our Grand Parents." Homer's individualist conception of character triumphed, in *PL*, over Virgil's collectivist and stoic notions.

Yet if Milton leaned toward the Homeric conception of love and marriage*, it was from Virgil that he took his models of female disloyalty, infidelity, and impiety. Eve is a Nausicaa, but she is also a Helen and a Dido, and when Milton wished to invoke the horror of her impious act he turned to that *monstrum horrendum* of Virgil, the "marriage" of Dido and Aeneas. At that fatal moment of consummation, Virgil writes,

. . . prima et Tellus et pronuba Iuno
dant signum; fulsere ignes et conscia aether
conubiis, summoque ulularunt vertice
  Nymphae.
(4. 166–68)

Primeval Earth and Juno the bridesmaid give the sign;
fires flash out high in the air, witnessing the union,
and nymphs cry aloud on the mountain-top.
(Harding trans.)

Milton's treatment of the theme of guilt is certainly both deepened and embellished by his Virgilian background. The Homeric world is a shame-culture, and the chief exemplar of this shame-culture is Hektor, who rashly exposes himself and his city to destruction because he is ashamed to do otherwise. Shame is the motive for Satan's obduracy, as it is for Turnus's rash intransigence, which underlies this soliloquy :

O then at last relent: is there no place
Left for Repentance, none for Pardon left?
None left but by submission; and that word
Disdain forbids me, and my dread of shame
Among the Spirits beneath, whom I seduc'd
With other promises and other vaunts
Than to submit, boasting I could subdue
Th' Omnipotent.
(4. 79–86)

The model for this is Hektor's soliloquy as he stands alone at bay, outside the walls of Troy, waiting for Achilles' attack :

Now, since by my own recklessness I have ruined my people,
I feel shame before the Trojans and the Tro-jan women with trailing
robes, that someone who is less of a man than I will say of me :
"Hektor believed in his own strength and ruined his people."
Thus they will speak; and as for me, it would be much better
at that time, to go against Achilleus, and slay him, and come back,
or else be killed by him in glory in front of the city.
(22. 104–10)

The words Lattimore translates as "my own recklessness," *atasthaliesin emesin,* really mean criminal folly. Shame has led Hektor to actions that will lead to the destruction of the city he is supposed to be defending. Hektor's last concerns before the fatal encounter with Achilles are not his family or his city but the preservation of his body from desecration. Here is the negative side of Homeric individualism, which obviously informs the character of Satan.

The *Aeneid* is often supposed to have introduced the concept of history into the epic tradition. Although Homer has a fairly strong sense of the past, his notion of the future is very weak. Of prophetic passages in either the *Iliad* or the *Odyssey* there is nothing to compare with Jupiter's declaration of Aeneas's future in Book 1 or Aeneas's visions of the future of Rome in Book 6. What has been referred to here as the collectivist emphasis of Virgil as against Homer's individualism is also reflected in Homer's preoccupation with the fate of a single hero like Achilles or Odysseus in contrast to Virgil's larger vision of Aeneas as a representative of the imperium Romanum. Virgil greatly expanded the epic sense of time, and Milton, we might say, added eternity*. Both poets anticipated a future time that would, in some measure, redeem the sufferings of the present. Thus

the prophetic books with which *PL* ends are deeply indebted to Virgil and his interest in history. In both poems a major event that has already occurred (the founding of Rome, the coming of Christ) is treated as a future event, thus enhancing its climactic importance as a shaping influence over everything that led up to or followed it. For Virgil the flowering of the Roman empire was the purpose of history; for Milton, the Redemption was the central and climactic event that would fulfill history and ter-minate it. A small example of the way Milton built upon Virgil's prophetic theme, derived from Grandsen, occurs in *PL* 12. 369ff., where Michael speaks to Adam of Christ's advent :

he shall ascend
The Throne hereditary, and bound his Reign
With earth's wide bounds, his Glory with the Heav'ns.

Here Milton is building on the model of Jupiter's utterance to Venus in *Aeneid* 1. 286ff. :

nascetur pulchra Troianus origine Caesar,
imperium Oceano, famam qui terminet astris,
Iulius, a magno demissum nomen Iulo.

From this noble line shall be born the Trojan Caesar,
who shall limit his empire with ocean, his glory with the stars,
a Julius, name descended from great Iulus.
(trans. H. R. Fairclough)

Milton absorbs and extends the Virgilian example, at the same time substituting for Virgil's rather secular vision the ultimate apotheosis.

Scholars who have paid close atten-tion to Milton's Latin and Italian epic models have shown how creatively he imitated them in assimilating their exper-iments in adapting *their* models to the vernacular. According to B. A. Wright, Milton's employment of Latin idiom and syntax were "devices for attaining in English some of the effect of the loaded line of Latin verse, which is a legitimate aim in a poem that deliberately emulates Virgil" (*Milton's "Paradise Lost"* [1962], p. 65). F. D. Prince, in *The Italian Element in Milton's Verse*, shows how Milton followed the example of Italian poets and theorists such as Bembo, Tasso*, Della Casa*, and others, who were striving to import into the Italian vernacular some of the qualities of the Virgilian sublime.

No contemporary Miltonist has explored the language of *PL* more profitably than Christopher Ricks, whose book *Milton's Grand Style* (1967) employs a happy combination of sound theory, an intimate knowledge of Milton's classical models, and an acute ear for subtle effects of rhetoric, diction, and prosody. Space does not permit more than a sample of his elucidation of the Miltonic grand style as he turns the suggestions of earlier critics to good account. He pursues Bagehot's allusion to the poem's "haunting atmosphere of enhancing suggestions"; he follows up Addison's perceptive discussion of Milton's Ovidian "turns"; he opens himself up to the insights of the great eighteenth-century editors* and commentators like Newton*, Hume*, and the Richardsons*. Following the example of Empson, he shows in detail how ambiguity in Milton can coexist with precision as well as richness of expression.

One cannot escape the conclusion that some of Milton's best critics are those who are grounded in the classics. Perhaps Milton's "fit" audience was "few" because not many of his contemporaries could hope to share his extensive and minute understanding of the classics, especially Homer and Virgil. Fortunately for those of us who do not share Milton's classical learning, generations of scholars and critics have made plain the vast indebtedness of *PL* to the classical epic and the corresponding indebtedness of the epic tradition to *PL*, for Milton's poem is an exegesis, as well as a palimpsest, of the *Iliad*, the *Odyssey*, and the *Aeneid*. There is no better guide to Milton's classical sources and analogues than New-

ton's annotated edition of 1749. In this learned bishop Milton had an ideal reader. An example may be taken from his commentary on the ninth Book, beginning with Adam's horrified reaction to Eve's trespass and concluding with her penitent plea. As Adam

Astonied stood and blank, while horror chill
Ran through his veins, and all his joints
     relax'd,

Newton, following Hume, directs us to Sinon's pretended response to the Delphic oracle in *Aeneid* 2. 120, "obstipuere animi, gelidusque per ima cucurrit / ossa tremor" ("our hearts were numbed, and a cold shudder ran through our inmost marrow") and also to the poem's next-to-last line, on the death of Turnus, "illi solvuntur frigore membra" ("his limbs grew slack and chill"). The Turnus allusion suggests the climactic and fatal character of Eve's act (as Adam sees it), while the Sinon reference suggests the specious and histrionic element in Adam's response (so generous, in some respects), since her act is fatal only if he concurs in it.

On the next line and a half, "From his slack hand the garland wreath'd for Eve / Down dropp'd," Newton remarks:

The beauty of the numbers as well as of the image here must strike every reader. There is the same kind of beauty in the placing of the words *Down dropt* as in this passage of Virgil: Ut tandem ante oculos evasit et ora parentum, Concidit.

The lines describe one of the most horrible moments in the *Aeneid*, when Polites is slain before his mother and father: "When at last he came before the eyes and faces of his parents, he fell." It is the climactic horror of the fall of Troy, and placing of *concidit* has a finality about it like that of *Down dropt*.

On Eve's plea to Adam,

                              that all
The sentence from thy head remov'd may light
On me, sole cause to thee of all this woe,
Mee mee onely just object of his ire.
                              (10. 933–36)

Newton notes that Milton is imitating the plea of Nisus to the Rutulians to spare his beloved friend, Euryalus:

me, me adsum qui feci, in *me* convertite ferrum.

(9. 427)

He also suggests the way in which Milton amalgamates classical and biblical sources here by directing us to Abigail's speech to David in 1 Samuel 25 : 24—"Upon me, my lord, upon me let this iniquity be." Newton completes his exploration of this deceptively simple but richly allusive passage by citing as a parallel the Son's plea in 3. 236–37 that he pay the penalty for man's sin :

Behold mee then, mee for him, life for life I offer, on mee let thine anger fall.

Thus with exquisite subtlety Milton suggests that in her moment of penitence and self-sacrifice Eve is not only imitating the heroic love of classical and biblical predecessors but is closer than at any other time in the poem to her Redeemer. "The greater fortitude" is this *imitatio Christi*.

Milton's treatment of Virgil (and of countless other models as well) is thus extremely original and independent, neither slavishly programmatic nor recklessly innovative. The enhancing suggestions in such a brief passage extend enormously the thematic, rhetorical, and metaphorical resonances of the poem. Consider how a delicate balance is kept not only in the guilty Eve's penitence but in the modulation of Adam's situation by the allusions to Sinon and Turnus, the one a fallen champion of a ruined city, the other, the lying contriver of Troy's ruin. They imply that Adam, "yet sinless," has already begun the process of deception that will ruin him—and us—while the enhancing suggestions behind Eve's plea point to eventual redemption.

The variety that marks Milton's rhetoric, prosody, and syntax is also to be found in his diction. In his adaptation of Virgilian phrases and words he was selective, as Helen Darbishire observes:

How is it, then, that Milton's language remains alive—is not throttled by the learned words? To begin with, he is not pedantic in his pursuit of these. He will echo a beautiful phrase of Virgil about the poet's love of the Muses, *ingenti percussus amore*. But instead of using the word percussed (Bacon used it) he chooses a strong, hard monosyllable—English of the English: "smit with the love of sacred song." ("Milton's Poetic Language," *Essays and Studies* [1957], p. 45)

As B. A. Wright says, his "sonorous Latin words are usually accompanied by simple native words : 'so thick bestrown / Abject and lost lay these' is characteristic." Here *abject* retains its Latin sense of cast down, as the modern sense of dejected. There is an intermingling of polysyllabic Latin words and native monosyllables : "dark opprobrious den," "to perplex and dash maturest counsels," and so forth.

The Latin words are important for their evocative power. "The void profound of unessential Night" follows Lucretius's* *inane profundum*; *liquid air* is Virgilian and *conscious night* Horatian*. *Speed succinct* though post-Augustan, exemplifies in its incisiveness and brevity the kind of creative relation to the Latin language that Milton achieved, just as Virgil did with the Greek language.

Finally, we should note an important class of polysyllabic words derived from Latin with a negative prefix, sonorous and suggestive words that help to evoke the ineffable character of Milton's subject. Among them Miss Darbishire lists *loss irreparable, inextinguishable fire, immutable, immortal, infinite*. As she says, "Milton needs a large infusion of them because the horizon of his subject is the infinite. He wants words that deny and defy the finite, and contradict earthly limitation" (p. 45).

Almost every critic has remarked on the principle of irrelevance that Milton in his similes seems to have imitated from Homer through the addition of details in the vehicle that have no apparent relation to the tenor. As in Homer the "irrelevant" details are vital to the imaginative life of the simile, and although they do not have a logical connection with the tenor, they often have an emotional one. Bowra has shown (*From Virgil to Milton* [1948], p. 240) the "enhancing suggestions" behind the famous simile of the fallen angels :

Thick as Autumnal Leaves that strow the
    Brooks
In *Vallombrosa,* where th'*Etrurian* shades
High overarch't imbowr.
(1. 302–4)

Behind this lies Bacchylides' account of Heracles' visit to Hades; Virgil's simile for the ghosts of the unburied dead in *Aeneid* 6. 309–10 (quam multa in silvis autumni frigore primo / lapsa cadunt folia); and Dante's ghosts pressing to cross Acheron :

Come d'autumno si levan le foglie
L'una appresso dell'altra, fin che'l ramo
Vede alla terra tutte le sue spoglie.
(*Inferno* 3. 112–14)

After tracing the simile through Tasso and Marlowe, Bowra concludes that Milton's "instinctive genius shows his affinity to classical art when he gives a real place to the fallen leaves. His Vallombrosa is as exact as Bacchylides' Ida and has the immediacy of Greek poetry" (pp. 240–41).

At its best, the style of *PL* befits the theme in all its extraordinary ramifications. No English writer has come closer than Milton to creating an idiom that can be both sublime and "simple, sensuous and passionate." His intimate and profound knowledge of Homer and Virgil was a necessary precondition to this achievement. His poem lives in theirs and theirs in his. [GdeFL]

EPISTOLARUM FAMILIARIUM.

Thirty-one personal letters, all in Latin, were published in *Epistol* in May 1674 by Brabazon Aylmer*. Only nine or ten more personal letters from Milton have been discovered. These additional letters are : six Latin letters to Hermann Mylius* (dated between November 7, 1651, and February 21, 1652), and four English letters, one to an unknown friend, one

to Bulstrode Whitelock* (dated February 12, 1652), one to John Bradshaw* (dated February 21, 1653), and one perhaps to Christopher Milton. The last item is not certainly Milton's, but if it is and if it is addressed to Christopher, it probably would have been sent in January 1658. Three letters printed in 1674 have been found in manuscript. The dates attached to the letters in *Epistol* are often suspect, and may sometimes represent Aylmer's misreading of Milton's notations. Important recipients are individually entered in this Encyclopedia.

In addition, as the title page announces, the volume contains seven college prolusions, of varying lengths, which Aylmer in his foreword says comply with his request for some more material "to counterbalance the paucity of letters, or at least occupy the blank." The dates and occasions of the prolusions are not really certain, the assumption that they are printed in chronological order being unreliable. Nos. 4 and 5 are properly disputations (exercises in logical argument), and the remainder are declamations (exercises in rhetorical persuasion). The form of argument, the procedural techniques, and the traditional rhetoric of these prolusions were to influence Milton's prose and poetry repeatedly in later years. Quite obviously not all of them have survived; the only additional one that has been found is entitled, "Manus citus lectum fuge." It was discovered in 1874 by Alfred J. Horwood*, along with the *CB,* on a loose leaf of paper that transcribes *CarEl* on the reverse. [JTS]

EPITAPH ON THE MARCHIONESS OF WINCHESTER, AN.

This 75-line poem appeared in both the 1645 and 1673 editions of Milton's poems. A seventeenth-century manuscript in the British Museum (Sloane MS 1446) probably represents an earlier version, which Milton revised for publication.

The occasion of the poem was the death on April 15, 1631, of Jane Paulet*, the Marchioness of Winchester. Only twenty-three at the time of her death, she was noted for her loveliness and charm. When far advanced in pregnancy, she had an abscess on her cheek lanced and died of the infection, though not before she had borne a dead son. Since the Chancellor of Cambridge University was a kinsman of hers, it seemed likely that a memorial volume would be forthcoming, and Milton may have written his poem in anticipation of that volume, though if it was produced, it has subsequently disappeared without a trace. Poems on the Marchioness's death by Ben Jonson*, William Davenant*, and others also survive.

The opening line of Milton's poem —"This rich Marble doth enterr"—calls attention to the genre to which he assigned it, for the epitaph is a poem suitable for inscription upon a tombstone. Though longer and more elaborate than most epitaphs, *EpWin* retains the characteristics of the genre in that it identifies its subject, describes her station in life, and gives her age. In a larger sense, Milton's work belongs to the tradition of funerary poetry that was so popular in the seventeenth century. Milton himself had contributed to the tradition with a number of poems ranging from conventional Latin commemorations of university dignitaries to the English verses on the death of his niece, Anne Phillips.

EpWin represents a distinct advance over these earlier performances, but he continued to adorn his poetry with such classical and biblical allusions as reflect the background he shared with other well-educated men of his day. Beyond this, *EpWin* reveals an expanding literary awareness and sophistication in the use of sources. Lines 61–70, for example, suggest a Dantean influence. As Dante* in his *Paradiso* had placed Beatrice and Rachel, both mothers who died in childbirth, together in the third rank of the celestial rose, so Milton in his work linked the Marchioness and Rachel together "Far within the boosom bright / Of blazing Majesty and Light. . . ." These lines do far more, however, than suggest that Milton had been reading

Dante. The poem divides into two definitely contrasted parts. In the first forty-six lines, the Marchioness is referred to in the third person, and the pathos of her early death is emphasized; thereafter, she is directly addressed, and consolation is derived from her present happy state. The poem moves from past to present and, not surprisingly, from dark to light. Thus the lines quoted above take their place as a pendant to the earlier description of the Marchioness housed "with darkness, and with death."

Because *EpWin*, *L'Al*, and *IlP* are all written in octo- and heptasyllabic couplets (a meter sometimes employed by Ben Jonson), the three poems have often been considered to constitute one distinct phase in Milton's metrical development. However, Michael Moloney (*Modern Language Notes* 72 : 174–78) has shown that the couplets in *EpWin* differ from those in the companion poems in their greater reliance upon monosyllables and in their more heavily emphasized caesuras. In this, they reflect the influence of Jonson. Octo- and heptasyllabic couplets had more traditionally been used in English literature to create light effects, but Jonson, whose accomplishments in funerary poetry were considerable, had demonstrated that they could achieve a dignity commensurate with serious subjects. In *EpWin*, Milton followed his example with some success, creating couplets that are slow and stately in feeling. [ERG]

EPITAPHIUM DAMONIS was probably written in late 1639 or early 1640 and first published privately and anonymously, probably in 1640. It commemorates the death of Milton's close friend Charles Diodati*, who had died in August 1638 while Milton was in Italy. Milton had written his first and sixth Latin elegies as verse letters to Diodati; his fourth sonnet (in Italian) is addressed to him; and two prose letters from Milton to him survive.

EpDam takes the form of a pastoral* epicedion in which Milton assumes the guise of the shepherd Thyrsis mourning his dead friend Damon, both of these names being traditional in pastoral poetry. It is written in dactylic hexameters. The furniture of the pastoral tradition included sheep, rural scenery, nymphs, shepherds named Lycidas, Damon, Thyrsis, Daphnis, and so on. Quite frequently a pastoral poem used a refrain, and the subject of the poem was often sorrow for a shepherd who was lovelorn or dead.

EpDam centers on the poet's loneliness, "suam solitudinem," as he says in the headnote, and progresses to his vision of his friend in the company of the saints in Heaven. This upward impetus takes place through a series of steps in which the poem gradually moves out of its pastoral mode, emerging from what Mark Pattison calls "the dilapidated debris of the Theocritean world" to an ecstatic fusion of neo-Platonic*, Dionysiac, and Christian joy and love*. Milton manages this progression by means of two important structural devices. The first is the refrain ("Ite domum impasti . . . ," "Go home unfed, my lambs . . ."), which is repeated seventeen times in the poem, nominally without variation, but in its different contexts taking on new meanings that carry the poem forward. The second device is the use of the pastoral tradition itself, first as a mode for the statement of grief early in the poem, and then increasingly as a consciously inadequate ritual from which the poem emerges as it achieves its concluding transcendent vision.

EpDam opens in conventional pastoral grief and then for a moment bursts out passionately (and not necessarily pastorally):

Tum verò amissum tum denique sentit amicum,
Cœpit & immensum sic exonerare dolorem.
(16–17)

(Then truly, then at last, he felt the loss of his friend, and he began to pour out his tremendous sorrow in words like these—Trans. M. Y. Hughes.)

Then comes the first occurrence of the refrain:

Ite domum impasti, domino jam non vacat, agni.

(Go home unfed, for your master has no time for you, my lambs.)

Here the refrain seems simply to be a conventional pastoral: the sheep (i.e. distracting responsibility, etc.) are an annoyance in his time of grief.

The poem is conventionally pastoral in the early lines. In echoing such conventions, Milton is also creating an important structural tension between his lonely grief and the rituals of his pastoral form. For example, lines 69–72 closely echo Virgil's* tenth eclogue (42–43), but as Thyrsis rejects the charms of the cool waters, so the poem rejects Virgil's eclogues and the pastoral tradition. It is Diodati who is dead, and the old rituals have no power on such an occasion.

The section on the pairing of animals (94–112) is central to the poem; loneliness is a peculiarly human curse, and the herds—of cows, birds, or sheep—merely emphasize the loss in the death of his friend. Thyrsis's rejection of his flock has developed from an expression of annoyance in line 18 to an anguished realization, in lines 94–112, of the tragedy of being human.

He goes on now to feelings of regret for his absence at Damon's death, to his activities in Italy, and—as would have been natural between them had Damon not died—to a sketch of his plans for serious poetry, for something "grand," loftier than a pastoral. The wordplay is quite complex: "vos cedite, silvae" echoes Virgil's farewell to pastoralism ("concedite, silvae") in the closing lines of his last eclogue. So here, Milton's last pastoral poem is emerging from its last traces of pastoralism. But "silvae" are not only the forests of the shepherds and their flocks; the word also means "minor poems" or "sketches," and *EpDam* is indeed one of the last poems before the appearance of the great epic. And in

1645, when Milton republished *EpDam,* it was the final poem in the collection he entitled "Sylvarum Liber," the "Book of Minor Poems." Now, Milton is saying, he is ready for his great epic, and the refrain, repeated here for the next-to-last time, has developed into a declaration of his poetic position—his readiness now to transcend pastoralism and turn to heroic verse.

The verse paragraph (162–79) that follows sets forth his plans for an epic poem on British history and the adventures of King Arthur*, and the paragraph concludes with the final appearance of the refrain; now the dismissal of the lambs no longer reflects annoyance or grief but buoyant expectation as it brushes aside pastoralism for the heroic poem that lies ahead to be written.

He now tells of the two cups given him by Mansus*, introducing an element that carries the poem further: the cups portray various Resurrection symbols, but especially the figure of Amor, the mighty god whose arrows enflame the hearts of men. Milton depends heavily here on the Neoplatonic tradition of love as a force that draws men up from earthly beauty (such as the cups, or Milton's present poem, or his projected epic) to the eternal beauty of God.

So Amor lifts the poet to a true vision of Damon in Heaven, where Damon has cast aside his shepherd garments, just as the poem has cast aside its pastoralism, to assume his true (in several senses) name, his "divino nomine," "Diodotus," "Gift of God," even though "silvisque vocabere Damon" (211, "while in the forests you will keep the name of Damon"). The poem closes with Diodati transfigured, in the eternal love of the celestial marriage feast; and the poem, like the cups of Mansus, has been instrumental in lifting the poet from earthly grief and loneliness to an ecstatic epiphany of Heavenly joy.

Critical judgment of *EpDam* has been sharply divided; Dr. Johnson*, E. K. Rand, E. M. W. Tillyard*, and Douglas Bush consider the poem far from Milton's best, although Tillyard admits that it contains "perhaps the most beautiful passages" of the Latin poems. Rand objects to the unvarying refrain: "Lambs that have to be liturgically shooed away seventeen times are either unusually hungry or unusually inquisitive; at any rate they become unusually monotonous."

But David Masson* thought the poem was "beyond all question the finest, the deepest in feeling of all that Milton has left us in Latin, and one of the most interesting of all his poems, whether in Latin or English." James Holly Hanford* thought it "incomparably the best of the Latin poems," and A. S. P. Woodhouse* called *EpDam,* with *Lyc,* "the crowning achievement of Milton's earlier verse." [RC]

ERASMUS, DESIDERIUS (1466?–1536). Although the principles of Christian humanism came under attack in the early seventeenth century, the works of Erasmus still exerted a powerful influence on English literature and education. More often assumed than documented, that influence had its impact on John Milton, "the last great examplar of Renaissance humanism." The allusions to Erasmus in Milton's works, with one exception, show Milton's esteem for the sixteenth-century humanist. Erasmus was the wonder of his age (*Tetra* 4:223–24), a paragon of learning (*Erasmo doctissimo: 3Def* 9:111), the equal of Bucer*, both "men of highest repute for wisdome & piety" (*Tetra* 4:230–31); and in the company of Bucer, Fagius, and Martyr, one of the "illustrious divines" (*3Def* 9:61). *In Praise of Folly* ranked with the works of Homer*, Socrates, and Cicero* (*Prol* 6 12:221).

Erasmus appeared as the enemy when Milton lauded Luther's* vehement defense of his religious principles. The humanist's opposition to Luther served as a foil to Milton's praise. For Milton, moderation in debate was weakness, for had not Luther "reapt nothing but contempt from both Cajetan and Erasmus" when he moderated his temper (*Apol* 3:315)? Milton's own attack on the prelates implied that his readers ought to "take the course that *Erasmus* was wont to say *Luther* took against the Pope and Monks. . .." (*Apol* 3 : 366; from Erasmus, *Discourse on Free Will* 4. 5–6).

Milton's wide knowledge of Erasmus derived in part from his grammar school and university studies, for the seventeenth-century curriculum still included study of the *Adagia, Colloquia, Apophthegmata, De conscribendi epistolas* and *De duplici copia*. The colloquies were required reading in the Third Form at St. Paul's School*. *De copia*, or texts based on it, was a guide to essay writing; for example, Johannes Susenbrotus's *Epitome troporum ac schematum* (1608), an adaptation of *De copia*, was used by Alexander Gill*, Senior, one of Milton's tutors* at St. Paul's. Many schoolmasters adopted Aphthonius's *Progymnasmata* as a model for themes, after Erasmus's recommendation; others used Erasmus's own manuals, *Parabolae, sive similia* and *Apophthegmata*, both later abridged in Conrad Lycosthenes' editions. Further reading of Erasmus's colloquies and, as Joseph Mead's* book-sales lists suggest, *De lingua, Encomium Moriae,* and *De Instituto principis*, was required by university tutors. Erasmus's editions of such classical authors as Quintus Curtius Rufus provided further edification for the student.

As a result of his humanistic education, Milton followed many rhetorical* standards fostered by Erasmus. In spite of the Ramist* challenge to that classical rhetoric Erasmus admired, Milton remained loyal to Ciceronian style, exemplified in the periodic sentence and the frequent use of paired synonyms. Erasmus, while ridiculing the excesses of that style in *Ciceronianus*, noted its characteristic features, including the special use of synonyms. Such usage was not peculiar to Cicero's style alone, but found its way into English prose, appearing frequently in English translations of Erasmus's works. Besides continuing the Ciceronian tradition then, Milton borrowed many examples directly from Erasmus's manuals. In the theme on early rising, for

example, the commonplace "A good ruler should not grow fat in endless slumber" echoes Erasmus's adage *Non decet principem solidam dormire noctem* (*Omnia Opera* 2 : 635). The *Apophthegmata* provided another allusion for the same theme: death is viewed as a kind of sleep (*Apophthegmata* [1550], p. 1039). The figure *litotes* occurs in Milton's allusion to the author of *In Praise of Folly*, "a work not by a writer of lowest rank" (*non infimi Scriptoris opus, Prol* 6 12: 221). Milton's familiar letters, especially those to Richard Jones*, followed the rules laid out in Erasmus's *De conscribendi epistolas*.

In addition to his adopting Erasmus's standard of style and usage, Milton absorbed his humanistic ideals. Indeed, Milton seems to have embraced Erasmus's vision of the Golden Age—"the restoration of piety, letters, and Christian concord." In his *Educ*, Milton replicated the educational ideal of St. Paul's school, collaboratively enunciated by John Colet and Erasmus. Like Erasmus, Milton believed in the value of reading the best ancient authors; the precepts from their works laid a foundation for living a more nearly perfect life. Erasmus viewed *eruditio*, or *sapientia* as "learning in use" or "wisdom interpreted." He and Milton agree that the study of theology or ethics yield the greatest profit, for it expands man's capacity to make the best of his life. The cultivation of the spirit, more than the intellect, was most important to them both. But Milton did not share Erasmus's sanguine view on the educability of women; unlike Erasmus, he valued modern languages and considered training in military skills necessary.

Nevertheless, Milton understood the evils of war* just as well as Erasmus did. To Milton, war bred only more war (*Sonn* 15, line 10), an echo of Erasmus's observations, "one war springeth of another" (*Bellum Erasmi* 7). Milton seemed to have borrowed further from Erasmus's commentary on war, for several lines in *PL* (2. 496–505) parallel Erasmus's statement "The wicked spirits, through whom the concord and peace of those that be in heaven and of men was first broken . . . are now in league among themselves, and defend their tyranny . . . with consent and agreement" (*The Complaint of Peace,* ed. Hirten, p. 10).

Milton's allusions to Erasmus's comments on divorce* show that he had searched thoroughly for a corroborating view. He knew not only the annotations in Erasmus's Greek New Testament, but the *Responsio ad Phimostomi de Divortio* and *The Censure and Judgment of . . . Erasmus.* Milton called Erasmus's annotation of 1 Corinthians 7 an "eloquent and right Christian discours" (*Bucer* 4 : 60). Erasmus thought divorce "a Doctrin so *charitable* and *pious, as, if it cannot bee us'd, were to bee wisht it could*" (*Colas* 4 : 266). Both Bucer and Erasmus had written their tracts in and for England, Erasmus professing that he had written "out of compassion, for the need he saw this Nation had of some charitable redresse heerin . . ." (*Bucer* 4 : 60). Erasmus believed that the souls of many were endangered by an unfortunate marriage (*The Censure and Judgement of . . . Erasmus,* [sig. A, viii]). Milton noted that Erasmus saw other causes for divorce besides fornication comprehended in Christ's teachings, and that, furthermore, fornication ought to mean more than mere bodily intercourse (*Tetra* 4 : 223–24).

Milton turned to Erasmus's New Testament for opinions on other questions, acknowledging his reliance on Erasmus's text : "Erasmus, Beza* and other learned men . . . edited from the different manuscripts what in their judgment appeared most likely to be authentic readings" (*CD* 16 : 277). In a philological discussion of the question "Is it lawfull for a man to *put away* his wife?," Milton noted that Erasmus cited Hilary's rather harsh interpretation of the words *put away* (*Tetra* 4 : 145). Regarding another issue, the magistrate's power in spiritual matters, Milton observed that his Presbyterian* opponents might just as well grant the magistrate power to excommunicate ; they would "turn spiritual into

corporal, as no worse authors did then Chrysostom*, Jerom*, and Austin [Augustine*], whom Erasmus and others in their notes on the New Testament have cited to interpret that *cutting off* which St. Paul wish'd to them who had brought back the Galatians to circumcision. . . ." (*CivP* 6 : 17).

On the question of the Trinity*, Milton cited 1 John 5 : 7 as "the clearest foundation for the received doctrine of the essential unity of the three persons." But this verse was lacking in the Syriac, "Arabic, [and] Ethiopic versions as well as in the greater part of the ancient Greek manuscripts. . . . And not only Erasmus. but even Beza, however unwillingly, acknowledged (as may be seen in their own writings) that if John be really the author of the verse, he is speaking here . . . of an unity of agreement and testimony" (*CD* 14 : 215).

Milton turned again to Erasmus's text as an authority for the meaning of the word *God.* As Milton pointed out, some of the church fathers did not find the word in Romans 9 : 5, "if we may believe the authority of Erasmus; who has also shown that the difference of punctuation may raise a doubt with regard to the true meaning of the passage, namely, whether the clause in question should not rather be understood of the Father than of the Son" (*CD* 14: 261). The text of 1 Timothy 3 : 16 was clarified in a similar way; Erasmus asserted, according to Milton, "that neither Ambrose nor the *Vetus Interpres* reads the word *God* in this verse, and that it does not appear in a considerable number of the early copies (*CD* 14 : 265).

When Milton discussed the problem of the death of the body, he relied on Erasmus's understanding of Matthew 27 : 52–53. The passage in question illustrated Milton's interpretation of the time* element in bodily resurrection. According to Matthew, the graves of the dead opened the same day as the earthquake that accompanied the expiration of the crucified Christ; "the dead came out, . . . and having come out, at length after the resurrection of Christ they went into the holy city; for so, according to Erasmus, the ancient Greeks pointed the passage; and with this the Syriac agrees" (*CD* 15 : 245).

In retrospect then, Erasmus's influence on Milton seems all inclusive : Erasmus's rhetorical standards, his humanistic view of man and the world, and his Christian idealism played a part in shaping Milton's thought and literature. [RMa]

ERASTIANISM, the doctrine named for Thomas Erastus (1524–1583), Swiss theologian, asserting the power of the state over the church. Hooker accepted the theory in his *Ecclesiastical Polity,* as did the Tudors and Stuarts in practice. Enforcement, however, by Archbishop Laud* in the 1630s resulted in disastrous consequences in Scottish and then English resistance to a state-imposed religious conformity. As the Presbyterians* came into power in the 1640s, they replaced enforced conformity with the Church of England by enforced conformity with Presbyterianism. A strong group in the Westminster Assembly* (e.g., John Selden*) were Erastians, vehemently opposed by Independents*, who generally were anti-Erastian. At issue was the separation of church and state and, even more fundamentally, toleration (see W. K. Jordan, *Development of Religious Toleration in England,* esp. 3 : 347ff.).

Milton must have been an Erastian (if he thought about the matter) when he penned his college Latin pieces in favor of King James*. Even *Lyc* may be Erastian if the "two-handed engine" that will correct church abuses is some state power. But with the anti-prelatical tracts he moves in the direction of Independency on this issue, and the entire argument of *Areop* assumes an anti-Erastian view. Thus Milton came to see the "New Forcers of Conscience" as using the instrumentality of the state to force religious (i.e. Presbyterian) conformity.

The inauguration of the Commonwealth raised new hopes for disestablishment of the state church, but they were dashed despite Milton's fears of "new foes" who are "Threat'ning to bind our souls with secular chains" (*Sonn* 16). Indeed, Cromwell* never moved as far in this direction as Milton wished. Accordingly, after the Protector's death Milton addressed his fullest anti-Erastian statement to Parliament in *CivP*, arguing that he has written "heretofore against *Salmasius** and regal tyranie over the state; now against *Erastus* and state-tyranie over the church" (6 : 17). But nothing happened, and with Charles's* return the following year Erastianism was firmly continued in England. Modern Erastianism develops an idea of Hobbes* that political representatives, even though they are nonprofessing, may legislate upon religious matters. [WBH]

ESCHATOLOGY. Eschatology (from the Greek meaning *last, farthest*) is the branch of theology that deals with the last things, such as death*, resurrection, judgment, glorification, and damnation. Milton characteristically formulates his own eschatology by extracting all pertinent biblical texts and making a synthesis, although, except for mortalism*, his conclusions are orthodox. Death is the punishment of sin*. Since in Milton's view when Adam and Eve sin they are guilty in soul* as well as in body, soul and body alike are punished by death. Indeed, for Milton soul and body are indivisible, one being unable to exist without the other, and both are transmitted through the seed of the father to his offspring (see TRADUCIANISM). Thus all men, having within themselves seed originally derived from Adam, partake of his sin and suffer death in body and soul. There are four degrees of death. The first consists of all evils that lead to death : guiltiness, terror of conscience, forfeiture of divine favor, and degradation of mind. The second is the death of the spirit brought about by sin, for sin causes the loss of divine grace* and of right reason*. The third is the real death of the body and the soul. The fourth, the final degree of death, which is not experienced by good men, is eternal damnation. Man is rescued from the necessity of undergoing the final degree of death by the redeeming sacrifice of Christ, who to fulfill eternal justice, undergoes the "rigid satisfaction, death for death." Perhaps no implication of Milton's mortalism is more disturbing to the orthodox than this—that Christ must die both body and soul. Resurrected by God from the "loathsom grave," Christ ascends in his human body to his pre-ordained seat in Heaven at God's right hand, and thereafter he is no longer ubiquitous. Every individual, once dead, remains so, body and soul, until his own resurrection, when he will rise "numerically one and the same person." (16 : 353)

The time of the judgment is known only to God, and it will be sudden in its advent. Certain signs, however, will signal its coming, some of which are the destruction of Jerusalem, the coming of false prophets, false Christs, wars, pestilences, persecutions, earthquakes, famines, the decay of faith* and charity*, impiety, apostasy, and the Antichrist. The advent of the Son as judge will be glorious and terrible. Then will take place the resurrection of the dead in body and soul and a wondrous change in the living. Each man will be individually judged according to the "Rule of Judgment," which takes into account the measure of light enjoyed by him, for even among pagans may be found those who have lived commendably, having acted by God's law written in their hearts. During and perhaps after the very lengthy process of judgment, Christ will reign upon earth for a thousand years; then Satan will again rage, only to be defeated and, with Sin and Death, cast finally into Hell for eternity. To each man a place will be assigned. The evil will be imprisoned with Satan in Hell*, where, though their punishment is eternal, all are not punished with equal severity. The nature of their punishment is twofold : first, the punishment of loss, of alienation from God and goodness; and second, the punishment of sense, the fierce pangs of Hell. Good men will at the time of their reward receive perfect glorification, though the glory of one will not necessarily be equal to the glory of another. Heaven and earth will be renewed, and the blessed will become one in Christ, who, when his reign is ended, will become one with God. The universe, Milton's "World," will very probably become dematerialized to merge with Chaos, which the poet characterizes as "the Womb of nature and perhaps her Grave" (*PL* 2. 911). And at last even Chaos, sublimated into primal material, will be absorbed by God, who will then once more, as He was in the beginning, be "All in All."

The views summarized here appear throughout *PL;* they are concentrated in *CD* 1 : 33, which deals with the second coming, the resurrection of the dead, and the end of the world. [HFR]

ESSENCE: *see* METAPHYSICS.

ETERNITY. By *eternity* is meant timelessness or a state without beginning or end. On this subject Christian thinkers have generally followed the views of St. Augustine* (*The City of God* 11. 6 and 12.16) and Boethius* (*De Trinitate* 4): God alone is eternal in that He lives in a present that contains what is past, present, and to come. In *CD* Milton states that nothing is eternal but "what has neither beginning nor end" and that only God can be so described. The concept is rendered in the Greek of the New Testament by the word signifying "always existent." But in the Old Testament the words used to describe eternity often mean only antiquity or a vast extent of time*, for example, in the phrase "mighty men which were of old" (Gen. 6 : 4) and in the prophecy that the throne of David would exist forever (2 Sam. 7 : 13). From these and similar texts, it appears that the idea of eternity is conveyed in Hebrew by comparison and by deduction rather than by explicit words (14 : 43–45). (See Laurence Stapleton, *Harvard Theological Review* 57 : 9–21).

In *PL* eternity is generally attributed to the Father* alone, but the invocation to Book 3 is susceptible to a different interpretation. There it is stated that "God is Light," and "never but unapproached light / Dwelt from Eternitie dwelt then in thee" (3. 3–5). But it is also suggested that Light may be co-eternal, and William B. Hunter, Jr., argues that this Light is equated with the Son (*Bright Essence* [1971], pp. 149–56). Elsewhere there is less ambiguity. Raphael asks the question of why "the Creator in his holy Rest / Through all Eternitie" was moved to create the physical world (7. 90–93). The Father is explicit on this point, declaring himself to be "alone / From all Eternitie, for none I know / Second to mee or like, equal much less" (7. 404–7). This statement is generally interpreted as ruling out co-eternity with the Son*.

PL contains two views on the question of whether time and motion can exist in eternity. The affirmative is expressed by Raphael in explaining that the exaltation of the Son took place "on a day / (For time, though in Eternitie, appli'd / To motion, measures all things durable / By present, past, and future) on such day . . . (5. 579ff.). This view conforms to what is expressed in *CD* (15 : 35). On the other hand, Adam concludes that this world, "the Race of time," is transient and that time will eventually "stand fixt : beyond is all abyss, / Eternitie, whose end no eye can reach" (12. 553–56). Adam's words recall those of the angel of Revelation who swore that after the end of the world "there should be time no longer" (Rev. 10 : 6). Perhaps what is meant is that duration is measured by time in the "eternity" before the creation* of the world but not after its dissolution. [RF]

ETERNITY AND TIME. Time is a basic Hebrew and Christian concept, in that God's will must be understood as revealing itself in history. Accordingly, much of the Old Testament is a history of the Jews, their rewards and punishments culminating in the long night of the Babylonian Captivity. Ultimately their goal is to repossess the Promised Land. New Testament writers extend this historical time to the appearance of Jesus and finally to the supposed conclusion of time in Revelation, an apocalyptic* vision elaborated from similar temporal promises developed in Jewish traditions in the intertestament period. One was expected to examine his own life to discover in it God's divine purpose and to anticipate its continuing revelation. Conversion, the immediate visitation of divine grace for the individual, took place in each person at God's good pleasure in time*. In the study of history one could discover on a larger scale the same revelation of the divine will and its teleology. History, then, is God acting in time. The historical account of the last two books of *PL*, moving from Adam to Jesus, is a fine example of this intense concern for time inherited by Western civilization.

The metaphysics* lying back of this concern is ultimately Aristotelian* : time is the measure of motion (or change). It must be admitted that a totally motionless, changeless time is beyond conceptualization. Milton plays with this idea in *Carrier 2* : Hobson* stopped moving and so left time; he died. The Aristotelian definition is expressly quoted in *CD* (15 : 35; see also *PL* 7. 177, where motion and time are treated as synonymous). But ultimately owing to Plato's* *Timaeus* is the complementary idea of eternity, which in contrast is utterly without motion or change and thus somehow exists in the Aristotelian timeless state. This became identified in Christian thought with a God who existed in a timeless heaven and who yet revealed himself through time in history. The interplay of eternity and time, of fixity and flux, is an extraordinarily difficult concept.

Various Church Fathers dealt with the problem—Gregory Nazianus and Augustine*, for instance. The latter (*City of God* 11. 6), accepting Aristotle's definition, argues that time and the world began simultaneously. If by *world* is meant the creation of our universe, Milton does not accept this definition in *PL*, because events leading to the fall of the angels happen in time before this moment (see Laurence Stapleton, *Harvard Theological Review* 57 : 9ff., and *Philological Quarterly* 45 : 734ff.). Perhaps more basic to his thought is the development of the concept of eternity in Boethius, who argues that " 'God is ever' denotes a single Present, summing up His continual presence in all the past, in all the present . . . , and in all the future." Thus "ever [semper]" has a different meaning when applied to God : " 'ever' is with Him a term of present time, and there is this great difference between 'now,' which is our present, and the divine present. Our present connotes changing time . . . ; God's present, abiding, unmoved, and immovable, connotes eternity" (*De Trinitate* in *The Theological Tractates*, trans. H. F. Stewart [1962], p. 21). The same idea, a definition of God existing in an eternal present, concludes his *Consolation of Philosophy* (5, prose 6).

Milton appears to have reached a similar position in his maturity. In *Logic* (11 : 93, 95), time is defined as "the duration of things past, present and future"—and God so exists, but "eternity, not time is generally attributed" to him. In *PL* time as applied "To motion, measures all things durable / By present, past, and future" (5. 581ff.), but this time itself is "in Eternity." God, on the other hand, is defined as being "in his holy Rest [i.e., motionless] / Through all Eternitie" (7. 91ff.). He has "Dwelt from Eternitie" in light (3. 4ff.); Milton wishes to "assert Eternal Providence*" (1. 25). In Boethius's terms, "that then which comprehendeth and possesseth the whole fulness of an endless life together . . . may always be present to itself, and have an infinity of movable time present to it." From this results God's Eternal (that is, ever-present) Providence : "the divine sight beholding all things disturbeth not the quality of things which to Him are present, but in respect of time are yet to come" (*Con. Phil.* 5, prose 6). Providence is the knowledge of God in his eternal present of things temporally future or past. As *PL* states, God looks "from his prospect high, / Wherein past, present, future he beholds" (3. 77ff.). In a sense Milton's whole poem is present in a similar way to the reader, who knows it in its entirety, its past and future story, but who reads it in an eternal present.

The temporal sequence occupies an important place in many of Milton's poems. It is carefully manipulated in *PL*, which begins in the middle of the story and then moves back to its earlier stages and then down to its later ones, furnishing a present, past, and future —the fictional present being the Garden episodes themselves. Efforts have been made to work out an exact time sequence for the entire epic of thirty-three days (see Grant McColley, *Paradise Lost* [1940], and, more recently, Gunnar Qvarnström, *The Enchanted Palace* [1967]), but, exact though many details are as to their time (at midnight Satan returns to the Garden, 9. 58; at noon Eve eats the fruit, 9. 739) there is not really enough information for construction of a rigorous calendar for the poem. At the end of the poem and of time "God will be All in All"—everything will partake of eternity, in other words—and "time [will] stand fixt" (12. 555) in Eternity.

Elsewhere, Milton shows something of the same concern that Marvell* had for "Time's winged chariot," worrying that "Time [is] the sutle theef of youth" (*Sonn* 7) but responding that "Time . . . and the will of Heav'n" are leading him to yet unrealized goals—the Christian's concern with God's direction of each individual in time. Finally, the poem *Time,* supposed as being an inscription on a clock, addresses the movement of each person through time to the last change, death, when "long Eternity shall greet our bliss," and there "we shall for ever sit, / Triumphing over Death, and Chance, and thee O Time." Indeed, the movement from time into Eternity underlies the consolatory responses of all of Milton's poems that are concerned with death. [WBH]

ETHICS, MILTON'S. Early in the twentieth century Leslie Stephen in *The Science of Ethics* suggested that ontology, metaphysics*, and formal religion* are irrelevant in ethical study. Stephen's work reflects the inclination of modern philosophy either to abandon ethics as an unprofitable field or to relegate it to the aegis of "science." Milton's ethics cannot be studied under such restrictions. Milton was neither a moral philosopher in the traditional sense nor an ethical scientist in the modern sense. He was moral and didactic in the tradition of Edmund Spenser*, whom he considered "a better teacher then Scotus* or Aquinas*" (*Areop* 4 : 311), and he believed like Spenser that the best teaching was by example, a fact that would quite properly suggest that Milton's ethical notions are exemplified in his poetry. Many scholars have noted the ethical content of Milton's creative works, a subject that is indeed difficult to avoid. The primary purpose here is to demonstrate the doctrinal base for his ethics and to summarize his system of virtues* that is reflected in his poetry. In this regard the important source is *CD*, although his *Areop*, his *CB*, his tracts on education and divorce*, as well as others, contain important ethical views.

Milton does have a definable and, in certain respects, unique ethical system that is not without relevance to the modern world. But to view his system through the lens of the moral scientist would be unprofitable; for any effort to wrench free his ethics from his concomitant theological, psychological*, and political* notions would be to destroy the system root and branch. Milton's ethics are organic, evolutionary, and eclectic. Rooted in and growing from his theological and psychological concepts, his ethical aim for man was the ultimate attainment of a *summum bonum*, a happiness arising from a freely willed achievement of physical and spiritual harmony of being and an ultimate salvation.

In his youthful *Prol* he had argued that "nothing can be recounted justly among the causes of our happiness, unless in some way it takes into consideration both that eternal life and this temporal life" (12 : 255), a notion he retained throughout his life, though his emphasis may have shifted more to the "eternal." The word *eclectic* is frequently seen in Miltonic studies, and certainly it has legitimate application to his ethics, which blend the Hellenic and Judeo-Christian traditions. Plato*, Aristotle*, Xenophon, Cicero*, Augustine*, Aquinas*, the Bible*, Spenser*, Hooker*, Shakespeare*, and Bacon* are some of the names that critics have offered as influences upon Milton's ethics. Brief note will be taken here of a few of the discussions of the Platonic, Aristotelian, and stoical influences.

A striking similarity between the ethical notions of Milton and Plato appears evident to many scholars. J. H. Hanford calls Milton a Platonist, arguing that his "true philosophy is antique rather than medieval" and that "temperance, not asceticism, is his real principle of action" (*Studies in Philology* 15 : 178, 186). Hanford finds the Platonic subordination of man's lower faculties to his higher faculties the "central doctrine" in Milton's philosophy, but says that Milton avoided the "danger of asceticism" that was inherent in Plato. Hanford ultimately prefers to place Milton in the tradition of Christian humanism because of his "assertion of the spiritual dignity of man," his rejection of the ascetic principle, and his trust in man's reason and intuition as instruments of knowledge (*Studies in Philology* 16 : 143–45). In *Milton and Plato* Herbert Agar also notes the Platonic nature of Milton's ethics by suggesting that his belief in man's "capacity to attain knowledge in the moral world" and his equation of virtue with knowledge, wisdom, or reason* are main tenets of Platonism ([1965], p. 6). Irene Samuel, like Hanford, tempers her Platonic view of Milton's ethics by asserting in *Plato and Milton* that his guiding principles "do not belong to any one philosophical system" ([1947], p. 3), but she nonetheless offers the most extensive and persuasive argument for Platonic influence. Samuel contends that Plato's works served Milton not merely as a source and stimulant but "acted as a catalytic agent on the heterogeneous materials of pagan, Biblical, and Christian learning in his mind" (p. viii). She notes that Plato and Milton both viewed ethics as "the inclusive study of moral theory for the individual, and political theory for the State" (p. 16), and she agrees with Agar in suggesting that Milton, like Plato, attributes a greater importance to ethical knowledge than knowledge of the physical world. She also believes (pp. 133–34), as does William B. Hunter, Jr. ("Milton on the Nature of Man" [Dissertation, Vanderbilt University, 1946], p. 165), that Milton drew upon the Platonic doctrine of innate ideas in arriving at his notion of elemental virtue.

Aristotle's greatest influence on Milton's ethics may be reflected, as William J. Grace observes (*Ideas in Milton* [1968], pp. 62–63), in Milton's subscription to the classical idea of moderation, the notion of virtue as a mean between excesses and deficiencies. But the most perceptive views regarding the Aristotelian influence are perhaps those which argue that Milton's ethics revise Aristotle. In "An Ethical Distinction by John Milton" (*The Written Word and Other Essays* [1953], p. 79), Hardin Craig takes issue with T. C. Hall's claim (*History of Ethics Within Organized Christianity* [1910], pp. 435–37) that Milton's ethics are only Aristotelian scholasticism in a scriptural framework. Craig argues that Milton's doctrine of voluntary morality distinguishes his notions from the Aristotelian concept of goodness as habit. For Milton, Craig says, "the achievement of goodness in human life means being something virtuous rather than doing something virtuous" (p. 82). Ernest Sirluck, who finds Milton's "whole conception of virtue" to be "more strenuous than Aristotle's," agrees with Craig's distinction in arguing that for Milton there could be "no safety in habit," since right choice "was always dependent upon reason" (*Modern Philology* 48 : 95–96). John M. Steadman also views Milton as revising Aristotelian ethics; and in *Mil-*

ton's Epic Characters he suggests that Renaissance moralists derived from Aristotle their notion of heroical virtue as being an excess of virtue and brutishness as being an excess of vice, but regarded this definition as too fragmentary (p. 25). Steadman notes, for example, that Milton, in his use of the ethical conception of the metamorphosis of Satan into a beast, was exploiting a well-established tradition; but in Milton's hands, Steadman says, the convention "becomes an Aristotelian reversal" since Satan, rather than assuming the image of God as he attempts, "assumes that of a beast" (pp. 207–8).

S. B. Liljegren and Martin A. Larson agree in placing Milton in the stoic tradition. Making "Roman Stoicism the chief foundation of his modes of thought and action," Milton largely abandoned a purely Christian system of ethics, Liljegren contends (*Studies in Milton* [1919], pp. 139–40). Larson sees as stoical Milton's notions of self-dependency, his beliefs that virtue derives from wisdom and knowledge, that happiness derives from consciousness of right actions, that good comes from within, and that the passions should be subordinated (*The Modernity of Milton* [1927], p. 104). The problem with the stoical position, as with other positions, is that correspondence of ethical views does not necessarily ascertain influences; and in the realm of ethics where there are so many similarities among the tenets of Platonism, Aristotelianism, stoicism, and Judeo-Christian values, the task of assigning influences becomes difficult and questionable in its rewards.

Though Milton was a child of the tag-end of the Renaissance, the spirit of Christian humanism continued to pervade his moral thought; and though he may have applauded and subscribed to much of the wisdom of the pagan moralists, he conceived of the gift of revelation as essential to his ethical system. To justify God's ways to men he had not only to assert God's supreme providence but had to establish man's power of rational choice as precursory to moral action. Milton was both a product and an advocate of a humanistic system of education that sought to exalt man's spiritual dignity and provide for his temporal estate. In his own tract *Educ*, Milton claims that the "end" of learning is "to repair the ruins of our first Parents by regaining to know God aright, and out of that knowledge to love him, to imitate him, to be like him, as we may the neerest by possessing our souls of true vertue, which being united to the heavenly grace of faith makes up the highest perfection" (4 : 277). And a "compleat and generous Education" was one that fitted a man "to perform justly, skilfully and magnanimously all the offices both private and publick of Peace and War" (4 : 277). Douglas Bush says that in Milton's stress upon "religion and virtue, the training of the moral judgment and the will, he only adds a personal earnestness to what had been the chief object of Christian humanism in all ages and countries" (*English Literature in the Earlier Seventeenth Century* [1945], p. 375). Imitating God, being "like" him in this world, required an accounting for the dignity of oneself and one's neighbor, of providing useful service and leadership, all of which demanded the proper exercise of moral judgment. For his students to contemplate "with some judgement . . . upon moral good and evil," Milton recommended "moral works" in the humanistic tradition. His course in ethics would include Plato, Xenophon, Cicero, and Plutarch* (4 : 284).

The humanist tenet most essential to Milton's ethical concepts was monism. His view of the universe as an organic whole of a substance originally and necessarily good allowed his ethical man to concern himself not only with the glory of God but with the condition of his own estate. "Original matter," Milton says, "diffused and propagated" by the will of God, "is not to be looked upon as an evil or trivial thing, but as intrinsically good, and the chief productive stock of every subsequent good" (*CD* 15 : 23). The moral life might ultimately be rewarded with restoration of spirit and body, both released from mortality. In the Renaissance tradition, Milton's psychology represented man as a creature of faculties, the essential ones being his reason*, will, and passions, with his moral life dependent upon the proper ordering and subsequent harmony of the faculties. Proper order and harmony demanded self-knowledge and self-government. In the tradition of Aristotle, Milton's ethical man sought self-knowledge both within himself and in the external world. He had to realize himself as a creature of the temporal world, seeing himself in the mirror of the world's stage, and he had to understand his own inner nature. More important, self-scrutiny and scrutiny of the universe brought one to a knowledge of the creator of both.

Comprehension of one's inner nature meant the understanding of one's divine nature, his likeness to God, and the ethical incumbency to act as God would act and according to God's will. In the Renaissance tradition the faculty that established man's likeness to God was, of course, his reason. Man being fashioned like God in reason, "it followed as a necessary consequence that he should be endued with natural wisdom, holiness, and righteousness" (*CD* 15 : 53). Milton's notion of a bifurcate reason, intuitive and discursive in its nature, may owe much to Neoplatonism*. In any case, his concept of a higher intuitive reason, which he frequently terms "right reason" or simply "conscience," differs little from prevailing seventeenth-century notions of casuistry, especially among the Cambridge Platonists*. For example, Nathaniel Culverwel's "candle of the lord," Benjamin Whichcote's "first inscription," and Henry More's "boniform faculty" or "right reason" all define a faculty that enables man intuitively to understand principles of innate "natural" and moral law that had applications in theological, ethical, and political realms. Hence, in *PL*, God says He will place within man "as a guide" His *"Umpire Conscience"* (3. 194–95). In *CD* Milton argues that the "rule of conscience" is "innate, and engraven upon the mind of man" (15 : 179, 181) and that it is "an approving judgment of the mind respecting its own actions" (17 : 41). This faculty, "whether we term it conscience, or right reason," is not entirely absent even in the worst of us (14 : 29). In *PR* Milton appears to identify this faculty with Christ and the Holy Spirit. After silencing the pagan oracles, God sends "his living Oracle / Into the World, to teach his final will, / And sends his Spirit of Truth henceforth to dwell / In pious Hearts, an inward Oracle / To all truth requisite for men to know" (1. 460–64). Milton's ethics, derivative from "moral law" and accessible to "right reason," are therefore ideal in nature (Marjorie H. Nicolson, *Studies in Philology* 23 : 414–33; also Hunter, pp. 146–74).

In his explanation of the difference between man and angels in *PL,* Raphael tells Adam that reason is the "being" of the soul, "Discursive, or Intuitive; discourse / Is oftest yours, the latter most is ours, / Differing but in degree, of kind the same" (5. 487–90). In this regard, Northrop Frye claims that the "point at which revelation impinges on reason is the point at which discursive understanding begins to be intuitive." For Adam, Raphael's account of the fall of Satan is knowledge received, and as such it allows reason to operate discursively in the free man (*The Return of Eden* [1965], p. 74). The higher reason, Milton suggests, is not to be equated with virtues, either sought or achieved, which are "means" rather than "ends" and are therefore under the proper government of the moral judgment or discursive reason, a "choosing" faculty. Following Ramus*, Milton says that "in ethics progress is from the end, to wit, beatitude, to the means, namely, the virtues" (*Logic* 11 : 479). In training the moral judgment in the deliberation of "means," education played an important role. In *Educ* Milton says that since the "understanding cannot in this body found it self but on sensible things, nor arrive so clearly to the knowledge of God and

things invisible, as by orderly conning over the visible and inferior creature, the same method is necessarily to be follow'd in all discreet teaching" (4 : 277). Although ethical habit of choice may be developed, the emphasis, again, is upon the training of the moral judgment as a choosing faculty. In *Educ,* after prescribing for his students curriculums of grammar, mathematics, natural science, and poetry, Milton says, "By this time, years and good general precepts will have furnisht them more distinctly with that act of reason which in *Ethics* is call'd *Proairesis* : that they may with some judgement contemplate upon moral good and evil" (4 : 284). The term *proairesis,* uncommon in Milton's day, would suggest right judgment in choice of means that academic training could develop and thereby lead to good moral habits. Milton apparently used *proairesis* rather than *synteresis,* a term common to the seventeenth century, to give emphasis to the importance of training the discursive reason in its role of choosing particular means to ends in the ethical life since the latter term (*synteresis*) suggested insight into moral law and choice of good ends (see John F. Huntley, *Philological Quarterly* 43 : 40–46).

Unquestionably, Milton, being in the Christian humanist tradition of such men as John Colet, Thomas More, Thomas Elyot, and Edmund Spenser, viewed formal education, like poetry, as providing example and means to perfection of the moral life in both spiritual and temporal realms. As previously noted, in *Educ* he maintains the "end" of learning to be "regaining to know God aright," a knowledge that enables one to love and "imitate" God "by possessing our souls of true vertue, which being united to the heavenly grace of faith makes up the highest perfection" (4 : 277). The two great Christian commandments are implicit here : faith* and love* in knowing God aright and loving imitation of Him in dealings with oneself and neighbor. A person's spiritual relationships and his temporal relationships, then, depended upon choices made, and an educable reason was the faculty of moral choice. Knowledge acquired through study was not, however, to be equated with temporal virtue, nor was it by necessity viable in the spiritual life. Hence Satan, incapable of understanding this distinction, is frustrated in his temptations* of Christ in *PR*. Knowledge alone was never an assurance of ethical wisdom: a man might be "learned without letters" or "lettered without learning" (*1Def* 6 : 69).

Again and again Milton equates reason with choice. In *Areop* he says that God trusts man with the "gift of reason" so that he may "be his own chooser" (4 : 310). In the same work he maintains that when God gave Adam reason, "he gave him freedom to choose, for reason is but choosing; he had bin else a meer artificiall *Adam*" (4 : 319). And in *PL* God tells the Son that "Reason also is choice" (3. 108). Reason then had to be king of the faculties in ethical choice with the will as its instrument of free choice. The freedom of the will is dependent upon personal choice. The will is "free" in the sense that it may be governed either by reason or by the lower faculties. Paradoxically, once the lower faculties usurp reason in the rule of will, the will's indeterminism is lost. Hence the angel Michael tells the fallen Adam that once "upstart Passions catch the Government / From Reason" man is reduced to "servitude" who was "till then free" (12. 88–90). But it should be remembered that the passions were not by nature deleterious to moral health. They were on the contrary the raw materials of a virtuous life, for why would God have created "passions within us, pleasures round about us, but that these rightly temper'd are the very ingredients of virtu" (*Areop* 4 : 319). As things sensed are the "subjects" of the senses, things "related to virtues and vices" are their subjects. Virtues and vices are thus "made plain in ethics by this argument, temperance and intemperance by pleasure, fortitude and cowardice by perils, liberality and avarice by riches" (*Logic* 11 : 85).

The passions might be the matter of sin but were not by necessity sinful. Herein lies an essential dualism basic to Milton's concept of evil and explicable in terms of his theology.

For Milton the tree of knowledge of good and evil, whatever else it may have been, was a test of Adam's obedience. It is important to note that in *PL* the only accusation the Son makes when he comes to judge the fallen Adam is that he failed to know himself "aright" and govern himself accordingly. Had he done so, he would not have transgressed. Essentially what Adam should have known about himself was that his rational self should rule his passions even in affairs of the heart. The essential dualism in man, Milton argues in *CD*, is a legacy of Adam's disobedience*. In addition to man's having a propensity to good, subsumptive to his likeness to God, man's nature is characterized also by an "evil concupiscence," a propensity to evil: "Evil concupiscence is that of which our original parents were first guilty, and which they transmitted to their posterity, as sharers in the primary transgression, in the shape of an innate propensity to sin" (15 : 193). Man thus has an aspect of self like his divine creator and an aspect of self unlike his creator. The self-like-God, identifiable with reason, allows him access to an immutable moral law, a law of nature*; while the self-not-like-God, identifiable with the passions, contains the propensity for destructive evil if the higher self is rejected.

The essential tension of *PL*, at least on an ethical level, is a tension between these two aspects of self. Satan and his forces, we are told, are those "who reason for thir Law refuse, / Right reason for thir Law" (6. 41–42). Earlier God had told the Son that men, indeterminately free, must be "Authors to themselves in all / Both what they judge and what they choose" (3. 122–23). Satan, once he has scorned and absolutely rejected immutable law, no longer is "author to himself" but asserts that he is author *of* himself, the creator of his own moral being; but for Satan, of course, the moral order is reversed : passion is his conscience, and evil, therefore, will be his good. Thereafter, Satan *is* "evil concupiscence," symbol of consummate pride born out of rejection of moral law, with Sin being the offspring of his incestuous affair with himself. The conflict between these two aspects of self that later involves Adam, consequent to his failure in meeting the test of obedience, mirrors precisely the cosmic conflict between God and Satan; in both instances powerful factors of reason and passion are at war. God's judgment upon Satan is irrevocable, Milton explains, because Satan was self-tempted. In contrast the grace* accorded to Adam, with the Son acting as mediator and redeemer, was consequent to his being Satan-tempted. But as ethical man he was thereafter on his own, a free-willed creature with impulses to both good and evil.

In Milton's view God "eventually converts every evil deed into an instrument of good" (*CD* 15 : 79), but more immediately important for the moral life was the value of evil in the attainment of virtue. Since good and evil are "as twins clinging together" (*Areop* 4 : 310), and since "we know good only by means of evil" (*CD* 15 : 115), knowledge of virtue must therefore be "attested by evil," must be "illuminated and trained" by it (*CB* 18 : 128). Good and evil, then, comprise the field in which the reason makes ethical choices. True honor in the moral life or in the worship of God should never be sought in cloistered virtue. Neither forced virtue nor sheltered virtue prospers since "virtue is chiefly exercised" by evil and by evil "shines with greater brightness" (*CD* 15 : 115).

The two great commandments of Christianity are the taproots that produce and support the trunk, branch, stem, and leaf of Milton's ethical system. Following Adam's failure to honor the one prohibition in Eden, man is ethically bound by the covenant of Moses until he is at last liberated by the Son's redemption. Released from the law of the covenant,

man is then free to discover the laws of God "written in the heart." For Milton, there was no fundamental difference between the laws written in the heart (or the "law of nature") and the scriptural injunction to love God and neighbor. In *CD* he claims that the "unwritten law is no other than the law of nature given originally to Adam," a remnant of which "still dwells in the hearts of all mankind; which, in the regenerate, under the influence of the Holy Spirit, is daily tending toward a renewal of its primitive brightness." The "law," he suggests, means "heavenly doctrine in the abstract, or the will of God" (16 : 101). In spiritual and ethical matters the law of nature, the Mosaic law, and the gospel law are essentially the same; for although the gospel "abolished" the Mosaic law, "the sum and essence of the law is not hereby abrogated, its purpose being attained in that love of God and our neighbor, which is born of the spirit through faith" (16 : 141). The difference, he claims, is that under the new law men are freed to determine their own destiny, "loosed as it were by enfranchisement," becoming "sons instead of servants, and perfect men instead of children" (16 : 153, 155). Here in Milton's definition of "Christian liberty*" is found an important tenet of his ethical doctrine. The "actions" of virtue must always be "elective & unconstrain'd. Forc't *virtue* is as a *bolt* overshot, it goes neither forward nor backward, and does no good as it stands" (*DDD* 3 : 495). For man to develop as a moral being by means of rational choice, there need be no irrational constraints, either in his civil or religious life : "to be free is precisely the same thing as to be pious, wise, just and temperate, careful of one's own, abstinent from what is another's, and thence, in fine, magnanimous and brave—so, to be the opposite of these, is the same thing as to be a slave" (*2Def* 8 : 249, 251).

"Love, or the worship of God," Milton suggests in *CD*, must be predicated upon "Faith, or the knowledge of God" (14 : 23). As previously noted, knowledge of God proceeds from knowledge of self, discovery of one's own rational (and thereby divine) nature; and again, it is that "feeling, whether we term it conscience or right reason" that may prove the existence of God (14 : 29). To know God is to be obedient to His will; hence ethical man, as original man, must continue in the test of obedience. Paradoxically, obedience to God in Milton's view was what set man free as an ethical being; for to obey God was to love and worship Him, and the essential way to demonstrate love of God was to demonstrate love of neighbor, to do "good works" and thereby return glory to God. Hence Milton argues that faith and love, though "distinct in their own nature . . . cannot be separated in practice." In this regard he quotes Romans 2 : 13 ("not the hearers of the law, but the doers of the law shall be justified") and says that "obedience and love are always the best guides to knowledge" (14 : 32, 25).

Milton thus argues that ethical life in the temporal world is dependent upon a knowledge of God and obedience to His will. As man's knowledge of God is dependent upon self-knowledge, so his worship of God by love of neighbor and "good works" is dependent upon self-government. Book 2 of *CD* deals with the "worship of God" and contains a highly detailed system of virtues intended as a guide for a moral life. Milton sometimes used the word *virtue* as a specific moral attribute to suggest truth in living with God, self, and others, as in *PL* when Adam, after learning that "to obey is best" (12. 561) is told by Michael to "add / Deeds to thy knowledge answerable, add Faith, / Add vertue, Patience, Temperance, add Love" (12. 581–83). But as a generic word in *CD,* virtue is equated with "good habits" and "duties" that result in deeds, that is to say, "good works." "The true worship of God," he argues, "consists chiefly in the exercise of good works" (17 : 3); the "true essential form" of good works is "conformity . . . with the unwritten law," that is, faith (17 : 9). The intended purposes of good

works are "the glory of God, the assured hope of our own salvation, and the edification of our neighbor," the last admonishing us to "become examples to others" (17 : 5, 13). The "primary efficient cause" of good works is, of course, God; but the "proximate causes" are "good habits, or, as they are called, VIRTUES; in which is comprised the whole of our duty towards God and man" (17 : 27). The aim, then, of virtuous habits is the glory of God and man's salvation, but it must be remembered that good works occur in the temporal world where "the external service even of God is sometimes to be postponed to our duties toward men" (17 : 195).

Although Milton declares that "there can be no excess in piety and charity" (17 : 17), the ethical habits prescribed in *CD* are Aristotelian and Spenserian in their emphasis on moderation, each virtue having "opposites" and usually representing a mean between extremes. His system is complex and at times confusing largely because of the duplication of terms among the various categories of virtues. He first classifies his virtues as either "general" or "special," but this division is not really an equal one. The "general" virtues, pertaining to the "whole duty of man," belong either to the "will" or to the "understanding" and encompass both his spiritual and temporal natures. The "general" virtues, rooted in the two great commandments, thus comprise the trunk of his ethical tree with the "special virtues" being the "particular branches" of the "whole duty." The two branches of the special virtues are "duty towards God," divided into "internal" and "external" worship, and "duty towards men," the latter having a more complex division. Duty to "self" and duty to "neighbors" are the two branches of duty toward men, these virtues distinguished as general or special with the special virtues regarding "self" classified as relating either to a desire for external good or a resistance to evil, and the special duties toward neighbors distinguished as being either "internal" or "external." An additional category of "reciprocal" virtues is either "public" or "private," the private virtues divided as "domestic" and non-domestic and the public virtues as "political" and "ecclesiastical."

The general virtues pertaining to man's "whole duty" are wisdom and prudence, which belong to the "understanding," and sincerity, promptitude, and constancy, all virtues of the "will." Wisdom is inferable from the first commandment since it is the consequence of ethical man's searching out and learning the will of God and governing his actions accordingly. Opposites of wisdom include an ignorance or false understanding of God's will, the pursuit of forbidden knowledge "after the example of our first parents," and "human or carnal wisdom." In each of Milton's three great works, the achievement of this primary virtue is exemplified in his heroes : Adam achieves a "wisdom," a true understanding of self and the will of God only after the Fall; Jesus rejects Satan's offer of "carnal and human wisdom" as ungrounded in God's will; and Samson acts according to God's will only after he achieves wisdom. Concomitant to wisdom, the virtue of prudence enables us to discern proper actions once God's will is manifested. Hence the general virtues of the will govern our actions once proper actions have been discerned. Sincerity demands right actions in all situations and would reflect a readiness (promptitude) and a determination (constancy) to act rightly.

"External" worship, as a branch of "special" duties owed to God, is concerned largely with propriety and form in private and public worship. More important to ethical life, "internal" worship requires the "acknowledgment of the one true God" and the cultivation of "devout affections" of love, trust, hope*, gratitude, patience, and obedience*. Again, these virtues are inferable from the first commandment and reflect man's need to acknowledge "the one true God" as a just but merciful supreme judge in whose providence* man's hopes for salvation reside. Thus, to achieve the virtue of

patience is to rely on God's providence and to bear evil with equanimity. Patience does not, however, appear to be a passive virtue but a willingness to rely upon God, even under the most severe duress, until one becomes aware of God's will as it regards a particular action. In this regard, Milton's Samson exemplified patient suffering until God's will became apparent, and he was then able to act to the greater glory of God. In the last of the internal affections the ethical thrust is clear, for "obedience" to God is to make His will the "paramount rule of our conduct" (17 : 69).

In the category of duties toward men, the second great commandment is obviously implied, but "even in these we may be considered as serving God" (17 : 193). The general duties to self and man are love and righteousness, both pertaining to temporal as well as eternal good. In its "wider sense," Milton says, love means holiness, but here love pertains to deed and truth rather than word. Righteousness is a matter of rendering what is due to oneself and neighbor. As it regards "self," righteousness demands proper self-government (specifically the regulation of the internal affections) and resistance or endurance of external evil. Love or "charity" as it regards a neighbor consists in loving one's neighbor as himself, a neighbor defined as anyone "to whom we have the opportunity of rendering service or assistance" (17 : 255), which would include even our enemies. Charity to a neighbor is either "absolute or reciprocal," absolute charity including the virtues of humanity, good will, and compassion. Reciprocal charity includes brotherly love, the strongest of "affections," and friendship.

In man's duty to self, the first class of "special" virtues comprehends temperance and moderation in his desire of external good while the second class requires fortitude and patience in his resistance to or endurance of evil. Temperance prescribes the limits to bodily gratification, decorous language, dress, and appearance. Moderation governs the desire of goods and includes contentment, frugality, industry, and liberality. These virtues allow Milton's ethical man to use his talents in providing for himself and to enjoy a comfortable and even elegant temporal life, free from excess. To repel evil, or at least meet it with equanimity, one needs the virtue of fortitude*. Patience in duty to self is defined as the "endurance of misfortunes and injuries" (17:253), but there is again the suggestion that patience is not a stoical virtue, that patience is as much a waiting as an endurance. One of his biblical references in his explication of patience is to Proverbs 19:2: "the discretion of a man deferreth his anger," which suggests a postponement of action. Among the opposites of patience are effeminacy and "Stoical apathy." "Sensibility to pain, and even lamentations," we are told, "are not inconsistent with true patience" (17:253).

Of the "special" duties owed to one's neighbor, his "internal" good demands a regard for his safety and honor. Regard for his safety in both his spiritual and temporal life demands an avoidance of voluntary injury and giving or taking offence, and readiness to forgive an injury. Honor implies a high regard for a neighbor's "personal modesty"; specifically, it is the avoidance of fornication and adultery. Regard for a neighbor's "external" good requires the protection of his good name and worldly interests. His good name may be preserved by our avoiding "injury" to his name in other's eyes, by our "deportment" toward him, and by our "conversation" with him and about him. Proper conversation entails the virtues of veracity (truthful speaking in a neighbor's behalf) and candor (acknowledgment of his talents and a favorable interpretation of his words and actions). A neighbor's "worldly interests" are promoted by the virtues of integrity and beneficence. Integrity is defined simply as the "refraining from the property of others" (17:331), but Milton's essential concern in this category is with business ethics, for integrity more specifically concerns "commutative justice," which includes "all transactions of purchase and sale, of letting and hire, of lending and borrowing, of keeping and restoring deposits" (17:335). The primary ethical concern here is with honesty in dealing and truth in lending. In view of his father's business life, it is interesting to note that Milton finds usury "in itself equally justifiable with any other kind of civil contract" (17:341). Beneficence, the second virtue of worldly interests, requires a sharing of our abundance with our neighbor, especially the poor.

As noted above, "reciprocal" duties to neighbor are either public or private. The private "domestic" duties embrace "reciprocal obligations of husband and wife, parent and child, brethren and kinsmen, master and servant" (17:349). Milton's notions here reflect the traditional Elizabethan view of correspondence between God who rules His realm with justness and compassion and the king and husband who should likewise rule their estates and families. But there should be mutual love between parents and common responsibility for inculcation of discipline that is neither indulgent nor excessively severe. Reciprocal non-domestic private duties include an unostentatious almsgiving to relieve the poor, and hospitality that is, when necessity demands, receiving into one's own house the poor and strangers. Milton's final category of reciprocal duties comprises those public virtues regarding political and ecclesiastical life. Political duties include mutual obligations of magistrates and citizenry and their relations with other nations. Concerned primarily with honesty in governmental and judicial affairs, Milton in the tradition of his Elizabethan predecessors suggests that magistrates and ministers should be men of true wisdom and understanding. Obedience to law is owed by the people, but obedience to the unjust magistrate "has no foundation in Scripture" (17: 403). And though religion should be encouraged and protected by the magistrate, it should never be "forced upon the people" (17 : 395).

In Milton's view, although ethical habits could be developed, moral living was rational and decorous choosing; and his ethics are thus intimately concerned with all areas of life—personal, religious, political—that were inseparable in ethical matters : "The Judiciall law can serve to no other end then to bee the protector and champion of Religion and honest civility . . . and is but the arm of morall law, which can no more be separate from justice then justice from vertue" (DDD 3 : 471–72). Basic to Milton's concept of ethics was his understanding of religious and civil liberty, which was never license. Liberty was rather freedom to choose and thereby basic to man's test of obedience. Liberty did not obviate duty but made duty incumbent upon ethical man. Man's virtues are what he *owes* to God, self, and neighbor, but to pay or not to pay is ultimately a personal choice. For Milton, outward liberty is only a manifestation of inward liberty; true liberty was never license because with license the passions enslaved the will, a condition to which whole nations were susceptible as well as individuals. In *PL* Michael tells Adam that nations sometimes decline so "From vertue, which is reason, that no wrong, / But Justice . . . / Deprives them of thir outward libertie, / Thir inward lost" (12.97–100).

Although emphasis on moderation characterizes Milton's system of virtues, it is important to remember that virtues, ethical habits, are attained only by means of personal choice, by proper exercise of the moral judgment, with the essential choice being between good and evil. In this regard Milton, throughout his creative life, gave decided emphasis to the spiritually elevating power of good as opposed to the imbruting power of evil. As early as his prolusions we find this to be a recurrent theme. To instruct the moral judgment in its primary responsibility was indeed the purpose of "divine poetry" which, with its heaven-given power, rouses "to high flight the mind, buried in earthly dross, establishes quarters among the temples of the sky; and . . . instils in a measure heavenly blessedness and suggests a kind of immortal joy" (12 : 163). In *Prol* 7, he suggests that by living "modestly and temperately" we may "subdue the primary impulses of the ungovernable age through reason" and thus preserve "the heavenly vigor of the mind pure and unharmed from all contagion and defilement" (12 : 275). In *Mask*, the Lady is able to understand that nature is a "good cateres" who "Means her provision only to the good / That live according to her sober laws / And holy dictate of spare Temperance" (763–66) and thus may reject Comus's lustful offer of marriage and know his "lickerish baits" are "fit to ensnare a brute" (699). The Elder Brother knows that his sister's "saintly chastity" protects her from a spiritually enervating lust, a passion that "Imbodies and imbrutes" the soul "till she quite loose / The divine property of her first being" (467–68).

This same concern with the imbruting power of evil is manifested as well in Milton's three major poems. In *PL*, following their succumbing to the serpent's temptation, Adam and Eve and nature itself suffer a devastating change. "Outrage from liveless things" began; beasts warred with beasts and "Devourd each other" (10. 707–12). Adam and Eve fall away from their temperate marriage to a bestial lust. Their nakedness must now be clothed with "Skins / Of Beasts" (10. 220–21). In *PR* the imbruting temptation that Satan offers Jesus is ironically forced back upon himself. Satan tempts Jesus to "expel this monster," the Roman emperor, "from his Throne / Now made a stye" (4. 100–101) and ascend the throne himself. In rejecting the temptation, Jesus says, "I shall, thou say'st, expel / A brutish monster; what if I withal / Expel a Devil who first made him such?" (4. 127–29). When Satan at last falls from the pinnacle from which he hoped "to see his Victor fall," Milton compares him to "that *Theban* Monster" who devoured her victims, but who, when her riddle was "once found out and solv'd . . . / Cast herself headlong from th' Ismenian steep" (4. 571–75). In *SA*, Samson is himself an example of one victimized by bestial forces. He sees himself as "Inferiour to the vilest now become / Of man or worm" (73–74); and the Chorus depicts him as a "Dungeon" of himself and a mirror for mankind (155–65). He calls Dalila a "Hyaena," a beast fabled to entice men from their houses and devour them; and he views himself as being "to Ages an example," having become "Entangl'd with a poysnous bosom snake" (763–65). But Samson achieves an important ethical awareness and can thus say to Dalila, "I to my self was false e're thou to me" (824). In the simplest terms of Milton's ethics the imbruting of both Adam and Samson was the consequence of their free choices of evil over good, while the spiritual elevation of the Lady and Jesus proceeds from their choices of good over evil. Basic to Milton's "whole ethic," John Diekhoff says, "is the doctrine of free choice and the correlative doctrine of individual responsibility for individual actions . . ." (*Milton's "Paradise Lost"* [1946], p. 140). Virtues, or ethical habits, thus proceeded only from right choices made by the moral judgment.

In Book 5 of *PL* Raphael uses the image of the tree to explain to Adam that all things proceed from God "and up to him return, / If not deprav'd from good" (5. 470–71). Milton's ethical system, like Raphael's tree, proceeds from God, from his twin commandments, and provides the organic structure by which man ascends to happiness in this life and ultimately to salvation, if not "deprav'd from good" by irrational choosing. Milton's ethical doctrine is then one of comfort, but rational responsibility and obedience to divine moral authority are always demanded. [AWF]

EURIPIDES: *see* DRAMATISTS, GREEK.

EUROPEAN JOURNEY: *see* ITALIAN JOURNEY.

EUSEBIUS OF CAESAREA, Church Father and Bishop of Caesarea from about 313 until his death about A.D. 339. He achieved prominence both when he aided the exiled presbyter Arius and when he proposed the confession that became the basis of the Nicene formula. As an arch-enemy of Sabellianism, Eusebius has been suspected of Arianism*, although he actually followed Origen's* emphasis on the subordination of the Son* to the Father*. Milton mentioned neither Origen nor Eusebius, however, in his own subordinationistic passages in *CD*. Eusebius's two greatest historical works are his *Chronicle* (to A.D. 325), featuring a synchronism of Assyrian, Hebrew, Egyptian, Greek, and Roman history in parallel columns; and a *Church History* from apostolic times to his own era. Careful, comprehensive excerpts from original sources made his work indispensable to later scholars; and his constant affirmation of God's action within human history completely divorced his work from Graeco-Roman historical method. His *Life of Constantine,* more eulogy than history, is nevertheless valuable for its incorporation of numerous documents; and his *Praeparatio evangelica* attempted to prove the excellence of Christianity over every pagan religion and philosophy.

Milton cites Eusebius more than seven times in *CB* (18 : 136, 138, 146, 147, 163, 168, 170), most interestingly on his proof of apostles' marriages and his frequent mention of bishops' wives and children. He made heavy use of Eusebius, "the ancientist writer extant of church history," to undercut the authority of unwritten tradition and to battle prelacy (3 : 20, 21, 30, 85, 87, 91, 93, 97, 178, 211–12; 4 : 64). In *3Def* Milton rejects charges of obscenity by identifying with "the ancient fathers of the church" (including Eusebius), who might also have been charged with obscenity for their derision of "the obscene mysteries of the old religions" (9 : 111). In *Brit* he cites Eusebian details, once in disagreement (10 : 80) and once in agreement (10 : 93). In *Tetra* Milton twice cites Eusebius to help prove that charity should be the "supreme resolver of all Scripture" (4 : 136, 207–8); and in *Areop* he describes the "vision recorded by *Eusebius*" in which Dionysius Alexandrinus was granted freedom to read whatever came into his hands because he was "sufficient both to judge aright, and to examine each matter" (4 : 308).

Milton's imagination was apparently fired most by the *Praeparatio evangelica.* In *TM* "Outlines for Tragedies," the seventh entry suggests a tragedy on Dinah drawn from that work (18.235); and stanzas 19–25 of *Nat* draw upon the *Praeparatio*'s treatment of history surrounding the legend that all oracles ceased at the birth of Christ. [VRM]

EVAGRIUS (ca. 536–ca. 600), surnamed Scholasticus, a Syrian legal adviser to Pope Gregory and patriarch of the church in Constantinople. He wrote an *Ecclesiastical History* in six books, covering the period 431–493, thus continuing the work begun by Eusebius*, "the Father of Church History," about 200 years earlier. In bringing the work down to 493, Evagrius may not always be considered trustworthy, but he is consistently impartial and bases his narrative on primary sources. His *History* is listed among Milton's reading in *CB* and cited in *PrelE* (3 : 84). [PMZ]

EVE. "Mother of human Race" (*PL* 4. 475), "Mother of All Mankind" (11. 159), and "Mother of all things living" (11. 160), Eve is one of the chief characters in *PL*. Before her appearance (4. 288ff.), Milton pays her scant attention : in the manuscript proposals for a tragedy (18 : 228ff.) and in two of the divorce tracts (*Tetra* 4 : 83ff., 170; *DDD* 3 : 441). In *PR*, she is dismissed as a "facile consort" (1. 51), but as a character in *PL,* she is one of Milton's most satisfying creations.

Her name in Hebrew, *hawwāh,* means "mother of all living" (Gen. 3 : 20), mentioned once in the Old Testament and twice in the New. She and Adam together are

              the lovliest pair
That ever since in loves imbraces met,
Adam the goodliest man of men since borne
His Sons, the fairest of her Daughters *Eve.*
                (4. 321–24)

She is called "our general Mother" (4. 492) and associated through her motherhood with the "great" and "all-bearing Mother" Earth (5. 338; 5. 11, 281). She is also figuratively linked with the Moon as Adam is with the Sun, each being respectively "Male and Femal Light, / Which two great Sexes animate the World" (8. 148–51). Thus, Eve is at once a character from biblical history and a mythological earth, moon, and mother goddess who expresses with Adam the fundamental male-female principle of the universe : "male and female created he them" (Gen. 1 : 27).

Apart from her biblical and mythical associations, Eve is a warmly human character, beautiful to behold, susceptible to a blameless vanity and curiosity that Satan uses successfully to deceive and seduce her into sin*. Her beauty is such, as Adam explains, that "Wisdom in discourse with her / Looses discount'nanc't" (8. 552–53). Milton's descriptions of her in Books 4 and 8 constitute some of his best poetry, and his characterization is the subtlest and most extensive in world literature.

Milton's chief perception about Eve's "loveliness" is that it is both creative and potentially destructive. As long as Eve stands in relation to Adam as a subordinate or "inferior," acknowledging his absolute rule, the divinely created order of their marriage* will be sustained. It will, moreover, be fertile and prolific, as when Zephyr breathes on Flora (5. 16). God created Eve from Adam's rib in order that she be a suitable companion ("helpmeet"). She is made for him, and for God in him (4. 299). Eve herself admits that "beauty is excelled by manly grace / And wisdom, which alone is truly fair" (4. 490–91). Milton's undeviating conviction is that man's is "the Perfeter sex" (*DDD* 3 : 306), following Aristotle*, and that God has granted "superior rights to the husband" (*CD* 15 : 121), who has "despotic power / Over his female in due awe" (*SA* 1054–55), a view based on St. Paul (1 Cor. 11) and widely supported by the majority of Milton's contemporaries. Deplorable as such views may now seem, it was this arrangement of domestic affairs that Milton celebrated as an ideally creative union.

But whereas Adam's is the "more attentive mind" (10. 1011), Eve's is more responsive to the current of nature* within her (8. 500–510), thus reflecting the traditional association of Adam with reason* and Eve with passion. Should her womanly nature go unruled, she can disrupt the created harmonies both within herself and without through her domestic and natural relationships. She is thus destructive when Adam yields to his "effeminate slackness' (11. 634), as Michael calls it, which is Adam's excessive delight in Eve's beauty, such that he is incapable of restraining her curiosity when she wants to work alone in the Garden. The result is the Fall*, wherein Adam "scrupl'd not to eat / Against his better knowledge, not deceav'd, / But fondly overcome with Femal charm" (9. 997–99).

Just before the Fall, Eve, although still "sinless" (9. 659), is described as "unwary" (9. 644). She is a victim of Satan's deceit, having fallen "into deception unaware" (9. 362), as both Raphael and Adam had warned. Adam, however, is not "deceived," at least not in the same way that Eve is. Instead, he subordinates his wisdom to Eve's beauty, places her above God in an idolatrous act and submits, as the Narrator says, "to what seemd remediless" (9. 919). Eve falls deceived by the Serpent; Adam falls through "vehemence of love" (9. Argument). As the Narrator comments at the beginning of Book 10, Satan "in the Serpent had perverted *Eve*, / Her Husband shee" (lines 3–4). Eve, or more exactly Eve's beauty, had been suborned by Satan and used to "pervert" Adam. As Eve understands her transgression, she became Adam's snare, though she was ordained to be his "help" (11. 164–65).

Although Milton has been accused of misogyny by some of his critics, epitomized by Dr. Johnson* who said Milton had a "Turkish contempt of females," the worst that can be said of his portrait of Eve is that in his idealization of woman he makes her superhuman. Milton's account goes a long way toward restoring the original splendor and polish of an image of Eve tarnished by the outspoken antifeminists of the sixteenth and seventeenth centuries. The grace and quiet "domestic" honor of Eve before the Fall, the glorification of the ideal marriage of Adam and Eve, the strength and intelligence of Eve's reasoning with the Serpent even amidst her failure, the honest humility of Eve's repenting before Adam after the Fall, and Eve's acceptance of the role as mother of the Seed (Christ) and direct link to "blest *Marie, second Eve*" (5. 387), all argue that Milton intended Eve to be a "perfect" woman.

Milton's two references to Mary as a "second *Eve*" (5. 387; 10. 183), show how carefully he worked out the elaborate symmetry and parallelism for which *PL* has been justly praised. Following the commentaries of many church fathers (among them, Jerome*, Augustine*, and Irenaeus), Milton incorporates the following terms of the patristic comparisons between Eve and Mary (see Mother Mary Christopher Pecheux, *Publications of the Modern Language Association* 75 : 359–66) :

1. The persons : both Eve and Mary were virgins. Milton's Eve is not a virgin in the technical sense, though she expresses "Virgin Modestie" (8. 501) and "Virgin Majestie" (9. 270), which details emphasize her innocence and figuratively accommodate the tradition to his own views.

2. The actions of the two angels: the fallen angel visited Eve, who listened to him readily, believing his deceiving words, and disbelieved God; the good angel visited Mary who, at first troubled by his words, believed the good tidings he brought from God.

3. The actions of the two women : Eve disobeyed, Mary obeyed.

4. The results : Eve brought forth death, Mary life.

Thus, Adam, the first man, fell through the instrumentality of a woman; whereas Jesus, the second Adam and new man, was born of a woman and began the Redemption. Eve is the "mother of all living" according to the flesh, but with the Fall she becomes the mother of the spiritually dead, and it is left to Mary, the second Eve, to fulfill the meaning of her name when she becomes the mother of Jesus.

Eve, as Milton's portrait of the ideal wife, may reflect, as some readers have suggested, the kind of woman the poet wished to marry but never found, certainly not in Mary Powell, his first wife. Milton's poetic idealization doubtless reflects something of his personal experience, but his portrait of Eve is poor evidence for biography except as it shows a poet capable of soaring (as Voltaire* said) "not above human, but above corrupt Nature." [RCF]

EVELYN, JOHN (1620–1706), diarist and author. Educated at the Middle Temple and Balliol College, Oxford, Evelyn left without a degree, traveled on the Continent extensively, and finally settled at Sayes Court, Deptford, Essex, in February 1652. A Royalist, he lived there quietly until the Restoration, investigating horticulture and establishing what became a public garden and museum. His *Acetaria. A Discourse of Sallets* (1699; 1706, two editions) refers to Milton with quotations from *PL* on pp. 93 and n., 188–89 and n. Compare also remarks on pp. 146–48. His friends before and after the Restoration were the scientists John Wilkins and Robert Boyle. It is not surprising, thus, that he aided in the establishment of the Royal Society and was one of the first fellows chosen. Milton's nephew Edward Phillips joined the Sayes Court household on October 24, 1663, to be Evelyn's son's preceptor. Evelyn's diary entry is interesting : "This

gentleman was nephew to Milton who writ against Salmasius's* *Defensio,* but not at all infected with his principles, and though brought up by him, yet no way tainted" (E. S. de Beer, ed., *Diary* [1955], 3 : 364–65). Phillips left on February 27, 1665, and Ralph Bohun became tutor to the younger John Evelyn (1655–1699), who became a translator in adult life. A poem by him, "To Envy," contains an allusion to Milton; see John Nichols, ed., *A Select Collections of Poems: With Notes, Biographical and Historical* (1780), 3 : 135. Evelyn recommended Phillips as tutor on September 16, 1677, to Henry Bennet, Earl of Arlington (*Diary,* 4: 120–21). On June 9, 1686, Evelyn noted that Milton's brother, Christopher, had been sworn one of the barons of the Exchequer on April 24 and called him a papist (*Diary,* 4 : 514). [JTS]

EVIL. Evil is that which is undesirable, that which is to be resisted directly or indirectly. It may be regarded as passive or physical (that which befalls us) and active or moral (that which we do). Concerning passive evil, Milton vigorously proclaims that although "all things ill / Are but as slavish officers of vengeance" (*Mask* 217–18), it is man's responsibility to try to alleviate the social results of his own sin* by hard work : "There is no evil in the state that the Lord hath not let in, Amos 3. Famine, plague, sedition, a public enemy—is there a single one of these that the state will not strive with all its might to shake off? Shake them off it will if it can, though it know them to be sent by God," he writes (*1Def* 7 : 181). His point here, of course, is to urge the state's responsibility to rid itself of Charles I*.

But it was with active or moral evil, with the cause rather than the effect, that Milton chiefly concerned himself, for he knew that the problem of evil is central to any attempt to justify the ways of God to man. If God is omnipotent and good, why does evil exist at all? To answer that question, Milton concentrated on several important factors, including the parasitical character of evil, a distinction between the positive and permissive will of God, and the reality of free will* in all created moral beings.

Like the ancient Greeks and the Neoplatonists*, St. Augustine* taught that because what we call bad things are really good things perverted, evil is parasitical and cannot exist without good (*The City of God* 14. 11). Similarly, Milton's Satan is perverted from his original goodness by pride (becoming more interested in himself than in God); but at first his original glory is not completely obscured (*PL* 1. 591ff.), and becomes so only gradually as he continues to negate all that he was originally intended to be. Thus Satan is magnificent at the beginning of *PL* because he is the negation of one of God's finest creations : Lucifer, the Light-Bearer (cf. *PL* 7. 131ff.). And in another sense he is the Antichrist, the negation of the love and selflessness that are the Son*.

Milton's description of sin in *CD* emphasizes its negative character : "not that sin is properly an action, for in reality it implies defect; but . . . it commonly consists in some act. For every act is in itself good; it is only its irregularity or deviation from the line of right, which, properly speaking, is evil" (15 : 199). Thus Milton asserts that the creation* is good, that no act or thing is intrinsically evil, and that evil is the abuse or misuse of the good and the real (cf. *PL* 4. 110).

This is not the same as to say that evil is only an illusion or a mirage, having no genuine reality. Evil, according to the Christian tradition (and Milton), is a genuine but inferior power, terrible in its impact on fallen man but negligible when compared to the power of God. Evil is goodness that has been perverted from its normative goals. In Paul Tillich's phrase, it is "the elevation of something conditional to unconditional significance"; hence, evil is basically a lie, a falsification of its own nature. Thus, Satan boasts that he made himself (*PL* 5. 860–64), knowing all the while that he is lying

(*PL* 4. 42–45). Inevitably, therefore, evil is self-enslaving and self-destructive.

Both Heaven* and prelapsarian Eden prove that good can exist without evil; but evil cannot exist without good, for there must first be something good before its perversion can be accomplished. Because of the Fall*, however, man's perception has become limited so that his knowledge of good is dependent upon his knowledge of evil : "It was called the tree of knowledge of good and evil from the event; for since Adam tasted it, we not only know evil, but we know good only by means of evil. For it is by evil that virtue is chiefly exercised, and shines with greater brightness" (15 : 115).

God is the author of evil only in the sense that He created goodness and gave to His creatures the free will by which they could either affirm or pervert it. Because both reason* and free will would be hollow terms without genuine choice, the *possibility* of evil is clearly necessary; hence the placement of the Tree of the Knowledge of Good and Evil in the midst of the Garden, and hence God's injunction not to eat of it. Adam and Eve were created "fallibly perfect"—free to disobey as well as to obey. The impetus for their fall came not from God, nor from their own unconscious minds, but from Satan's conscious mind.

There was, however, a sense in which Satan was the tool of God, for ultimately God would bring good out of his evil (*PL* 1. 216–20). Furthermore, Satan could make no move at all without God's permission; as Milton says in *CD*, "God . . . is concerned in the production of evil in only one of these two ways; either, first, he permits its existence by throwing no impediment in the way of natural causes and free agents . . . or, secondly, he causes [physical or passive] evil by the infliction of judgments, which is called the evil of punishment" (15 : 67). Thus Milton, like many other Renaissance apologists, distinguished between the positive will of God, which produces goodness, and the permissive will of God, which allows evil (*PL* 1. 212, 366; 2. 1025; 3. 92, 523ff.,

685; 6. 674; 10. 622ff.). At times, however, God does exert restrictions over evil activities, for His permissiveness in no way reduces His control over His creatures (*PL* 4. 1006–10; 6. 699–703).

The context of *PL* 5. 117–19 makes clear that in this passage Milton is not ascribing evil to God, but rather is saying that the presence of evil as an object of thought in the mind of God or man does not contaminate the mind, in that only the approval of the free will can bring about contamination. Thus the theory that there is evil latent in the Infinite God receives no support in Milton's works.

The many parallels between good and evil in *PL* (Trinity* and Anti-Trinity, hierarchies and councils in Heaven and in Hell, and so forth) exist not only to strengthen the epic's unity, but also to demonstrate the parasitical nature of evil and to clarify meanings for the reader, who as a member of a fallen race can understand goodness only by means of evil. (One of the best ways to understand Milton's concept of the Trinity, for instance, is to study the relationships between Satan, Sin, and Death.) In *Apol*, Milton demonstrates that he had found this technique among Christ's own methods: "Doth not Christ himselfe teach the highest things by the similitude *of old bottles and patcht cloaths*? Doth he not illustrate best things by things most evill? his own *comming* to be *as a thiefe in the night,* and the righteous mans *wisdome to that of an unjust Steward*?" (3 : 311–12). [VRM]

FAIRFAX, THOMAS (1612–1671), parliamentary general whom Milton extolled in *Sonn* 15 and in *2Def*. He came of an old Yorkshire family with a strong fighting tradition. After a period at St. John's College, Cambridge, he was sent at seventeen to the Netherlands to learn the art of war under Sir Horace Vere, whose daughter he later married. When the Civil War broke out he was a committed parliamentarian, and he commanded the cavalry in the Yorkshire forces raised and led by his father. His

dash and skill in the actions at Wakefield, Winceby, Nantwich, Selby, and Marston Moor gained him a growing reputation, and when the New Model Army was formed in 1645 he was appointed its Captain-General. He commanded it at Naseby and in all the subsequent actions that clinched Parliament's victory. He was unhappy about the army's defiance of Parliament and seizure of the king in 1647, but he had no hesitation about leading it next year against the royalist insurrections in the southeast. These ended when he penned up the insurgents in Colchester—the occasion of Milton's sonnet. He was now Lord Fairfax, having recently inherited the Scottish barony purchased by his grandfather.

Sonn 15 was an appeal to Fairfax to save England from the corruption and extortion of which Milton believed the Parliament and its agents to be guilty. But for all his integrity Fairfax was out of his depth in politics. He played a vacillating, equivocal part in the events that led, five months after Colchester fell, to the execution of Charles I*. He claimed that the army "purged" the Parliament in December without his knowledge—a strange admission for a commander-in-chief. He claimed too that he did all he could to prevent the execution of Charles I, but whatever his efforts, they left no ripple on the surface of events. Though increasingly alienated by the course of English politics, he did not resign his command until June 1650, when he was ordered to lead an army against the Scots.

Milton probably came into occasional contact with Fairfax in the Council of State* of which the general was a member in 1649–1650. Later Andrew Marvell* formed another link, for he had been tutor to Fairfax's daughter Mary just before he became Milton's colleague and friend. But long before Milton wrote his page of tribute in *2Def*, Fairfax had completely retired from public life—less because of ill health, as Milton professed to believe, than because he disliked the political tendencies of the Commonwealth and (still more) the Protectorate. When at length he allowed himself to be elected to the Parliament of 1659 he associated with the Protectorate's republican opponents, but any sympathy he had with them was quickly dissipated, for at the beginning of 1660 he led a rising of the Yorkshire gentry that had as its ultimate, though unavowed, object the restoration of the king. Four months later, in recognition of this signal service, he headed the commission that the Convention Parliament sent to attend Charles II* at the Hague. In spite of his good standing with the restored monarchy, however, he again retired to his home at Nun Appleton, this time permanently. [AW]

FAITH, in the religious sense, is the subjective state reached by a Christian believer as the result of the operation in him of divine grace*. One of the theological virtues together with hope* and love*, it must be understood as an activity or a response to religious matters. As such it is seated in the will, but a will illuminated by the understanding, producing "works" that are external manifestations of its inward being.

Following Paul, Luther* had taught that man is saved by faith alone. The New Testament book of James, however, had emphasized the importance for salvation of works. In Article 11 of the *39 Articles* man is "accounted righteous . . . by Faith" alone and not by works, though the next Article recognizes them to be the "fruits of Faith" and "acceptable to God." The Presbyterian* *Westminster Confession* (14) is somewhat more detailed, arguing that faith springs from an inner conviction, itself derived from God, which is assisted by sacraments* and prayer with recognition of the psychological fact that it may exist in varying degrees of conviction though in the elect it is never wholly obliterated.

Milton's writing shows his continuing concern for the vitality of the religious experience—that is, with faith—though he is not always consistent in his handling of its details. Thus according to *CivP*

(6:21), faith originates in the understanding or jointly from the understanding and the will, but *CD* places its seat in the will alone (15:407). In any case, however, the original impulse comes from God. As Milton explains, it is part of the religious experience of conversion; repentance precedes it, and the sense of divine mercy leading to repentance should not be confused with the faith that results (15:387). The convert may begin with the experience of implicit or unreasoned faith, a divine assurance, and proceed to develop a true faith or full persuasion (15:397–99). The voluntarism of Milton's definition is strikingly shown in his emphasis upon its being exercised: "Our faith and knowledge thrives by exercise," he wrote in *Areop* (4:333), an idea somewhat twisted by Eve: "what is Faith, Love, Virtue unassaid / Alone, without exterior help sustain?" (*PL,* 9. 335ff.), yet more temperate than Sir Thomas Browne's "me thinks there be not impossibilities enough in Religion for an active faith" (*Religio Medici* 1. 9).

In *CD* Milton tries to bring into harmony the vexed question of the relationship between faith and works, arguing that there is no dichotomy between them but that a living faith cannot exist without works (16:39). On the other hand, man cannot take any merit from them inasmuch as the faith itself that produced them derives from the operation of the Spirit in him (41). Thus in *PL* Jesus' merits save men, "not thir own, though legal works" (12. 410). At the same time works are necessary to evince true faith; as Michael tells Adam (and the reader) "onely add / Deeds to thy knowledge answerable, add Faith" (12. 581ff.). Accordingly, if Adam had abstained from eating of the Tree of Knowledge* he would have pledged his obedience* and faith (8. 325). [WBH]

FAITHORNE, WILLIAM (the elder) (1616–1691), designer and engraver of the standard portrait of Milton (age 62), an eminent English engraver of the seventeenth century. He was born in

London, became a pupil of Robert Peake, under whom he worked for about four years, and then followed in support of King Charles* during the Civil War. Faithorne was arrested and confined in Aldersgate, but allowed to resume his profession in confinement. He was released but exiled, went to France, studied under Robert Nanteuil, and finally returned to England in 1650. The influence of Nanteuil improved his work considerably, and Faithorne had a good deal of success as a printer and bookseller. He retired from his shop in 1680, but continued to engrave and draw crayon portraits. Faithorne's *The Art of Graving and Etching* (1662) is an early standard in the field.

Faithorne's reputation may have drawn him the commission from James Allestry to draw from life and then engrave a portrait of Milton for the 1670 (first) edition of Milton's *Brit.* Both the crayon drawing and the engraving itself were copied by at least forty-five artists in the ensuing two hundred years. It is known also as the Bayfordbury portrait, having been owned by William Buber, who resided there. (See John Rupert Martin, *The Portrait of John Milton at Princeton and Its Place in Milton Iconography* [1961].) The drawing, now at Princeton, seems to be the original of the etching, and it shows a man with light brown hair and a softer expression than is depicted on the engraving. The head is turned slightly to the left in the drawing, while the reverse process of printing makes the engraving a mirror image of the drawing. Milton's third wife did not like the engraving, and apparently disliked the drawing as well; but Deborah Milton, the poet's daughter, exclaimed on the drawing's fidelity when she first saw it in 1721 or 1725.

Faithorne did numerous other engraved portraits, including portraits of Thomas Hobbes*, William Laud*, Henry Lawes*, and a good many members of the English and continental nobility. His portraits and engraving techniques are still respected, though his attempts at historical engravings are considered failures. For a description of his work, see Louis Fagan, *A Descriptive Catalogue of the Engraved Works of William Faithorne* (1888). [SW]

FALL AND RESTORATION OF MAN, THE. The Protestant theory of the Fall is an extension of the views that St. Augustine* had formulated in the heat of controversy. In opposition to Pelagius*, who, more than all others, minimized the effects of Adam's sin* on his descendants, Augustine shifted the emphasis from the human plane to the divine by stressing mankind's dependence upon the Creator, the inability of the human race to raise itself unaided, and the primacy of divine grace* in each and every act undertaken by man. The Augustinian doctrines of depravation and predestination*, of free will* and the damnation of unbaptized infants, cannot be divorced from his reiterated conviction that divine grace through the Son* of God is the fundamental tenet of the Christian faith.

Basic to Augustine's approach was the conclusion that, ever since the Fall, the will of man is naturally inclined toward evil*. This disposition of the will applies not only to a few individuals but to the whole human race considered as the direct successors of Adam and heirs of his sin. Mankind, Augustine maintained, was present in the first man *in semine* or *in germine* (in his seed); and as a result of Adam's heinous crime, we have all inherited the *originis reatus* no less than the *originale peccatrix*, becoming a *massa peccatrix*, indeed a *universa massa perditionis* (*De gratia Christi* 2. 34).

Augustine's views were upheld in even harsher terms in the theology of the Reformers, notably Luther* and Calvin*. Luther's view was unequivocal. As he claimed in his commentary on Galatians, "Whatsoever is in our wil, is evil: whatsoever is in our understanding, is errour. Wherefore in spirituall matters man hath nothing but darknes, errours, ignoraunce, malice, and perversenes both of wil and understanding" (anon. trans. of 1575, fol. 82). For his part, Calvin redefined the Augustinian doctrine of original sin as "the inheritably descendynge perversnesse and corruption of our nature, poured abroade into all the partes of the soule" (*Inst.* 2, i, 8; trans. Thomas Norton, 1561). Moreover, mankind was present in Adam not merely "seminally," as Augustine held, but "federally," so that we are "all borne evell and corrupted," "we bryng with us from the wombe of our Mother a viciousnesse planted in our begetting" (2, i, 4–8; etc.).

By the time of Milton the precise extent to which Adam's disobedience* affected both his own free will and that of his descendants had become a matter of earnest controversy. No orthodox Protestant expositor, however, was prepared to minimize the gravity of Adam's rebellion. Widely regarded as a *summa omnium vitiorum,* his action in the Garden is expressly said in *PL* to have been a "manifold" sin (10. 16)—for it comprehended, as *CD* informs us, "at once distrust in the divine veracity, and a proportionate credulity in the assurances of Satan; unbelief; ingratitude; disobedience; gluttony; in the man excessive uxoriousness, in the woman a want of proper regard for her husband, in both an insensibility to the welfare of their offspring, and that offspring the whole human race; parricide, theft, invasion of the rights of others, sacrilege, deceit, presumption in aspiring to divine attributes, fraud in the means employed to attain the object, pride, and arrogance" (15: 181–83).

But the "manifold" sin of Adam and Eve may ultimately be reduced to one —pride—for "there is no sinne almost but pride doth participate with it" (Miles Smith, *Sermon preached at Worcester* [1602], p. 15). As love is centrifugal, pride is centripetal. Love "seeketh not her own" (1 Cor. 13 : 5), "drives a man out of himselfe, and makes him nothing in himselfe" (John Preston, *The Breast-plate of Faith,* 5th ed. [1634], 1 : 58). Pride is

selfishness : "It hates Superiors, It scorns Inferiors, It owves no equalls" (Francis Quarles, *Enchyridion* [1640], sig. F2). It is the state of any creature *incurvatus in se,* as Luther phrased it, "curved inwards upon himself." "It was by reason of this *Self-will,"* Ralph Cudworth argued, "that Adam fell in Paradise; that those glorious Angels, those *Morning-starres,* kept not their first station" (*A Sermon* [1647], pp. 19–20). Milton, in agreement, condensed within a few lines the whole tradition pertaining to Lucifer's sin :

> his Pride
> Had cast him out from Heav'n, with all his Host
> Of Rebel Angels, by whose aid aspiring
> To set himself in Glory above his Peers,
> He trusted to have equald the Most High.
> (1. 36–40)

Milton's Eve also fell "by reason of this *Self-will."* Her Fall itself is forecast by two incidents that alike testify to her centripetal tendencies. The first occurred the moment after she was created, when she regarded with "sympathie and love" the reflection of her own image in a lake (4. 465). The Monarch of Hell, overhearing Eve's account of her experience, promptly brought about the second important incident, Eve's "high exaltation" in a dream (5. 30–93). Satan's foremost desire was to instill in Eve a "sense of injur'd merit" similar to his own (1. 98; 4. 80). He therefore plants in her mind the idea that she deserves to be "among the Gods . . . a Goddess" (4. 77ff.), cultivates it during the temptation* at high noon (9. 547ff., 568, 612, 684, 732), and finally sees it come to fruition when Eve falls, appetent after "God-head" (9. 790). Now "curved inwards" Eve plunges into a soliloquy. Should she permit Adam to partake of her happiness? Were it not better to retain it all herself so as to be "more equal" to him, perhaps even superior? But what if the "great Forbidder" should render her extinct and give Adam another Eve? Her final decision is not just immersed in irony; it is drowned in it :

> I resolve,
> *Adam* shall share with me in bliss or woe:
> So dear I love him, that with him all deaths
> I could endure, without him live no life.
> (9. 830–33)

So she bows before the Tree of Knowledge. The gesture may be symbolic of her intention to "live independently of God." It amounts to idolatry*.

Whether Adam also fell "by reason of this *Self-will*" is a matter of controversy. His decision to share Eve's fate has been termed variously "true love," "half-nobility," "fullness of passion," and even "frivolity." The first of these labels—"true love"—seems to have raised the most objections, yet many Renaissance commentators *did* claim that Adam's motive was "love." Adam, it was maintained, fell "partly by the provocation of the woman, whome greatlye he loued," "who beeing his wife, yea, his onely companion, was no doubt a great pleasure, joy, and delight vnto him" (John Udall, *Certaine Sermons* [1596], sig. B8ᵛ; Thomas Morton, *The Three-fold State* [1629], p. 23). Adam's decision about Eve was indeed grounded on love, but when we consider the obligations they shouldered, other than toward each other, his "true love" turns into irrational love—even, in Milton's phrase, into "compliance bad" (9. 994). Eve herself naturally does not think so. She greets Adam's decision with the cry,

> O glorious trial of exceeding Love
> Illustrious evidence, example high!
> (9. 961–62)

Milton rarely hit upon greater irony, for her cry is but a dreadful parody of the Son's "unexampl'd love" (3. 410).

The Christian tradition postulates also that Adam sought to assume to himself —in the words of St. Ambrose*—"that which he had not received, that thus he might become as it were his own master and creator, and arrogate to himself divine honour" (*Ep.* 73. 5). We may think that this interpretation bears no relationship to *PL*, yet Adam *is* discovered to be "puffed up." Fascinated by Eve's argument that she grew "up to Godhead," he

observes explicitly that the possibility of becoming "Gods, or Angels Demi-gods" is an "inducement strong" to violate any divine command (9. 877, 934–37). As the Geneva Bible of 1560 asserted in a marginal note to Genesis 3 : 6, Adam fell "Not so muche to please his wife, as moved by ambicion at her persuasion." Seen thus, Adam's "true love" recedes again into self-love. We might consider that love is not love when it is mingled with regards that stand aloof from the entire point.

The most disastrous consequence of the Fall is stated at the outset of *PL*: Adam's disobedience "Brought Death into the World" (1. 3). Death and disorder simultaneously penetrated the fabric of the entire universe which now "resembleth a chaine rent in peeces, whose links are many lost and broken, and the rest so slightly fastened as they will hardly hang together" (Sir Richard Barckley, *The Felicitie of Man* [1598], p. 6). As Milton wrote in *SolMus* (19–24),

> disproportion'd sin
> Jarr'd against natures chime, and with harsh
> din
> Broke the fair musick that all creatures made
> To their great Lord, whose love their motion
> sway'd
> In perfect Diapason, whilst they stood
> In first obedience, and their state of good.

The effect of Adam's disobedience on the macrocosm of nature corresponds to its effect on the little world of man. Adam's conduct after the Fall, when he raves and grows more fierce and wild at every word, demonstrates an idea often repeated that sin is "anomy," and expresses dramatically the sort of behavior castigated in innumerable Renaissance treatises on the passions. Hence the significance of Adam's description in *PL* as one who is "in a troubl'd Sea of passion tost" (10. 718). Earlier the metaphor was applied to both Adam and Eve :

> They sate them down to weep, nor onely
> Teares
> Raind at thir Eyes, but high Winds worse
> within

Began to rise, high Passions, Anger, Hate,
Mistrust, Suspicion, Discord, and shook sore
Thir inward State of Mind, calm Region once
And full of Peace, now tost and turbulent.
(9. 1121–26)

Another way of looking at the effects of
the Fall was stated in an Elizabethan
homily : "In stede of the ymage of GOD,
[man] was become nowe the ymage of the
Devyll" (*The Second Tome of Homelyes*
[1563], sig. zzz4). As Michael observes in
PL, referring to the descendants of Adam,

Thir Makers Image . . .
Forsook them, when themselves they villifi'd
To serve ungoverned appetite, and took
His image whom they serv'd, . . . since they
Gods Image did not reverence in themselves.
(11. 515–25)

Expanding this theme, Michael sub-
sequently informs Adam that

Since thy original lapse, true Libertie
Is lost, which alwayes with right Reason
    dwells
Twinnd, and from her hath no dividual
    being:
Reason in man obscur'd, or not obeyd,
Immediately inordinate desires
And upstart Passions catch the Government
From Reason, and to servitude reduce
Man till then free.
(12. 83–90)

But even as Renaissance apologists never
lost an opportunity to denounce Adam's
crime, they also never tired of stressing
the vast difference between God's attitude
toward fallen man and his attitude toward
the rebellious angels. Lucifer and his
disciples were "cast downe" without any
hope of restoration, but Adam and Eve
were "cast out" with promise of the
redemption to come. The Augustinian
thesis that "man had sinned less than the
devil" (*De lib. arb.* 3. 10) was used to
account for such differences in the divine
disposition. The distinction was made
because the angels disobeyed through
"willfull pride" whereas man was merely
"misse-lead"—or as one apologist phrased
it, "the Angels fell of themselves, but
man by the suggestion of another" (Rich-
ard Field, *Of the Church*, 3d ed. [1635],
p. 5). In the words of the Father* in *PL,*
the angels

by thir own suggestion fell,
Self-tempted, self-deprav'd : Man falls
    deceiv'd
By the other first : Man therefore shall find
    grace,
The other none.
(3. 129–32)

We now see why a drastic difference exists
between the two judgments described by
Milton. When the angels are judged after
the War in Heaven*, the Son of God
appears "full of wrauth," "Gloomie as
Night," with a terrible countenance "too
severe to be beheld," and mercilessly
drives them out of Heaven (6. 824ff.).
When Adam and Eve are judged, God
appears "without revile," "gracious,"
"mild," and so compassionate that he
covers their nakedness with the skins of
beasts (10. 96, 118, 211ff.; cf. 1046–48).
Still more important, however, God pro-
claims the "mysterious terms" of the
woman's seed.

The promise of the "seed" was em-
phasized by Protestants in a manner quite
without parallel in the teaching of other
Christians. The most relevant passage is
embedded in the sentence that God
passes on Satan in Genesis 3 : 15, restated
by Milton thus :

Between Thee and the Woman I will put
Enmitie, and between thine and her Seed;
Her Seed shall bruise thy head, thou bruise
    his heel.
(10. 179–81)

To prevent any misunderstanding, Mil-
ton proceeded to explain that these
"mysterious terms" were

                          verifi'd
When *Jesus* son of *Mary* second *Eve,*
Saw Satan fall like Lightning down from
    Heav'n,
Prince of the Aire; then rising from his Grave
Spoild Principalities and Powers, triumpht
In op'n shew, and with ascension bright
Captivity led captive through the Aire,
The Realm it self of Satan long usurpt,
Whom he shall tread at last under our feet.
(10. 182–90)

But the persuasion that Genesis 3 : 15 is
the "first gospel"—the *protevangelium**—
involved also the acrimonious controversy

between Protestants and Catholics concerning the exact reference of the pronoun in the biblical phrase *it shall bruise*. The varied interpretations, with a censure of the obvious culprits, were summarily stated by Nicholas Gibbens in *Questions and Disputations* (1601): the pronoun

> may onlie be translated, as some do *it*; that is, that same seed; but much better, *he*: namelie, that one person; as manie other, & even *Hierome* himselfe, and the Septuagint translation, and our English [i.e., the Geneva Bible] hath it. But some of the Fathers, misguided by the translation of *Aquila,* of *Symmachus,* and *Theodotion,* which chieflie in their time were in use, doe read it, *she shall breake*: so also doth the Jewish Targhum which those translatours followed, as Jewish heretikes: yet none of these expound it of any other woman then of *Heva,* saving that in a mysticall sense, they take it for the affections of the minde. But the church of Rome will needes read it, *she shall breake,* & understand it of the virgin *Marie,* giving unto her the glorie of breaking the Serpents head. (p. 146)

Few aspects of Catholic devotion succeeded in stimulating the ire of Protestants more than the elevation of the Virgin to the rank of redeemer. "They have made her," sneered Bishop Miles Smith, "the very dore by which we enter into Paradise, shut by *Eve,* opened by her" (*Sermons* [1632], p. 32). But under no circumstances, Smith continued, should Mary be regarded as "the Mediatresse of Reconcilement and Propitiation"—not even, added Richard Sheldon, "if all *Austens,* all *Bernards,* all *Gregories,* all *Angells* from heaven should affirme it" (*The First Sermon* [1612], p. 42).

Concurring with the prevalent Protestant opinion, Milton expressed himself in violent opposition to the occasional Catholic claim that "the obedience of *Mary* was the cause of salvation to her selfe, and all mankind" (*PrelE* 3 : 94). His contrary view, as we have seen, took the form of the explicit equation of the seed with the Christ, which is precisely the identification insisted upon by his contemporaries and immediate predecessors. Thereafter in *PL* the prophecy is

recollected at a crucial moment in the relations of our "grand parents." Long after it was first uttered by God, Adam attempts to console his repentant wife with these words:

> let us seek
> Som safer resolution, which methinks
> I have in view, calling to minde with heed
> Part of our Sentence, that thy Seed shall bruise
> The Serpents head.
>
> (10. 1028–32)

For the time being, however, the terms are still mysterious to both. But not for long. The archangel Michael was already receiving his charge from God to

> reveale
> To *Adam* what shall come in future dayes,
> As I shall thee enlight'n, intermix
> My Cov'nant in the womans seed renewed. . . .
>
> (11. 113–16)

In line with the divine behest, Michael —"milde," "benigne," "gentle"—unfolds the future before an expectant Adam. But the key word is not mentioned until the appearance of Abraham in the vision, whereupon Michael states that "in his Seed / All Nations shall be blest" (12. 125–26). Shortly after that, the word is repeated—with a significant addition:

> all Nations of the Earth
> Shall in his Seed be blessed; by that Seed
> Is meant thy great deliverer, who shall bruise
> The Serpents head; whereof to thee anon
> Plainlier shall be revealed.
>
> (12. 147–51)

Michael's failure to be precise is calculated: being an excellent storyteller, he increases the suspense by withholding the information Adam is seeking until the appropriate moment. So the gradual identification of the seed continues. The intricate doctrine of typology* is next resorted to, so that Adam is informed

> by types
> And shadowes, of that destind Seed to bruise
> The Serpent, by what meanes he shall achieve
> Mankinds deliverance.
>
> (12. 232–35)

At the mention of David, Michael pauses to look both before and after:

> of the Royal Stock
> Of *David* (so I name this King) shall rise
> A Son, the Womans Seed to thee foretold,
> Foretold to *Abraham,* as in whom shall trust
> All Nations, and to Kings foretold, of Kings
> The last, for of his Reign shall be no end.
> (12. 325–30)

Then, at long last, the Nativity:

> His place of birth a solemn Angel tells
> To simple Shepherds, keeping watch by night;
> They gladly thither haste, and by a Quire
> Of squadrond Angels hear his Carol sung.
> A Virgin is his Mother, but his Sire
> The Power of the most High; he shall ascend
> The Throne hereditarie, and bound his Reign
> With Earths wide bound, his glory with the
> Heav'ns.
> (12. 364–71)

As Michael falls silent, Adam joyously exclaims:

> O Prophet of glad tidings, finisher
> Of utmost hope! now clear I understand
> What oft my steddiest thoughts have searcht
> in vain,
> Why our great expectation should be calld
> The seed of Woman. . . .
> (12. 375–79)

But Adam has not in fact "understood" as yet. Patiently, therefore, Michael explains what is meant by the stroke that is to "bruise the Victors heel." This leads to an account of the redemption, to Adam's acknowledgment of that wondrous mystery, and to Michael's final statement explicitly linking his narrative with the mysterious terms of the *protevangelium*:

> The Womans Seed, obscurely then foretold,
> Now amplier known thy Saviour and thy Lord.
> (12. 543–44)

In the moving confession of faith that follows, Adam acknowledges the seed to be his "Redeemer ever blest" (12. 573). He has finally "understood." At last he has become a Christian.

Milton's interpretation is securely grounded upon the peculiarly Protestant doctrine of justification *sola fide.* Adam, it was repeatedly maintained, was not merely aware of the future advent of the Messiah, but apprehended its precise nature "by faith alone" and was saved. As the popular Swiss theologian Rudolph Gwalter observed, there was "no doubte" that Adam believed in the revealed Christ; indeed, "it is evident that he dyd put his whole hope and trust in Jesus Chryst alone, which was that promised seede of the woman. Therefore *Adam* was a christian man, and beleeved that he and his posteritie should be delivered and saved from the tyrannie of the Divell, through the merite of Chryst onely" (*Homelyes . . . upon the Actes,* trans. J. Bridges [1572], pp. 852–53). Inevitably, of course, every patriarch since Adam was also saved by a similar acceptance of the redeemer "by faith only." For Protestants, in other words, the history of salvation began with Adam and thereafter proceeded in terms of the faithful individuals, who in *PL* include Abel, Enoch, Noah, Abraham, Isaac, Moses, Joshua, and David (11. 436ff. to 12. 321ff.).

As already noted, in *PL* the prophecy of the "first gospel" is reinforced by the "types and shadowes" alluded to by Michael (12. 239–40). Milton's advance from a consideration of the *protevangelium* to an affirmation of typology in general is not without numerous precedents among the theologians of his age. Benjamin Whichcote, the Cambridge Platonist*, typically observed that the promise of the "seed" made to Adam was "often repeated to the Patriarchs successively one after another; to *Abraham,* to *Isaac,* to *Jacob*: As also in the Types and Shadows that were under the Mosaicall Dispensation" (*Select Sermons* [1698], p. 331). The orthodox thinkers of the Renaissance maintained the validity of these "types and shadows" with a unanimity impressive in its contrast to our own skepticism. Typology, present in Christian theology ever since the time of the early apologists, was now extended significantly to include any number of persons and incidents in the Old Testament. Bishop Griffith Williams in *Seven*

Goulden Candlestickes (1624) adequately summarized the conventional attitude :

> [The Christ] is the *First*, hee is the *Last* . . . , The beginning of the *Law*, and the end of the *Gospell*; *Velatus in Veteri, revelatus in Novo Testamento*: Veyled and shadowed in the Old, reveiled and exhibited in the New Testament; *promised* in that, *preached* in this; there *shewed* unto the Fathers in *Types*, here *manifested* unto us in *Truths*: for the *Tree of Life*, the *Arke* of *Noah*, the *Ladder* of *Jacob*, the *Mercy Seat*, the *Brazen Serpent*, and all such mysticall *Types*, and typicall *Figures* that we read of in the Old *Testament;* what were they else but *Christ;* obscurely *shadowed* before he was fully *reveiled;* and so all the men of Note, *Noah, Isaac, Joseph, Moses, Aaron, Josua, Sampson, David, Salomon*, Kings, Priests, Prophets, Titles of Dignities, Names of Honour, or whatsoever else was ascribed to them to expresse their *Soveraignty;* they were onely used to expresse those *transcendent excellencies,* which these personall types did *adumbrate,* and shew most properly to belong unto this *King of Kings*. (p. 258)

Of the types mentioned here, two in particular are of interest to the student of Milton. First, Samson was said to have prefigured the Christ "both by his life and deedes." Second, Jacob's Ladder —which is introduced in *PL* 3. 501–15— was accepted as a prefiguration not only of the dual nature of the Christ but also of his reconciliation of heaven and earth.

The advent of the Christ within the historical process was interpreted by theologians in a variety of ways (*see* ATONEMENT). One consequence of that advent was noted by Richard Carpenter in *Experience, Historie and Divinitie* (1642), where it is reported that "God hath so play'd the good Alchymist, with the sinne of our first Parents, extracting many goods out of one evill, that some curiously question, whether wee may, or may not be sorry, that *Adam* sinn'd" (1 : 68). The reference here is to the well-attested paradox of the "fortunate" Fall, which in *PL* is reiterated by Adam immediately after the termination of Michael's prophecy of the Incarnation* :

O goodness infinite, goodness immense !
That all this good of evil shall produce,
And evil turn to good; more wonderful
Then that which by creation first brought forth
Light out of darkness! full of doubt I stand,
Whether I should repent me now of sin
By mee done and occasioned, or rejoyce
Much more, that much more good thereof
    shall spring,
To God more glory, more good will to Men
From God, and over wrauth Grace shall
    abound.

(12. 469–78)

Most commentators did not question the theory of Adam's "happy fall" because they wished to establish that the work of the Christ gained for us "a better estate then *Adam* was in before his fall" (R. Snawsnel, *A Looking Glasse* [1610], sig. F6). But Milton, aware of the theological traps inherent in the paradox, sagaciously allowed Adam to give tongue to it while remaining "full of doubt" about its validity. At the same time, he accepted an accompanying tradition that man's salvation is more wonderful than the act of creation.

The Christ's restoration of man led Milton to regard the God-man as a "Most perfet *Heroe*" (*Passion*, line 13), and his deeds as "Above Heroic" (*PR* 1. 15). Milton is by no means the innovator of this concept of the God-man's "heroism." It was adapted from the "Hero Christology" of the Bible, which in turn yielded the tradition of Jesus as "the hero of heroes." Milton, having accepted this sacrosanct interpretation, welcomed also the validity of the *imitatio Christi*. As Michael observes in *PL,* the disciples of Jesus were charged with the preparation of the faithful "in mind . . . , if so befall, / For death, like that which the redeemer dy'd" (12. 444ff.). But the Redeemer's life and death could also be imitated by the faithful few who lived before his advent, "types" such as Samson. Hence the appropriateness of Milton's ascription of a "Heroic magnitude of mind" to the protagonist of *SA,* for he, like the historic Christ, exemplified "the truest fortitude" that consists in the patient acceptance of afflictions even unto death (lines 654,

1279). Manoa's epitaph on his dead son applies to Samson as to the "Most perfet *Heroe*":

> *Samson* hath quit himself
> Like *Samson*, and heroicly hath finish'd
> A life Heroic.
>
> (1709–11)

The "truest fortitude" celebrated in *SA* is the ideal immemorially commended by the Christian faith: "an Heroicall fortitude of minde," as Hieronymus Zanchius* observed, "in bearing all grievous Crosses" (*The Whole Body of Christian Religion,* trans. R. Winterton [1659], p. 123). But the invitation is not to passive resignation but to action, the action specified by the Congregationalist minister Jeremiah Burroughs when he remarked in 1638 on the "true Heroicall spirit" of man sanctified by grace. As he put it, "none have such brave heroicall spirits as Gods servants have, it is not discouraged by difficulties, it will set upon things a sluggish spirit thinkes impossible, . . . it breakes through armies of difficulties, that it might goe on its way, and accomplish its worke" (*The Excellency of a Gracious Spirit* [1638], pp. 63–64).

Milton's thoughts on the essence of "heroism" are admirably summarized in the opening lines of the ninth book of *PL.* Just as Virgil* had criticized the heroic ideal he inherited, so Milton claimed that his own argument is "Not less but more Heroic" than Homer's* and Virgil's—more heroic indeed than the subject matter of Christian poets such as Tasso*, Ariosto*, and Boiardo*:

> hitherto the onely Argument
> Heroic deemd [was the] chief maistrie to
>   dissect
> With long and tedious havoc fabl'd Knights
> In Battels feign'd, . . . or to describe Races
>   and Games,
> Or tilting Furniture, emblazon'd Shields,
> Impreses quaint, Caparisons and Steeds;
> Bases and tinsel Trappings, gorgious Knights
> At Joust and Torneament; then marshal'd
>   Feast

> Serv'd up in Hall with Sewers, and Seneshals;
> The skill of Artifice or Office mean,
> Not that which justly gives Heroic name
> To Person or to Poem.
>
> (9. 28–41)

Milton's reproach to the Italian poets resembles that of the humanists' attack on "depraved" romances that set forth—as Roger Ascham compained of Malory— "open mans slaughter and bold bawdrye." The humanists would have commended Milton's attitude in Book 9 as they would have commended the subsequent commentary by Michael on the "slaughter and gigantic deeds" destined to sweep the earth:

> To overcome in Battle, and subdue
> Nations, and bring home spoils with infinite
> Man-slaughter, shall be held the highest pitch
> Of Human Glorie, and for Glorie done
> Of triumph, to be styl'd great Conquerours,
> Patrons of Mankind, Gods, and Sons of Gods,
> Destroyers rightlier call'd and Plagues of Men.
> Thus Fame shall be achiev'd, renown on
>   Earth,
> And what most merits fame in silence hid.
>
> (11. 691–99)

Michael's words are supplemented by Jesus in *PR*:

> if there be in glory aught of good,
> It may by means far different be attain'd,
> Without ambition, war, or violence;
> By deeds of peace, by wisdom eminent,
> By patience, temperance.
>
> (3. 88–92)

Echoes of *Lyc* in these passages heighten the significance of Milton's claim at the outset of Book 9 that his higher argument concerns "the better fortitude / Of Patience and Heroic Martyrdom" (31ff.). Within *PL* this ideal is celebrated in connection with the "true Heroicall spirit" that Adam and Eve manifest when they repent in "humiliation meek" and later abandon Eden to face the sufferings of an inhospitable world in "meek submission" before Divine Providence* (10. 1092, 1104; 12. 597). Yet such "heroic" conduct, Milton avers, would have been impossible had not the God-man volunteered his "unexampl'd love" (3. 410), which made it possible to send to man the speediest of the divine messengers, grace—the grace involved in the sacrifice of the Son of God for man, and the grace that anticipates man's inclination Godward (11. 3). [CAP]

FATE denotes a principle or force that predetermines all events. Early Christian thinkers, faced with the pervasiveness of this concept, recognized that it conflicted with such tenets as the omnipotence and providence* of God as well as free will* and moral responsibility in man. Yet, because of its etymology (*fatum,* "that which is spoken"), it was sometimes used in the sense of a decree expressing the will of God (St. Augustine*, *The City of God* 5. 1. 8). Ralph Cudworth recognized as "being really the same thing" the concept of "Fate, and the Laws or Commands of the Deity, concerning the Mundane Oeconomy" (*True Intellectual System of the Universe,* 1678). Milton rejects the pagan concept of fate but likewise states that the term can mean "a divine decree emanating from some almighty power" (14 : 27). It is in this sense that he speaks of Fate in *Nat:* "But wisest Fate says no, / This must not yet be so" (149–50).

The use of the term in *PL* is the subject of a study by Ben Gray Lumpkin (*Studies in Philology* 44 : 56–68). Aside from a few passages where "fate" appears as a synonym for death, misfortune, and the like, it is employed in one or the other of two opposed senses : fate as an active, blind force superior to God and controlling the affairs of the universe, and fate as a divine decree or the will of God. Satan uses the term in the former sense because he is unwilling to admit the omnipotence of God or is doubtful about it. God and those on His side, including Milton in his role as commentator, use it in the latter sense to assert God's omnipotence and to refute the words of Satan. When, early in the rebellion, Satan is challenged by Abdiel, he claims that "We know no time when we were not as now; / Know none before us, self-begot, self-rais'd / By our own quick'ning

power, when fatal course / Had circl'd his full Orb" (5. 859–62). Later, when beginning to recover after the defeat, he attempts to encourage Beelzebub by insisting that "since by Fate the strength of Gods / And this Empyreal substance cannot fail" (1. 116–17). But the Father* refutes such claims; He asserts that His actions are free from necessity or chance and that what He wills is "Fate" (7. 170–73). Hence the Father equates fate with predestination*. [RF]

FATHER, THE. "Omnipotent, / Immutable, Immortal, Infinite, / Eternal" is the description of God the Father sung by the angelic choir, and that description neatly poses Milton's problem of making the Father a character in *PL* (3. 372–73). "Omnipotent" is the only positive term employed, and it suggests a power entirely beyond human experience. The other four terms are all negatives, part of the *via negativa,* which approaches God by denying categories that make other beings intelligible to man. All other beings are traceable by their limits, both physically and psychologically, but God the Father is infinite and eternal, and so there are no boundaries to identify. Many characters are defined by the way they die, but this is of no help with an immortal being. And, perhaps most important of all, the Father is immutable, which rules out the changes of development or degeneration that make most characters interesting and intelligible. That the Father is also "invisible" and "inaccessible" further compounds the difficulties (3. 375, 377).

No wonder, then, that Milton's task was one "unattempted yet in Prose or Rhime" (*PL* 1. 16). Dante* had carefully avoided bringing God directly into the action of his *Divine Comedy,* presenting Him symbolically in the circling of lights of beatific vision upon which his epic ends. We know that Milton's earlier plan to write a drama on the Fall of Man had not involved bringing God on stage, but the shift to the epic form laid down the challenge of an active God, and Milton accepted the challenge.

God the Son* raises lesser problems, for though he shares in the divine substratum of the Father, he is visible and directly accessible, the operative agent of deity. Whenever something needs doing, the Son does it magnificently, which gives him a literary viability that Milton effectively exploits. The role of the Father in *PL,* on the other hand, is largely one of talking, of explaining. And as He is, by virtue of His deity, all-knowing, the Father does not need to seek knowledge. Nor does He need to seek solutions to problems—for all solutions are immediately self-evident to Him. He is, among other things, pure intellect, pure reason, unmixed with passion or uncertainty, so that He simply and instantaneously knows what is right, correct, or wise. As paternal deity, He does not seek truth—He establishes it.

Now this theological understanding will be familiar and relatively acceptable to theists in general and Christians in particular, whereas nontheists will disagree with and even disapprove of the conception. But all that is quite beside the point for a literary treatment. Milton, like any other poet, has the right to posit the internal conditions of his poetic universe, and he chose to posit the divine Father in these explicitly theistic terms. Critically, the key question concerns the poetic success of his treatment. Alexander Pope* said that Milton made his God the Father speak like a school divine, and Marjorie Nicolson described him as "a somewhat querulous schoolmaster at a glorified desk." As a literary creation, the Father has again and again been seen as the least successful feature of Milton's epic. It has been suggested in defense of Milton that many people who say they dislike Milton's God really dislike God himself, but this argument is scarcely satisfactory, for many readers who are willing to accept Milton's conception of the Father (either provisionally or ultimately) find themselves seriously dis-

satisfied with his literary characterization. The problem will be clarified if it is considered in two categories : first, Milton's overall conception of the Father's thoughts and actions, and second, the speeches and style in which he has developed the Father's expressions of these.

The Father's establishment of man's freedom is clear and unequivocal, and forms the basis for Milton's justification of God to man. The fact that God foresees man's fall is due to the divine omniscience, but in no sense implies predestination of the Fall : it is a matter of divine knowledge, not causation (3. 86–134). God's creatures were all formed free, both man and angels*, and remain free "Till they enthrall themselves" (3. 125). Man's fall comes by the temptation of Satan, so that man is defrauded, whereas Satan is fraud itself. Man can thus be forgiven, and even before his defection a plan is established that will redeem him, or rather those of his race who accept their redemption, for freedom is present from first to last.

Throughout, furthermore, the epic posits the Father's love for His creatures. In this regard, we should recognize that Milton's God is the only character in Western literature who is entirely responsible for his own environment, so that the environment He establishes is an important part of His characterization. That environment is a "communion sweet" of "immortalitie and joy" (5. 637), while on earth God "fram'd / All things to mans delightful use" (4. 691ff.). Men and angels alike live in perfect love, and God showers gifts upon them "With copious hands, rejoicing in thir joy" (5. 641). Both men and angels are endowed with reason, though in different degrees, and for both this is sufficient to guide their choices in accord with the values that their creator incorporated into creation. The environment is thus as close to perfection as the mind of man can conceive.

The fall from this state of perfection comes when man repudiates existence in the image of God and seeks to establish an independent identity "as Gods" (*see* ADAM). The result is a distortion and perversion of being, self-willed and self-achieved. God's response is at once a repudiation of the sin* and an appeal for reconciliation with the sinful creature —an appeal that reaches its ultimate expression in the sacrifice on the cross. Throughout, the actions on God's part are generous and loving in the extreme, for even the divine hatred of sin is inextricably bound up with the divine love for the sinful creature.

It is difficult to fault this overall conception of the Father's thoughts and actions, and although a few critics have objected strenuously at one or another point here, this aspect of the characterization does not appear to be the greatest source of difficulty for most readers. The greatest difficulty seems to lie in the manner and style with which the Father expresses Himself. Douglas Bush summarizes the problem: "God suffers, paradoxically, through being the mouthpiece for the very doctrines which clear him of arbitrary cruelty and justify the ways of God to men." The Father seems too defensive in stance and His speeches too often strike us as self-serving. Whether or not we accept what the Father says as true—and perhaps especially if we do— most of us are uncomfortable in the presence of a self-serving deity, God presented as a literary character on the defensive. In having the Father explain Himself, Milton too often suggests an attitude of smug self-satisfaction. Finally, in seeking to establish a simplicity of style appropriate to divinity, Milton perhaps moves too far from the rhetorical* and logical* tropes and schemes that enliven his other styles in the epic, so that by contrast the Father's speech appears flat, unvaried, even dreary and unimaginative.

This issue of the poetic effectiveness of God the Father is perhaps the most fundamental critical problem in the epic. Even if Milton's treatment to a certain extent fails, as has been suggested, that failure must be appraised in relation to the massiveness of the difficulties that Milton faced. In this way the failure (which at worst is only partial) will be seen to be more impressive than many earlier successes in literature. Within the total achievement of the epic, furthermore, such flaws as may exist here are placed in perspective by the great achievement of the whole. And it can be argued that the speeches of the Father can be entirely justified as simple, modest, and impressive statements on the part of one who is absolutely sovereign in power, knowledge, justice, and love.

And it is surely true that Milton's epic employment of the Trinity* contributes greatly to dramatize the deity, making it literarily effective. At every crucial point in the epic story, there is a colloquy between Father and Son, in which each exhibits "a conscious mutual deference; the pattern of their speeches is like that of a dance, a dance expressing perfect love," as H. V. S. Ogden put it. By these conferences, Milton interjects into his narrative something very like a process of thought, almost even of debate, so as to dramatize the self-evident conclusions of deity. The heavenly councils are a brilliant device for obviating many of the problems inherent in a literary treatment of deity. [RMF]

FEATLEY, DANIEL: *see* ANTAGONISTS.

FELICITY. *Felicity* is what I. A. Richards calls a "key word" in theology, philosophy*, politics*, poetry, and rhetoric*. It is usually regarded as the enjoyment of the highest good; its most common synonyms are "happiness" and "beatitude."

In ethics*, this chief meaning of *felicity* is the most frequently cited sense. The signification of "highest good" varies, however, according to the scope and ends of each philosophical viewpoint. Milton delineates some of the variant viewpoints and schools in Christ's speech (*PR* 4. 285–321). Some philosophers thought themselves wise by claiming to know nothing or by doubting all things; some by expressing truth in myths or fables;

"Others in vertue plac'd felicity, / But vertue joyn'd with riches and long life" (4. 297–98); and still others (the Stoics) boast of their virtue, a virtue that was but "Philosophic pride." Christ's judgment on these schools of thought was forcefully simple: "Alas what can they teach, and not mislead . . . ?" (4. 309). Instead, "he who receives / Light from above, from the fountain of light, / no other doctrine needs, though granted true. . . ." (4. 288–90). *Felicity* for Milton in religion* can be attained only through the exercise of right reason* combined with grace*, not through knowledge, money, and power. Adam and Eve and Samson are the chief characters who learn through disobedience* and obedience* about the means of achieving felicity. Raphael instructed Adam and Eve about the power and properties of God, the reasons for creation*, the fall of Satan and his followers, their own special creation, and what they must do to maintain their place within creation and to achieve eternal life. Choosing to disobey, they fell, but later, through experience and through Michael's instruction, relearned the proper conduct of life. As Adam tells Michael:

Henceforth I learne, that to obey is best,
And love with fear the onely God, to walk
As in his presence, ever to observe
His providence, and on him sole depend.
(*PL* 12. 561–64)

Michael's response to Adam's comment sums up Milton's view of felicity. Felicity is not to be gained through knowledge of natural principles, through wealth, or through political power, but only through right moral action coupled with faith*, virtue*, moderation, and charity*.

This having learnt, thou hast attaind the summe
Of wisdome; hope no higher, though all the Starrs
Thou knewst by name, and all th' ethereal Powers,
All secrets of the deep, all Natures works,
Or works of God in Heavn, Aire, Earth, or Sea,

And all the riches of this World enjoydst,
And all the rule, one Empire; onely add
Deeds to thy knowledge answerable, add Faith,
Add Vertue, Patience, Temperance, add Love
By name to come call'd Charitie, the soul
Of all the rest: then wilt thou not be loath
To leave this Paradise, but shalt possess
A paradise within thee, happier farr.
(12. 575–87)

Felicity, according to Michael, not only means the *visio dei* in heaven, but it is also a condition known to men on earth as a psychological state and is a foretaste of heavenly existence. Milton believed that since the Fall*, felicity is possible on earth only within the souls of individual believers and only in an enduring state in heaven.

Milton's conception of felicity is consonant with Christian tradition. All men, St. Augustine* argues, desire happiness, but few attain it: some fail because of lesser or evil choices. Felicity consists of possessing that which is highest and eternal; it means, finally, to St. Augustine, the possession of God by man (*De Moribus Ecclesiae* 1. 3, 4). In part 1 of the second part of the *Summa Theologica*, St. Thomas Aquinas* surveys the various opinions about the nature of felicity or happiness. He asks whether felicity consists of wealth, honor, fame or glory, power, any good of the body, pleasure, in any good of the soul, or in any created thing, and concludes that felicity is found in none of these because they do not offer lasting, but only contingent, happiness. In objection, St. Thomas concludes that happiness is uncreated, is the supreme good, and is the last end toward which man's will tends. His conclusion is that "final and perfect happiness can consist in nothing else than the vision of the Divine Essence" (2. 3. 8). More mystical and personal is St. Bonaventure's conception of beatitude. He makes a distinction between ecstacy and beatitude: ecstacy is the experimental knowledge of God here on earth, prepared for through prayer and discipline and completed by the infusion of grace by Christ the mediator; beatitude is the experience of eternal life in heaven ("The Tree of Life," §48, *Mystical Opuscula*).

Besides the reference to felicity in *PR* (4. 297), there are four other specific instances of the word's use in Milton's works: in *EpWin* 68 ("Through pangs fled to felicity"); in *RCG* (3:185–86), and twice in *Way* (6:122, 126). Three other senses of *felicity* also require mention. First, felicity, or the attainment of highest good, is the final cause of various arts and sciences. According to Plato*, Aristotle*, Minturno, Piccolomini, Melanchthon, Hall, Curcellaeus, Henry More, Bodin, and others (see John M. Steadman's *Milton's Epic Characters*, pp. 105–22), ethics, politics, poetics, rhetoric, and theology are all oriented toward felicity as their final cause. Milton, in *RCG*, held that the poet had power to "inbreed and cherish in a great people the seeds of vertue and public civility." Second, discussion of felicity in deliberative rhetoric was a *topos*, and found expression as the end of rhetorical exhortation or, if the end proposed would not lead to felicity, rhetorical dehortation. Important instances of this rhetorical exploitation of felicity occur in the Infernal Debate of *PL* 2, and the temptations and rejoinders between Christ and Satan in *PR*. Finally, felicity is an end or final cause in poetics. Benedetto Varchi, in his *Lezzioni*, held that the purpose of poetry was to remove "the vices of men and [to incite] them to virtue, in order that they may attain their true happiness or beatitude." In his famous letter to Can Grande, Dante* maintained that morals or ethics ruled the meaning of the *Divina Commedia* and that "the end of the whole and of the part is to remove those living in this life from the state of misery and lead them to the state of felicity." Similar views are maintained by Tasso* in his *Gerusalemme Liberata*, by Spenser* (see *The Faerie Queene*, 1.10), and by Gratiani in his *Il Conquisto di Granata* (see the "Allegoria del Poema"), and are implied in Milton's conception of literature as a divine calling. [WAG]

FELTON, NICHOLAS (1556–1626), a Cambridge scholar and former Master of Pembroke College. He was one of the translators of the Bible and a close friend of Lancelot Andrewes*, whom he succeeded as Bishop of Ely. Milton wrote a Latin elegy, *In Obitum Praesulis Eliensis*, in honor of Felton, who died October 5, 1626. Milton very likely heard Felton speak at Cambridge only a few months before his death, where the bishop supported Thomas Howard, Earl of Berkshire, over George Villiers, Duke of Buckingham*, for the chancellorship of the University in the upcoming election. [WM]

FENTON, ELIJAH (1683–1730), poet and editor. A friend of Alexander Pope*, Fenton reputedly produced books 1, 4, 19, and 20 of Pope's translations of the *Odyssey*. His own poetry had little success. His *Poems on Several Occasions* (1717) contains "The Eleventh Book of Homer's Odyssey. Translated from the Greek. In Milton's Style," pp. 84–127; it has a five-line epigraph from *PL*. There are also allusions to Milton in letters sent to William Broome, dated January 29 and September 7, 1726; see George Sherburn, ed., *The Correspondence of Alexander Pope* (Oxford, 1956), 2:365, 398. But of most importance is his life of Milton, which prefaced his edition of *PL* in 1725, "The Twelfth Edition." It was very frequently reprinted in the British Isles and the colonies during the eighteenth century. The life was often abbreviated in later editions, however. It is the basis for the biography in Paolo Rolli's translation* *Del Paradiso Perduto* (Londra, 1729), Books 1–6, and the French *Le Paradis perdu* (Paris, 1729) by Raymond de Saint-Maur, revised by C. J. Chéron de Boismorand, three volumes. Both translations, with these versions of the life, were reprinted in later years. The biography* is based on John Toland's*, although it does make some corrections. Using such an intermediate source, however, led Fenton to make such assertions as the following, which thereby became established. He called Katherine Woodcock the subject of Milton's last sonnet, though it was obviously only an inference drawn from Toland, and Toland's embellishment of Edward Phillips's comment about Milton's annoyance at adverse criticism of *PR* became a positive statement that Milton preferred *PR* over *PL*. The life includes Fenton's own appreciations and critical judgments of the poems, which are worthy of note. He also undertook to amend the punctuation of *PL*, and a postscript on textual changes in the second edition was added. The postscript often accompanies reprints of the life in later editions.

Fenton was the anonymous editor of *Oxford and Cambridge Miscellany Poems* [1709], which included printings of Thomas Yalden's "On the Reprinting Mr. Milton's Prose-Works, with His Poems Written in His *Paradise Lost,*" pp. 177–78, and the anonymous "An Extempore upon a Faggot, by Milton," pp. 286–87. In 1729 he edited the works of Edmund Waller with copious notes. It includes Francis Atterbury's "Preface" to *The Second Part of Mr. Waller's Poems* (1690) with its allusion to Milton, p. 445, and Fenton's "Observations on Some of Mr. Waller's Poems" (new pagination) with several references to Milton and quotations from *PL* as well as a reprint of *Sonn* 13 to Lawes, pp. lvi–lvii. The edition was frequently reprinted. [JTS]

FESTING, MICHAEL C.: *see* ADAPTATIONS.

FICINO, MARSILIO: *see* NEOPLATONISM.

FICTION, BIOGRAPHICAL. Not surprisingly, most fictional accounts of Milton concern the private, rather than public, man. To be sure, Milton's poetry and politics are not eschewed, but they are clearly subordinated to the mysteries of his life and character. Did this harsh schoolmaster beat his nephews? Why did Mary, his first wife, depart so soon after

their marriage? Was Milton thrashed by William Chappell* and subsequently rusticated from Cambridge? More important, what must this genius have been like in his less sublime moments, not atop that poetic (and perhaps moral) pinnacle where traditionally we place him, but trapped in the depths of common life? In one fashion or another these questions have tempted fictional biographers for better than a century.

In *The Maiden and Married Life of Mary Powell* (1849), Anne Manning restored the most intriguing hiatus in Milton's life, the marriage to Mary. Cast as a journal, the book is Mary's record of her change from scatterbrained coquette to endearing wife. In her own words, " 'I lost, or drove away a child, and have found a Woman' " (p. 257). With uneven characterization and occasional fancy, *Mary Powell* alternates between the seriocomic and sentimental. In time Mary matures sufficiently to deserve Milton, who takes her back without demur. *Deborah's Diary* (1859), the sequel to *Mary Powell,* is Manning's account of Milton's later years when, blind and dependent, he used his two younger daughters as amanuenses*. On cue, the book rings with tunes we have heard before. Mary comes to hate her father; Anne is thwarted in her marriage plans; John Phillips becomes a coarse hack writer; Christopher wars with his brother over politics*. And Elizabeth, Milton's third wife, is what rumored history would have her—a shrewish troublemaker. Deborah, however unappreciated, remains Milton's "best daughter," while the poet is himself cast as gentle, affable, and amusingly tolerant of life's inversions.

A very different portrait of Milton is offered in Robert Graves's *Wife to Mr. Milton* (1944), yet another version of that famous first marriage. Mary's tedious, though sometimes amusing, retrospection is salted with fierce idol-smashing. Milton is made a bizarre compound of hair fetishist and ideological turncoat, not to mention misogynist and domestic tyrant;

as a case study in arrested development, he displays acute sexual repression. Of particular interest for the Milton student is Graves's persistence in using apocryphal history, for scarcely a rumor or anecdote about Milton is left untouched. A similar recourse to hearsay provides the plot for *The Binding of the Strong* (1908), Caroline A. Mason's novel appropriately subtitled "A Love Story." The mysterious Miss Davies (or Davis)—here Delmé Delon, stepdaughter to Dr. Davies—is the major character in an old-fashioned triangle with Mary Powell at the other corner and Milton at the apex. As Milton's starry-eyed pupil, Delmé is overlooked by her master until it is too late; forced, then, to choose between his wife and the woman he loves, Milton behaves with predictable nobility.

This romanticizing of Milton is carried to excess by Max Ring in *John Milton and His Times* (1868), a rambling historical novel that betrays the confusion implicit in its title. Among these fictional biographies it is perhaps the most inventive. Certainly it is the most liberal in adapting history. The young Milton, irresistibly gallant, is courted by numerous belles, among them Alice Egerton* and Leonora Baroni*. (The latter turns out to be the anonymous Italian charmer of Milton's Cambridge days!) Overtly Protestant and republican in its bias, Ring's work is a curiosity piece for still other reasons. The idealized Milton is rather like a nineteenth-century romanticist, while the book as a whole reflects an aesthetic entirely at odds with the period it purports to survey.

Another type of fictional biography is represented by two modern works, Flora Strousse's *John Milton: Clarion Voice of Freedom* (1962) and Edmund Fuller's *John Milton* (1967), a revision of a 1944 endeavor. As "biographies" for the young reader these are not, properly speaking, novels; but Fuller remarks that his book "employs some of the techniques of the novel," and both works use fictional dialogue as fanciful as anything Landor wrote of Milton in *Imaginary Conversa-*tions. The result is a hodge-podge of truth and invention, fiction and biography, criticism and paraphrase. Milton's actions are recorded with passing accuracy (though Fuller is far more conjectural than his introductory note suggests), but the poet's character and personality reflect a Milton made palatable for teen-agers. Both Strousse and Fuller exaggerate Milton's adolescent self-consciousness as well as his poetic dedication. Their biographizing of his works is more disturbing, however, for it misrepresents him badly. The young Milton, especially, was no austere prophet, but in many ways a common youth not above posturing and occasional braggadoccio. Finally, mention must be made of Leonard Bacon's fine blank verse poem, "An Afternoon in Artillery Walk," a soliloquy spoken by Mary Milton, who unconsciously displays her complete inability to understand her husband.

It can well be asked what value these fictional biographies have for one's understanding of Milton. As literature they are generally unimpressive and dull. As biography they are often frustratingly inaccurate. Their choice of subject, too, is usually more sensational than helpful: Milton's amours (however many there were), his sexual problems his family relationships, his unspoken personal agonies. Some of these works particularly those for the young reader are even mildly pernicious in circulating hearsay as fact. In defense, of course, one can argue that these books are simply not subject to the constraints of scholarly biography, and, furthermore, that this license is beneficial. Aberrant speculations are forbidden the inductive biographer, whatever their truth and whatever he may think of them personally, yet precisely this kind of leap often sparks a real insight—not only into the life and personality of the poet but into his art as well. Only the superficial reader, probably, can finish Graves or Manning without some urge to glance again at Milton's texts; only the most remarkable finds his responses unaltered. At their best, then, fictional biographies contribute to our understanding of Milton's art. At their worst they conjure up wildly fanciful "explanations" for certain of the poems and pamphlets. In truth, the value of these fictional studies is likely more neutral than positive. They shock us, thereby restoring momentarily what we often set aside, namely, the sense of Milton's human fallibility. By oversimplifying his life and laying blame at will, they caution us away from similar pitfalls. They are admirable handbooks of stock-in-trade gossip about Milton, much of it suspect. Even more than authentic biography, they often re-create vividly the poet's milieu. But finally their value is largely an ironic one, for by explaining all, they emphasise how much of Milton's life is simply unknown. [DBC]

FILMER, SIR ROBERT: see ANTAGONISTS.

FIORETTI, BENEDETTO: see ASSOCIATES, PERSONAL.

FIRST DEFENSE: see PRO POPULO ANGLICANO DEFENSIO.

FISHER, ELIZABETH, a maidservant who apparently entered Milton's household thirteen months before his death, and who testified on December 15, 1674, concerning the poet's nuncupative will*. She said that she heard Milton express his intention of leaving all his possessions to his wife Elizabeth. She also testified that Milton told her that his daughter Mary had remarked to a previous maid, upon hearing that he was going to marry again, that that was no news, but if she could hear of his death that would be something. Further, Miss Fisher said Milton accused his daughters of stealing his books and cheating him when they could. She placed Milton's death on Sunday, November 15, though he was buried on November 12; her testimony, therefore, suggests Sunday, November 8, the now-accepted date. [WM]

FLEETWOOD, CHARLES, (ca. 1618–1692), lieutenant-general under Cromwell* and warmly praised by Milton in *2Def.* His father had been a baronet and a royal official and his eldest brother was a royalist, but Charles was a deep-dyed Puritan and fought for Parliament from the start. By 1644 he commanded his own cavalry regiment, which became known as much for its preaching officers and soldiers as for its fighting qualities. He entered Parliament in 1646, but although an Independent* in politics as in religion, he refused to take any part in the trial of Charles I*. He remained a member of the Rump, however, and after further distinguished military service in the Dunbar and Worcester campaigns he was elected to its Council of State* in 1651. This brought him into personal contact with Milton, who may (as some biographers have assumed) have known him earlier, though there is no real evidence. In 1652 he strengthened his already close ties with Cromwell by marrying the latter's daughter Bridget. Very soon after, he went to Ireland as commander-in-chief, and in 1654 he became Lord Deputy.

Milton acclaimed him in *2Def* for being fearless in battle, merciful in victory, and civil, gentle, and courteous at all times. All this was true; but Fleetwood was also weak and partial in political judgment, indecisive in a crisis, and malleable as putty under the emotive rhetoric of his fellow "saints." These shortcomings became so apparent in Ireland that in 1655 Cromwell as tactfully as possible recalled him. Yet he remained so high in the Protector's favor that he was tipped as a possible successor, though in the end Cromwell almost certainly nominated his own son Richard.

During Richard's brief Protectorate, Fleetwood was flattered by some agitation in the army to have him made commander-in-chief, and resentful of Richard's reliance on conservative civilian advisers. Aware too that very many of his officers were becoming wholly alienated from the Protectorate, he made fatal overtures to the republican politicians who were leading the attack on it in Parliament. In April 1659 he summoned a General Council of Officers and unleashed forces that he could not control —forces that led to the overthrow of the Protectorate and the recall of the Rump. He was duly made commander-in-chief, but he was totally out of his depth in the political turmoils that followed, especially after the army again turned the Rump out in October. On December 23 he resigned what was left of his authority to the Speaker, confessing that "the Lord had blasted them and spit in their faces."

At the Restoration he escaped any further penalty than permanent disqualification from public office, and he lived for another thirty-two years in quiet retirement. Milton's acquaintance with him may have become closer after 1660. Mrs. Anne Fleetwood, from whom Milton rented the cottage at Chalfont in 1665-1666, was a somewhat distant kinswoman, but Martha Fleetwood, whom Milton's nephew Thomas married in 1672, was Charles's niece. [AW]

FLESHER, MILES: *see* PRINTERS.

FLETCHER, ROBERT: *see* INFLUENCE ON THE LITERATURE OF NINETEENTH-CENTURY ENGLAND, MILTON'S.

FLETCHERS, THE, AND MILTON. The Fletchers hold a singular place in the history of English literature. In addition to influencing John Milton's work, Giles Fletcher, his sons Phineas and Giles, and their first cousin, John, the dramatist, comprise one of England's largest, most significant family of writers. Their works form part of the same great renascence in English literature as Milton's. Their lives span that most important hundred years in English cultural history, 1550-1650, which includes Renaissance, Reformation, and the revolutionary Civil Wars, and forms the essential background of John Milton's life, thought, and writings. Also, Phineas and Giles, Jr., form a major literary bridge between

Milton and the master of the sixteenth century, Edmund Spenser*.

Giles Fletcher (1549-1611) enjoyed a successful career in London and at Elizabeth's court as civil servant, foreign emissary, ambassador, and diplomat. His writings well reflect the literary fashions of the 1580s and 1590s, which centered in the court. *Licia* (1593) exemplifies the Elizabethan sonnet cycle as well as the courtly love tradition it embodied. His narrative poem, "Rising to the Crowne of Richard the Third" (1593), reflects the age's near passion for history and chronicle materials, just as his prose account "Of the Russe Common Wealth" (1591), which appeared also in Hakluyt's and Purchas's* *Voyages*, exemplifies the vogue of travel literature. Like most university-educated courtiers, he also wrote miscellaneous Latin poems. In both career and writings, he fits the pattern of the leading writers of the day, such as Sidney*, Spenser*, Ralegh*, Daniel, and Lodge. His work was known by Milton and there are interesting points of relation. Milton used Fletcher's account of Russia, probably the Hakluyt and Purchas versions, as one of the several "Eye Witnesses" from which he wrote his *Mosc.* He commended it particularly: "Dr. Giles Fletcher went Ambassadour from the Queen to Pheodor then Emperour; whose Relations being judicious and exact are best red entirely by themselves" (10:378). Fletcher's Latin poem *De Literis Antiquae Britanniae* (edited and published by Phineas in 1633) contains among other old legends and myths the story of Sabrina, which Milton used in *Mask* in 1634. In this poem, in the poem on Richard III, and in the plan he submitted to Queen Elizabeth to do an official history of her reign, Fletcher reveals the same devotion to national history as Milton in *Brit.*

The second generation of literary Fletchers—Giles's sons Phineas (1582-1650) and Giles, Jr. (1685[6]-1623), and his nephew John (1579-1625)—reflect a different age as well as very different career patterns. John Fletcher remained in London after his father, the Bishop of London, fell from Elizabeth's favor and died. He became a leading dramatist on the public stages, not only writing over fifteen plays by himself, but also collaborating with the other leading dramatists of the day, such as Shakespeare*, Jonson*, Massinger, and Tourneur. His collaboration with Francis Beaumont from 1608–1616 proved to be the most popular and successful of the period and it produced a new kind of theater. The full extent of the influence of his *Faithful Shepherdess* (1608) on Milton's *Mask* becomes obvious only upon reading both pieces. However, its pastoral* and masquelike elements and its emphasis on the theme of chastity and virginity are clearly leading factors in that influence. Effects of the play have been detected also in Milton's *Arc* and *EpDam*. The beginning of *IlP* sounds much like a song from *Nice Valour,* a play Fletcher wrote with Beaumont.

It is clear, from abundant allusions in Milton's early poetry, that he visited, knew, and enjoyed the London stage during the period when John Fletcher was probably its leading light. Still, of the four Fletchers, it is Phineas and Giles, Jr., who exerted the strongest influence upon Milton.

Phineas Fletcher followed his father's footsteps to Eton and Kings College, Cambridge. In 1600 he commenced an academic career at Cambridge that lasted fifteen years; it included scholarship, B.A. (1604), M.A. (1607), and, in 1611, ordination, B.D., and a college fellowship. In 1615, however, he lost the fellowship (perhaps for political-religious reasons or Calvinist leanings) and had to leave Cambridge. A whole career of youthful hopes and effort was shattered. He was rescued, literally, by Sir Henry Willoughbie, who made him his household chaplain at Risley Hall, Derbyshire. Later, Phineas was made Rector of Hilgay Church, Norfolk (1612), a post he held until his death (1650).

Phineas proved a prolific poet throughout his long career. In size, scope, and variety, the body of his poetry exceeds that of most of his now better-known contemporaries like Donne*, Herbert, Jonson*, Herrick, or any of the cavalier poets. He wrote epic, drama, and a variety of pastoral poems, epithalamia, elegies, long and short narratives (romantic, theological, nationalistic), a sizable and diverse body of occasional verse and devotional pieces, psalms, hymns, translations, and amorous and erotic songs. He also wrote three books of religious prose.

His best-known works are probably *Piscatorie Eclogues* (seven pastoral autobiographical poems), *Locustae* or *Apollyonists* (a narrative poem in both Latin and English versions on the Gunpowder Plot of 1605), *The Purple Island* (an allegorical epic that combines the pastoral mode, human anatomy, and a war of good and evil spirits), and *Poetical Miscellanies*. Most of his works were published at Cambridge between 1627–1633 while Milton was a student there.

Giles Fletcher's career is much like that of his older brother. He followed Phineas to Cambridge in 1602 (Trinity College), though by way of Westminster School, London. His academic career also lasted fifteen years and almost duplicates Phineas's : scholarship, B.A. (1606), minor fellow at Trinity, Lector in Greek (1615), B.D. (1618). He too had to leave Cambridge, perhaps also for political-religious reasons. In 1619, through the patronage of Sir Roger Townshend and Sir Francis Bacon*, he became Rector of the country church at Alderton, Suffolk. Unfortunately, he died within four years (1623). Thomas Fuller wrote that his "clownish" parishioners "valued not their pastor, according to his worth, which disposed him to melancholy and hastened his dissolution." His short life is matched by a slim volume of work.

Like Phineas, he first published in University anthologies. He wrote several English and Latin poems commemorating the death of Elizabeth (*Sorrowes Joy,* 1603) and Prince Henry (*Epicedium Cantabrigiense,* 1612), and a book of religious prose, *The Reward of the Faith-*

ful (1623). His major work is *Christ's Victorie and Triumph,* a sacred heroic poem or epyllion in four books, which was published by the university press in 1610; this work proved significant in the literary history of the century. Among other things, it clearly and heavily influenced Milton; it has proved also the basis of his reputation as a poet.

For over two hundred years now, editors, critics, scholars, and students of the literature of the period have been commenting upon Milton's literary debt to Giles and Phineas Fletcher. The kind of terms they have used is indicative: borrowings, source, debt, influence, model, precursor, and predecessor. Milton is silent on the subject; but discernible are very clear and specific debts of one work to another as well as the most suggestive kinds of similarities and affinities, large and small. To begin with, when Milton arrived at Cambridge, already an ardent young poet, awaiting him was what some critics call "the School of the Fletchers." As H. E. Cory writes, "they founded a distinct school of poetry. . . . In Milton's day, most of the Cantabrigians, Crashaw, Joseph Beaumont, Thomas Robinson, and others wrote more or less in their manner. In his boyhood, Milton was enlisted in the School of the Fletchers and their influence is traceable even in his mature poems." J. H. Hanford describes them as "Milton's principal masters at this time [ca. 1625–1634] in the art of poetry." M. W. Mahood notes, "At Cambridge in 1625 or 1626 this did not mean that Milton was returning to an outworn Elizabethan mode, but that he was feeling the influence of a group of Cambridge poets, with Giles and Phineas Fletcher as its nucleus. . . . Since mid-century poets so varied in temperament and allegiance as Joseph Beaumont, Crashaw, Milton, and More were among the poetic heirs of the Fletchers, these brothers deserve to be regarded as the disseminators of a new poetic manner. . . ."

Phineas had gathered a whole "pastoral" coterie around him at Cambridge.

Some of the writers known to have been involved initially were Giles, the two musician-poet brothers, John and Thomas Tomkins, and Samuel Woodford. Later, Francis Quarles, Edward Benlowes, Isaac Walton, and perhaps Abraham Cowley* associated themselves with Phineas. Still other contemporary writers who have been mentioned as reflecting his influence include Fuller, Herrick, Peacham, Habington, and Owen Feltham.

Direct influence of specific works by Phineas and Giles Fletcher has been noted in numerous works of John Milton. The list of "verbal echoes" and paraphrastic or parallel passages that scholars have detected scattered throughout Milton's poems is impressively long. The single most influential work appears to be Giles's *Christ's Victorie and Triumph* (1610). This English Christocentric epic focuses upon four events in Christ's life : nativity, temptation by Satan in the wilderness, crucifixion, and resurrection/ascension. During his Cambridge years, Milton began writing something of a *Christiad* himself with *Nat, Passion, Circum,* and later *PR* (the temptation). The influence of *CVT* on these works as well as on *PL* has been variously said to involve subject, episode, character (Satan especially), meter, style, and stanzaic pattern.

The impact of Phineas on Milton appears more scattered. His *Locustae* has been described as the model for *QNov,* and its Satan as the model for that of *PL* as well. The figures of Sin and Death in *PL* may be step-children of those in *The Purple Island.* The rather unusual stanza in Milton's *FInf* was one used often by Phineas. And the blend of pastoral, fraternal, and college spirit in *Lyc* echoes the tone, spirit, and setting of the *Piscatorie Eclogues.*

Besides direct influence, there are a number of other areas in both the lives and poetry of Phineas, Giles, and Milton that closely relate them. For example, they all came from middle-class, somewhat Calvinistic* backgrounds; were educated in the same type of schools in London and at Cambridge; received the same Christian-humanist education, and at about the same time. All three were deeply committed to poetry, to university, to intellectual and religious lives; and all three display these concerns with similar spirit and intensity. One result of this, in Hanford's words, is that "the Fletchers are Milton's immediate precedents in a kind of poetry that puts a religious subject matter in terms of sensuous beauty." Moreover, the concept of the *vates*, the poet of Sacred Song, is a notable and self-conscious aspect of the work of these three as well as something of an innovation in England at this time. In *CVT* Giles makes an impressive case for what Milton would later describe as "the inspired gift of God rarely bestowed" (*RCG*).

Not only are they fervid religious poets, but they reflect the same propensity to sing both "divine and heroical matters" (in Giles's words). They write heroic and religious narratives or epics*. Furthermore, these poems—*CVT, Apollyonists, The Purple Island, PL*, and *PR*—are essentially versions of Christian divine history and draw upon the same long tradition that produced masterworks by Prudentius*, Dante*, Andreini*, Grotius*, Vida*, Du Bartas*, and many more. In this capacity, they operate alike and quintessentially as Christian mythologists*.

Many of the poets who strongly influenced the Fletchers also influenced Milton. The impact of Spenser on both the Fletchers and Milton has been noted often; and not uncommonly, the Fletchers have been described as "Spenserians" as well as the literary "bridge" from Spenser to Milton. However, the influence of Virgil* appears equally significant. Phineas and Milton both began with distinct pastoral periods, moved to longer, mixed poems, and finally to epic, following the pattern of Virgil. (Spenser also followed the Virgilian pattern.) Less noted but equally significant and clearly credited is the influence of continental and baroque poets, especially Du Bartas, Sannazaro, and Marini*. From these must have come at least some of the baroque features of

style that first appear so notably in England in the Fletchers' verse : the highly rhetorical* language, constructions, and ornamentation—especially the elaborate conceit, the paradox, hyperbole, and excessive parallelism; the "wit," sensuous imagery, and the general grandiloquence of style.

Modern readers may learn with surprise that the reputation of Phineas and Giles Fletcher as poets appears to have exceeded considerably that of Milton in the seventeenth century. Their critical reception since, however, has varied far more. The eighteenth century ignored them; the nineteenth revived and progressively enlarged their audience; the twentieth century, since the 1920s, has allowed them to sink into virtual obscurity. Critical estimates of them over the centuries have varied widely, too. Most commentators, however, agree that "the family of Fletcher was rendered illustrious in the literary history of the 17th century by a constellation of poetic power" (Cattermole) and that John Milton was more than a little affected by them. [FSK]

FLORENCE OF WORCESTER (d. 1118), chronicler. Among other monkish sources that Milton read in preparing his *Brit* was the *Chronicon ex Chronicis* by Florence of Worcester. Florence based his work on the chronicle of Marianus, an eleventh-century Irish monk. Like Marianus, Florence conceived of his work as a universal history. Its value lies chiefly in its being based in part on a now lost version of the *Anglo-Saxon Chronicle*; for the most part the other sources are derived from Bede*, Asser's* life of Alfred* and the *Lives* of Dunstan, Oswald, and Aethelward*. Milton referred at least thirty times to this chronicle, using the edition that included Matthew of Westminster's* *Flores Historiarum* (Frankfurt, 1601). He incorporated some of the information not found in Wheloc's* edition of the *Chronicle* (e.g., the deeds of King Ida, the reference to the Danes' lack of fidelity to Edmund [*Brit* 10:

238]); occasionally he confused what came from which chronicle, stating that Florence called the Mercians South-umbrians, whereas that really was found in Henry of Huntingdon* (Fogle, in Yale *Prose* 5 : 225n). More often, Milton's confusion on a particular subject (e.g., whether William the Conqueror took or built a fortress after landing [*Brit* 10 : 312]) derives from his sources. Florence stated that he strengthened one; Huntingdon that he built one (Fogle in Yale *Prose* 5 : 398–99n). [RMa]

FLUDD, ROBERT (also spelled Flud, Latinized as de Fluctibus and in Fuller's *Worthies* spelled Floid), an Englishman of Welsh origin, born in 1574 in Bearsted, Kent, son of Sir Thomas, "sometime treasurer of war to Q. Elizabeth." He was educated at St. John's, Oxford, taking the B.A. in 1596, the M.A. in 1598. For nearly six years he lived on the Continent, supporting himself by tutoring in noble families while he pursued the study of medicine in France, Spain, Italy, and Germany. He returned to become a member of Christ Church, Oxford, and in 1605 was awarded the degrees of M.B. and M.D. He was licensed to practice by the College of Physicians in 1606 but, because apparently of disagreements on medical topics with members of that body, was not elected a Fellow until 1609; he served as Censor, 1618, 1627, 1633–34. His residence and practice rooms, where he retained his own apothecary, were in Fenchurch Street, later Coleman Street, London. He died, unmarried, in 1637 and was buried, as he had directed, in the parish church at Bearsted.

Fludd's most ambitious work, and the one that brings him within the purview of Milton scholarship, is *Utriusque Cosmi Maioris et Minoris Metaphysica, Physica atque Technica Historia, in duo Volumina . . . divisa,* the two tomes bound together in one folio volume, each with its own pagination and titlepage: Oppenheim, 1617 and 1619. "The History of the Greater Cosmos" undertakes the orderly presentation of the Mosaic account of creation in terms of Neo-platonic* theories of emanation, succeeding levels of emanation being adapted to the work of each of the six days of Genesis. Fludd's cosmos is Platonic*, not Copernican*. His assimilations of Neo-platonic doctrines to Genesis, frequently with the aid of the Cabala, are presented in a style that is, at the same time, reverent (even if not infrequently doctrinally heterodox) and blandly persuasive. And his argument is plentifully illustrated by engravings of strikingly pictorial effectiveness. The second tome "On the Supernatural, Natural, Preternatural and Contranatural History of the Microcosm" is an elaborate argument of correspondences, with sections on the divine numbers and on internal and external harmony. Bound also into this volume with new pagination and an undated title page as *Tomus Secundus, Sectio Secunda* under the title *De Technica Microcosmi historia* are seven sections relating various technical arts to the grand scheme. The legend *Tractatus I* occurs as a running title at the top of each leaf throughout the three paginations of this volume.

Another folio volume, one pagination of almost eight hundred pages, was issued in Oppenheim in 1618; this carries as title and running title *Tractatus Secundus*. The title page continues: *De Naturae Simia seu Technica macrocosmi* [for *microcosmi*?] *historia in partes undecim divisa.* It is clear that Fludd wished these eleven sections, each concerned with an art (techne) in which man the microcosm apes nature the macrocosm, to be read as addenda filling out the design of the other volume. This second volume, as well, is remarkable for the quality and the quantity of its illustrative plates. Especially striking are those illustrating types of military fortifications, siege guns and other engines of war*, and the movements of armies in the field and on parade.

The number that survive indicate that many copies of both of these volumes were printed and, presumably, widely distributed during the years of Milton's adolescence in the 1620s. It seems not unlikely that the young Milton had access to them, perhaps owned them, and that they had their part in feeding the intellectual and visual imagination of the future author of *PL*. (*See* MINERALOGY.) [EHD]

FOREKNOWLEDGE. The foreknowledge of God is a necessity of His omniscience. Although certain theologians, notably the Socinians*, have denied God's foreknowledge of the actions of free agents because they felt it to be inconsistent with human freedom, most have attempted to cope with the paradox as stated by Rabbi Akiba in the first century A.D. : "All is foreseen, and free will is given." The free will* of man is well documented in the Bible; but so is God's foreknowledge (Acts 2 : 23, 4 : 28, 15 : 18; Rom. 8 : 29–30, 11 : 2; 1 Peter 1 : 2). Milton makes use of these and many other passages in his discussion of foreknowledge, predestination*, and free will (14 : 55–57; 63–175).

St. Augustine* distinguished between foreknowledge and necessary decree. The Council of Trent* (1545–1563) adopted the Augustinian principles that God is absolute master by His grace* of all determinations of the will, that man remains free under the action of grace, and that the reconciliation of these two truths rests in the divine government.

The Reformers, however, eager to refute Roman ideas of authority, stressed personal election rather than the church's machinery of grace, with the result that predestination assumed a basic and controlling stance. Calvin's* *Institutes* (1564) went so far as to assert predestination to life and death, irrespective of merit*, by a decree* of God in which foreordination and foreknowledge are inseparable. But Arminius* (1560–1609) argued a predestination conditional on foreseen faith, and a grace that men could resist but that provided to all men the means sufficient for salvation.

Milton follows Augustine in distinguishing between foreknowledge and

necessary decree (14 : 75, 85–87); and unlike Calvin, he accepts only election, the positive aspect of predestination: "The principal special decree of God relating to man is termed Predestination, whereby God in pity to mankind, though foreseeing that they would fall of their own accord, predestinated to eternal salvation before the foundation of the world those who should believe and continue in the faith" (14 : 91; cf. 14 : 99). In other words, God predestined or elected all those who would believe of their own free will (14 : 123). The foreknowledge of God concerning particular individuals has no bearing on the essence of election, which applies generally to the whole body of those who would believe (14:125). Thus, individual merit is not the issue; belief is.

"So extensive is the prescience of God," Milton explains, "that he knows beforehand the thoughts and actions of free agents as yet unborn, and many ages before those thoughts or actions have their origin" (14 : 57; cf. *PL* 2. 188–90; 3. 78; 5. 647, 711ff.; 10. 5–7). Milton does not stress the theory that God lives in an Eternal Present, incapable of division into past, present, and future; rather, he sees past, present, and future as a panoramic sequence within the mind of God, who "perfectly foreknew in his own mind from the beginning what would be the nature and event of every future occurrence when its appointed season should arrive" (14 : 75). Foreknowledge is, in short, "that idea of everything which God had in his mind . . . before he decreed anything" (14 : 65; cf. *PL* 7. 551–57). And from this panorama God permitted Michael to show Adam certain selected scenes, and to describe others (*PL* 11 and 12).

Foreknowledge in no way forces upon man the necessity of acting in any certain way, for "the issue does not depend on God who foresees it, but on him alone who is the object of his foresight" (14. 83; cf. *PL* 3. 116–18). It is impossible to experience anything like the full dimension of *PL* without understanding Milton's resolution of the paradox of man's freedom and God's foreknowledge. [VRM]

FOREST HILL, OXFORDSHIRE. A town in Oxfordshire, Forest Hill was the home of Milton's in-laws, the Powells, his first wife, Mary, having been baptized there on January 24, 1625. His father's family came from Stanton St. John, less than a mile from Forest Hill, and this fact probably accounts for the relationship with the Powells. On June 11, 1627, Milton's father loaned Richard Powell £300, on which interest was to be paid, but financial difficulties beset Powell and apparently it was default in payment that caused Milton to travel to Forest Hill around June 1642. Here he met and married Mary, whom he brought home to London but who returned to her family soon after, around August.

The Powells owned the manor and rectory at Forest Hill, as well as land in nearby Wheatley and other places. In a suit in 1647 to recover the loan and back interest that was again accruing, Milton may have expected to obtain this or some other land, though it was the Wheatley property that was transferred to him on November 20. Sir Robert Pye had, by June 1646, acquired the Forest Hill property from Powell, through another debt, however. The Powell family received the land back after the Restoration. Milton's in-laws resided here through the rest of his life. [JTS]

FORM: *see* METAPHYSICS.

FORTITUDE, or courage, is the third of the four cardinal virtues*. In *CD* Milton couples fortitude with patience* as the two virtues "which are exercised in the resistance to, or the endurance of evil*." The former is defined as the virtue that is "chiefly conspicuous in repelling evil or regarding its approach with equanimity"; the latter, as consisting in the "endurance of misfortunes and injuries." The great pattern of fortitude is "our Saviour Jesus Christ, throughout the whole of his life, and in his death";

patience is exemplified by Job and other saints who suffer and lament but with endurance (17 : 247–53). Here Milton treats the two virtues as related but distinct, in contrast to the traditional view, which considers patience to be a species of fortitude. Cicero* in his *De Inventione* (2. 163) taught that fortitude consists in both active strength (highmindedness, confidence) and passive endurance (patience, perseverance). St. Ambrose* and subsequent Christian moralists tended to place greater emphasis on the latter quality; patience in adversity was regarded as an indispensable virtue for every Christian, with the martyr rather than the soldier its highest exemplar.

In *SA* Milton followed the traditional view in depicting patience as a part of fortitude, in fact, its noblest manifestation. This aspect is the subject of a study by William O. Harris, *ELH: A Journal of English Literary History* 30:107–20. Early in the poem the Chorus refers to the wisdom of those ancients and moderns who have extolled "Patience as the truest fortitude" (654). Later the Chorus states that "patience is more oft the exercise / Of Saints, the trial of thir fortitude," adding that Samson may become numbered among those "whom Patience finally must crown" (1287–96). Another aspect of traditional teachings is that rational direction and control are necessary elements in true fortitude; without wisdom or prudence, courage is nothing more than physical prowess and degenerates into rash and reckless behavior. Samson as an embodiment of the *sapientia et fortitudo* formula is discussed by A. B. Chambers (*Publications of the Modern Language Association* 78 : 315–20). Samson confesses that as a young warrior he took pride in his physical strength and walked about "like a petty God"; then, "swoll'n with pride," he fell into the snares of sensuality (521–39). Through suffering he has learned wisdom, and now he is ready to use his physical strength in a just cause prompted by the divine will. Guided by the concept of fortitude, Milton has, in the words of

Chambers, transformed "the muscle-bound Samson in the Book of Judges to the tragic figure of Samson Agonistes."

In *CD* Milton follows the Aristotelian* teaching of virtue as a mean between the extremes of excess and defect. Fortitude is opposed on the one hand by rashness, "which consists in exposing ourselves to danger unnecessarily," and on the other hand by timidity. The epic council of *PL* contains an embodiment of these extremes in the respective figures of Moloch and Belial. The rash and impetuous Moloch pleads for an immediate renewal of the war against heaven, while Belial, "timorous and slothful," counsels "ignoble ease, and peaceful sloath." The golden mean of true fortitude is absent in hell. [RF]

FOSTER, ELIZABETH (1688–1754), Milton's granddaughter. The daughter of Deborah and Abraham Clarke and the wife of Thomas Foster, a journeyman weaver, Elizabeth Foster is particularly important to Milton's biography because of the information that she supplied to Thomas Birch* and John Ward* about her grandfather. Her reports concerning him or his family directly were, of course, stories that her mother had told her, and thus they are once in a while uncertain or inaccurate. She was born in Ireland in November 1688 and came to England about 1703; however, her mother had returned to England earlier "during the troubles in Ireland under King James II" and was certainly established in London in 1698. Her father died after 1687, possibly in 1688, and probably about 1702. The discrepancies in dates concerning the family movements are unexplained, if accurate. Her husband is referred to between 1719 and 1750, but their marriage date is unknown and he probably survived her. By 1738 they had had seven children, all of whom had died in infancy or at birth. Deborah lived with her daughter from sometime before her death in 1727 at the Fosters' home in Pelham Street, Spitalfields, Middlesex. A public appeal was made to aid Deborah

on April 29, 1727. Elizabeth's brother Urban Clarke, a weaver, came to live with her also and may have remained with the Fosters in their successive changes of residence. Elizabeth kept a chandler's (grocer's?) shop here to supplement her husband's meager income. They moved to Lower Holloway, Middlesex, around 1742 and here her cousin Catherine, daughter of Christopher Milton, resided with her. In 1749 the Fosters moved to Cock Lane, near Shoreditch Church, where Elizabeth also maintained a chandler's shop. In 1750 they changed residence to the Sign of the Sugar Loaf, opposite the Thatched House, in Islington. Elizabeth died on May 9, 1754, having been ill with asthma and dropsy. Her funeral, at which Birch officiated, occurred on May 14.

She was first visited by John Ward on February 10, 1738, and by Thomas Birch the next day. Birch was able to include some information in his biographical preface to his edition of the prose, which was then going through the press. Birch again visited her on January 6, 1750, and November 13, 1750. Information gathered then was used in the revision of his edition of the prose works (edited by Richard Baron) in 1753. Ward's notes are found in the British Museum, Additional MS 4320, f. 232, and Birch's in BM, Additional MS 4244, ff. 52–53; Additional MS 4472, f. 3; Additional MS 4478c, f. 248b (notice of burial); and Additional MS 35, 397, f. 321b (a letter to a Mr. Yorke, dated November 17, 1750). Bishop Thomas Newton's* life of Milton printed in *PL* (1749) also focused on Milton's descendants and particularly on the financial plight of the Fosters. Samuel Johnson* proposed to David Garrick and a Mr. Lacy, managers of the Drury Lane Theater, that a benefit performance be given of John Dalton's* *Comus*. For this performance Johnson contributed a prologue, published as *A New Prologue Spoken by Mr. Garrick, Thursday, April 5, 1750. At the Representation of Comus, for the Benefit of Mrs. Elizabeth Foster,*

Milton's Grand-Daughter, and Only Surviving Descendant (London, 1750). In this representation was added a dramatic satire called *Lethe*. After expenses, the proceeds amounted to £130/4/–, of which £100 was invested by the Fosters and the remainder used to move to Islington. According to Masson (6 : 760) the sum collected was £147/14/6, expenses were £80, but contributions brought it up to £130. Johnson, in his *Life of Milton*, says that Newton brought a large contribution and that Tonson* gave £20. A further subscription for Mrs. Foster's relief was asked in December 1750 (see *Gentleman's Magazine* 19 [December 1750] : 563). [JTS]

FOURDRINIER, P.: *see* ILLUSTRATIONS.

FOXE, JOHN (1516–1587), commonly called the martyrologist. Born at Boston, Lincolnshire, he was educated at Magdalen College, Oxford, where he proceeded A.B. in 1537, and A.M. in 1543. Two years later he resigned his fellowship at Magdalen because of the ecclesiastical obligations it entailed. Thus began an active career of dissent, which lasted throughout his life. Though he later accepted Holy Orders in the Anglican Church, he never was reconciled to the wearing of a surplice. The accession of Queen Mary in 1553 warned Foxe of impending danger, and, within a year, he escaped to the Continent, where he joined the Marian exiles, first at Strasbourg, subsequently at Frankfort, and finally at Basle. He was already the author of many tracts expounding Reform doctrine and defending dissenters. When he arrived at Strasbourg, he had with him the first part of a Latin treatise on the persecution of the Reformers. It dealt primarily with Wycliffe and Huss, and was the beginning of his monumental *Actes and Monuments,* popularly known as the "Book of Martyrs." The work was first published at Frankfort in 1554 as a Latin octavo of 212 pages. As Foxe added accounts of persecutions that took place after 1500, especially those of Mary's

reign, the book grew rapidly, and a second edition, still in Latin, was published in a folio of 750 pages in 1559. The first English issue was printed in 1563 at London. The effect of the book was greatly enhanced by the inclusion of a large number of wood blocks, vividly depicting scenes of torture and execution. Before Foxe's death, enlarged editions appeared in 1570, 1576, and 1583; and in the century after he died five new editions were published. Copies were placed in the cathedrals and the principal parish churches, where they were chained to the lecterns beside the Bible. Although on occasion, he accepted hearsay as fact, he normally admitted doing so. When he had personal animus, it was so transparent that his prejudice nullified itself. His use of letters and documents was accurate and honest, and his style gained strength from its directness and its homeliness. His writing was vivid because of its content, and he never sought effect through rhetorical elaboration.

Milton obviously had intimate acquaintance with *Actes and Monuments.* In his prose works he specifically cites or refers to the book more than forty times, a number of references that places the work high among his favorite writings. More important, however, is the fact that he accepted and embodied in his own historical comments and full-length accounts of British history a philosophy that is fundamental to Foxe and characteristic of many other commentators who were of Foxe's school of historical thought. In *The Elect Nation* (1963), William Haller gives a full account of Milton as historian and of his relationship to Foxe (see also Yale *Prose* 5. xix–xlix). Throughout *Brit,* and in *Areop, Ref, DDD,* and *Tetra,* Milton reasserts Foxe's belief that God spoke first of Reformation to His Englishmen and that Wycliffe was the morning star of the new dispensation. And Milton again follows Foxe in his expression of the idea that this British primacy in reform was aborted by priests and prelates for selfish motives. It may be said, therefore, that, though

Milton never doubted the superiority of the Roman historians over "monkish chroniclers," he accepted the authenticity of the point of view that pervaded *Actes and Monuments*. Like Foxe Milton failed to comprehend the reasonableness of the Elizabethan Settlement and persisted in public adherence to radical Puritanism. But Foxe remained within the orbit of the Church. Soon after his return to London from the Continent in 1559 he was ordained to the priesthood by his close friend Edmund Grindal, who had recently been consecrated Bishop of London. He became closely associated with the printer John Day, who published English editions of his great work, and he continued to bring out controversial tracts on doctrinal matters. In 1563 Bishop Jewell appointed him a prebendary of Salisbury Cathedral, and later he was preferred to the same office at Durham, but he continued to refuse conformity to Anglican usage. Despite his nonconformity he developed a wide correspondence concerning Anglican practice, and he rose to a vehement attack on the papal bull that excommunicated Elizabeth. In later years he was in financial straits and his health failed. He died in 1587 after great suffering and was interred in St. Giles, Cripplegate, London, where he rests in death with Milton. A list of his writings, exclusive of the editions of *Actes and Monuments*, appears in J. F. Mozley, *John Foxe and His Book*, pp. 243–45. [DAR]

FRANCINI, ANTONIO, poet and member of the *Apatisti* (the "passionless") academy of Florence, who wrote an 84-line Italian ode to Milton, which included praise of Milton's mastery of six tongues (English, Latin, Greek, French, Spanish, and Tuscan). Milton included it in the 1645 *Poems*. He also mentions Francini in both *EpDam* and *2Def*. And in his letter to Dati* (*Epistol* 10; April 21, 1647), he sends greetings to Francini, which are returned (12 : 315; December 4, 1648). [WM]

FREE WILL. No doctrine is more vital to Milton than that of freedom of the will both in God and in His creatures. But immediately a troublesome problem arises : if an omnipotent, infinite God acts freely, in what sense can His finite creatures also act freely? Are they free to contradict and contravene His will?

Philosophers and theologians have, of course, answered these questions in a variety of ways. Determinists (Hindus, Moslems, Naturalists, and so forth) have made of freedom an empty term. Calvin* scandalized Roman Catholics by his concept of loss of free will through a predetermined fall, and Luther* envisioned man as a beast standing between God and Satan and alternately led about by each of them. François de Croi (trans. 1620) proclaimed that "the holy Scripture, and the Councels that are of sound judgement, have overthrowne the doctrine of free will." On the other hand, Pelagius* (fl. 400–A.D. 418) defended man's freedom to the detriment of God's sovereignty; and Arminius* (1560–1609) was maligned as a reincarnation of Pelagius when he modified Calvin's absolute predestination* into a predestination conditional upon the choice of man.

The wisest of philosophers, theologians, and artists (Homer*, Shakespeare*, and the like) have recognized a paradox and learned to live with it. Even those who emphasized one pole or the other often did so in reaction to an opposite extreme; as Bullinger warned in 1572, the outcries against free will should not be interpreted in isolation but only in relation to "that proud and arrogant doctrine concerning the merites of men." Similarly, extreme proponents of free will were reacting against the destruction of moral responsibility by deterministic theories. The fact is that freedom and necessity are the two alternating poles of human experience, and any attempt to harmonize them is bound to be a continually shifting and open-ended dialogue. Consequently, the Bible has it both ways (cf. Phil. 2 : 12–13).

As is his habit, Milton meets the paradox head on. God is "perfectly free," both in His decrees and His actions (14 : 73); He begat the Son* of His own free will, not of necessity as most orthodox Trinitarians would claim (14: 187); and the Holy Spirit* had likewise been produced "by the free will of the agent" (14 : 403). He freely decreed the reasonableness, and therefore the free will, of men and angels* (14 : 83; cf. *PL* 9. 351–52), and He would become mutable were He to obstruct that freedom by yet another decree. "It follows, therefore, that the liberty of man must be considered entirely free of necessity, nor can any admission be made in favor of that modification of the principle which is founded on the doctrine of God's immutability and prescience" (14 : 77; cf. *PL* 3. 120–28). Furthermore, "the will of God . . . is not less the universal first cause, because he has himself decreed that some things should be left to our own free will, than if each particular event had been decreed necessarily" (14 : 81). God decreed nothing absolutely which He Himself left in the power of free agents—"a doctrine which is shown by the whole canon of Scripture" (14 : 65). In other words, God's freedom is limited by His own consistent being, His own purpose, and His own works, but by no external force.

Although God foreknows what man will do, man's actions are nevertheless free. God's foreknowledge, like man's occasional foreknowledge, is intransitive and has no external influence; therefore, it cannot be "considered at all as the cause of free actions" (14 : 85; cf. *PL* 3. 111–23; 10. 43–47). Thus the angels, Adam, and Eve were created free agents who were sufficient to stand but free to fall (14 : 81–83; *PL* 3. 98–102; 5. 535–40). The only alternative to this "fall-able" perfection was, as Henry King put it in 1643, the condition of marionettes (cf. *PL* 8. 640–43). When Adam and Eve fell, their freedom was seriously impaired. Indeed, it could be regained only through regeneration or supernatural renovation, which "create[s] afresh . . . the inward man" (15 : 367; cf. 15 : 357). And man

becomes more and more free as he willingly cooperates with the divine will (14 : 135; 8 : 249–250). Conversely, he becomes more and more enslaved as he seeks to negate that will, as is symbolized by the gradual degrading of Satan's form in *PL*.

The belief in man's freedom of choice, or reason*, is absolutely central to Milton's justification of God's ways to man. For if God "inclines the will of man to moral good or evil, according to his own pleasure, and then rewards the good, and punishes the wicked, the course of equity seems to be disturbed; and it is entirely on this supposition that the outcry against divine justice is founded. It would appear, therefore, that God's general government of the universe . . . should be understood as relating to natural and civil concerns, to things indifferent and fortuitous"; God could not properly enter into a covenant with mankind if man's personal religion were not in some degree dependent upon himself (14 : 213–215; cf. 14 : 139–41). And when God "hardens the heart" of a sinner, as in Exodus 7: 2–3, He does so not by infusing an evil disposition and thus thwarting freedom, but by employing the kind methods that ought to reclaim the sinful heart (15 : 81; cf. *PL* 6. 789–91). It is the refusal of the sinner to respond to this kindness that simultaneously hardens his heart and proves his freedom to resist God's gracious overtures.

Upon his belief in the free will of the regenerate man Milton based his doctrine of Christian liberty*, which in turn formed the basis for his attacks on tyrannical bishops, kings, and customs, on oppressive canon laws, on state-controlled religion, and on prepublication censorship. For whatever stifled religious, domestic, or political freedom prevented the Christian from the exercise of right reason and thus thwarted his proper humanity. [VRM]

FRENCH, J(OSEPH) MILTON (1895–1962), scholar, who earned all of his degrees from Harvard University. After a series of brief academic appointments he moved to Rutgers University, with which he was identified as professor and chairman of English for the remainder of his career. Aside from a selection of Charles Lamb's *Essays and Letters* (New York, 1937) and work on George Wither, his publications were devoted largely to biographical facts about Milton. His *Milton in Chancery* (New York, 1939) reports new material about Milton and his father's various legal suits, giving insights into a previously neglected area of his life. This book led to the *Life Records* (1949–58). In a period noted for its cooperative editorial projects, these five volumes are the biggest undertaken by a single individual. They attempt to give a day-by-day account of the poet's life, reproducing every known document with interpretive commentary. The final volume also updates and corrects some of the entries of the preceding ones. [WBH]

FRENEAU, PHILIP: *see* INFLUENCE IN AMERICA, MILTON'S.

FRESCOBALDI, PIETRO: *see* ASSOCIATES, PERSONAL.

FRIENDS: *see* ASSOCIATES, PERSONAL; ASSOCIATES, POLITICAL.

FRIENDS, SOCIETY OF; *see* QUAKERS.

FRONTINUS, SEXTUS JULIUS, first-century Roman soldier and governor of Britain (as Milton mentions in *Brit*). Author of *Strategematicon*, Frontinus is cited only in *CB* on "Duels." [WBH]

FROST, GUALTER (WALTER): *see* ASSOCIATES, POLITICAL.

FULLER, THOMAS (1608–1661), canon of the Savoy and chaplain in extraordinary to Charles II* after the Restoration. A moderate Royalist and an Anglican, Fuller is remembered as the author of *The History of the Holy Warre* [the Crusades] in 1639, *The Holy State and the Profane State,* a collection of characters and essays, in 1642 (rptd. 1648,

1652, 1663), and *The Worthies of England,* a description of England county by county with anecdotes and brief biographies of people associated with each, in 1662. A reference to the anonymous author of *Ref* in *The Holy State* appears in the "Life of Bishop Ridley," Book 4, chapter 11, pp. 291–92 (1st, 2d. eds; pp. 279–80, 3d, 4th eds.). It is one of the earliest allusions* to Milton and includes quotations from the tract. Fuller criticizes Milton for his attitude toward Protestant martyrs and his abusive language. [JTS]

FUSELI, HENRY (1741–1825). "One of the greatest imaginations" of his age and one of the leading forces behind the romantic movement ("the first of the Romantics," according to Sidney Colvin), Fuseli, the son of a painter, began his professional life in Zurich as an ordained minister. With Lavater, he wrote a pamphlet called *The Unjust Magistrate,* which detailed the acts of oppression committed by a prominent government official. Though the charges made in the pamphlet were validated, the incident itself created so much discomfort for Fuseli that he left Zurich in 1763, went to London, and thereupon commenced a new life as critic and painter. By 1780, having received encouragement from Sir Joshua Reynolds, Fuseli was regularly exhibiting his paintings at the Royal Academy, to which he was elected an associate in 1788 and a member in 1790. In 1799 he became Professor of Painting and five years later was elected Keeper of the Royal Academy. Besides contributing numerous pieces to the *Critical Review* and *Universal Museum* between 1767 and 1768 and to the *Analytical Review* between 1788 and 1798, Fuseli translated Winckelmann's *Reflections on the Painting and Sculpture of the Greeks* (1765), Dragonetti's *Treatise on Virtues and Rewards* (1769), and Lavater's *Aphorisms on Man* (1788). The translation of Lavater's work led Fuseli to write a complementary volume, *Aphorisms on Art,* which he worked on from 1788–1818 but which was not published until six years after his death. By the time Fuseli began this project, he had already published his *Remarks on Rousseau* (1767), he had achieved his first great success as a painter with *The Nightmare* (1782), he had made substantial contributions to Boydell's Shakespeare Gallery, and he had established important professional connections with Cowper* and Blake*. He was about to begin work on the Milton Gallery, and he was yet to write a series of twelve lectures delivered before the Royal Academy between 1801 and 1825, as well as his *History of Art in Italy*. Though some of the lectures were published during Fuseli's lifetime, they were not collected together until the appearance of John Knowles's *The Life and Writings of Henry Fuseli* (1831). Fuseli's *Aphorisms* and his *History* were published in the same volume, and these works, together with the *Lectures*, constitute a significant body of neglected criticism on Milton.

An illustrator of many poets, including Homer*, Dante*, Shakespeare*, and Spenser*, Fuseli put his full talents and his greatest efforts into a series of illustrations for Milton. The success of Boydell's Shakespeare Gallery inspired the Milton project. In 1790, J. Johnson, the publisher, engaged Fuseli to illustrate the edition, then underway by Cowper, with thirty designs to be engraved by Sharpe, Bartolozzi, and Blake. Cowper's subsequent illness and pressure from Boydell, who feared competition, caused Johnson to abandon the project. Nevertheless, Fuseli continued the work, devoting his time exclusively to it, despite financial difficulties, which were eased in 1797 when six friends—Coutts, Lock, Roscoe, G. Steevens, Seward, and Johnson—agreed to support Fuseli until the Milton Gallery was completed. Thomas Lawrence and John Opie offered another kind of assistance, each wishing to contribute paintings to the Gallery. Fuseli declined their offers, preferring to complete the project himself in order to avoid discontinuity of style and purpose.

Even before the exhibit of forty paintings opened on May 20, 1799, the newspapers began to attack Fuseli's work both for its execution and subject matter. The paintings in the exhibit were of enormous size (*Satan calling up his legions*, 13′ x 12′; *Satan, Sin and Death*, 13′ x 10′; *The Lazar House*, 11′ x 10′; *Christ on the pinnacle*, 10′ x 7′); and of the forty paintings *The Lazar House* was judged to be the best. Judgments on the complete exhibit, however, were so harsh that it closed, only to be reopened on March 21, 1800, under the patronage of the Royal Academy, which hoped, through Fuseli's work, to restore historical painting to favor. Seven new pictures were added to the exhibit; but reception was once again hostile, and thus the second exhibit closed four months after it was opened. Despite the general dissatisfaction with Fuseli's work, a few associates praised it : Benjamin Haydon thought the Milton Gallery "showed a range of imagination equal to the poet's"; Southey proclaimed that Fuseli "doubled the pleasure I derived from Milton"; and Roscoe saw in Fuseli's designs the "glowing outline" of Milton's thought. Though Blake lamented that his country "must advance two centuries in civilisation before it can appreciate [Fuseli]," there were at least these few men of his time who could share in his sympathy for Fuseli.

Next to Blake, Fuseli, who came to know Milton through Bodmer's translation of the poet, is Milton's best illustrator*-critic. Before the Milton Gallery ever opened, Fuseli was being celebrated in the *European Magazine* as the "Blest commentator of our Nation's Bard." In contrast to the ordinary critic who speaks to the common understanding, Fuseli is praised for presenting flashes of revelation that cause Milton's vision—in all of its complexity and in all of its grandeur—to unfold. Intent upon subverting the old orthodoxies and upon provoking "a total revolution" in the arts, Fuseli points to Milton as a model for much of the transforming work that needs to be done. Milton's poetry embodies those "genuine principles of Art" that during the eighteenth century had disappeared from the national character; like a Michelangelo painting, it reveals "the indestructibility of forms and thoughts" and, through its exquisite employment of the epic mode, demonstrates that "sooner or later . . . every work propped by baser materials and factitious refinements" must be swept into oblivion (see Eudo Mason, *The Mind of Henry Fuseli* [1951], p. 218). Moreover, Milton demonstrates that the "puny laws of local decorum and fluctuating fashions" that may bind the "meaner race of writers" are to be spurned by the epic poets who, writing "for all times and all races," may claim "the lasting empire of the human heart" (see *Analytical Review* 15 [1793] : 1–2). Milton, himself a revolutionary artist, was from Fuseli's point of view, then, an appropriate model for the artistic revolution he sought to precipitate at the end of the eighteenth century.

Acutely aware of the uniqueness of Milton's achievement in *PL,* Fuseli was also profoundly sensitive to those dislocations in the poem that detract from it. Genius, says Fuseli, is sometimes surprised by "lethargic moments," as when "Milton dropt the trumpet that astonished hell, left Paradise, and introduced a pedagogue to Heaven" (Mason, p. 318). Furthermore, Fuseli felt that *"Paradise Lost* would have acquired additional dignity" if Milton were to have remained outside the poem. It is not the "digressions" in the prologues to individual books that bother Fuseli; rather it is the allegations, the sternly obstrusive commentary, "the unbecoming epithets, the Christian's indignation descending to vulgar passion" (*Analytical Review* 13 [1792] : 126). Yet in his criticism, verbal and nonverbal, Fuseli chooses to emphasize those moments which are the true objective of religious art—those moments when "the veil of eternity is rent" and "time, space, and matter teem in the creation" (Knowles, 2 : 158). Believing that epic poetry belongs to "the loftiest species of human conception," Fuseli recognized

that the introduction of allegory* could destroy the poem's "credibility"; but he also defended Milton's use of allegory against the strictures of Addison* and Dr. Johnson*, by insisting that "the Sin and Death of Milton are real actors, and have nothing allegorical but their names" and by explaining that through the intermittent use of allegory in *PL* Milton "amalgamates the mythic or superhuman, and the human parts" of his story (see *Analytical Review* 13 [1792] : 123; 23 [1796] : 351; and Knowles, 2 : 196, 200). Fuseli is also reported to have regarded Book 2 of *PL,* along with the first three acts of *Hamlet,* as the highest flights of human imagination and to have said that "the speech of Adam to his Creator requesting a Mate was equal to anything" in English literature (see Mason, p. 345).

By refusing to observe the usual distinction between poetry whose medium is action and painting whose medium is form, Fuseli elicited the disapproving words of Goethe, who said he "has no business addressing himself to the imagination in the same way that the poet does"; and yet by blurring the usual distinction between the sister arts, Fuseli achieved the distinctive qualities of his Milton illustrations. The very qualities that Fuseli expected to find in a great work of art—"a monumental structural principle operating in it centripetally, a maximum density and firmness of substance, clearness and incisiveness of outline" (Mason, p. 61)—are qualities that Fuseli found in Milton's poems and ones that he translated into his illustrations for them. Fuseli's illustrations can scarcely be called representative of eighteenth-century Milton illustration; but that is because, as Allan Cunningham reminds us, "his main wish was to startle and astonish—it was his ambition to be called Fuseli the daring and the imaginative, the illustrator of Milton and Shakespeare, the rival of Michaelangelo." [JAW]

GABRIEL, an angel* who figures in *PL* chiefly in Book 4 as commander of the

Cherubim that guard Eden before man's Fall*. Two of his guard take Satan by surprise as he crouches at the ear of sleeping Eve to suggest sin to her (4.800) and conduct him to a rhetorical confrontation with Gabriel and his troop. A "celestial Sign" of the hopelessness of violent resistance causes Satan to flee. In Book 6 God names Gabriel as second to Michael in prowess and rank among the heavenly host, and during the battle Gabriel overthrows Moloch.

Luke 1 : 19 tells of Gabriel's appearance to Zechariah to prophesy the birth of John the Baptist, and Luke 1 : 26 of the annunciation to the Virgin, a role in which Satan mentions Gabriel to Christ in *PR* 4.504. The Hebrew of Gabriel means "Man of God" and is prominent in Judeo-Christian angelical tradition. Milton pays little overt attention to the tradition in *PL,* though probably he intended Gabriel to be thought one of the seven angels who, he says in *CD,* serve God "in particular." In *PL* he is explicit about only Uriel as such a servitor, but traditional listings of the seven before the Throne always included Gabriel, and in Luke, Gabriel mentions that his place is in the presence of God.

Many critics of *PL* have noted that Gabriel's services are inconclusive. He hurt Moloch but did not finally harm him, and he and his guard could not adequately protect Adam and Eve. To Peter, Gabriel is so "unimpressive" that Michael suffers in the reader's eyes because "Gabriel was placed next in the military prowess to him" (*A Critique of Paradise Lost* [1960], p. 29). As for the angelic guard, it seems so ineffective, Peter thinks, that we feel that God had to intervene to keep Satan from beating it (p. 25). William Empson, as scathing in a different direction, thinks that the guard might have been effective but proves at last to be "just for show; as soon as the guards look like succeeding [God] prevents them (*Milton's God* [1961], p. 112). Dennis H. Burden, however, points out that God's intervention is conditional in a way treated in *CD* : the guard would

have prevailed had Satan resisted it (*The Logical Epic* [1962], p. 28). Joseph H. Summers notices that the guard does drive Satan out, and holds that achievement to be one "evidence of God's continuing providence in giving 'only good' " (*The Muse's Method* [1968], p. 82). Still, J. B. Broadbent says with some cogency that "the need for sentries in Paradise, their failure to prevent Satan's approach to Eve, and God's release of Satan after his arrest are absurd" (*Some Graver Subject* [1960], p. 200). But, answers Stanley E. Fish, what is "absurd is what has been absurd before, the efforts of any agent to cause effects apart from the will of God. . . . Good intentions and a willingness to serve do not assure success, which comes only if God wills it. If the existence of Gabriel's patrol is to be justified only in terms of need and sufficiency, Empson is right; it is for show." Later, however, "when the battles and events of Book VI have unfolded, we shall realize that Gabriel is heroic here because he admits that, in the conventional sense, he cannot be" (*Surprised by Sin* [1967], pp. 175–76).

A telling criticism of Gabriel is that Milton simply does not give him action and speech that comports with the estimate Milton wants us to form of him. Gabriel, according to Peter, answers Satan "Disdainfully half smiling" in a way that suggests "supercilious vanity," and in speech his "egotism . . . seems very nearly as touchy as Satan's." These things appear "most unnatural in an angel as valiant and august as Gabriel". (p. 26.) In a similar vein Broadbent feels that the absurdities of Gabriel's confrontation with Satan probably are "relics of Milton's early plans" for a dramatic version of *PL.* Every time these relics enter the poem "they spoil it, not so much because they are ex-generic but because the genre they belong to is less serious than *Paradise Lost*" (p. 200). At any rate, Gabriel seems intended as a committed servant of God, impressive in his faithfulness and even in his prowess and dignity, compared with man, however insignificant compared with God. [RHW]

GADDI, JACOPO (d. 1668), Florentine poet and scholar, the intellectual and social arbiter of the city, second only to the Grand Duke. He founded the Svogliati Academy. At least one, and probably all, of the meetings were at Gaddi's magnificent house, and one tradition has it that Milton stayed here during his visit to Florence. Milton fondly remembers the "Gaddian" academy in his letter to Dati*, *Epistol* 10, and mentions Gaddi in *2Def* (8 : 122) as one of the numerous Italian friends he made. [WM]

GALILEO, MILTON AND. To illustrate the danger of a censured press, Milton cites the Catholic Church's suppression of Galileo in Italy :

> There it was that I found and visited the famous *Galileo* grown old, a prisoner to the Inquisition, for thinking in Astronomy otherwise than the Franciscan and Dominican licensers thought.

On the basis of this single but explicit piece of autobiography from *Areop* it is generally assumed that Milton met Galileo during his Italian journey, 1638–39. There is, however, considerable mystery surrounding the visit. Indeed, it cannot be proved from external evidence that Milton actually met and talked with the old astronomer. At the time of Milton's visits to Florence, Galileo was confined to his house when not in church, and the Inquisition discouraged visits by foreigners, especially Protestants. Milton was very outspoken on religious matters while in Italy, and rumors of Jesuit plots against him arose before he left for England. In addition to the ideological barrier, Galileo's failing health also restricted the reception of visitors. Galileo was blind by 1638 and died in 1642 at age 77.

If Milton did meet Galileo the meeting was likely arranged through the friends he made among the two academies he frequented while in Florence, the Svogliati* and the Apatisti. These private academies, among about twenty in Florence, concerned themselves with literary,

philosophical, and religious debates, including problems presented by their most renowned citizen, Galileo. Milton may have arranged to meet the "Tuscan artist" through one of these acquaintances who were close to the astronomer. Vincenzo Galilei, the scientist's natural son, and Carlo Dati*, a former pupil, were among this circle of friends who entertained Milton while he was in Florence.

Galileo's impact on Milton was typical of his impact on the seventeenth century in general. For Milton's immediate poetic predecessors, the moon was the dwelling place of mythological figures and the source of its own mysterious light. After Galileo's invention of the telescope and the subsequent publication of his *Sidereus Nuncius* (1610), there occurred a tremendous amount of scientific speculation among technical writers and frequent realistic treatment of the moon in poetry. Milton could write not only of the moon as myth, but of the moon as a possible world, the habitation of mortals, as well as the reflector of "borrow'd light."

As important as Galileo was to Milton's conjectures on extraterrestrial nature, it is not necessary to conclude that Milton formulated the many cosmological questions and conclusions that occur in *PL* solely from direct contact with Galileo or his writings. A number of semi-scientific arguments of great popularity, such as John Wilkins's *Discovery of a New World in the Moon* (1638) and even Robert Burton's* *Anatomy of Melancholy* (1621), theorized on all the possibilities Milton considers in *PL*.

Nevertheless, the younger Milton's cosmology* as it appears in those poems preceding the Italian journey is decidedly more medieval than the universe of *PL*. In fact, each of Galileo's most famous discoveries is reflected in one or more passages in the epic. Among them are the countless newly sighted stars (7. 382–84), the nature of the Milky Way (7. 577–81), the phases of the planet Venus (7. 366), the four newly discovered moons around Jupiter (8. 148–51), the new conception of the moon (7. 375–78), the nature of moon spots (1. 287–91; 5. 419–20; 8. 145–48), and the nature of sun spots (3. 588–90). In addition to these explicit references to Galilean astronomy, the vastness of Milton's cosmological canvas may be due, in part, to Galileo's expansion of man's notion of the universe and, perhaps, to Milton's own observation of the heavens through a telescope.

It is important to note that though Milton used the Church's suppression of Galileo as an example of injustice, he did not commit himself to Galilean anti-Ptolemaic conclusions. When in Book 8 Raphael considers the Copernican theory through a catalogue of Galilean particulars, it is only by way of negating the importance of such theorizing, advising rather to be "lowly wise." Though Milton shared Galileo's humanistic reverence for reason*, he did not trust that faculty with the devotion of science*. "Reason is but choosing," and the writer of *PL* did not trust man always to choose well.

But for Milton, Galileo was a supremely impressive man. In addition to the statement in *Areop*, Milton refers explicitly to Galileo three times in *PL*. In Book 1 Galileo appears in an epic simile likening Satan's shield to the moon (287–91). Here "the Tuscan Artist" views the topography of "new Lands" appearing as moon spots. The passage sets Galileo in Fiesole, an ancient Etruscan village high above Florence and the original seat of the Florentine people, or in Valdarno, probably a reference to the upper Arno valley generally or, perhaps, to Florence itself. He is an "Artist" not only because he fashioned the telescope, but also because of his sensitively written appreciations of the masterpieces of fine art. In Book 3 the reference is within a simile describing Satan's landing on a sun spot, "a spot like which perhaps / Astronomer in the Sun's lucent Orb / Through his glaz'd Optic Tube yet never saw" (588–90). The third reference occurs again within a simile. Describing the clarity of Raphael's view of earth from heaven (5. 261–63), Milton compares the sight, by inverting the viewpoint, to Galileo's telescopic examination of the moon's particulars. Above all, these passages bear witness to a high esteem for the great Florentine. These three references to Galileo are the only passages in *PL* honoring a contemporary. [FBY]

GALLIARD, JOHN ERNEST: *see* ADAPTATIONS.

GARRICK, DAVID: *see* ADAPTATIONS.

GAUDEN, JOHN (1605–1662). Chaplain to Charles II*, confessed author of *Eikon Basilike*, and later Bishop of Worcester, Gauden acknowledged his authorship to a few in high places after the Restoration, but as the Earl of Clarendon* said, the news was such as to "please none but Mr. Milton" (see French, *Life Records*, 4 : 369; 5 : 459). It is not certain whether Milton learned of Gauden's authorship. [WM]

GENESIS B: *see* ANGLO-SAXON.

GEOFFREY OF MONMOUTH (1100–1154), British historian. Milton referred many times to the *Historia Regum Britanniae* by Geoffrey of Monmouth in *Brit*, including a citation traceable to Geoffrey in *CB* (18 : 132) and two allusions in *Ref* (4 : 39). In *Mask*, Milton much elaborated the portrait of Sabrina, the water nymph, after Geoffrey, whom he knew through J. Commelin's edition in *Rerum Britannicarum . . . Scriptores* (Heidelburg, 1587). At one point, Milton thought Geoffrey important enough to warrant a separate treatise, inasmuch as he was the principal author of various tales about the origins of Britain. He referred to the fact that Geoffrey had gathered the basic materials for the Arthuriad* in which Milton was most interested.

Milton did not consider Geoffrey's work as serious history, adding fanciful details of his own (e.g., the story of Leir and his daughters) or moralizing from Geoffrey's evidence. He was openly critical, identifying Geoffrey as "The British

Author, whom I use only when others are all silent, hath many trivial discourses of Caesar being heer, which are best omitted" (*Brit*, 10 : 46). [RMa]

GEOGRAPHY AND MILTON. "In the poetry of Milton geography is rivaled in importance by none of the sciences* except astronomy." Thus wrote Allan H. Gilbert in *A Geographical Dictionary of Milton* (1919), p. vii. And Milton has himself declared his fascination for the subject. In the Preface to *Mosc* (10 : 327) he writes, "The study of Geography is both profitable and delightfull," and he goes on to say how he had eagerly followed the Russian travelers, "who yet with some delight drew me after them." It is clear that the subject takes an important place in his curriculum, for in *Educ* (4 : 283) he advises the pupil "to learn in any modern Author, the use of the Globes, and all the Maps; first with the old names, and then with the new." And even after he went blind we find him appealing to his friend Peter Heimbach (12 : 83–85) to learn for him what are the best atlases, "which of the two issues, that of Blaeu or that of Jansen, is the larger and more correct." All this reveals the attitude of a scholar deeply and naturally interested in geography.

As is well known, geography was in a transitional stage during Milton's lifetime. Authorities such as Mela* and Diodorus Siculus* and Marco Polo had been accepted for centuries. And it is not until we near Milton's own century that we find the old information and theories being discarded. It is significant that the most important of the "correctives," Richard Hakluyt's mammoth three-volume work, *The Principal Navigations Voyages Traffiques and Discoveries of the English Nation,* appeared in the years 1598–1600. Samuel Purchas's* even more voluminous *Pilgrimes* came twenty-five years later. Never again were Englishmen going to accept to the same extent the "absurd Superstitions, Ceremonies, quaint Habits, and other petty Circumstances" that Milton so deplored in *Mosc.*

In the course of Milton's long career there are three stages in his attitude toward geography. In the first he is, quite naturally, under the spell of the Bible* and the classics. Aware of the associational value to his poetry of the older terms and concepts, he does not hesitate to use them prodigally. Thus we find his lines liberally sprinkled with such allusions as Mount Niphates, Enna and Proserpina, Rhodope and Orpheus, the Hellespont and Xerxes, Pelorus, Libyan sands, Dodona, Atropatia, Ophiusa, and Arachosia. Needless to say, Milton was fully conscious of the poetic worth of these names. When we come to the second, we note a radical change. It is impossible to overestimate the influence on his geographic outlook of the researches he was doing to write *Mosc.* Here we find him in direct contact with the resources of those two great cosmographers, Hakluyt and Purchas. *Mosc* is little more than a brilliantly skillful digest of their pertinent materials. If he is himself to avoid the "absurd Superstitions," he must critically select what is authentic and up-to-date. We can call this what we will, but it amounts to a growth of the geographic conscience. Moreover, if the writing of *Mosc* is connected with his tutoring of the Phillips brothers, as seems quite likely, Milton would have been particularly careful to include only accurate information. The government posts that he later held would confirm this tendency and would have the further effect of extending his geographic knowledge. It is at this time that he insists on including only material that has been "observ'd at several times by Eye-witnesses." It is not, however, to be thought that there is anything definitive about these three periods. It is like the development of Chaucer*, whose so-called "French" period merged with his "Italian," and that in turn with the "English." So it was with Milton. At no time did he hesitate to use a biblical or classical reference, even after he was intellectually convinced of its wrongness, so long as it served his poetic purpose. It is simply a matter of emphasis.

The other factor to be kept in mind is that not infrequently the new travel books confirmed what the older ones had said and thus gave their material status. A typical example occurs in *PL* 2. 592–94 :

A gulf profound as that *Serbonian* Bog
Betwixt *Damiata* and mount *Casius* old,
Where Armies whole have sunk.

The ultimate source, as Verity says (*Paradise Lost*, p. 415), is probably Diodorus Siculus. But the passage is substantiated and elaborated on by George Sandys in his *Relation of a Journey* ([1621], p. 137), who adds that "whole armies have bene devoured."

The importance of *Mosc* in the whole development of Milton's geographic knowledge has clearly been underestimated. It was not merely that he saw the chance to present an accurate picture of one country about which comparatively little was known outside of Giles Fletcher's *Of the Russe Common Wealth* (1591); he wished also to make his little history a kind of "Pattern or Example." He chose Russia, partly at least, because it was opened up to English trade by the ill-fated Willoughby-Chancellor expedition, which went in search of the northeast route to Cathay. Milton leaves no doubt on that point when he speaks (10 : 327–28) of "the more northern Parts thereof, first discovered by *English* Voiages." There is ample evidence to prove that the northeast passage was thought of as a distinctively *English* project. In other words, it represents one side of his nationalism. Another way in which his nationalism is represented is in his patent condescension to northern peoples. He thought of the Russians as being ignorant and barbarous and as living in a country paralyzed by cold for more than half the year. In this respect Milton did not differ from most of his countrymen, who had some tendency to be condescending to all foreigners. Where he did differ was in conceding that the country had its redeeming qualities; the rulers sometimes refused to tolerate "new forcers of conscience," and in Russia a man was at perfect liberty to separate himself from a wife who had proved her unfitness. Nor is there any suggestion of giving the devil his due; perhaps there is rather something of Milton's objective to make the picture as complete as a digest would allow.

The northwest passage was also for many years an English concern, and it is therefore surprising that America plays so small a part in Milton's writings. His reference to the "savage deserts of America" may give the answer. For the rest we recall, in the famous passage where Michael reveals to Adam the future kingdoms of the world, the mention of,

Rich *Mexico* the seat of *Motezume*,
And *Cusco* in *Peru,* the richer seat
Of *Atabalipa,* and yet unspoil'd
Guiana, whose great Citie *Geryons* Sons
Call *El Dorado.*

(*PL* 11. 407–11)

With his anti-Spanish bias Milton may be glancing at the exploits of Cortés in Mexico and of Pizarro in Peru. The notorious case of the treacherous, barbarous mistreatment of the Inca ruler Atabalipa would make the reference especially telling to his English readers. At any rate Milton had concerned himself with that kind of mistreatment if the *Declaration Against Spain* (1655) is his. The "yet unspoil'd *Guiana*" and "*El Dorado*" were intimately associated in his readers' minds with their hero Ralegh*.

Europe also looms less large than one might expect. It is possible that, since the "grand tour" was already in operation especially with his "fit audience," Milton might have felt that there was something almost commonplace to allusions to familiar countries. In this light the passage in *PL* 1. 289–303 that includes references to Italian place names, "Fesole," "Valdarno," "Vallombrosa," must be regarded as something of an exception.

By the time he came to write *PL* Milton had read (or had had his amanuenses* read to him) the travel books deeply enough to know which one to go to for the particular knowledge he needed for the occasion. His favorite of all was clearly Peter Heylyn*, whose *Cosmographie* had been printed in 1652, 1657, and 1660. It was precisely the kind of digest that the poet would be apt to resort to in his blindness. It mainly lies behind the two long geographic passages in *PL* (11. 385–411) and *PR* (3. 269–321), in the first of which the angel Michael gives Adam a preview of the world's future kingdoms and in the second Satan does the same for Christ, though with a completely different purpose. In an age of loose orthography the very spellings of geographic entities are identical. It is well known that geographies of that period took a philosophic and historic outlook in their long introductions. There was much in Heylyn's attitude that would appeal to Milton, though the two differed widely in politics and religion.

Probably the geographer next in importance to Milton was Samuel Purchas. Milton makes it perfectly clear from marginal notes to what extent he was dependent on *Pilgrimes* in *Mosc*. But for the rest of his works he approached Purchas in a different mood. His huge volumes, which Milton was unlikely to read in their entirety, were rather a storehouse of information from which he might cull an incidental detail here and there. The alternate title was *Hakluytus Posthumus,* and Purchas fell heir to Hakluyt's reputation for authenticity. Here too the poet was appealed to by the quietly religious cast to the cosmographer's thought.

A third favorite was George Sandys's *Relation of a Journey begun An. Dom 1610* (1615, 1621). Verity goes so far as to say that the work was probably his "main authority for the topography of Palestine." It was a popular book, there being seven editions before 1660. Sandys, though unduly credulous, had a positive flair for what was notable and interesting. The other aspect that undoubtedly appealed to Milton was that he gave the impression of having viewed the sights with his own eyes, whether he had or not. Throughout his career Milton became increasingly skeptical about hearsay geography; perhaps this is one reason why Mandeville puts in no appearance. Sandys's pages are full of some countries in which Milton was deeply interested, Egypt and the Holy Land, Greece and Italy. And it can be justifiably said that Sandys served Milton as a modern geographer who retold stories from the Bible and the classics and succeeded in conveying the impression that such stories were contemporary.

Another geography that Milton had doubtless read and that influenced his outlook on the Holy Land was Thomas Fuller's* *Pisgah-Sight of Palestine* (1650). Some of Fuller's preoccupations and attitudes would have found a sympathetic audience in the poet, for instance his insisting that he chooses to follow "modern Travellers who have been eye-witnesses of the country." Milton would like also Fuller's art in giving a reader the impression of being taken on a personally conducted tour. It is not merely the text of *A Pisgah-Sight* that is important but the fairly numerous graphic maps and images that Fuller includes. Thus the never-to-be-forgotten picture of the devil-god Dagon (*PL* 1. 457–63) has its ancestor in *A Pisgah-Sight* where Fuller's image has every detail to be found in Milton. What present-day readers are inclined to forget is that seventeenth-century geographies are much more than geographies. The same holds true for the great atlases. Probably the one Milton used most was Ortelius's* *Theatrum Orbis Terrarum* (1570), which Charles Lamb* fondly called "old Ortelius." The fascination of these early maps lies in the elaborate decorations the artists indulged in, filling the spaces representing lands and seas that they did not know with detail out of their fertile imaginations. Any poet would have his own imagination stirred by these details. And Milton was no exception. There is evidence that he pored over Ortelius's pages with some care, and lifted from them some of his geographic names and terms for use in his poetry.

It is quite clear that throughout his career Milton was capable of using geographical references, however outmoded, so long as they contributed to the associational value of his poetry. But though his procedure must be termed eclectic, a pattern can be traced. In his earlier verses he was much more apt to use allusions of a general nature such as "the nice Morn on th' *Indian* steep" (*Mask* 139), whereas in *PL* (2. 638–39) he is more apt to localize, as when he describes Satan flying toward the gates of hell and compares him to a ship in the East Indian trade sailing past the tiny spice islands "Of *Ternate* and *Tidore*." Still later, in *PR* (4. 75), he creates the same effect with his mention of "utmost *Indian* Isle *Taprobane*."

Thus we find Milton using geography in a way that is typical of the rest of his work. His mind reaches back freely for allusions to classical and biblical material. But at the same time he will make full use of the new information presented by the men of his own great century. Passage after passage in *PL* reveals an interesting amalgam of the two. [RRC]

GIANTS. Giant lore distinguishes between biblical and classical giants. In biblical, or Hebrew, story, giants were humans of abnormal strength and size, averaging about twelve feet tall, while those in classical myth were superhuman, reaching to the skies, standing in relation to the gods. Milton used both kinds of giants. Harapha is obviously in the biblical tradition, "of stock renowned / As Og or Anak and the Emims old" (*SA* 1079–80) —alluding to Og, king of one giant race called Raphaim, and to two other races called Anakim and Emim. Harapha himself was famed to be the father of the more notorious Goliath (*SA* 1248) and indeed of the whole Raphaim race. The King James Bible and Edward Phillips's *New World of Words* (1671) identified him with "the Rapha" of 2 Samuel 21. Besides the Raphaim, Anakim, and Emim, Milton also alludes to still a fourth race of giants, the antediluvian Nephilim of

Genesis 6 : 4—"giants in the earth . . . men of renown." Commentators like Calvin* associated them with force, tyranny, and violence through reading the name as denoting both "fallen men" and "violent men," thus making a connection with Satan and his angels*. Milton makes the same connection with respect to Satan and his fallen angels, ascribing to them violent nature in their fallen condition. They, like the Nephilim, are as great in sin as in size, models of a vicious, spurious heroism* that contrasts with the true pattern of a Christian hero.

Milton sometimes blended biblical and classical characteristics. *SA* 1120 speaks of Harapha's spear as "A weaver's beam," echoing 1 Samuel 17 : 7, but also speaks of his "seven-times-folded shield," echoing the shield of Ajax that was made of seven layers of hide. Still, he was well aware of the difference between the two kinds of giants, distinguishing the former, for example, in *PL* 11. 688, where he echoes Genesis 6 : 4 while punning on the giants' size by calling them "men of high renown," and earlier when he speaks of those who came "from ancient world" in *PL* 3. 464, "with many a vain exploit, tho then renowned." In using the classical myths, Milton retains the traditional distinction between Titans who were heaven-born and ordinary giants who were earth-born, a distinction sometimes obscured by the practice of ancient writers themselves, who occasionally confused the War of the Titans and the War of the Giants. Milton, however, speaks of the heaven-born Titans and earth-born giants in *PL* 1. 198.

Milton uses Hesiod's* *Theogony* as his basic source for both wars. The War of the Titans, echoed in *PL* 1. 510–21, features Kronos as the antagonist of Zeus. Kronos (Saturn) was last of the twelve Titans born to Uranus and Ge. On advice of his mother, Kronos castrated Uranus and forced him to flee. Kronos then wed his sister Rhea, and from that union came Hestia, Demeter, Hera, Hades, Poseidon, and Zeus—second-generation Titans, as it were, but soon to be Olympian gods. Learning that he was to be overthrown by his son, Kronos ate all male offspring, but Zeus escaped because Rhea substituted a stone in his swaddling clothes. She hid him in Crete until he was old enough to return and trick Kronos into disgorging his siblings, who then joined Zeus in overthrowing their father and banishing their aunts and uncles, except Oceanus, to the deepest pit of Tartarus; that is, Kronos, his brothers Coeus, Crius, Hyperion, and Japetus, and his sisters Rhea, Thea, Themis, Mnemosyne, Phoebe and Tethys. Kronos's eating of his children lies behind some lines of Milton's *Time*: "Fly, envious Time, til thou run out thy race . . . And glut thy self with what thy womb devours. . . ."

The War of the Giants was, in effect, a continuation of the earlier war. According to Hesiod, the first giants were conceived when the blood from the castration of Uranus fell upon his wife Ge (i.e., earth). Later, more out of envy than revenge, the giants banded together to attack Zeus and his followers luxuriously throned upon Mount Olympus. So powerful were the giants that they easily made a scaling ladder by piling Mount Pelion upon Mount Ossa (cf. *QNov* 174). With aid from the mortal Heracles, the Olympians beat back the attack. Zeus killed Porphyrion in the act of ravishing Hera. Athena overcame Pallas. Poseidon mashed Polybotes with a huge rock that turned into an island. Apollo shot Ephialtes, Hermes slew Hippolytus, Dionysus trapped Eurytus in his vine and slew him along with many other giants. The victorious Olympians then buried the fallen giants under Mount Aetna.

Milton transformed the story of the giants from Hesiod into the battle scenes of *PL,* especially in the crushing defeat of the giant rebels and their nine-day fall (*PL* 1. 50; 6. 871), along with such details as the angels using rocks, waters, woods, and hills as missiles that blotted out the sky (6. 644–66), or the ruler of heaven withholding his most potent weapon until

the troops reached stalemate. With these parallels, Milton (like others) saw the War of the Giants as an analogue of the angelic rebellion. He even includes the Titans and their brood in the catalogue of fallen angels (1. 508–14) as types of deceivers because they disseminated fraudulent myths about themselves. But this fraud did not weaken their myth as an analogue. Fabulous, no doubt, but such tales as the giants' defeat on Olympus could easily be understood "as an ethnic version of a comparable fall by the 'rebellious rout' " (Hughes, p. 208). In 10. 579–84, Milton alludes to a tradition also used by George Sandys in commenting on Ovid's* *Metamorphoses* 1. 151–55: "Pherecides the Syrian writes how the Divels were throwne out of heaven by *Jupiter* (this fall of the Gyants perhaps an allusion to that of the Angells) the chiefe called *Ophioneus,* which signifies Serpentine : having after made use of that creature to poyson *Eve* with false ambition" (1632 ed., p. 27). For the most part, then, Milton made just so much use of Hesiod as would suit his purpose, not hesitating to shape the basic myth with materials from other traditions or contemporary commentary.

The practice is seen at its most complex in *PL* 1. 198–99, with its allusion to "Titanian, or Earth-born, that warr'd on Jove, Briareos or Typhon." The allusion to Briareos is simple enough, with an earlier appearance in *Eikon* (5 : 221) where he is one of "those Giants who threaten'd bondage to Heav'n," especially apt there because with his hundred hands he symbolized those who grasp for political power. Milton's use of Typhon is much more complex. For some reason, Typhon is identified with Ephialtes in *Prol* 4 (12 : 173), but Ephialtes was the victim of Apollo in the War of the Giants, while Typhon was vanquished by Zeus himself—setting Mount Aetna afire in the process of burying him. In popular lore, Typhon was known for his monstrous size, his head reaching the skies, and for having sired such more famous monsters as Geryon, Gorgon, and Cerberus.

To Hesiod and thus to Milton, he was a fearsome adversary in the War of the Giants, with a hundred heads that could utter the sounds of many different beasts, and a hundred hands and feet that could have done much damage to Olympus if Zeus had not stopped him. Thus, despite the confusion with Ephialtes, he is a fitting symbol of rampant Error rebelling against Truth (12 : 173). In *Nat* (226) he appears conflated into another Typhon of Egyptian mythology, a deity representing the cosmic principle of divisive energy, who appears also in *Areop* as a butcher of truth (4 : 338). Milton is clearly creating another analogue for Satan. Spenser* named Typhon with Procrustes, Ixion, and Prometheus among the giant heroes (*Faerie Queene* 7. 6. 29), but for Milton he is less hero than allegorical* figure, whose fate once more gives testimony to the truth of Christian history. [PMZ]

GILDAS, sixth-century British priest. Milton relied heavily on *Liber Querulus de Excidio Britanniae* by Gildas for many of his ideas about early British customs and history. Over forty examples of his use of Gildas's chronicle can be adduced from *Brit, CB, Tenure, 1Def*, and *2Def*. Milton did, however, confuse Gildas sapiens or Badonicus, the historian, with at least two other Gildases, at one point calling him a British poet (*Brit* 10 : 12).

In considering Gildas "the most ancient historian," Milton approached him somewhat critically; for example, "if Gildas deserve belief" (*Brit* 10 : 111) "if we mistake not Gildas" (*Brit* 10 : 137). He knew Gildas through Jerome Commelin's* edition in *Rerum Britannicarum* (Heidelberg, 1587); his notes on his comparison of Polidore Vergil's 1525 edition with the text testifies to his careful reading (Marginalia 18 : 258–29). Unfortunately, Gildas's work has little independent literary merit, being chiefly "a tract for the times" (G. O. Sayles, *Medieval Foundations of England*, p. 4). The information

he did provide is incidental to his theme, a denunciation of the Britons whose evil life and violent habits brought on their destruction. But it was this very element that Milton found most useful in his polemical tracts, comparing the wickedness of leaders of his own day with those of the past (Fogle, Yale *Prose* 5 : 420). [RMa]

GILDON, CHARLES (1665–1724), miscellaneous writer and editor. Gildon was a hack writer who engaged in two controversies of note and who edited poems and essays with Miltonic relationships. Remarks accompanying his editorial work are also often pertinent, although for the most part his ideas are trite and their concerns are the current questions over Milton's verse, style*, and decorum*. Born a Roman Catholic, Gildon later espoused deism but converted to Anglicanism through the influence of Charles Leslie's works; see his *Deist's Manual* (1705) with a preface by Leslie. His *New Rehearsal* (1714) attacked Alexander Pope's* "The Rape of the Lock" and the ensuing feud (which involved Gildon's memoirs of William Wycherley) continued after Gildon's death with Pope's barbs in *Epistle to Dr. Arbuthnot* (1724 and 1735) and *The Dunciad* (1728).

Gildon's edition of *Miscellany Poems upon Various Occasions: Consisting of Original Poems, By the Late Duke of Buckingham, Mr. Cowley, Mr. Milton* [etc.] (1692) erroneously attributes two poems to Milton, a long Latin epitaph on Cardinal Mazarin and a six-line Latin epigram on Pope Urban VIII, pp. 29–33, which ascriptions were repeated in other volumes. In *Miscellaneous Letters and Essays, on Several Subjects* (1694; reissued, 1696), pp. 41–44, he printed "To Mr T. S. in Vindication of Mr Milton's Paradise lost," by "I. I." Gildon has sometimes been alleged to be the author. The letter commends the language as appropriate to the subject and the speakers; it recognizes that there are levels of style within the poem. There are also two allusions on p. 81 on blank verse* in "Some Reflections on Mr Rymer's Short View of Tragedy" and "Attempt at a Vindication of Shakespeare, in an Essay Directed to John Dryden Esq." *Chorus Poetarum: or, Poems on Several Occasions* (1694; reissued, 1696), p. 19, prints the Latin verses to Queen Christina*, perhaps written by Fleetwood Shepherd, as Andrew Marvell's*; they had appeared in Marvell's *Poems* (1681) and in later collections and manuscripts. But the poem persists in eighteenth- and nineteenth-century editions of Milton's minor poems, having been noted as possibly Milton's by John Toland* (1698; 1 : 38–39). It was included in Thomas Newton's* 1752 variorum and following. One of the first appearances of John Phillips's* parody* of style, "In Imitation of Milton" (later titled "The Splendid Shilling") was in Gildon's *New Miscellany of Original Poems on Several Occasions* (1701), pp. 212–21.

Various other volumes allude to Milton or quote from his works. *Examen Miscellaneum. Consisting of Verse and Prose* (1702) discusses the verse of *PL* with quotation from Milton's statement, pp. [xv–xvi], and prints "The Vision. A Fable, Inscribed to Dr. Garth," pp. 44–64, an anonymous imitation with appropriations from *PL* and a specific allusion on p. 63. In *The Complete Art of Poetry. In Six Parts* (1718), two volumes, there are very frequent references and quotations, most from *PL* but also from *Educ* and *SA*. Gildon was fond of repeating the cliché that Milton is "worthy of the Fraternity of Homer and Virgil" (1 : 269). In *The Laws of Poetry* (1721) he is cited as "immortal" and his works as "truly perfect and admirable" (p. 34); there are five further references as well as one in John Sheffield, Lord Buckingham's "Essay on Poetry." Other volumes produced by Gildon that are to be noted are his revision of Gerard Langbaine's* *An Account of the English Dramatick Poets* (1698 or 1699); *The Post-Boy Robb'd of His Mail* (1706), with two allusions to Milton, and 1719, with three different allusions; *Libertas Triumphans* (1708),

p. 6; *Memoirs of the Life of William Wycherley* (1718), p. 19; and *A Grammar of the English Tongue. With the Arts of Logick, Rhetorick, Poetry* (n. d., various eds.), *passim,* and with a comment on the style of *SA*. [JTS]

GILL, ALEXANDER (SENIOR) (1564–1635).

Milton's first schoolmaster, Alexander Gill (Senior) was appointed high master of St. Paul's School* on March 10, 1608. His influence on Milton probably lay most significantly in three areas: religion*, poetry, and spelling*. He was author of *A Treatise concerning the Trinitie* (written 1597, published 1601), reprinted in his *Sacred Philosophie of the Holy Scripture* (1635). It argued against the anabaptist* Thomas Mannering that Jesus was indeed "very God of very God." The later work is a commentary on the Apostle's Creed*. Gill read much and often quoted from recent English poets, his favorite being Spenser*. He was respected as a learned man and a noted Latinist. And his *Logonomia Anglica* (1619, rev. 1621) has been cited as offering Milton theory and example for phonetic spelling such as he does seem to employ. What Gill's influence was is difficult to determine exactly, but at least in all these areas Milton was to become concerned and the subconscious presence of his old schoolmaster's beliefs may have colored his own. In addition Gill maintained the teaching of Hebrew in his school, and Milton may first have learned that language under his guidance. Gill died in his home in St. Paul's Churchyard on November 17, 1635. [JTS]

GILL, ALEXANDER, JR. (1597?–1644?),

schoolmaster, poet, and friend of Milton. Gill was appointed under-usher at his father's St. Paul's School* in 1621, teaching the lower forms; thus he was not one of Milton's tutors*. But they became good friends and Milton seems to have sought Gill's advice from time to time in the years ahead. Gill himself had been educated at St. Paul's, Wadham College, Oxford (B.A., 1616), and Trinity

College, Oxford (M.A., 1619; B.D., 1627; D.D., 1637). He had some reputation as a Latin and Greek poet, his collection of occasional poems entitled *Parerga* being published in 1632. The collection has a dedication to the king and a poem addressed to William Laud*, although Gill had had official difficulties with them shortly before. An infamous episode in his life developed out of John Felton's assassination of George Villiers, Duke of Buckingham*, Charles I's* much hated adviser, on August 23, 1628. On September 1, in the wine cellar of Trinity College, Gill and some friends talked of the assassination. Gill remarked on the king's stupidity and Felton's courage, and assured his auditors that Buckingham was in hell. William Chillingworth overheard the talk and reported it to his godfather Laud. Three days later Gill was apprehended, examined, and sent to the Gatehouse. Letters and verses found in the rooms of his friend William Pickering of Trinity College evidenced his attitude toward the king and Buckingham. The decision of the Star Chamber on November 6 was to confine Gill to the Fleet, fine him £2000, degrade his ministry, strip him of his degrees, and pillory him at Westminster and have his ears cut off (a symbol of inability to pursue God's ministry further). However, all that occurred by November 22 was that Gill was imprisoned and degraded. He was promised a pardon on October 18, 1630, and this was granted on November 30 by the king. Gill was high master of St. Paul's upon his father's death, from November 18, 1635, through January 7, 1640. He was reputed to have a savage temper and to whip boys fitfully. Satiric poems circulated at the time alluding to his excessive severity; an example was written by Ben Jonson*. He is said to have died at St. Botolph's, Aldergate, in 1642, and on the other hand he is reported to have been headmaster of Oakham Grammar School, Rutland, in 1643–44.

There are three extant letters from Milton to Gill, and it is argued that one of Milton's poems is directly indebted to one of his. The first letter to Gill is dated May 20, 1628, but on the basis of an allusion to Gill's poem on the capture of Hertogenbosch by Frederick-Henry of Nassau on September 14, 1629 (entitled "In Sylvam-Ducis" and published in *Parerga*), it has been redated 1630. The letter was evoked by receipt of verses from Gill. The second extant letter is dated July 2, 1628, and concerns Milton's student associates* and commencement exercises, for which Milton ghost wrote some verses for one of the Fellows of his college. The verses are said by Milton to be printed, but this apparently means for local distribution at the exercises only. What verses Milton alludes to is debated; usually *Naturam* and/or *Idea* are advanced. The date of the letter is not very plausible for various reasons and it has been argued that the date should be 1631. The third letter is dated December 4, 1634, and discusses Greek verses sent by Gill to Milton some time before. Gill's poem provoked Milton to attempt his first composition in Greek since his days in school. Suggested as the verses referred to is Milton's Greek translation of Psalm 114; it perhaps was composed during the week of November 23–29. The letter also makes an appointment with Gill, which, if it was kept, probably took place at a bookseller's in London on December 8. That Milton's "Philosophus ad regem" is somehow a result of this meeting is a mere guess. And finally it should be noted that Milton's *AdP* has seemed to have been influenced by Gill's "In Natalem Mei Parentis," written in 1624 and published in *Parerga*. [JTS]

GILLES, PIERRE (1571–?) author commissioned by the Waldensian* church to write its history, which appeared in 1644, *Histoire Ecclesiastique des Eglises Reformées . . en Quelques Valées de Piedmont*. In *CB* Milton quoted a statement from it about the Waldensians' skill in languages. A sentence from the same passage appears in *Hire* to support his idea that ministers be trained in self-supporting trades. Milton's almost lifelong interest in these early reformers was based on such standard authorities as this. [WBH]

GIRARD, BERNARD DE (1535–1610), historian. Milton collected seventeen entries for his *CB* from the *Histoire de France* by Girard, sieur de Haillan. Three of these were later incorporated into *Tenure* (5 : 24) and *1Def* (7 : 265, 415). In the latter work Girard is identified as the eminent historian of France, as indeed he was officially. Milton found no use for his notes from Girard on his account of the introduction of the organ into France and of the invention of the musical scale (*CB* 18 : 140). Nor were his references under the topics, The Knowledge of Literature, Marriage*, Concubinage, and Divorce* of use. He did, however, employ Girard's statements to prove that kingship was not hereditary, that tyrants may be deposed, and that parliamentary power is superior to royal power: for example, he inferred from Girard's statement about tenures of fief being created by Charles Martel that all who held in fief were "in a manner servants" (*CB* 18 : 180). Such ideas were very useful indeed in his polemical works.

Mohl notes that Milton's page references indicate his reading from the *Histoire* (1576), but Hughes cites *De L'Estat et Success Des Affaires de France* ([1609] Yale *Prose* 1 : 378; 3 : 178). [RMa]

GLASS, GEORGE HENRY: *see* TRANSLATIONS OF MILTON'S WORKS.

GLUTTONY. Gluttony, traditionally a deadly sin, in the broad sense of the term denotes excess in both eating and drinking, although Milton in *CD* follows a common practice in distinguishing between gluttony and drunkenness on the basis of whether food or drink is the object of excessive indulgence. Milton was abstemious in his personal life, and, in *El 6* addressed to Charles Diodati*, he explains the necessity for a sparse diet in the regimen of the dedicated poet.

Gluttony receives various depictions in the poetical works. Comus, the offspring of Bacchus and Circe, is "much like his Father, but his Mother more" (58); accordingly, he is the drunken reveler who attempts to subvert the chastity* of the Lady. Eve is in part influenced by physical appetite to eat the forbidden fruit; as the hour of noon approaches, there is aroused in her "an eager appetite, rais'd by the smell / So savorie of that Fruit, which with desire, / Inclinable now grown to touch or taste, / Solicited by her longing eye" (9. 739–43). The immediate effect of the Fall* on both Adam and Eve is one of intoxication (9. 793–95, 1008–11). Milton explains in *CD* that gluttony is one of the sins comprehended in the original sin of Adam and Eve (15.181–83). Later in *PL* Michael presents to Adam a vision of a lazarhouse wherein are punished those who gave way to "gluttonous delight" (11. 466–546); their sin and consequent punishment is twice attributed to the sin of Eve (11. 475, 519). Gluttony forms the substance of one of the temptations, the banquet scene, in *PR* (2. 337–406). Gluttony is also one of the elements in the so-called "triple equation" discussed by Elizabeth Pope in *Paradise Regained: The Tradition and the Poem* [1947], pp. 50–69). Exegetes have seen a parallel between the Fall of Man and the temptations* of Christ in the wilderness. The sins of gluttony, vainglory*, and avarice* constitute the essence of man's fall; these same sins are embodied in the temptations that Jesus resists in his encounter with Satan. [RF]

GOD: *see* FATHER, THE; SON, THE.

GODFREY, THOMAS: *see* INFLUENCE IN AMERICA, MILTON'S.

GODWIN, WILLIAM (1756–1836), philosopher, novelist, and historian. He derived the plot of his anonymous *Imogen: A Pastoral Romance* (1784) from *Mask*. In the tongue-in-cheek preface, the authorial persona claims first that he has translated the tale "from the Ancient British" of the bard Cadwallo. He speculates next that Milton saw the same manuscript while preparing *Mask* "upon the borders of Wales." Finally he decides that Rice ap Thomas (1449–1526) wrote *Imogen* at the end of the seventeenth century. Godwin apparently intended the preface to parody various learned testimonials to the authenticity of James Macpherson's Ossianic forgeries.

Godwin's most influential work, *An Enquiry concerning Political Justice* (1793) finds "considerable virtue" in "Milton's devil," although "his energies centered too much in personal regards." Satan maintained "the spirit of opposition" after his fall "because a sense of reason and justice was stronger in his mind, than a sense of brute force; because he had much the feelings of an Epictetus or a Cato, and little those of a slave. He bore his torments with fortitude, because he disdained to be subdued by despotic power. He sought revenge, because he could not think with tameness of the unexpostulating power that assumed to dispose of him" (3d [1797], 1 : 323–24). This view of Satan anticipates that held by Godwin's son-in-law, Percy Bysshe Shelley*. It also bears a superficial similarity to William Blake's* statement in *The Marriage of Heaven and Hell* (1790–93) that Milton was "of the Devils party without knowing it." Blake and Godwin, although associates in the radical salons of the day, probably did not influence each other directly.

Godwin's *The Enquirer* (1797), Part 1, Essay 15, "Of Choice in Reading," characterizes *PL* as "a sublime poem upon a strange story of the eating of an apple, and of the eternal vengeance decreed by the Almighty against the whole human race, because their progenitor was guilty of this detestable offence" (p. 135). Were it not for tradition and prejudice, Godwin continues, the books that celebrate "so tyrannical a despot" as Milton's God "could inspire nothing but hatred" (pp. 139–40).

The man Milton appears in Godwin's *The Lives of Edward and John Philips, Nephews and Pupils of Milton* (1809) and in his *History of the Commonwealth of England* (1824–1828). The former work reprints Edward Phillips's "The Life of Milton" (1694) and mistakenly claims to print for the first time the manuscript of John Aubrey's* "Collections for the Life of Milton." Godwin's empiricist view that character and belief are entirely the product of sense impressions and education makes it difficult for him to account for the Phillipses' Royalism. *History of the Commonwealth* discusses *DDD* (1 : 350–51), *Areop* (1 : 352), the Secretaryship for Foreign Tongues* (3 : 36–37), and *1Def* (3 : 241–45).

"Of English Style," the concluding essay of *The Enquirer*, quotes *RCG* and *Areop* at great length (pp. 403–12). Godwin considers the latter "admirable" and "eloquent," despite "the occasional stiffness and perplexity of its style." In a letter to Shelley (December 17, 1812), Godwin declares that "Shakspeare, Bacon, and Milton are the three greatest contemplative characters that this island has produced. Therefore, I put Shakspeare and Milton at the head of our poetry, I put Bacon and Milton at the head of our prose."

Brief quotations from Milton's poems illustrate Godwin's other works, especially the novels *Mandeville: A Tale of the Seventeenth Century in England* (1817) and *Cloudesley* (1830). He also quotes *PL* 8. 540–42, and misquotes 4. 300–301, in *Of Population* (1820). Godwin's argument in this section of his answer to Malthus is that because "woman is the weaker vessel, and more a slave to passion," she is no more "capable of abstinence and self-government than our own sex" (pp. 532–33). [JHR]

GOODMAN, GODFREY: *see* HAKEWILL, GEORGE.

GOODWIN, JOHN (1594?–1665), Puritan minister and pamphleteer, graduate of Queens College, Cambridge, and Vicar of St. Stephens in London. In 1645, ousted by Presbyterian* opponents, he established an independent church but was restored to his parish by Cromwell in 1649.

Goodwin was one of the earliest ministers to support the Parliamentary cause and wrote pamphlets in its behalf; later in *Obstructours of Justice* (1649) he supported the regicides and referred favorably and at some length to Milton's *Tenure*. *Obstructours* was publicly burned in 1660, along with *Eikon* and *1Def*, and an order was issued for the arrest of both authors, who went into hiding. Goodwin finally participated in the general amnesty but was forbidden henceforth to hold public office.

Aside from his political activity, he was well known as the most forthright English Arminian* of his day, a major reason for Presbyterian opposition to him. In this respect he and Milton share an important area of religious belief, but unlike Milton he held the traditional Christian belief in the Trinity* and the Incarnation*. [WBH]

GOSTLIN, JOHN (1566?–1626), a physician and later Master of Gonville and Caius Colleges. He was Vice-Chancellor of Cambridge University at the time of his death on October 21, 1626. Milton's Latin elegy *In Obitum Procancellarii Medici* mourns his decease. It is the first of four poems commemorating persons who died in the fall of 1626. [WM]

GOTT, SAMUEL, 1613–1671, author of *Novae Solymae* (1648), erroneously attributed to Milton by the Reverend Walter Begley in his translation of 1902. Son of a London ironmonger, Gott attended the Merchant Taylor's School and St. Catherine's College, Cambridge, taking his B.A. in 1632. He entered Gray's Inn the next year and was called to the bar in 1640. He published (anonymously) *Novae Solymae* in 1648, *An Essay of the True Happiness of Man* (under his own name) in 1650, and *The Divine History of the Genesis of the World*. S. K. Jones is correct that Gott establishes a much more

musing and tentative tone than Milton, as for example when he complained of his age, in which "if any Books he read, they are only such as we disdain to read twice; Pamphlets and Stories of Fact, or angry Disputes concerning the Times" or when he stated he wrote as an "antidote against Idleness" ("Preface," *An Essay of the True Happiness of Man*). Milton, who loved controversy not wisely but too well, was incapable of either thought. Gott seems to have retired from the practice of the law and from political or military combat and to have set no great store by literary fame. While his explication of Genesis, often droll for all its high-flown metaphysics, shows a kind of interest to be found in Milton, his *Novae Solymae*, a sort of utopian travel fantasy, constitutes a retreat from the vexed and tumultous affairs of England. With a wit slightly reminiscent of Sir Thomas Browne, a complex philosophical diction, and a penchant for the contemplative rather than active life and thought, Gott is not without his interest as an author, partly because of the dissimilarities between him and Milton. [BMB]

GOTTSCHED, JOHANN CHRISTOPH (1700–1766), coming to Leipzig in 1724, joined a students' poetry club immediately, the Deutschübenden poetische Gesellschaft, thereby showing his interest in poetry, in the German language (Latin still dominated the literary and academic worlds, as it was to do for most of the century), and his tendency to work through already established organizations. Later he was to form, and encourage the formation of, other groups modeled upon this poetry club; he also started or took over critical journals, like the *Beiträge zur kritischen Historie der Deutschen Sprache, Poesie, und Beredsamkeit,* and encouraged friends and former students to start their own periodicals. It was in such journals that the decisive battles over the form and content of German poetry were fought out against such opponents as the two Swiss professors Bodmer* and

Breitinger, as well as battles over "proper" drama and the regularizing of literary German.

In the basic literary disagreement that marked the entire eighteenth century in Germany, that between the group favoring an aesthetic "norm" and those favoring literary tolerance, Gottsched belongs to the first, for reasons of personality as well as poetic philosophy. His linguistic and literary preoccupations are unified by his belief in the political destiny of Germany under the leadership of Prussia as the major political power. Germany, he thought, must have a national culture, interlinked and closed, rational, moral, proper. For this reason, he advocated the replacement in literature of the many German dialects with a single, "pure" form of the language, that spoken around Meissen; to this end, too, he demanded a literature and drama comparable to those of other nations. With his typical energy, he drew up a rank-order of compositions, the high and the low. The heroic epic* and tragedy* are "high," comedy, the novel, and the pastoral* poem are "low." On the stage he showed his conception of correct drama, not only with his own play, *Der Sterbende Cato,* but had access to a superb acting company, and a good actress, Karoline Neuber, with whose help he fought against the impromptu comedy (Stegreifkomödie), with its coarse humor and buffoonery, and against the formless, decayed, vaguely historical tragedy called Haupt- und Staatsaktion.

Since he was a rationalist, a follower of Christian Wolff, Gottsched's final attitude toward Milton and *PL* is predictable. In his journal, *Der Biedermann,* he had already attacked the supernatural and the fantastic. Nevertheless, he approved at first of Bodmer and praised his translation* of *PL,* because he had read Bodmer's letter exchange with Francesco Algarotti, an Italian count, dealing with elevation and sublimity in tragedy, poetic justice, and reason* as the guide to the eternal sources of beauty, and believed, mistakenly, that Bodmer was his ally.

In terms showing his ambivalence, Gottsched praises Bodmer's prose translation in the first issue of *Kritische Beiträge,* saying that though some Englishmen believe that the language "sank under Milton, too weak to set forth the elevated thoughts of his soul in their full power," Bodmer's translation in German shows such strength that "one could say Milton thereby gains more power and impresses more than in his mother tongue." Gottsched also remarks, "Milton has so succeeded that all English poets following him have admired and tried to imitate his ingenious style, but have had to confess their failure."

The difference of opinion between Gottsched and the two Swiss, Bodmer and Breitinger, was originally not great. Both were against the extravagances of late baroque* writing, for example, and both considered "imitation of nature" a desirable goal for a poet. They differed strongly, however, in their conception of the possible and in poetic method.

The controversy started in earnest with the fifth chapter of Gottsched's *Dichtkunst* (1730), "Von dem Wunderbaren in der Poesie." For Gottsched, the marvelous can concern itself with gods and spirits, with human beings and their deeds, and with animals and lifeless things. All instances must be treated "correctly," according to ascertainable rules, else the effect is laughable and childish. The use of angels* and devils in literature should be minimal, for "no reasonable person believes in them." Besides, no particular art or skill is needed to depict these creatures, nor does their depiction improve a poet's abilities. Rather, the use of the supernatural is evidence of lack of skill.

Gottsched held, too, that reason must lead to the unchanging rules of art; the artist, learning these, will understand what forms these rules lead to in individual types of works. One should start with the moral he wishes to teach, then follow the rules for the type of work that should embody this moral. Gottsched saw the poetic gift as basically intellectual, and poetry as a craft that could be taught to any diligent student. [MM]

GOUT. His frequent state of ill health was a result of Milton's developing blindness* and, in his last years, attacks of the gout. He was described as being of ruddy complexion and a very cheerful humor in his later years. Yet gout developed possibly during 1664–1666, and attacked most painfully during the spring and autumn. The term *gout* was often used inexactly, but whatever the specific affliction, he had great pain in his fingers and hands, and his knuckles became stiff. At times the attacks of gout in his feet and legs made any walking impossible. His death has been attributed to gout, but it probably was due to heart failure as a result of hardening of the arteries. (See Edward A. Block, *Bulletin of the History of Medicine* 28 : 201–11.) He died in his sleep apparently on Sunday, November 8, 1674. [JTS]

GOWER, JOHN (ca. 1330–1408), poet. A moral and erudite English poet, Gower dedicated his greatest work, *Confessio Amantis* ("The Lover's Confession"), an English poem of some 30,000 lines, to King Richard II. Though closely connected with the Church, he apparently never became a priest. In his later years he lived in the Priory of St. Mary Overies, Southwark. Perhaps blind by 1400, he died there in 1408. His tomb is now in Southwark Cathedral.

Milton makes two references to Gower. In *CB,* under the heading "Of War," he notes two passages in the *Confessio* (London, 1532 ed.) concerning the rightness of "holy warre as they call it" (18 : 211). In these passages Gower suggests that killing Turks and Saracens is not exactly a high Christian calling; love is better than hate, endurance better than aggression. Then in *Apol* Milton quotes "our old Poet *Gower"* against the Roman Emperor Constantine's establishment of Christianity as the state religion. Both Gower and Milton regarded this act as temporal meddling with spiritual affairs

(*Apol* 3 : 359–60), and Milton echoes Gower's passage again in *Eikon* (5 : 187: Constantine's poison in the Church). The same quotation appears without ascription in *Hire* and *2Def*. Thus Milton's reading of the *Confessio Amantis* around 1640–1642 bore later fruit as he labored for separation of church and state. [GLM]

GRACE, according to Christian belief, is the aid given by God directly to man so that he may be saved. Except to the heretical Pelagians*, fallen man is understood to be quite helpless to overcome his sinful state, powerless to be good without such divine assistance. Thus the individual may never merit* his own salvation through his own unaided efforts. The visitation of divine grace has often been understood as the operation of the Holy Spirit*. In any case, grace is at the center of the religious experience itself.

According to strict Calvinism*, God does not waste such efficacy on foreseen sinners; it is visited only upon the Elect, who respond accordingly to its irresistible power (see, e.g., *Westminster Confession,* 10). But for the Dutch Remonstrants, such divine grace comes (in varying degrees) to everyone, who then has the freedom to accept or reject it. Following Augustine* in part, these Arminians* thus developed the concept of prevenient grace : grace that is antecedent to conversion, the free gift of God, as distinguished from subsequent grace, which cooperates with man after his conversion. The visitation of prevenient grace upon one thereupon permits him, according to Arminian belief, to exercise his own newly freed will* to choose good or evil*.

As a Christian Milton frequently employs these concepts, finding, for instance, that the illumination provided by divine grace is a better guide than nature (*Animad* 3 : 142). Acting on both the understanding and the will (*CivP* 6 : 21), such grace in his later thought is understood essentially in the Remonstrant sense: God imparts grace to all but not in equal measure (*CD* 14 : 147) though everyone receives sufficient attention that he may be saved (15 : 321). Likewise in *PL*, God predicts that after his Fall* man will find grace (3. 131) with which God himself will endow him (3.174). The actual operation of this "prevenient grace" in Adam and Eve after the Fall is described in the opening lines of Book 11, a manifestation of the "Covenant of Grace made to man by God as detailed in *CD* (16 : 99ff.). [WBH]

GRAHAM, SIR RICHARD (1648–1695). Sir Richard, Viscount Preston, owned Milton's *CB* and made entries in it on pp. 20, 58, 59, 78, 79, 80, 81, 82, 177, 187, 189, 195, 197 199, 200, 201, 202, 203, 204, 205, 248, 249. Milton had written the start of a heading on p. 20 and used pp. 177, 187, 189, 195, 197, 248, 249. The manuscript remained at Sir Richard's ancestral estate, Netherby Hall, Longtown, Cumberland, until discovered in 1874 by Alfred Horwood*, who obtained the approval of its then owner, Sir Frederick Graham, for publication. Sir Richard probably received the manuscript from Daniel Skinner* when Skinner entered his service in Paris. Sir Richard, created Viscount Preston in 1680 for his efforts in behalf of James the Duke of York's succession, was appointed envoy extraordinary to the Court of France in May 1682, a post held until 1685 when James II ascended the throne. After the Revolution of 1688 he was frequently under arrest for his efforts for restoration. He retired to Yorkshire in 1691. When Lord Preston may have entered his own notes in the *CB* is uncertain. [JTS]

GRAMMAR, MILTON'S. To establish Milton's English grammatical practice, it is necessary to examine both characteristic seventeenth-century usage and the potential, inherent in English itself without recourse to classical or other modern languages as paradigms, for variation from that practice. Such an examination shows that Milton's grammar, far from being excessively dependent on that of other languages, especially Latin, as has regularly been charged or implied, is

sound English grammar well within the main patterns of modern English. It also shows that Milton's distinctive practice differs from that of poets contemporary with him and of our own time, not so much in the basic grammar he shares with them as in the choices he makes within its limitations. What it reveals most is a mind bent on explaining but explaining with compression, precision, and balance, and a mind concerned less with action than with the origins, the motivations, and the fruits of action.

Because of a provincial failure to recognize that the language of one's own age cannot be made the standard for another, it has been a commonplace among the critics, beginning with Johnson*, that Milton's English is somehow not sound. Undoubtedly prompted by their awareness of Milton's humanistic education, as well as of the image he had of himself as Virgil's* heir and the general Renaissance disesteem of the vernacular in relation to Latin, they have attributed the source of the trouble to Latin influence. The truth is that Milton's education made him not simply a Latinist but also learned in Greek, Hebrew, Aramaic, and several modern languages at the same time that it gave him as teacher Alexander Gill*, headmaster at St. Paul's*, who thought enough of English to write an English grammar. Milton's own tribute to his language in *Vac*, beginning "Hail native language," clearly indicates his early awareness of the importance and distinction of English.

It also must be pointed out that Latin, either directly or indirectly through French, is the source of over three hundred among the thousand most commonly used English words—the result of Church dominance in medieval Western education, the Norman conquest, and the utility of Latin as a source of abstract terms in the Age of Science.

Those who argue a preponderant Latin influence on Milton, as against its influence in general on the vernacular, often have not come to terms with the frequently un-English sound of the good

English of Milton's age to our ears. Janette Richardson, for example, (*Comparative Literature* 14 : 325) cites as a Virgilianism or usage "strange to English ears but . . . typical of Virgil's style": "thee I revisit *safe*" (*PL* 3. 21), apparently not recalling how often seventeenth-century writers practiced functional change, in this instance the substitution of adjective for adverb. The following examples—from many that could be cited—are from the work of that man of "little Latin," Shakespeare* :

> Which the false man does *easy* (*Macbeth* 2. 3. 143).
> Raged more *fierce* (*Richard* II 2.1. 173).
> It shall *safe* be kept (*Cymbeline* 1. 6. 209).

Italian also is claimed to have influenced Milton's syntax through the neoclassical manner advocated by Bembo and adopted by Tasso* and Della Casa*, and undoubtedly Milton imitates this manner in some measure to enrich his epic. But we should not overestimate the influence of the Italian of Milton's contemporaries, for some of its distinctive features were not without precedent in English.

The Cicero* who serves most Renaissance writers as the model for rhetoric* of course serves Milton too; but neither Ciceronian formalism nor the newer neoclassical manner significantly alters the syntax of his poetry, which contains more than four times as many loose sentences as periodic ones.

It is in flamboyant examples of inversion that critics have found most support for charges that Milton's word order is unidiomatic. But considering his prose and poetry together, we see that in fewer than fifteen percent of his clauses does Milton invert the English order that is largely fixed for us but was less so in Elizabethan times ("Him keepe with, the rest banish," says Falstaff to Prince Hal, *1 Henry IV* 2. 4. 462), the language not yet having moved all the way from its inflected stage with relative flexibility in word order to the analytical one in which the subject-predicate order is usually pre-

determined. And as important as his much-discussed clausal inversions, which often heighten poetic effects, is the essential looseness of Milton's sentence structure, for it is an essentially English looseness. With the important exception of the practice of such Latin-learned writers as Wyclif, the typical Middle English sentence of any length was a succession of loosely joined clauses, often paratactic, that gave the main idea first. In Milton's prose, which is never the familiar essay but in which rhetoric is the technique of purposeful goals, loosely structured sentences are made to share place with periodic ones, in which the main idea is held suspended until the end. But in the poetry, though periodic structures appear in emphatic positions, as at the opening of *PL*, it is the native, unruffled, loose sentence that defines the mode and lends a foundation of directness and composure.

Milton's characteristic use of the parts of speech is as eminently English as his syntax and, where choices are available to him, usually is surprisingly modern. With respect to nouns, it is notable that although he qualifies what he says more than many poets and gives less weight to actions, he uses the same proportion of substantives in his sentences as do Shakespeare* and T. S. Eliot*. More than any of the major poets preceding him, as might be expected, he uses the historically newer -*s* plural to the virtual exclusion, after *Mask*, of the archaic -*en* terminal. And like Shakespeare and other contemporaries, he still occasionally gives abstract nouns the concrete quality lent by plural form, as in *insolencies, vehemencies,* and *compliances.* In the singular he can use *turbulency* as well as *turbulence* and *fluence* for our *fluency,* with the freedom characterizing Elizabethan practice.

Milton's use of pronouns is much like ours, differing from that of the present day mainly in his retention of *thou* for the second person singular in his poetry, probably under the influence of biblical usage for his biblical themes. But, with his time, he no longer uses the *you-thou* social forms of the pronoun to distinguish relationships between equals, inferiors, and superiors, forms still employed, though not consistently, by Shakespeare. He avoids *its,* still considered a rude intruder into the language as the second successor after the awkward *it* to *his,* the original neuter possessive.

That part of speech most characterizing Milton's grammar is the adjective, which he uses with far greater frequency than do any of his predecessors among English poets except Spenser*. His strong penchant for the descriptive adjective marks the cast of a mind that must discriminate and a style that, habitually, essentially qualifies. Apart from the abundance of Milton's adjectives, however, it is their position that has occasioned comment. Although he does not adopt Spenser's use of synonymous adjective pairs (*faithful true* or *guiltless innocent*) or his use of massed adjectives (Most *lothsom, filthie, foule,* and *full* of *vile* disdaine), he does, with restraint, use compound adjectives and adjective pairs (*seven-times-folded* shield : *SA* 1122; thy *last* and *deadliest* wound : *PR* 4. 622). And probably under the influence of Italian neoclassicism, in any case to secure appropriate epic elevation, he sometimes positions adjectives both before and after a noun (*haughty* Nation *proud: Mask* 33; *Towred* structure *high* : *PL* 1. 733).

That Milton uses proportionally fewer verbs than Eliot and far fewer than Shakespeare results from his desire to explain the ways of God to men, the strength of virtue, and the justification of divorce* and, in his one drama, *SA,* to provide ethical* debate and reportage rather than direct presentation of Samson's dramatic vengeance on the Philistines. That he uses proportionally more action verbs and fewer copulatives than either Eliot or Shakespeare adds to the evidence of his consistent desire both to avoid empty words and to gain compactness and precision. And the frequency of his passive constructions, which he uses twice as often as Shakespeare and over three times as often as Eliot, shows equal

concern for the object of an action as for its agent. (See also Seymour Chatman, *Publications of the Modern Language Association* 83 : 1386–99.)

Milton's practice does not permit the Elizabethan deviations from *-st, -est* for the present verb form governed by *thou* that Shakespeare adopts in "thou *affects*" (*Antony and Cleopatra* 1. 3. 71) and "thou *should* know" (*Taming of the Shrew* 4. 3. 147; F₂), Milton preferring, for example, "thou / *Revisit'st*" (*Hamlet* 1. 4. 52–53; F₁). But, though Alexander Gill regarded the innovation of the third person singular *-s* terminal among the Elizabethans as a poetic freedom, Milton favors it to the relative exclusion of the *-th* terminal other than in *hath.* And he avoids the third person plural *-en* terminal that had been used, though rarely, by Shakespeare—"the whole quire . . . *waxen* in their mirth," *Midsummer Night's Dream* 2. 1. 52–53; "All *perishen* of man, of pelf," *Pericles* 2. 1. 35; Q₁— and was to be heard beyond Milton's time in the border counties.

In keeping with his contemporaries Milton sometimes permits preterits the form of past participles and, conversely, past participles the form of preterits as in "I who . . . the happy garden *sung*" (*PR* 1. 1), "his snares are *broke*" (*PR* 4. 611), and "in triumph had *rode*" (*PR* 3. 36). Examples of his now-archaic forms are *strook, struck'n, loaden, indu'd, unautoritied* and, in the early *L'Al, ycleap'd.* But though Milton's use of them deserves note, it is infrequent. [RDE]

GRAY, THOMAS: *see* INFLUENCE ON SEVENTEENTH- AND EIGHTEENTH-CENTURY LITERATURE, MILTON'S.

GREENE, BENJAMIN: *see* SERVANTS, MILTON'S.

GREGORAS, NICEPHORAS (ca. 1295–1360), author of *Byzantinae Historiae Libri XI,* covering events contemporary with his own life, cited by Milton in *CB* under "Kings" for an example of appointive heirs. Under "Property and Taxes" the history is quoted upon the freedom of the seas, and finally, under "Athletic Games," its accounting of jousts and tournaments as being of Latin origin is given. But Milton did not refer to Gregoras outside these notes. [WBH]

GREGORY OF NYSSA (ca. 330–ca. 395). Bishop of Nyssa and brother of St. Basil, St. Gregory revealed acquaintance with Platonic* and Neoplatonic* speculation in his theology; he expounded the doctrines of the Sacraments*, the Incarnation*, and the Redemption, and was an ardent defender of the Nicene doctrine of the Trinity*. In his most famous ascetical work, *Of Virginity*, he developed the notion that by virginity the soul becomes the spouse of God.

Milton's only significant allusion to Gregory of Nyssa is in *CB*, where he states that "Gregory of Nyssa is shown to have had a wife, in Volume 3 of de virginitate (pare) 116." Gregory's treatise *Of Virginity* is a complete study of the subject as a spiritual way of life (3.3ff. [Paris, 1638]). Milton may have had this work in mind while writing the divorce* tracts because chapter 3 of *Of Virginity* is "a recounting of the difficulties and troubles that arise from marriage" and the work expounds the joys and consolations of this state of life over the married state. In *CD* Milton uses the authority of Nyssa's treatise on the soul* for his teaching that the human soul is not created daily by the immediate act of God, but propagated from father to son in a natural order. [PAF]

GREVILLE, ROBERT, LORD BROOKE (1608–1643). Officer in the army of Charles I* in the Bishop's Wars (1639–1640) and then champion of the Parliamentary Party and general of the Parliamentary Army (1641–1643), Lord Brooke was an eloquent defender of nonconformity. After a brief stay in Parliament in his youth (1627–1628), Brooke attended to the affairs of his barony until called to public service again in the

hectic days of the 1640s. He was one of a group of men who petitioned Charles to settle the Scottish wars without bloodshed and was a party to negotiating the treaty of Ripon in 1640. Dismissed from the king's service for refusing to take an oath of fidelity, he assumed his seat in the House of Lords and was soon after elected Speaker. As leader of the army, he secured Warwickshire for Parliament and was killed in action at Lichfield in 1643.

Brooke wrote and published little: two political addresses (1642–1643), *The Nature of Truth,* a treatise on the nature of the soul (1641), and his justly praised *A Discourse opening the Nature of that Episcopacie, Which Is Exercised in England* (1641, 1642). The latter work Milton knew very well, for he speaks of Brooke and his stand for toleration in the warmest of terms in *Areop.* Milton argues that the Commons were left Brooke's dying charge, "so full of meeknes and breathing charity," to hear with patience and humility those who desire to live purely and according to God's ordinances as their consciences direct them. Milton adopts Brooke's argument that enforced conformity to the statutes of an established church encourages rather than suppresses sects and schisms, that enforced conformity achieves no more than a unity of ignorance. He agrees with the *Discourse* that even with a disparity of ecclesiastical views truth would inevitably emerge by means of open argument and that separate congregations should therefore not be outlawed in Christ's church. Although the *Discourse* and *Areop* show different attitudes toward the matter of "things indifferent," both accord in maintaining that a published decree establishing precisely what matters the church considers indifferent violates the right of free conscience in Christians.

There are strong similarities in the arguments of *Discourse* and *Ref,* although indebtedness is uncertain. Both refer to the dangerous implications in the statement of James I*, "No Bishop, No King," and decry the usurpation of royal prerogatives by the bishops. Both staunchly maintain that in matters that do not touch the state, as in the election of pastors to purely ecclesiastical posts, the state should not assume control. It has been argued that Milton is indebted to Brooke's *Discourse* in *RCG*, though Milton's claim that episcopacy breeds heresy and faction can be found in other contemporary sources besides Brooke. On the other hand, it seems reasonably sure that Brooke is indebted to *PrelE*, since the *Discourse* seems to quote directly some of the arguments and phrases from Milton's tract. [GHS]

GRIERSON, SIR H(ERBERT) J(OHN) C(LIFFORD) (1866–1960), Scottish scholar who earned degrees in classics from both the University of Aberdeen and Oxford. After several years as a member of the faculty of the former, he moved to Edinburgh, to become the Rector of the University there before his retirement. In the early years of this century he was one of the first modern scholars of English literature, bringing to its developing discipline rigorous training such as classics required. Besides editing the letters and writing a biography of Sir Walter Scott, he gave a major thrust to the popularity of John Donne in his two-volume edition of the poetry (Oxford, 1912), which first attempted the establishment of a text and canon (to which he brought the training of editing Aristotle's text) and sound annotation. It remained standard for many years and led to *Metaphysical Lyrics and Poems of the Seventeenth Century* (Oxford, 1921), which brought the metaphysicals* as a group to the attention of a generation of students.

Aside from various historical and critical studies of English literature, Sir Herbert edited a two-volume *Poems of John Milton,* arranged in chronological order, in 1925. He devoted a chapter of *Cross Currents in English Literature of the Seventeenth Century* (London, 1929) to Milton and wrote *Milton and Wordsworth: Poets and Prophets.* Many of

his Milton contributions were textual: attempts to date poems and to establish textual accuracy. He also wrote the Milton entry for Hasting's *Encyclopedia of Religion and Ethics.* [WBH]

GRIFFIN, EDWARD: *see* PRINTERS.

GRIFFITH, MATTHEW. a Royalist divine and chaplain to Charles I*, imprisoned several times during the Commonwealth. In March 1660, excited by the prospect of a Restoration, he preached and published his sermon *The Fear of God and the King,* which he dedicated to General Monck* ("It is a greater honour to make a King than to be one"), and which once again earned him imprisonment, since Monck was not yet ready to declare for Charles*. Milton answered Griffith in *BN* (early April 1660). After the Restoration, Griffith held several livings, and is said to have died as the result of a blood vessel's being ruptured while he was preaching. [WM]

GRONOVIUS, or GRONOW, JOHANN FREDERICK (1611–1671), German philologist and classicist. On the advice of Hugo Grotius* in 1634 he migrated to Holland, where he gained immediate acceptance by the best minds of the land. In 1658, he was named Professor of Greek, History, and Politics at Leiden, in effect as successor to Daniel Heinsius*, and in 1665 University Librarian, a post also held by the late Heinsius. Gronovius's years at Leiden were highly productive, and his elaborate variorum editions of Latin prose writers like Tacitus, Sallust, Aulus Gellius, Seneca, Pliny, Suetonius, or—his master work—Livy* have won for him a place as one of the most significant Latinists of the seventeenth century. To the dynasty of renowned humanists that had graced Leiden in the persons of Joseph Scaliger*, Heinsius, and Claudius Salmasius*, Gronovius and his eldest son, Jacobus, proved worthy heirs, and through them the fame of the university continued into the next century.

Gronovius's education and background

seem to have predestined him to record the quarrel between Salmasius and Milton. When Gronovius first arrived in Holland, he won immediate entrée to the Heinsius coterie at Leiden, probably through Virdung, who admired and emulated the poetry of the elder Heinsius. Although he then also acquired the friendship of Salmasius, as he did that of G. J. Vossius*, Petrus Scriverius, and many others of differing literary, theological and political persuasions in the United Provinces, intimacy at Leiden with Salmasius's arch-rival Heinsius and his circle inevitably meant strife with the proud Huguenot. Although initially circumspect in his dealings with the Heinsii out of respect for Salmasius, Gronovius shared like tastes and values with Nicolaas Heinsius*, and because their temperaments were complementary, the two became fast friends. Just as with Isaac Vossius* —another of Gronovius's close friends— or Alexander Morus* later, Salmasius turned on Gronovius too during his feuds with the Heinsii during the 1640s, Johannes successfully defending himself against attacks on his work, including the typically Salmasian charge of plagiarism, and Salmasius's influence with the University curators keeping Gronovius from a professorship at Leiden until after the haughty scholar's death. When Milton attacked Salmasius, Gronovius and his friends followed the skirmishing with understandable relish, Isaac providing intelligence from Stockholm, Nicolaas carrying the gossip about as he journeyed around Europe in a martyrdom of exile from the Swedish court, and Gronovius manning, as it were, a home office in the United Provinces. Hence, Gronovius's correspondence with his friends is one of the main sources for the chronology of events and rumors about the antagonists and their activities during Milton's clash with Salmasius. Although Gronovius's reputation for fair-mindedness and irenicism recommends his perspective of Salmasius as trustworthy, as Milton may have recognized, his reaction to the English poet is not "typical" of continental reception, if for no other reason than that he and his friends were more vitally interested in the quarrel than almost any other observers except the combatants themselves. [PRS]

GROTIUS, HUGO (1583–1645) graduated in his early teens from the University of Leiden, where he had studied under Joseph Scaliger. After practicing law he was elected representative to the States General. Against the dogmas of the Reformed churches affirmed by the Synod of Dort, he pleaded for religious toleration and especially for the Arminians*, who had been damned by that meeting. Arrested and sentenced to prison for life because of such activities, he escaped to Paris, where he lived for most of the rest of his life, representing Sweden at the French court from 1635.

Grotius was one of the last men of the Renaissance, accomplished in a wide variety of fields. He wrote a history of the Low Countries, for instance, and a study of the supposed origins of the American peoples, and published some poetry (1617, 1619, 1645). His knowledge of law is especially displayed in his arguments developing the concept of the Law of Nature and Nations in favor of freedom of the seas against John Selden*. As a devout Christian he published biblical interpretations and is especially remembered for a simple manual of religion put into Dutch verse for sailors and travellers, *De Veritate Religionis Christianae* (1622), which was quickly translated into various foreign languages and which reflects its author's religious tolerance and his lifelong efforts to unite the various Christian churches in a common cause.

Milton was personally acquainted with Grotius, having met him in Paris through the help of John Scudamore on his way to Italy in 1638. There is no record of their conversation nor is it even clear just how much Grotius's thought had influenced him by that time. By 1643, however, when he wrote *DDD*, Milton had found support from him in favor of his own liberal interpretations of the New Testament limitations upon divorce*, citing him there four times (3. : 384, 481, 487, 498). Similar employment of Grotius's biblical scholarship appears in *Bucer* (4 : 11) and *Tetra* (4 : 229). There are, however, no entries from him in *CB*.

More difficult to evaluate is the direct influence of Grotius's religious beliefs upon Milton. The Englishman knew *De Veritate,* for he cited it in the marginalia to Euripides' *Ion* (18 : 315) on the subject of the virgin birth. Furthermore, Grotius was the most famous contemporary Arminian, if not theologically the most systematic, and Milton adopted many of the tenets of the Remonstrants in his later years. No direct influence, however, has been proved in this respect; more likely they represent parallel developments from common sources, as may also be true of the religious tolerance that they shared. On the other hand, Milton quite probably held him in high esteem, a fact that may be reflected in the unusually favorable statements about Grotius in Edward Phillips's *Theatrum Poetarum* (1675).

A final area in which Grotius displayed his versatility is his composition of three neo-Latin plays, the *Christus Patiens* (1635; English trans. 1640), *Sophompaneas* (1635; English trans. 1652; a treatment of Joseph and his brothers), and *Adamus Exul* (1601), which has been argued to be one of the sources for *PL,* either directly or through the mediation of Giovanni Andreini's* *Adamo* (1613). Indeed, William Lauder* in 1747 and 1750 forged a translation of several lines of a Latin translation of *PL* into passages from Grotius (and others) in an attempt to discredit Milton as having deliberately plagiarized from the play. Although these absurd claims are long forgotten, the play and the epic correspond in remarkably interesting ways. Lauder published parts of the play in *Gentleman's Magazine* 17 (1747) : 312–14, 365–66. *Adamus* is a tragedy in classical form (somewhat as the outlines

in the Trinity MS show to have been in Milton's mind when he first considered the subject of *PL*). Satan is a major character in the play, proceeding from the despair of an opening soliloquy to the determination to ruin mankind. He unsuccessfully tempts Adam, who has been told at length about Satan's fall and the creation of the world (cf. *PL* 5–8); then as a serpent he persuades Eve to eat the forbidden fruit, to Adam's subsequent dismay and fall. In the last act, after Satan gloats over his success and Eve restrains Adam from suicide, God judges the couple and has them driven from the Garden.

The play is more similar to Milton's epic than to the outlines for his tragedies, and the epic is closer to it than to Andreini's work. It may be significant that the earliest part of *PL* (4. 32ff.) is a soliloquy of Satan, as is the first speech of *Adamus Exul.* The Satans of both works are fatalists. Dozens of suggestive parallels like these have been observed between the two works. It seems certain that Grotius's play is part of the background of *PL,* like DuBartas's *Divine Weekes* and Ariosto's* *Orlando Furioso,* though exactly how many of the similarities are due to the play itself and how many to a common tradition is probably impossible to state. [WBH]

GRYNAEUS, SIMON : *see* TRANSLATIONS OF MILTON'S WORKS.

GUICCIARDINI, FRANCESCO (1483–1540), Florentine lawyer, statesman, and historian. His most important work—the only one Milton is known to have read—is the *Storia d'Italia,* completed in 1540 and generally regarded as the finest historical work of the Renaissance. It is uncertain when Milton read it, though Parker (*Milton,* 2 : 921) suggests the period 1642–1645. Milton refers to it twice in *CB,* citing Guicciardini for his assertion that the royal power of Aragonese kings was not absolute and for his judgment that kings who have feared their subjects have generally kept them disarmed and untrained for war*. These two citations are recalled again, without reference to Guicciardini, the first in *Tenure* (5 : 10) and the second in *Way* (6 : 137). [DJD]

GUILLIM, JOHN (1565–1621), antiquary. A member of the College of Arms in London, Guillim wrote *A Display of Heraldrie* (1610), which became a popular reference tool. Milton cites it in *CB*, perhaps between 1639 and early 1641, under the heading "Nobility." Though in such a book Guillim is obviously interested in nobility of birth, says Milton, "our English herald" insists that true nobility includes virtuous living (18 : 195). The 1724 edition of *A Display of Heraldry* (p. 210) reports, probably from John Aubrey*, that John Milton, Sr., the poet's father, attended Christ Church, Oxford. [GLM]

GUNPOWDER PLOT, MILTON'S EPIGRAMS ON THE. Aside from the rather ambitious *QNov*, the poems that Milton wrote on the Gunpowder Plot are short epigrams. Four of them—"In Proditionem Bombardicam" (On the Gunpowder Plot) and three others entitled simply "In eandem" (On the Same)— may be treated as a single unit since they resemble each other both in brevity and in treatment of their subject. A fifth epigram—"In Inventorem Bombardæ" (On the Discoverer of Gunpowder)—is usually classed with them, although it clearly differs from the other four and may not be related to the Gunpowder Plot at all.

"On the Gunpowder Plot" and its companion pieces appeared in both the 1645 and 1673 editions of Milton's poetry, but with no indication as to date of composition. A reference in one of them to the death of James I*, which occurred in March 1625, helps only slightly. The tendency has been to assign them all tentatively to November 1626, the period when Milton was working on *QNov*, although—as Parker notes—such an ambitious performance "might well have discouraged the writing of other

verses on the same theme in that year" (*Milton,* p. 732). They do probably belong to Milton's Cambridge period, and the fact that each of them is a satiric variation on a single theme—the Catholics' desire to dispatch King James to the other world—suggests that they were probably composed at the same time rather than over a period of years. Their tone is all strongly royalist.

Their satire is in keeping with the nature of the epigram. A genre that originated in classical antiquity, the epigram is difficult to define; but basically it is a very short poem that attempts to capture the essence of a situation or action. Writers like Ben Jonson* used it for a variety of purposes—compliment and philosophical reflection, for example. Its brevity and tendency toward sententiousness, however, made it preeminently a medium of satire and therefore a natural medium for Milton to employ in commenting on the Gunpowder Plot.

The plot was to explode thirty-six barrels of gunpowder under the House of Lords as King James opened Parliament, November 5, 1605. The group of Roman Catholic gentlemen, led by Robert Catesby, who conceived it, hoped in the ensuing confusion to reestablish Catholicism as the state religion—if necessary with aid from abroad. Unfortunately for them, their agent, a professional soldier named Guy Fawkes, was discovered with the gunpowder on the evening of November 4 and under torture ultimately revealed the entire plan. Such was the story as Milton knew it. Modern Catholic historians have argued that the whole affair was contrived by the government as an excuse for anti-Catholic legislation. Whatever the truth in that argument, for Milton—and for most English Protestants—the plot was a recent and horrifying example of the evils of Catholicism; and the annual observances of November 5, which was made a national holiday by act of Parliament, were harshly intolerant in tone. Milton's epigrams

—like the many other poems written on the matter—share that tone.

Posterity has not accorded the epigrams a high place in the Miltonic canon. Among the reasons for their lack of appeal are their topicality and their Latinity. Yet a poem like Milton's sonnet on the massacre of Piemont, on the one hand, is no less topical; and, on the other hand, so accomplished a Latinist as Dr. Johnson* observed in his life of Milton that "some of the exercises on Gunpowder Treason might have been spared." A comment of William Cowper's* suggests a more basic reason for their unpopularity. Forbearing to translate them with the rest of Milton's Latin and Italian poems, he observed that "the matter of them is unpleasant, and . . . they are written with an asperity, which, however it might be warranted in Milton's day, would be extremely unseasonable now."

They are indeed written with asperity. Milton likens the Pope to the beast mentioned in the thirteenth and seventeenth chapters of Revelation; he scoffs that the gunpowder might have been better used to blow the priests and idols of Rome heavenward, their chances of getting there otherwise being feeble. The asperity is not, of course, uniquely Miltonic. Examination of poems like Phineas Fletcher's* *The Apollyonists* reveals how customary it was in treating the Gunpowder Plot; but if such examination is useful in restoring Milton's epigrams to their proper milieu, it does little to augment their appeal. [ERG]

HAAK, THEODORE (1605–1690), a German living in England during the 1640s; he became a naturalized citizen in the mid-1650s. As a friend of Samuel Hartlib*, he also met Milton and related to Hartlib during 1648 (see Hartlib's diary, *Ephemerides*) that "Milton is not only writing a Vniv. History of Engl. but also an Epitome of all Purchas Volumes." On this basis *Brit* and *Mosc* can be dated at least in part in 1648, although the latter seems already to have been completed. Haak, interested in education

as were Hartlib and Milton, was the founder of the Invisible College of Natural Philosophers, which served as one of the nuclei for the Royal Society after the Restoration. He was, of course, a Fellow of the Royal Society.

On June 26, 1650, the Council of State* ordered the "Declaration of the Causes of War with the Scots" translated into Latin by Milton (later assigned to Thomas May*) and into Dutch by Haak. On August 17, 1650, he was paid £50 for services in foreign areas, that is, by procuring intelligence of continental activities through correspondence. On November 8, 1652, he received £200 for translating a Dutch book into English. In all, Haak must have had numerous contacts with Milton through friends, through mutual interests, and through similar governmental service.

Sometime after the appearance of the first edition of *PL,* Haak translated into German verse Books 1–3 and the beginning of Book 4. Entitled "Das Verlustigte Paradeiss auss und nach dem Englischen I. M. durch T. H. zu übersetzen angefrangen—voluisse sat," the manuscript was discovered by Johannes Bolte in 1887 in the Landesbibliothek in Kassel (now the Murhard'sche Bibliothek der Stadt Kassel). It is catalogued MS Poet. 4° 2, being a holograph quarto of 56 pp. It was first printed by Pamela R. Barnett in *Theodore Haak, F. R. S. (1650–1690). The First German Translator of* Paradise Lost. ('S-Gravenhage : Mouton and Co., 1962), in Appendix 3, pp. 189–260. The date of the translation is uncertain, though it has been given as ca. 1667–ca. 1680. Since Haak used the first edition, it is more likely that the translation was made earlier in this period. Aubrey*, his "Minutes of Lives" dating around 1680–1681, notes the translation of "half" of the poem into "high Dutch" and the praise of Johann Fabricius, a well-known professor at Heidelberg. This information seems to have come directly from Haak. Apparently the translation was sent or taken to the Continent, remaining there in its incomplete state without Haak's returning to his project. Although he used the second edition of *PL*, Ernest Gottlieb von Berge, who translated the complete epic into German verse (Zerbst, 1682), knew Haak's translation and was influenced by it.

Haak, who continued to live in England, was buried on May 8, 1690, at St. Andrew's, Holborn. [JTS]

HAEMONY. Milton used the term *haemony* in *Mask* (629–41) for "a small unsightly root . . . of divine effect" whose magical and allegorical* properties have been interpreted by critics in various complementary or conflicting ways. Nineteenth-century editors popularized a geographic explanation of the word; it was derived, they asserted, from "Haemonia or Thessaly, the land of magic" where Medea practiced her subtle arts. Spenser*, they noted, had depicted "the grassie bancks of Haemony" as a region of magic plants (*Astrophel* 1. 3); in addition, Milton himself had used the term "Haemonio . . . succo" in *El* 2 (7–8). It was agreed, therefore, that "nothing could be more logical than 'Haemony' for a magic plant." Coleridge*, with a poet's allusiveness, suggested that Milton's term was derived from the Greek compound for "blood-wine," and that Milton meant his plant to signify "redemption by the Cross." Both of these ideas have survived in contemporary criticism. However, twentieth-century critics of Milton's masque have approached the problem of the meaning of haemony in more erudite and philosophical modes. Not only have they compared the differences and similarities between haemony and the classical and Renaissance forms of moly, but they have been concerned with the etymological derivations of Milton's term as well as with the aesthetic problems that the symbolic and allegoric meanings of the magic plant present within the context of structure and theme in *Mask*.

Additional explanations of haemony drawn from geographic place-names include Arcadia, which is explained as a synonym for Haemonia; Thrace, which offers an association with the Thracian physician in Plato's *Charmides*; Mount Haemus, which provides a close verbal link; Ephesus (with its worship of the chaste Diana), which offers a possible thematic link; and the River Haemon itself.

Of the possible etymologies that recent scholarship in Milton studies has produced, the following have received serious consideration. 1) The Greek adjective *haimon* (skillful), used by Homer* to describe Scamandrios (the hunter whom Artemis had trained), has several connotations that Renaissance lexicographers employed to define it: *wise, prudent, experienced*. In such dictionaries, available to Milton, *haimon* was also listed as a variant of *daimon*, thus suggesting *learning* and *knowing* as possible meanings of the word. In *Mask* haemony's effects are given in terms of knowledge and especially of divine knowledge, which is brought by a celestial messenger who remarks of the herb: ". . . by this means I knew the foul inchanter though disguis'd." Haemony gives the two brothers protection from Comus's magic dust, which has trapped the Lady with "blear illusion" and "false presentments." This etymological explanation of Milton's term provides a clue to both the literal and the allegorical meanings of the magic plant.

2) The Hebrew root-word, *aman*, and its variant forms, *amon, emet, emouna*, mean *knowledge, skill, belief, truth*, which parallel the multiple meanings of the Greek *daimon*. It has been suggested that Milton saw the far-ranging theological ramifications that the Hebrew word lent to the Greek term and that he consciously reinforced the connections between *daimon* and *aman* by creating haemony, which draws upon both languages for connotations.

3) Derivatives of the Greek word for blood (*aima*) have been the basis for twentieth-century speculations. The origin of moly was associated with blood at an early date when Eustathius related the myth of the giant Pikolous, who assaulted

Circe and was slain by Zeus. From the blood-soaked ground moly was said to have sprung. Because of the analogy and the fact that blood is a symbolic element in many religions and is usually associated with sacrifice and charity*, it has been suggested that Milton's haemony, in its Christian context, alludes to Christ's blood and is a symbol for the "grace given to those who are virtuous."

4) The Greek word for thorn tree, *hramnos,* has been suggested as a possible source for haemony. "Christ's thorn," or the rhamnus tree, was believed by many to have been the plant from which Christ's crown of thorns was made. It had "pricklie branches" and "floures . . . of a yellow colour." In Fletcher's* *The Faithful Shepherdess,* a play that apparently influenced *Mask,* Clorin sorts her simples, among which are rhamnus branches that "kill all enchantments, charms."

Some critics have insisted that haemony is only a magic herb without allegorical or symbolic meaning and that the "magical instruments of the masque are mere conveniences of the will." This view discounts in *Mask* the constituent parts of the Renaissance romance that contain overt elements of moral allegory. Critics who have worked with the medieval literary habit of amalgamating Christian values with classical myths have pointed to the standardized interpretations of Homer's moly not only as "temperance" but also as *paideia* (education) and Hermes, who gave the plant to Odysseus, as *logos.* The allegorical lesson depicted in the physical appearance of the black and white moly was commonplace: "Education, beginning with the black root of ignorance, culminates after many trials in the milk-white flower of radiant knowledge." This ages-old habit of applying moral allegory to literary texts, in this particular instance, had a basis in fact. Experts from Galen and Pliny to the Renaissance herbalists, Lyte and Gerard, identified moly with rue and listed among the many benefits of the plant both the capability of warding off

evil spirits, and of conferring a psychological and spiritual insight (cf. Michael's use of rue to remove the film from Adam's eyes, *PL* 11. 414). Heraclitus's pronouncement upon moly was famous: the plant produced *phronesis* (insight illuminated by reason*). This medical background with its attendant moral allegory is important for an understanding of Milton's haemony. The analogy strengthens the reading of Milton's herb as a symbolic plant denoting a higher form of knowledge.

Other suggestions concerning the meaning of haemony have accrued. One writer has called it a symbol of "the Platonic doctrine of virtue." Some see in haemony a symbol for an esoteric kind of philosophical knowledge that Ficino's system of Neoplatonism* cultured. Others insist that haemony offers something beyond philosophical aid because it brings a supraphilosophical assistance to the brothers. Hence, "abused and neglected Faith*" has been suggested as Milton's intended meaning; and another critic has labeled haemony "indeed, nothing else but Grace*." It has been suggested that the herb stands for a "spiritual understanding" that "rises above reason." And one critic has compared the meaning of the plant with perfected heavenly knowledge, which transcends the limited intelligence of earthly existence.

An equally broad range of suggestions has been offered concerning the interpretation of the other "Countrey" where haemony "Bore a bright golden flowre." Southern Europe where civilizations have flourished has been proposed. Circe's Isle is another possible locale. Dante's* Paradiso, the setting for the famed golden flower of the Beatific Vision, has been put forward, as has the Christianized Jove's Court of the masque. In addition, critics have sought to identify the shepherd lad who would "ope his leather'n scrip" and who gave the magic plant to Thyrsis. Among the candidates are Charles Diodati*, Milton's close associate at Cambridge, who studied medicine; Nathaniel Weld; Milton himself; and the Apostle Paul.

The student working with the interpretations of Milton's haemony should remember that the effects of the magic plant are limited. Haemony does not resolve the nodus of the plot. It provides protection for the brothers against Comus's magic charms, but it does not afford them success in their mission to destroy the magician or to free the Lady from his power. Comus, disquietingly, is left free, while Sabrina's powerful lustration is required to liberate the enchanted girl. [ALS]

HAKEWILL, GEORGE (1578–1649), an Anglican clergyman. He was principally important in the seventeenth century an an exponent of the belief in progress and as a voice in the controversy of the ancients versus the moderns. His major work, *An Apologie of the Power and Providence of God in the Government of the World* (1627, enlarged eds. 1630 and 1635), denies the opinion "of the Worlds decay . . . so generally received, not onely among the Vulgar, but of the Learned both Divines and others," which had been summed up in Godfrey Goodman's *The Fall of Man, or the Corruption of Nature, Proved by the Light of Our Naturall Reason* (1616). Goodman argued that since Adam's Fall both man and nature had been in perpetual corruption and decay: "me thinkes whatsoever I see, whatsoever I heare, all things seeme to sound corruption." Hakewill asserts faith in God's providence* in arguing that the doctrine of degeneration dishonors the majesty of God and hinders the commendable endeavors of men. Change that appears to be for the worse is explained through a theory of compensation in which loss in one part of the universe is matched by gain in another, and by the assumption that all change is cyclical: "There is (it seems) both in *wits* and *Arts*, as in all things besides, a kind of *circular progresse*: they have their *birth*, their *growth*, their *flourishing*, their *failing*, their *fading*, and within a while after their *resurrection*, and *reflourishing* again." Hakewill's massive study fed the arguments of those who argued for and against providential, or Baconian*, ideas of progress for over a century. His influence was sufficient for Boswell to mention him as one of the great authors who helped in forming Dr. Johnson's* style.

Since the early nineteenth century, Hakewill's *Apologie* has been seen as inspiring the philosophical disputation for which Milton wrote *Naturam*. This has also been denied, although there would seem to be neither positive nor negative evidence for either assertion. Milton shared Hakewill's optimism about the meaning of the Reformation, the providential influence of God over human history, and his belief in the undiminished nature of contemporary man. In his understanding of progress, he was closer to Hakewill than to Bacon; but whether his ideas in these or any other areas were advanced or confirmed by reading Hakewill is not known. [FM]

HALES, JOHN W(ESLEY) (1836–1914), editor, was educated at Christ's College*, Cambridge, and then held a variety of academic appointments including Trinity College, Cambridge, and King's College, London. In addition to various essays upon literary subjects, the Globe edition of the *Faerie Queene,* and general overseeing of Bell's handbooks of English literature, he edited *Areop* (1866, rev. 1882) in the standard form that it was to receive until the work of Hughes* and Sirluck. He also published several shorter essays on Milton, including discussions of his plans for a play on the subject of Macbeth (in the *TM*) and an analysis of his relationships with Christ's College. [WBH]

HALL, JOHN: *see* ASSOCIATES, PERSONAL.

HALL, JOSEPH (1574–1656), Bishop of Exeter and Norwich. Educated at Emmanuel College, Cambridge, Hall remained essentially a Calvinist* in doctrine and a Low Church Anglican. He was a Senecan in prose style, contributing the first collection of English Theophrastan *Characters of Vertues and Vices* (1608) as well as significant work in other genres. "He was commonly called our English Seneca for the pureness, plainness and fulness of his style; not unhappy at controversies, more happy at comments, very good in his characters, better in his sermons, best of all in his meditations" (Thomas Fuller, *Worthies* [1662], p. 320). His patron, Sir Robert Drury, introduced him to King James*, who in 1618 made him Dean of Worcester and envoy to the Synod of Dort.

Hall was an impressive preacher and popular writer of devotional literature. He expected advancement. With the accession of Charles I* and the supremacy of Archbishop Laud*, Hall's prospects were less assured, since Laud was sensitive to his Low Church leanings. Nevertheless, Laud recommended Hall for the bishopric of Exeter. Eager to win approval, Hall carried out all orders in his diocese and passed the inspection of Laud's spies. He earned the complete confidence of Laud and Charles in 1639 when he launched an attack upon the Edinburgh Assembly, which had urged abolition of episcopacy. Hall went so far as to embrace Laud's extreme view that the Reformed churches of Europe are not part of the true Church : "no Bishop, no Church." Hall published *Episcopacie by Divine Right* in 1640, each paragraph bearing Laud's silent imprimatur. Milton alludes to this "Popish" book by "one of our own *Prelats*" in *Ref* (1641).

In January 1641, Hall published a pamphlet called *An Humble Remonstrance to the High Court of Parliament by a Dutiful Son of the Church* exhorting Parliament not to approve the Root and Branch Petition. This petition, signed by numerous Londoners on December 11, 1640, called for abolition of episcopacy "roots and branches." In July 1641, Hall and twelve other bishops were impeached for treason, convicted of *praemunire*,

their estates forfeited. In November Hall became Bishop of Norwich, but in December he was committed to the Tower. His humiliations at this time are recounted in *Hard Measure* (1647). He died in 1656 at age 82.

Hall's *Humble Remonstrance* provoked an exchange of pamphlets with five Presbyterians collectively called "Smectymnuus*." Milton entered the fray in July 1641, with *Animad*. His unexpected, virulent attack upon prelaty and Hall elicited the anonymous *A Modest Confutation of a Slanderous and Scurrilous Libell, Entitled, Animadversions* (March 1642), to which Milton replied sharply in *Apol* (April 1642).

Animad was not essentially a personal attack upon Hall. Like Archbishop Ussher*, Hall was a prominent prelate, a Goliath. Milton joined his Presbyterian* friends in their campaign to persuade Parliament to abolish "a long usurpation and convicted Pseudepiscopy of Prelates, with all their ceremonies, Liturgies, and tyrannies which God and man are now ready to explode and hisse out of the land" (3 : 105–6). Milton attacks what Hall stands for—avarice, ignorance, vested interests—and assails the bishops' claim of antiquity and patristic sanction. In *Apol* Milton answers the Confuter's vindictive charges against his personal morality (bordellos, playhouses, a "rich Widow"), taking occasion to describe his youth spent in studies, his chastity*, his devotion to liberty. He turns a battery of vituperation upon Hall and that "lozel Bachelour of Art" the Confuter, "if they be not both one person, or as I am told, Father and Son" (3. 312). Which one, if any, of Hall's six sons this Confuter could be is a matter for conjecture.

Milton scores effectively against Hall in both pamphlets by exposing and pillorying two anonymous literary efforts of the venerable Bishop's youth, *Virgidemiarum . . . Toothlesse Satyrs* (1597, 1598) and *Mundus alter & idem* (1605), translated by John Healey as *The Discovery of a New World* (1609, 1614). The ineptitudes of the Toothless Satires are held up to scorn, and the imaginary voyage of "this petty prevaricator of *America,* the zanie of *Columbus,*" is shamed by mention of Plato*, More, and Bacon*.

Because Milton, the unexpected David, came into the controversy, the affair of Smectymnuus added to the discomfiture of the sequestered bishop. There is no question of good manners or charity in such disputes. Despite their differences, Audrey Chew suggests, Hall and Milton would agree on many points of ethics* and personal conduct. [TLH]

HAMILTON, NEWBURGH: *see* ADAPTATIONS.

HAMMERSMITH. During the seventeenth century Hammersmith was a small hamlet in Middlesex lying about six or so miles west of St. Paul's. Today it is a part of Greater London. It was a suburban residential area increasing in population as the residents of the old City of London pushed outward first to the area of Leicester's Fields (Westminster) sometime before 1630 and then to Fulham, Kensington, and Hammersmith sometime after 1630. While John Milton, Senior, maintained his home and business on Bread Street during the 1630s, he may have moved to some suburban area before 1632; and by September 1632, he was living in Hammersmith. A deposition of September 19–26, 1631, places him in Bread Street, perhaps referring only to his business, although it says that he lives there, and he seems to have retired from active business soon after this date. Four legal documents dated September 14, 1632; April 17, 1634; August 5, 1634; and January 8, 1635, place him in Hammersmith. It was therefore to this house that Milton returned from Cambridge with graduate work behind him, and it was here that his "studious retirement*" began. His letter to Alexander Gill, Jr.*, of December 4, 1634, is addressed "from our suburban residence." When and why the Miltons moved to Horton*, Bucks, is uncertain, but the move may have occurred in 1635 (and by 1637) and may

have resulted from the development of Hammersmith and environs. Perhaps the plague in London in 1636 was significant in the decision. [JTS]

HAMMOND, HENRY (1605–1660), divine. A graduate of Magdalen College, Oxford, Hammond was ordained in 1629, obtained the living at Penshurst, Kent, in 1633, and became Archbishop of Chichester in 1643. In this latter year he was chosen to sit in the Westminster Assembly*, but he never attended. A Royalist, he became one of the royal chaplains in 1645, and it was through assistance furnished by his nephew, Colonel Robert Hammond, governor of the Isle of Wight, that Charles* fled Hampton Court for Carisbrooke Castle on November 12, 1647. Hammond, canon (1645) and then sub-dean (1647) of Christ Church, Oxford, was imprisoned briefly when he would not submit to the Parliamentarian army. He removed to the home of Sir Philip Warwick in Clapham, Bedfordshire, through his brother-in-law Sir John Temple (father of the important statesman Sir William Temple), where he engaged in literary work. He moved to Westwood in Worcestershire in 1649 or early 1650, where he died. His biography was written in 1661 by John Fell (1625–1686), Bishop of Oxford; the life contains a probable allusion to Milton as a divorcer on pp. 67–68.

Hammond's most important works, which Milton probably was well acquainted with, are *Practical Catechism* (1644), A Vindication of *Dr. Hammond's Address,* &c., From the Exceptions of Eutactus Philodemus [i.e., Anthony Ascham*], *Humble Address to the Lord Fairfax and the Council of War, 15 January, 1648, to prevent the King's Murder* (1649), *&c. together with a brief Reply to Mr. John Goodwin's "Obstructors of Justice,"* as far as concerns *Dr. Hammond* (1649), and *Paraphrases and Annotations on the New Testament* (1653). He assisted Brian Walton* in his Polyglot Bible in 1657; Milton's efforts on Walton's behalf may have brought him into direct contact with Hammond. A few years earlier in 1653 Hammond had cited *DDD* (p. 122) and had given a general answer to Milton's arguments for divorce (pp. 123–27) in *A Letter of Resolution to Six Quaeres, of Present Use in the Church of England*. This was reprinted in *The Workes* (1674); the discussion is found in 1 : 457ff. A letter by Hammond, dated February 12, 1649, in Ballard MS 1.75 in the Bodleian comments skeptically upon the alleged authorship of *Eikon Basilike**, which had just appeared. [JTS]

HANDEL, GEORG FREDERICK: *see* ADAPTATIONS.

HANDWRITING, MILTON'S. Like others', Milton's handwriting underwent change during the period for which we have evidence, 1623–1663. Early the hand is smaller and more angular, often employing scribal formations for "c," "d," "e," and "r." At other times, "c," "d," and "r" have the more usual formations, and "e" is like a Greek epsilon. The scribal forms generally drop out of use before the time *TM* and *CB* were begun, sometime in the 1630s. These two manuscripts also show that the hand began to vacillate between smaller and larger writing at this time. The most significant change in Milton's handwriting, however, occurred around the time he was writing *Lyc*, November 1637. The hand becomes cursive, looser, "Italian," and it employs an Italian "e" (similar to a type "e"). The "e" in the manuscript of *Lyc* is Greek except in alterations made after the basic transcription : "whome," line 60 (p. 31), and "selfe," line 58 (p. 30), both examples. This evidence suggests that the change was starting around this time and that other materials might be dated, at least generally, on the appearance or extent of appearance of Italian "e" in Milton's script. The dates of entries in *CB*, dated by various and different means, are in agreement with the general principle that can be deduced : holograph showing only Greek "e" is datable up to around the end

of 1637, that showing mixed forms is datable around the end of 1637 and 1638, and that showing the Italian "e," from around 1639 on. Thus it is particularly curious to note that there are two examples of the Italian "e" in a stage direction near the end of the basic transcription of *Mask* in *TM* : "scene" (second "e") and "towne," between lines 957–58. The so-called pasted leaf of *Mask* on which Milton worked out lines 672–706 after having transcribed the earlier form of the poem shows eight Italian "e's." This evidence lends credence to the argument that *Mask* as we know it was worked out in 1637–38 and that its first publication dated 1637 may be old style and should thus be 1638 by modern reckoning.

The first draft in *TM* of what became *PL* (p. 35), seems to have been the first thing entered after Milton returned from the Continent : all "e's" are Italian. Dating of entries in *CB* corroborates the principle implied. It should be noted, however, that the manuscripts of *Sonn* 13, written February 9, 1646, show a Greek "e" in "exempts" (second "e," line 5, draft one, and first "e," line 5, draft two). [JTS]

HANFORD, JAMES HOLLY (1882–1971), educated at the University of Rochester and at Harvard, who inaugurated modern American studies of Milton with a series of yet-standard articles dating from the first decade of this century that establish with scholarly authority such issues as biographical* details, the chronology* of Milton's reading, and the temptation* motive in his writings. His best-known work is the *Milton Handbook*, a vademecum for generations of students since its first publication in 1926. His professional career was most closely associated with Western Reserve University, where he taught from 1928 to 1949. In his later years he was consultant to the Princeton University Library, and in 1957 he served as President of the Modern Language Association. In 1948 the Milton Society of America* named him its first honored scholar. [WBH]

HARAPHA. The "Tongue-doughty Giant" (his name is accented on the first syllable) is an intruder in the Samson story. There is no reference to him in the Book of Judges, and the allusions to him in Scripture suggest that Haraphah (literally *ha raphah,* "the giant*") was not a personal name. Though the Geneva Version refers to his giant brood as sons of Haraphah, the glosses on 2 Samuel 21 : 16 and 1 Chronicles 20 : 4 explain this phrase as "the race of Gyants," and as the "Rephaim" or "the gyants." The Authorized Version, in turn, omits Haraphah's name in both accounts, substituting the literal translation : "the giant." As Milton was well aware, this appellation may not be the Philistine's original name; and he possibly retains the note of ambiguity in the giant's self-introduction : "Men call me *Harapha.* . . ."

The allusions to Gath and to Harapha's "five Sons / All of Gigantic size, *Goliah* chief," serve as authenticating details, identifying him specifically with the giant of Samuel and Chronicles. Milton follows the former account (which describes the death of *four* giants at the hands of David's mighty men) rather than the latter (which mentions only three). These accounts of Harapha and his son stress their gigantic stature and the weight of their armaments. Like the giants in medieval and Renaissance romance and in classical myth*, the giants of Scripture served as whipping-boys for heroic virtue and / or divine wrath. Tyrannical and boastful, proud of their own brute strength and glorying in acts of violence, they usually invited destruction either at the hands of divinely chosen warriors or by the immediate acts of God. The first race of giants had perished in the flood. Later breeds had similarly been destroyed by the will of God. When Harapha compares his "stock renown'd" to the fame of "*Og* or *Anak* and the *Emims* old / That *Kiriathaim* held," the allusion con-

tains ominous and unconsciously ironic overtones. He is alluding to peoples who had been defeated and destroyed long before by the Israelites or their neighbors in conformity with a providential design. As Milton's readers were well aware, the giant races of the Bible were doomed to destruction, and their lands would be given to other peoples, the chosen of the Lord.

Harapha's character, his literary antecedents, his relation to the social and religious conflicts of seventeenth-century England and to Milton's polemical career, and his dramatic function in the development of the action and the evolution of Samson's character—these have been, and still are, centers of dispute. He has been characterized alternatively as a cowardly braggart and as a "good fighting man." He has been compared with figures in Euripidean tragedy, in classical and Renaissance comedy, in medieval and Renaissance romance, and with other biblical giants, most notably his own son Goliath. He has been regarded as a type of the Cavalier—a Philistine prototype of the royalists and episcopalians who supported the Stuarts—and as an image of Milton's adversary Salmasius*. The scene in which he appears has been explained as comic relief or as a dramatic crisis of intense moral intensity, as an episode that has no ostensible bearing on the outcome of the drama or that directly hastens the catastrophe.

As early as 1914, Allan Gilbert recognized the influence of the romances on the dialogue between Samson and Harapha, characterizing the Philistine giant as "a boastful knight, own brother to Spenser's* Braggadocchio"; see *Modern Language Notes* 19 : 161. Daniel C. Boughner stressed the analogy with the cowardly braggarts of Renaissance comedy and the possible influence of Renaissance conceptions of honor. Though some of Harapha's boasts resemble the "traditional brags of the Latin *miles gloriosus,*" very different "and also very modern is Harapha's emphasis on his 'honours,' which he has won by 'mortal duel,' his knightly disdain for Samson's feats of strength and unchivalric equipment . . ." (*ELH, A Journal of English Literary History* 11 : 297–306). William Riley Parker, on the other hand, argues that "Harapha had some Euripidean blood in his veins"; see *Times Literary Supplement*, 2 January, 1937, p. 12. "Harapha is a bully and a coward—and little else. He is wholly dependent on physical force : what Samson might have been without 'Heroic magnitude of mind.'" Most of the blusterers in Sophocles' dramas possess "some slightly redeeming features," but there are "possible prototypes" in the tragedies of Aeschylus and Euripides. The "masking of cowardice with rhetoric is a trick of characterization which we associate with Euripides alone"; see Parker's *Milton's Debt to Greek Tragedy in Samson Agonistes* (1969), pp. 122–24.

Commentators have also adduced biblical analogues. Waggoner has compared Milton's challenge scene with the challenge in 1 Samuel 17, where Goliath's defiance of the host of Israel is answered by David. Other parallels between these episodes have been noted by J. M. Steadman, *Milton Studies in Honor of Harris Francis Fletcher* (1961), pp. 178–87. Like Samson, David despises the gorgeous arms of his adversary. Like Samson and Harapha, David and Goliath exchange insults, each threatening to give the other's body to the fowls of heaven and the beasts of the field. The benediction with which Saul sends David into battle against the Philistine giant parallels the blessing that the Danites bestow on Samson as he leaves for the Philistine theater : "Goe and the Lord be with thee."

The glosses on this chapter in the Geneva Bible stress David's faith and his zeal for God's honor, the inward notions of God's Spirit, and the directing agency of divine Providence* in arranging this occasion for a Hebrew victory over the Philistines. They offer parallels not only to the glosses on the Samson story but also to some of the principal themes of Milton's play. Though Milton's Samson

is a fallen hero near the end of his career, and David an apprentice-hero on the threshold of his first great victory, both are heroes of the faith, trusting in God's aid and zealous for His honor; in both instances the hero's fidelity and zeal are tested and exercised through direct confrontation with a Philistine giant, the champion of an idolatrous faith and of rival gods. (See George W. Whiting, *Rice Institute Pamphlet* 38 : 16–35). There are, however, notable differences, of course, in addition to the obvious constrast between a famous, though fallen, Nazarite and an obscure shepherd lad.

The portrait of Harapha may also reflect the influence of other biblical (and classical) allusions to giants. The Chorus's allusion to "the mighty of the Earth" may contain a pun on the etymology of the word *giant*. According to classical myth, the giants were earth-born; and it may be significant that Milton's giant emphasizes his ties with the soil of his country ("So had the glory of Prowess been recover'd / To *Palestine*, won by a *Philistine*"). The term *rephaim* (giants) was, in fact, merely one of several terms applied to the Old Testament giants. The ancient giants of the Near East included Anakim, Emim, Zamzummim, Nephilim, and others; and medieval and Renaissance exegetes had stressed their violent and oppressive character. Nimrod was regarded as a tyrannical giant; and the Geneva Bible glosses the antediluvian giants of Genesis 6 : 4 ("giants in the earth . . . mightie men, which in old time were men of renowne") as "tyrants." Renaissance commentators stressed the tyranny of the ancient giants, their pride in their own strength, their desire for fame and vain titles, their devastation and rapine, their contempt of God and man; in *PL* Milton invests the antediluvian giants with many of these characteristics. Calvin* regarded them as the world's first nobility—a nobility that exalted itself "only through despite and contumely of others."

Though Harapha compares himself to the postdiluvian giants of Deuteronomy, his preoccupation with renown and glory link him with the "men of renown" of Genesis; and the words of the Chorus immediately after his departure recall the image that Renaissance theologians had formed of the biblical giants and that Milton retains in *PL* :

The brute and boist'rous force of violent men
Hardy and industrious to support
Tyrannic power, but raging to pursue
. . . the mighty of the Earth, th'oppressour,
The righteous and all such as honour
    Truth. . . .

                    (*SA* 1272–76)

Apparently Harapha exhibits some of the features of an earlier generation of giants as well as certain characteristics of the next generation—the giants of his own begetting. He is a man of noble and renowned stock—a "gentleman" in the literal Renaissance sense of this term. Nevertheless, like the antediluvian giants (the world's first nobility) and like many of the English gentry and nobility of Milton's generation, he is also a persecutor of the just and an adversary of truth. Harapha displays something of the traditional *ethos* of the world's first heroic age, and indeed of other and later heroic ages. Against the background of classical myth and biblical exegesis, it is ironical that the giant should brand the Hebrew champion as "A Murderer, a Revolter, and a Robber"—vices commonly ascribed to the biblical and classical giants and indeed to the epic* heroes of antiquity.

Several critics have detected allusions to seventeenth-century English history in the Harapha scene. David Masson, E. H. Visiak, C. E. Kreipe, and others have recognized in the Philistine giant the image of Milton's redoubtable adversary Claudius Salmasius, and in the blind Hebrew champion a figure of Milton himself. Nevertheless, such a statement is pure surmise. Though there may be some historical overtones in this scene, Merritt Hughes observes that it is "most impressive if Harapha is regarded

as the embodiment of classes and attitudes to which we usually give the name 'Cavalier' "; see his edition of the *Complete Poems and Major Prose* (1957), pp. 535–36. But W. R. Parker has justly protested against the "autobiographical fallacy" that equates Milton with Samson, Dalila with Mary Powell, and Harapha with Salmasius; see *Philological Quarterly* 28 : 145–66, an argument that Parker frequently repeated. The historical significance of Harapha depends in part on the larger question of the autobiographical* element in Milton's drama and the problem of its date.

Like the literary and historical origins of Milton's giant, his character and his dramatical significance have been controversial. For A. W. Verity, Harapha is "a type of blustering cowardice beside which the courage of Samson becomes the more conspicuous." The formula that best expresses his nature is "bulk without spirit"; see *John Milton's Samson Agonistes,* ed. Ralph E. Hone (1966), p. 150. Hanford describes him as a "boaster" (*John Milton, Englishman* [1950], p. 256), just as Marjorie Nicolson regards him as "a taunting braggart prizefighter, who has come to gloat over a fallen champion," a *"miles gloriosus,* a boasting braggart," who "wishes only to taunt a fallen foe," suggesting "that Samson had done what he did not by his own strength, but by black magic" (*John Milton, A Reader's Guide to His Poetry* [1963], pp. 367–69). George M. Muldrow adds that Harapha reveals himself as "a blusterer and coward" and may "have something in common with the braggart warriors of literature." Nevertheless the giant does not "serve as comic relief"; to "see him as comic is to make Milton commit the 'Poet's error of intermixing Comic stuff with Tragic sadness and gravity.' " Muldrow further observes that "Milton has described Harapha's type before, and he is never comic" (*Milton and the Drama of the Soul* [1970], pp. 201–9). Don Cameron Allen, arguing against Boughner's interpretation of Harapha as the *miles gloriosus* of comedy, maintains that the giant is sincere, that his first speech is "that of a genuinely valorous man." He is not a "coward or a blusterer from the moment of his entrance"; if "we admit his sincerity . . . we can watch the degeneration of Harapha's courage. Before our eyes a brave and knightly man will change into a coward and a blusterer." In Allen's opinion, this "amazing alteration in character" is "brought about by Samson's growing confidence in Jehovah and Harapha's intimation of the supernatural power apparent in Samson"; and it "tells us more than even the verse implies of God's impending triumph" (*The Harmonious Vision*, Enlarged ed. [1970], pp. 91–94). J. B. Broadbent, on the other hand, regards Harapha as "the gigantic bully of fairy-tale and school-yarn—a cowardly braggart"—who, "for the first time in the play, makes objective and so heals Samson's internal despair," evoking from Samson "his first expression of hope" (*Comus and Samson Agonistes* [1961], pp. 52–53).

Several critics have examined the imagery and typology of the Harapha episode. Whereas Hanford, Krouse, Woodhouse, and other scholars have denied that Milton's Samson is a type of Christ, W. G. Madsen argues that there are "implicit foreshadowings of Christ in Milton's Samson" and that it is "essential to the whole doctrine of typology that the type be different from as well as similar to the antitype." The scene with Harapha underlines "Samson's inability to rise to Christ's contempt for 'ostentation vain of fleshly arm' "; and "whether or not we regard Harapha's visit as a temptation, it is clear that Samson's response is seriously flawed." However admirable his trust in God and his acknowledgment of God's justice, "less admirable, at best, is his eagerness to engage Harapha in single combat, his pathetic belief that by clubbing Harapha to death he will demonstrate the glory of God. The language of the chivalric combat used by both Samson and Harapha places this encounter at a vast moral distance from the 'great duel, not of arms' in which Christ engages the Father of all the giants of the earth" (*From Shadowy Types to Truth* [1968], pp. 187–92).

L. S. Cox calls attention to the imagery of storm in both the Dalila and Harapha episodes and in the final scene. The storm imagery of the poet "reiterates the emphasis on the condition of strife which is man's native habitat, but which at the same time defines divergent or disparate conditions. Samson, a man on the way to regeneration, exhibits the stormy working of the elements; but the unregenerate Harapha is a tempest, too, albeit 'another kind of tempest.' " Samson, Dalila, and Harapha are also "pictured as ships or as possessors of something described in ship imagery" (*Critical Essays on Milton from ELH*, pp. 257–65). Waddington stresses the medical imagery in the play, noting that Harapha's "very name possibly suggests" the medicine that will alleviate Samson's apparently remediless condition (*Calm of Mind*, p. 277).

Like the "great-souled" heroes of classical epic and the Aristotelian* *megalopsychos* or "magnanimous man," Harapha is highly sensitive to personal honor and dishonor and painfully conscious of his own dignity. His allusions to conventional topics of the Renaissance code of honor reinforce the portrait of a secular magnanimity, which may seem heroic by worldly standards but is nevertheless specious and spurious in the light of Judeo-Christian *ethos*. For many Christian commentators the highest virtues of the Gentiles had been little more than "splendid vices," since they aimed at the personal glory of man rather than at the glory of God. In this scene Harapha is primarily concerned with his own honor rather than the honor of his deity. He is, in fact, proud rather than magnanimous; and the Chorus initially characterizes him in terms of a vice contrary to magnanimity—"pride, when a man values himself . . . more highly than his merits deserve" (*CD* 2. 9).

The moral oppositions in this scene, as well as its dramatic intensity, acquire greater force if the reader accepts D. C. Allen's thesis that Harapha is not initially "a coward or a blusterer" and that he is sincere. Courage is closely linked with confidence; and in the traditional matter of fortitude—death in battle—Samson's courage and Harapha's cowardice are intimately interwoven with their contrasting modes of faith: trust in God and carnal reliance. In replying to Harapha, Samson has converted the "mortal duel" —which the giant had seen as a trial of human strength (and perhaps there is an unconsciously ironic pun in the epithet *mortal*) into a theomachy, a monomachia between immortals.

Though he may not believe Samson's claims, Harapha is (if one follows Allen's interpretation) profoundly moved by them. Like Comus, sensing a superhuman and supernatural power, he experiences dread but dissembles and conceals his fear. Trusting in Jehovah for "invincible might" and "celestial vigor," Samson has routed one of the "mighty of the Earth," who trust in "Ammunition / And feats of War" and in "Armories and Magazines." Though the duel is abortive and he humiliates the giant by words rather than arms, the terms of his challenge and the opposition between true faith and vain trust in arms recall the essential features of his past triumphs—his exploits in the field where Harapha had longed to be present—and anticipate his role, as the ally and instrument of deity, in the catastrophe. Samson has begun to acquit himself like Samson again. In the challenge he reasserts his heroic identity as God's elected champion and Nazarite, humiliating the Philistine champion in terms reminiscent of his victory at Ramath-lechi. The scene is an exercise in spiritual warfare preparatory to his final act of deliverance—a dress rehearsal for his performance on the Philistine stage. *See also* Dramatists, Greek. [JMS]

HARDING, DAVIS P(HILON) (1914–1970), scholar, who after earning the doctorate at the University of Illinois was associated with Yale University from 1943 until his death. As a Milton scholar he produced two major works, *Milton and the Renaissance Ovid* (1946) and *The Club of Hercules: Studies in the Classical Background of Paradise Lost* (1962). Their basic research lies in documenting Milton's use of the classics, upon which they may have said the final word. [WBH]

HARDY AND MILTON. Although critics have pointed to details of Thomas Hardy's reading, to specific allusions to Milton's prose and poems, and to some of the inevitable similarities between *The Dynasts* and *PL,* there has been no comprehensive assessment of the precise nature and pervasive extent of Milton's influence upon Hardy. Frequently there are verbal reminiscences of some Miltonic diction*; in other contexts the allusions function to create a mood, invoke mythic* parallels to elevate or satirize Hardy's characters' actions, or supply moral and intellectual authority for some argument or traditional advocacy for some theme.

Although Milton's legacy is most serviceably invested in Hardy's poetry, his major fiction is likewise enriched when he draws upon Milton's example. Carl J. Weber, in *Hardy of Wessex* (1940), pp. 241–42, F. B. Pinion, in *A Hardy Companion* (1968), pp. 211–12, and Lennart A. Björk, in his edition of *The Literary Notes of Thomas Hardy* (1974), 1:351–52, provide long but incomplete lists of allusions in the fiction; however incomplete, they nevertheless reveal the earlier author's ubiquitousness in the later one's works. *Lyc* is quoted in four novels, including *Desperate Remedies* and *The Well-Beloved,* the first and the last to be published (in 1872 and 1897). *L'Al* and *IlP, Mask,* "On the Late Massacre in Piedmont," *DDD,* and *Areop* are other works from which Hardy quotes; to *SA* he less directly alludes. Sometimes he merely recalls a felicitous phrase, the "stocks and stones" from the Piedmont sonnet; or he may abstract a well-known axiom from *Areop* ("Almost as well kill a man as kill a good book") to express by analogy his moral indignation against the razing of ancient buildings (see F. E. Hardy, *The Life of Thomas Hardy* [1962], p. 352); or he may use a passage as the epigraph to set the theme and tone for a long section of a major novel, as in *Jude the Obscure* (1895), Part 4, where he quotes Milton's prefatory statement from *DDD*, condemning any man who prefers matrimony or any law before the good of man and the plain exigency of charity. As a final example, again taken from *Jude*, he may compare his innocent and honorable hero to a shorn Samson, a victim of a wily woman's cunning. These allusions, representative of many others of the same kinds, are found in Hardy's major novels, his short stories, his preface to *Select Poems of William Barnes* (1908), and his autobiographical *Life*, published posthumously in his second wife's name; the very range of these works and their span in time suggest how thoroughly Hardy absorbed and admired Milton's works, and how often he appropriated their resources for his art. Unlike Keats*, whose late disparaging remarks about the insidious influence of Milton upon his *Hyperion* poems have beclouded the true nature of his indebtedness, Hardy never mentions Milton except with sympathy and respect.

PL, of course, most frequently figures in Hardy's fiction. The epic is alluded to in no fewer than nine of the novels; again, the significance of the allusions may range from the relatively unimportant reminiscence of a phrase (the "darkness visible" in *Two on a Tower* [1882]) or a character ("Ithuriel's spear" in *The Return of the Native* [1878]) to the exceedingly meaningful evocation of a central theme and mood, as in Hardy's reference in the last sentences of *Tess of the D'Urbervilles* (1892) to the conclusion of *PL*, where Adam and Eve make their solitary way through Eden to seek their life in the world. Hardy effects many variations on Milton's temptation sequence : in an elaborate reworking of Milton's myth in *Tess*, Alec is the vicious

tempter of the novel's tragic heroine (see Alan Brick's "Paradise and Consciousness in Hardy's *Tess*," *Nineteenth Century Fiction* 17 [1962] : 115–34, for a full discussion of the novel's Miltonic elements); in *Far From the Madding Crowd* (1874), Farmer Oak spies on Bathsheba "in a bird's-eye view, as Milton's Satan first saw Paradise"; and, in a parodic[*] rendition of Eve's confession after the temptation, Hardy's Fancy Day lies to her future husband about her flirtation with a lecherous old Lucifer (Shiner is his name). The comic effect, so consistent with the tone in *Under the Greenwood Tree*, is reinforced by Dick's vacillation between desperate uxoriousness and equally desperate, though finally triumphant, penetration of Fancy's deceit and chastisement of her for it. This scene begins as an apple falls to disturb the silence just before Fancy confesses; and though Hardy's intention is clearly whimsical, the allusion to *PL*, however oblique and inverted, does not permit the reader to forget the seriousness of the implications of woman's vanity.

In numerous other passages, the influence of *PL* upon Hardy's fiction is felt. The calamitous murders and suicide by Little Father Time, in *Jude*, are attributed to the "rashness of his parents," a phrase that recalls *PL* 9.780. In the *Life*, p. 210, Hardy reports his attendance at a service at St. Mary Abbots, using a Miltonic allusion to describe the sounds he hears : "When the congregation rises there is a rustling of silks like that of the Devils' wings in Paradise Lost."

Before turning to the influence of *PL* upon *The Dynasts*, one may look briefly at the lyric and dramatic poems. Hardy's interest in *Lyc* has often been noted; and his *Veteris Vestigia Flammae* (published in *Satires of Circumstance* [1914]) has been associated with the great English elegies, including Milton's (see Kenneth Marsden's *The Poems of Thomas Hardy* [1969], p. 98). J. O. Bailey, in *The Poetry of Thomas Hardy: A Handbook and Commentary* (1970), pp. 134–37, 142, describes "At a Lunar Eclipse" as a

Miltonic sonnet and comments on the Miltonic elements in two other sonnets, "Lausanne: In Gibbon's Old Garden" and "Zermatt: To the Matterhorn." The latter is characterized by the Miltonic high seriousness of its sestet; while in the former, the last two lines state the theme by summarizing Milton's passage in *DDD* about the impossibility of soiling Truth, which never enters the world without casting ignomiy upon the one who brought her forth (3:370).

Bailey also notes Milton's use of "darkling" (*PL* 3.37–40) as one source for the famous poem "The Darkling Thrush." And he identifies an allusion to *PL* 9.925–26, in the moving "To Meet, or Otherwise." Hardy's "A Philosophical Fantasy" opens with a quotation, "Milton . . . made God argue," which sets the keynote in a poem that out-Miltons Milton (see Bailey, pp. 166, 268, 607–8). To Bailey's list may be added many other works in which Milton's presence may be discerned; at least two of these appear in Hardy's first volume of poetry, *Wessex Poems* (1898). On the third page of Hardy's *Collected Poems* (1925), there appears a very early sonnet called "In Vision I Roamed." Written in 1866 when Hardy was serving his apprenticeship to authors who would be his lifelong masters, the poem's style can be described as "Miltonic Keats-Shelley." His "Heiress and Architect" (*Collected Poems*, pp. 67–68) is a fanciful dialogue between a modern God the Father and Eve, the broad features of both characters being drawn with Miltonic allusions.

Though critical judgment is far from unanimous concerning the caliber of Hardy's achievement in *The Dynasts,* the scope of his undertaking has often been compared to Milton's heroic effort. It would be surprising if critics did *not* sense the affinities between these two great poetic works, particularly since Hardy so often asserts, however obliquely, his tutelage to his great English master. In the *Life,* p. 203, he makes some entries for 1887 that indicate his program of reading for the year and his struggle with the artistic challenges posed by his vast subject. At the top of his list of "Books read or pieces looked at this year" we find the name Milton, followed by other epic authors and epic poems. *Lyc* appears later in the list. Also, on the same page Hardy quotes from Addison* about Milton's observing Aristotle's* rule of lavishing the ornaments of diction on the weak, inactive parts of the fable. In the preface to *The Dynasts,* Hardy explicitly excludes "the celestial machinery of *Paradise Lost,* as peremptorily as that of the *Iliad* or the *Eddas";* but the reference reveals where Hardy took his schooling. Finally, in a letter defending the meliorism of his ending, Hardy writes to Edward Clodd on February 2, 1908: "Yes; I left off on a note of hope. It was just as well that the Pities should have the last word, since, like *Paradise Lost, The Dynasts* proves nothing."

In more recent years, as critics have been encouraged to analyze *The Dynasts,* they have been identifying more precisely the nature of some of the links between the two major English epics. Harold Orel (*Thomas Hardy's Epic-Drama: A Study of The Dynasts* [1963], pp. 67–85) has studied Hardy's major modifications of Milton's formal epic; he concludes that Hardy's necessary repudiation of the epic* tradition exemplified by *PL* amounts to an act of a major poet in a major poem, Hardy's own *magnum opus.* Walter F. Wright (*The Shaping of The Dynasts* [1967], pp. 16, 72, 74) examines Hardy's underlinings and marginal markings in his personal copies of Milton's works and notes the extensive influence of Milton's imagery*, unusual diction, and rhythms throughout *The Dynasts.* There are other specific parallels cited by Wright: the futility of the parliamentary debates of 1805 are compared to the fallen angels' discussion of philosophy; and the role of Hardy's conqueror is reminiscent of Satan's in *PL.* Frank R. Giordano, Jr., compares Hardy's Napoleon and Milton's Satan, arguing (in "The Degradation of Napoleon in *The Dynasts," Thomas Hardy Yearbook 1973–74,* pp. 54–64) that in his portrait of Napoleon Hardy was influenced by Milton's techniques of characterizing his villain. [FRG]

HARDYNG, JOHN (1378–1465?), chronicler. Milton's interest in military matters led him to paraphrase a reference to the office of knighthood in Arthur's Round Table in *CB* from the verse chronicle of John Hardyng. Milton read one of Richard Grafton's 1543 printings of the chronicle, not a particularly reliable source of Hardyng's thought since Hardyng recast his manuscript between 1457 and 1464 to suit his current patron's interests. Hardyng cannot be considered a serious historian of his age. Indeed, Sir Francis Palgrave proved as forgeries all the documents relating to Scottish-English feudal relations that Hardyng "collected" on royally subsidized trips to Scotland. [RMa]

HAREFIELD, MIDDLESEX, village four miles from Uxbridge. The Countess Dowager of Derby, Alice Spencer Egerton*, stepmother of the Earl of Bridgewater, lived at Harefield during 1601–1637. It is about ten miles from Horton* and sixteen miles from Ashridge, where the Egertons lived. *Arc,* an entertainment honoring the Countess, was presented out-of-doors on her estate, but for what occasion and on what date are unknown. Recently W. B. Hunter has suggested her seventy-fifth birthday (May 4, 1634) (*English Language Notes* 9 : 46–47). It is assumed that the entertainment was written before *Mask,* performed on September 29, 1634; it would have taken place when good weather was expected (spring or summer). Formerly, it was thought that Milton resided in Horton from 1632 through 1638, but his residence was in Hammersmith* until ca. 1635 and then in Horton. Either location had no influence upon Milton's writing the entertainment for the Countess, or the date may lie after *Mask* and the Miltons' remove to Horton. [JTS]

HARRINGTON, JAMES (1611–1677), political scientist, sometimes confused with his uncle, Sir James, a member of the Council of State*. Leaving Oxford without a degree, he traveled abroad but returned before the outbreak of the Civil War. Although he took no part in the fighting, he did become a member of Charles's* entourage for a while. He seems to have been something of a dilettante, trying his hand at poetry by translating part of Virgil*. His most important work is his *Oceana,* a utopian description of England's development into a republic based upon public elections and limitation of property holdings. Despite the presence of a prince and gentry, Harrington's system, in part an answer to Hobbes's* *Leviathan,* supports freedom and equality.

During the political turmoil following Cromwell's death he established a club, the Rota, which met at Miles's Coffee House. Through it he hoped to activate his political ideas. It gathered a good deal of interest during its brief existence from about November 1659 to the following February. Its name derives from the principle of rotation applied to the elected leaders projected for the state, a senate consisting of elected representatives serving up to three years apiece, a third of them to "rote out" every year so that by the end of nine years there would necessarily be an entirely new group.

The ideas of the Rota Club certainly influenced Milton's thinking at this time, as he was writing his *Proposals . . . for Preventing of a Civil War* and *Way.* In opposition to the principle of rotation, however, he opts strongly for a governing body possessing tenure for life. Perhaps as a result of his long experience in government and the near-anarchy of the times, he takes a dimmer view of popular representation than did Harrington.

Immediately answering *Way* was the anonymous *Censure of the Rota* upon it, a witty sixteen-page pamphlet supposedly taken from a discussion of Milton's book at a meeting of the Rota by "Trundle Wheeler, Clerk." Although ostensibly attributed to "J.H.," the author is not known, but his answer is a clever satire on the Rota's procedure of deciding everything by ballot and upon Milton's frantic attempt to block the return of the monarchy. [WBH]

HARTLIB, SAMUEL (ca. 1599–1662) owes his fame today largely to the fact that Milton addressed *Educ* to him. The dedication, however, actually expressed recognition of Hartlib's importance among the leading educational theorists of his age, for he was the honored associate of men like John Amos Comenius*, Sir William Petty, and other significant but less well known reformers of education. Born in Elblag, commonly called Elbing, Germany, he was the son of a Polish merchant and his British wife. He appears to have been educated at the University of Königsberg, where he was recorded as a matriculant in 1614. References in letters and documents to his being at Cambridge apparently indicate visits rather than academic residence. He was in England by 1628, but the circumstances of his going there are not of record. He was registered as a merchant though he was already acquainted with John Dury* and it is possible (Masson, *Life* 3 : 193) that he went actually as a proponent of the latter's plans for Protestant reunion and the reform of schools. On January 20, 1629, at St. Dionis Backchurch, London, he was married to Marie Burningham, a fact that suggests his intention to establish permanent residence. He was soon engaged in a broad correspondence with foreign scholars on such matters as aid to religious refugees, the education of the children of the gentry, the encouragement of agriculture and applied science, and the unification in doctrine and polity of all Protestants. Obviously Hartlib hoped, through his letter writing, to establish an international information bureau that would serve as an exchange for knowledge and theoretical investigation. The project never came to fruition, but Hartlib received positive support for Protestant unity from several Anglican

divines. He was even offered ordination in Holy Orders so that he might have a means of livelihood. Hartlib made himself poor by his benefactions and his support of projects. In a letter, dated June 30, 1635, Dury says that "endeavors of advancing the public good by way of schooling and education of children . . . were the first causes of his losses." The project nearest Hartlib's heart was "the education of children in the way of Christianity." He expresses his educational ideal as "erecting a little academy for the education of the gentry of this nation, to advance piety, learning, morality, and other exercises of industry, not usual in common schools." He attempted to embody his ideal in a small school at Chichester in the autumn of 1630. Though he gathered an excellent staff, the school lasted for only a year. Hartlib obviously was too engrossed in his numerous writings, his many nonpedagogical projects, and his associations with foreign scholars to give his school due attention. Outstanding among these associations was that with John Amos Comenius. It appears that Hartlib knew him before 1638, when Pym sought unsuccessfully to induce him to visit Britain, for he was a fellow student of Hartlib's brother at Heidelberg. It was not until 1641, however, that, largely through the inducement and the financial aid of Hartlib, he went to London, where his *Great Didactic* and his concept of Pansophia were known through Hartlib's writings. Parliament was not ready to consider educational reform when Comenius arrived on September 21, 1641, and he left for Sweden on June 20, 1642. Hartlib had high admiration for Comenius, especially for his ideas concerning the teaching of languages* and his emphasis on a child's familiarity with objects before it copes with ideas, but Comenius did not share Hartlib's belief in the religious purpose and basis of education. Hartlib's view was nearer to Milton's intention that education should "repair the ruins of our first parents."

Hartlib was recognized as one of the virtuosi of his age. Evelyn* (*Diary*, 3 : 162) refers to him as "honest and learned Mr. Hartlib, a public spirited and ingenious person, who propagated many useful things and arts." Hartlib wrote about his investigations on agriculture, animal husbandry, manufacturing, and mechanics. His inquiries are fully described and illustrated by Henry Dircks : *A Biographical Memoir of Samuel Hartlib* (London, 1865). In *Hartlib, Dury and Comenius* (London, 1947) George H. Turnbull presents a comprehensive summary of his activities and a definitive bibliography of his known writings. Hartlib's primary concerns, religion and education, are skillfully synthesized in his utopia, *A Description of the Famous Kingdom of Macaria* (1641). He died of renal calculus on March 10, 1662, in serious financial difficulties. [DAR]

HARTOP, JONATHAN (1653?–1791), an alleged benefactor of Milton, who is supposed to have died at the incredible age of 138. The year before his death a story circulated that he had loaned Milton £50 soon after the Restoration (a period when Milton was in financial difficulty). Milton repaid the money, although Hartop wanted to decline it, "with an angry letter which is extant among the curious possessions of this venerable man." The improbabilities of the story are many, but Hartop was supposed to have married as his third wife an illegitimate daughter of Cromwell* and to have had a portrait of Cromwell by Samuel Cooper, and these alleged facts have led some to credit it. No letter from Milton to Hartop is known. The story was told in *London Chronicle* 67 (March 23–25, 1790) : 284, and was repeated by other periodicals. [JTS]

HAUGHTON FAMILY: *see* RELATIVES, MILTON'S.

HAVENS, RAYMOND D(EXTER) (1880–1954), scholar. After completing his doctorate at Harvard University, he was associated with the University of Rochester until 1925, when he moved to the Johns Hopkins University. Besides assisting there with *Modern Language Notes,* he wrote an important study, *The Influence of Milton on English Poetry* (1922), one of the earlier critical works that set the standards for modern Milton scholarship. The book traces in some detail the effect that Milton's writing had upon the poetic styles of the later seventeenth century, and its growing importance in the next, especially for the pre-romantic and romantic writers and their successors. Less emphasis is put upon the influence of Milton's ideas. Havens's other important work is a study of Wordsworth, *The Mind of a Poet* (1941). [WBH]

HAYDN, FRANZ JOSEF: *see* ADAPTATIONS.

HAYLEY, WILLIAM (1745–1820). Milton's Romantic biographers* were the first to perceive the full dimensions of the poet's libertarianism and the first to celebrate him as the hero of political radicalism. They found support for their views in William Hayley's *Life of Milton.* The prototype for Romantic biographies, Hayley's *Life* was written with the double aim of correcting erroneous views of Milton purveyed by eighteenth-century commentators, especially Dr. Johnson*, and of restoring to view the whole Milton. As such, it was a shaping influence on criticism of the Romantic era; and it was the immediate inspiration behind Blake's* *Milton.*

The first edition of Hayley's *Life,* prefixed to *The Poetical Works of John Milton,* was published in 1794; a second edition, enlarged and substantially revised, was issued in 1796. The differences between these editions are of real significance. Besides changes obviously intended to achieve verbal precision or to correct earlier errors, there are those which bring into focus the biographer's original intentions and attitudes lost by the expurgations made by the publisher of the first edition. With few exceptions, the additions to the second edition reveal the political motives and ideals of Milton and exhibit the revolutionary character of his religious philosophy.

In the Preface to his encyclopedic life of Milton, David Masson* distinguishes between two kinds of biography: those which add to "the stock of facts" about an author and those which "vary the impression." Hayley's *Life* is of the second sort: it borrows its methods and materials from earlier biographers, but its organization and conclusions are Hayley's own. The first to make the division that has become a commonplace of Milton studies, Hayley presents his biography in three parts, corresponding to the three phases of Milton's literary career—lyric, polemic, and epic—focusing on the "middle" period as one of creative vigor and intense intellectual development that converted Milton into a "constant advocate for freedom, in every department of life" (2d ed., p. 88), that inspired his audacious independence of mind, and that kindled the "inextinguishable fire of imagination, which gave existence and perfection to his Paradise Lost" (p. 73).

There are some lapses into bardolatry, but they are to be expected in a biography that postulates with Tasso* and Milton that only God and the poet are creators. In his Appendix to the *Life of Milton*, Hayley suggests that just as God produces "wonders from the rude and unformed chaos," so from "the still ruder chaos" of the mind the poet must create his poem (pp. 287, 289). This analogy between God and the poet, between God's creation and the poem, if not the discovery of the Romantic era, is at least one of its major recoveries from Renaissance poetical theory.

When Hayley says that Milton gives "purer signification" to the word *hero* than is ordinarily acknowledged, he elects to emphasize the revolutionary character of Milton's art and thought. Hayley insists that when Milton said *PL* was "Not less but more Heroic" than the epics* of Homer* and Virgil* he was repudiating not only much of the atrophied machinery that comprised the classical epic tradition but also the conception of heroism it enshrined. The classical epic—from Milton's point of view, and from Hayley's—exhibited "too great a tendency to nourish the sanguinary madness in mankind, which has continually made the earth a theatre of carnage" (p. 276). Thus, Milton's aim in both *PL* and *PR* was to embody in his revolutionary epic mode a radical version of Christianity—"a purer religion" accompanied by "greater force of imagination" (p. 277). Hayley writes his biography, then, in order to show a perfect coincidence between Milton's prose and his poetry: both lock arms to effect a Copernican Revolution in the religious thought of Western culture; a new intellectual system, accompanied by a new scheme of values, emerges from Milton's prose and is given perfect embodiment in a radically new kind of epic poem represented by *PL* and *PR*. Views such as these find additional underpinnings in Hayley's *An Essay on Epic Poetry* (1782), which forges a new conception of epic poetry based largely on Milton's epic achievement, and in *Cowper's Milton* (1810), which Hayley, after the poet's death, saw through the press. [JAW]

HAYMAN, FRANCIS: *see* ILLUSTRATIONS.

HAYWARD, SIR JOHN (ca. 1564–1627), historian. Queen Elizabeth imprisoned him for praising Essex in the dedication of *The First Part of the Life and Raigne of Henrie the IIII* (1599) and released him only after Essex's execution (February 25, 1601). In 1610, James I* made him and William Camden* the two historiographers of the new Chelsea College. He was knighted in 1619. His *Life and Raigne of King Edward the Sixth* was published posthumously (London, 1630).

Milton knew this book well. In *CB*, under the heading "Of Allies," he cites Hayward's account of Edward's aid to continental Protestants (18:215), a context that appears again in *Ref* (3:8) and

Animad (3 : 134). He cites the book again in *Ref* (3 : 11), and *Animad* (3 : 119), using Hayward and other English historians as authorities. [GLM]

HAZLITT, WILLIAM. Hazlitt (1778–1830), the well-known Romantic critic, wrote extensively on Milton, and often opposed the views of Samuel Johnson*. He published discussions of *Lyc* and Milton's versification* (in *Round Table*, 1817), *Mask* (in *A View of the English Stage*, 1818), Shakespeare* and Milton, especially *PL* (in *Lectures on the English Poets*, 1818–19), and *Sonn* (in *Table Talk*, 1821). Hazlitt was one of the first to prefer *Lyc* to *Mask;* he answers the charge that it lacks feeling and is overloaded with learning by stressing the emotional value of the allusions and images. As for the poem's unity, Hazlitt argues that it is not made up of conflicting ingredients, but rather that one supreme imaginative reality pervades and unifies it. On *PL*, Hazlitt concentrates on the characters. Satan is the hero (Milton "unwittingly" assigned him that part), and one critic pronounces Hazlitt's discussion of Eve "the finest study of Eve in the whole history of Miltonic criticism." Hazlitt also sees Milton's verse, excluding Shakespeare's, as "the only blank verse* in the language that deserved the name of verse," thus refuting Johnson's condemnation of the "harsh and unequal" versification of the epic*. [WM]

HEAVEN. Although Milton suggests that earth may "be but the shaddow of Heav'n," he can write of Heaven only by "Lik'ning spiritual to corporal forms" (*PL* 5. 573–75). Therefore he writes about angels* as men "writ large" and about Heaven as if it were an earthly Paradise*, but somehow even more glorious and pure. To counteract the apparent materialism of his description, he uses suggestion rather than explicit statement of shape or dimension : the battlements of Heaven are "undetermind square or round." When he writes of the War in Heaven*, he seems to reverse Raphael's

assertion that earth may be the shadow of Heaven and to write of a Heaven that is a rather substantial "shadow" of earth. The War in Heaven is therefore frequently criticized as being too material, except by Johnson*, who thought that it should have been more classically material. As usual, though, Milton is following the precedent of the Bible*, which he regarded as a highly symbolic "accommodation" to man's necessary process of thought, which is concrete and not abstract.

Because man thinks in terms of time and process, because he understands by comparison and contrast, and because he requires variety, Milton describes an analogous Heaven in which there is motion, virtual or celestial time*, and even variety in the form of good change or "Grateful vicissitude." Even the glorious full light of Heaven alternates with a kind of twilight. And since there is process, there is perfectibility, although Milton conceives of God as perfect rather than perfectible.

As John R. Knott, Jr., points out (*Publications of the Modern Language Association* 85 : 487–95), Milton combines two biblical traditions of depicting Heaven : Jerusalem, the City; and Paradise, the pastoral* garden. Gold appears, but is usually minimized : Mammon, even in Heaven, admires the golden pavement excessively; the crowns of the angels combine gold with amaranth. The "pendant world" hangs on a golden chain from "Opal Towrs" and battlements of "living Sapphire" (*PL* 2. 1049–51). Christ rides forth in the chariot of cherubim, in which images of wheels, stars, fire, beryl, sapphire, "Amber, and colours of the showrie Arch" (*PL* 6. 759) combine to suggest the same sort of fluid and dynamic beauty that transcends any fixed image. Satan, on the other hand, is associated even in Heaven with gold, adamant, and diamond.

The heavenly pastoral life is expressed in terms of fruits and flowers, "rubied Nectar," cool breezes, living streams, and the Tree of Life. The cycle of rest and activity corresponds usually to the alternation of a kind of day with twilight (*PL* 6. 645). The activities of the blessed in *PL*, as in *Lyc*, are expressed primarily through music* and mystical dance as well as service of God and man. Thus

Melodious Hymns about the sovran Throne
Alternate all night long.

(5. 656–57)

And in serving man (Lycidas guards the shore, and Raphael and Michael are dispatched for Adam's education, for instance) and obeying God, the angels constantly manifest the freedom appropriate to Heaven, where God requires that they affirm love by "voluntary service." This is joy, except to those who prefer to be in Hell and scorn what they misinterpret as "Forc't Halleluiah's" (2. 243).

In addition, the angels enjoy the contemplation of God in a Heaven described in terms of light. Milton begins his third book by invoking holy Light and speaking of a divine fountain of light. Then he writes of God in the "pure Empyrean," where the

Sanctities of Heaven
Stood thick as Stars, and from his sight receiv'd
Beatitude past utterance.

(3. 60–62)

Yet the Son* is the radiant image of what the Father* ineffably is, and the angels must veil their eyes with their wings in the presence of a God whose skirts appear "Dark with excessive bright" (3. 380). [AG]

HEBRAISM, MILTON'S. The background of Milton's Hebraism is a permanent feature of what is sometimes called the Judeo-Christian tradition and as such constitutes a diffused influence in Western culture from the beginning of the Middle Ages to the present. Milton was as much exposed to this factor as anyone else in his time, a fact that would in part account for his moral earnestness and his emphasis on salvation, reward

and punishment, and free will*. The emphasis on theodicy ("to justify the ways of God to man") is also characteristic of the Hebraic trend in western Christendom (cf. Ps. 145 : 17 and Job passim).

In Milton's time, however, as a result of the forces at work in the Reformation and in the Puritan movement, Hebraism emerges as a new and radical trend separable in some respects from evangelical Christianity. And here Milton plays a significant role through his writings. In his divorce tracts he holds up the law of Moses, which permits divorce* (cf. Deuteronomy 24) against the received canon law* of the Church, which had normally denied it. Such revolutionary Hebraism is not uncommon in the Reformation. It is found among the Anabaptists* and Socinians* of the sixteenth century.

Puritanism provided the soil for these developments in seventeenth-century England. Ben Jonson* satirizes the Puritans in *Bartholomew Fair* (1614) with particular reference to their alleged Judaizing tendencies ("Rabbi Zeal-of-the-land Busy"). But the sharpest opposition to this trend came also from within the Puritan camp. William Prynne* (1600–1669) on the right wing was markedly anti-Judaic, while John Bunyan in *Pilgrim's Progress* (1678) has Christian warned at the beginning of his quest against seeking salvation by the way of Mount Sinai. Hebraism was clearly felt as a temptation against which the faithful were bidden to be on their guard.

Outside the Puritan camp, writers who were markedly influenced by Hebraism included the theologian Bishop Jeremy Taylor* (1613–1667), the chemist Robert Boyle (1627–1691), who was a friend of the Dutch Jewish philosopher Rabbi Manasseh ben Israel (1604–1657), and the Cambridge Platonists*, John Smith (1618–1652) and Henry More (1614–1687). Both these latter show themselves receptive in important points of doctrine to the ideas of the Jewish philosophers, Philo Judaeus* (1st century) and Moses

Maimonides (12th century). Milton has affinities with all these writers.

As for his knowledge of Hebrew, Milton had undoubtedly been stimulated by the Hebraic learning of his age, the golden age of Hebrew studies in England. He knew the work of the great Orientalist Edward Pococke (1604–1692), who edited a major work of Maimonides for the Oxford Press in 1655, of the Talmudist John Lightfoot (1602–1675), and of the jurist John Selden* (1584–1654), whose *Hebrew Wife* (1646) Milton cites approvingly in connection with the Jewish law of divorce. At Christ's College*, Cambridge, Milton would have come in contact with the great Semitic scholar Joseph Mead* (1586–1638).

Like many educated men of his time, Milton had himself a good reading knowledge of the languages of the Old Testament, Hebrew and Aramaic. In his address to Hartlib (*Educ*), he requires proficiency in those tongues from the pupils of his ideal school. This does not mean that Milton was an expert Hebrew scholar or that he had direct access to difficult texts of the earlier Middle Ages such as the Talmud or the classical *midrashim* (homiletics of the rabbis) as some scholars have supposed; but he evidently possessed and used a copy of Brian Walton's* Polyglot Bible (1657) and also the great annotated Hebrew Bible (*Mikraoth Gedoloth*) as edited by Johannes Buxtorf, the elder (Basle, 1618–19). This work brings together the Hebrew (or Aramaic) text of the Old Testament with Aramaic paraphrase (*Targum*) and the standard Hebrew commentaries of the later Middle Ages. These latter included the glosses of Rabbi Solomon Yitzhaki ("Rashi"), eleventh century; Rabbi Levi ben Gershon ("Ralbag"), thirteenth century; Rabbi David Kimchi ("Radak"), thirteenth century; and Rabbi Abraham Ibn Ezra, twelfth century. In addition, this edition recorded in the margin the variants and textual notes (*masorah*) of the original editors of the received Hebrew text. Milton was able to make intelligent use of this apparatus

and employs the commentaries freely in various parts of his prose works.

Of the earlier classical literature of Rabbinic Judaism he had no direct knowledge, but he probably knew something of it from various partial Latin translations and also from such compendia as Buxtorf's great *Lexicon* (1609–1639). Denis Saurat* has argued that Milton was much influenced by the occult literature of Judaism (the Kabbalah). But this view has been challenged by Maurice Kelley and by R. J. Z. Werblowsky. The fact is that the chief text of the *Kabbalah*, the thirteenth-century *Zohar* ("Book of Splendor"), was untranslated in Milton's time, and Milton was not equipped to study it in the original. He had probably met the writings of some early Christian kabbalists, in particular those of Johann Reuchlin (1455–1522) and Pico della Mirandola (1463–1494) and of his own English contemporary, Robert Fludd* (1574–1637), but from those he had derived only a few imperfect conceptions. Moreover, the bent of Milton's mind was not particularly occult. He was inclined toward a Hebraism of a more down-to-earth, everyday kind. As a Protestant seeking salvation in the Scriptures, he was inclined toward a biblical Hebraism. The word of the Bible* was his guide, and the Jewish scholiasts and grammarians were found helpful insofar as they illuminated the text and helped him to define a rational theology based on that text.

Hebraism certainly influenced Milton's style, although its base is hellenic. *Areop* takes us back to the golden oratory of Demosthenes, while *SA* is based avowedly on the model of the Greek dramatists, and the epic poems on those of Homer* and Virgil*. Nevertheless, there is a marked Hebrew counterpointing. In prose Milton is capable of a direct vehemence that is Hebrew rather than Greek.

The adversarie again applauds, and waits the hour. When they have brancht themselves out, saith he, small enough into parties and partitions, then will be our time. Fool! he sees not the firm root out of which we all grow, though into branches. (*Areop*)

There is a tendency here to fall into the parallelizing cadences of the Old Testament. The tone is also biblical; the writing has the scorn of the prophets rather than the irony of the Greeks. In *Areop* the dominant images of light ("We boast our light") and of streams of water ("Truth is compar'd in Scripture to a streaming fountain") are clearly biblical.

This biblical resonance comes as naturally to Milton as it does to many divines of all parties. Donne's sermons, for instance, are saturated in biblical language and parallelism. In Milton's case, however, this resonance is also linked with a revolutionary ardor, a desire to make reason and the will of God prevail, in the manner of Matthew Arnold*, another Hebraic writer later on.

A similar dialectical balance of Hellenic and Hebraic elements may be noted in *PL* The first books are dominated by mythological* patterns derived from the classical epics*, recalling in particular the wars of the Titans against Zeus, and there are many Homeric images, some of them actually taken from Homer* and Virgil, such as the comparison between the fallen angels and "Bees / In spring time" (1. 768–69). But crossing these are many image patterns drawn from the Apocalypse* and the Old Testament prophets. The account of the Son* riding to overthrow Satan at the end of Book 6 has as its central feature the "Chariot of Paternal Deitie," comprising "Four Cherubic shapes," a "sapphire Throne," and a "crysal Firmament," all from the famous description of the divine chariot in Ezekiel 1. But there are deeper and more sustained Hebraic images, too, which have a more controlling function in the poem. Such an image pattern is that which relates the entire story of the poem to the exodus of the children of Israel from Egypt. The fallen angels are compared in Book 1 to the "*Memphian* chivalry," whom the

"Sojourners of *Goshen*" saw drowned in the Red Sea (307–9). Later on the same angels are compared to the plague of locusts that Moses summoned "o'er the realm of impious Pharaoh." The matter of the exodus and the crossing of the Red Sea is again recalled in Book 6 when heaven opens its "Crystal wall" and the rebel angels move out through the gap into the "wastful Deep" (860–62) after which

Disburd'nd Heav'n rejoic'd, and soon repaird
Her mural breach, returning whence it rolld.
(6. 878–79)

This, as J. H. Sims has noted, was precisely the phenomenon that the children of Israel witnessed at the Red Sea in Exodus 14 : 28. The connection between the story of Adam and Eve in Eden and the story of the exodus was a frequent theme of the Jewish commentaries, where the serpent of Eve had been linked with the serpent that Moses displays before Pharaoh (Exod. 32 : 6). This association was evidently in Milton's mind in *PL* 9.1027. It was customary in hexameral* literature to interweave biblical material of all kinds into the story of the Creation and the Fall*, but Milton's tendency to environ the poem with images and associations that recall in particular the exodus and the sojourn of the Israelites in the wilderness has the effect of bringing the whole fable of the poem down to earth. The dimensions of history and geography are introduced. Instead of the events ocurring in the mythological realm, they are related to the political struggle of the Jews in Egypt, to nonmetaphysical battles in the wilderness, and to the sorts of temptations and challenges that might beset any nation in history. This demythologizing tendency (as Harold Fisch has argued) is one that Milton had evidently learned from the Hebrew scholiasts for whom the story of Adam and Eve had little or nothing to do with wars in heaven, but a great deal to do with wars on earth.

In the second half of *PL* there is less mythological enlargement, and the style is less weighted with epic simile. The half that still remains unsung, says Milton in the opening section of Book 7, is "narrower bound / Within the visible diurnal sphere." Milton now concentrates more on the domestic drama of Adam and Eve themselves, who henceforth take the center of the stage, and a Hebraic realism and simplicity tend to take the place of epic orotundity. Eve's thought in offering Adam the forbidden fruit—

> but what if God have seen,
> And death ensue? then I shall be no more,
> And *Adam* wedded to another *Eve*,
> Shall live with her enjoying, I extinct;
> A death to think.
> (9. 826–30)

is drawn from Rashi's commentary on Genesis 3 : 6. The simplicity of these lines should be noted, as well as their dramatic urgency. They introduce into the poem the human dimension, and with it the tensions arising out of human choice and human weakness. This is entirely in keeping with the nonepic Hebraic sources on which Milton leans at this point in his argument. It is significant that in this second half of the poem Satan the tempter is pointedly compared with "some Orator renound / In *Athens* or free *Rome*." The grand style (which had dominated the first half of the poem) is here clearly associated with the representative of evil.

The tendency in *PR* is once again toward a biblical austerity in keeping with the standard Puritan view derived from the apostle Paul ("Seeing we have such hope we use great plainness of speech," 2 Cor. 3 : 12). In the fourth book Milton's hero lauds the song and prophecy of the Hebrew Scriptures ("*Sion*'s songs, to all true tasts excelling") as superior to all the literary arts of Greece and Rome ("varnish on a Harlots cheek"). There are contradictions here, for an excessive dependence on Hebraic models of style could lead also in the direction of a rich and metaphoric style in poetry, as in Thomas Traherne, or in the direction of exoticism, as in Christopher Smart later on. In fact, St. Paul in the above-quoted passage from

Corinthians is really opposing the simplicity of the Gospel to the "veil of Moses," that is, the more adorned and less naked character of the poetry and prophecy of the Old Testament. Thus Puritan simplicity and bareness were not the only option that Christ's speech in Book 4 suggested, though it is the style that he seems to have as his model in *PR*.

But the most successful use of the Hebraic is in *SA*. That poem, lacking as it does any mythological background (whether of devils or angels), concentrates on the moral failures and victories of its very earthly hero. The direct dependence on the biblical story of Samson as presented in Judges 16 (with a collateral influence of the Book of Job in the dramatic patterning of the speeches of the tempters) is matched by a style and prosody informed throughout by the influence of the Hebrew Bible. This constitues once again a biblical counterpointing to the choric structure (derived from Euripides and the other Greek dramatists*), of which Milton speaks in the Preface. Many passages in *SA* are directly modeled on poetic texts from the Bible. For example, the Chorus greets Samson's new-found strength with the words :

> Oh how comely it is and how reviving
> To the Spirits of just men long opprest !
> When God into the hands of thir deliverer
> Puts invincible might
> To quell the mighty of the Earth, th'op-
>   pressour,
> The brute and boist'rous force of violent men
> Hardy and industrious to support
> Tyrannic power, but raging to pursue
> The righteous and all such as honour Truth.
> (1268–76)

This is evidently inspired by Psalm 18, describing how God avenges the suffering of those who believe in him :

> The Lord liveth; and blessed be my rock;
> And let the God of my salvation be exalted.
> It is God that avengeth me,
> And subdueth the people under me.
> He delivereth me from mine enemies:
> Yea, thou liftest me up above those that rise
>   against me:

Thou hast delivered me from the violent man.
Therefore will I give thanks unto thee, O
  Lord among the heathen,
And sing praises unto thy name.

Along with the verbal echoes we may note in Milton's passage the same loose versification* as in the English translation of this psalm. Critics have sometimes seen these metrical forms in *SA* as a kind of anticipation of modern free verse, or else as a carry-over from medieval accentual rhythms. Others, notably F. T. Prince (*The Italian Element in Milton's Verse*), have observed a parallel to Italian forms of versification. But one certain source is to be found in the parallelistic cadences of the Hebrew Bible, in particular, as J. F. Kermode has suggested, in the free movement of the Psalms and other poetic portions of the Bible in the English translation.

Above all, *SA* reveals the Hebraic concern with an active righteousness, and the Hebraic capacity for yoking human aggressions to moral purposes. Samson does not love his enemies but rather compasses their downfall and destruction. This is not precisely consonant with the ethics of the Sermon on the Mount, but it does fit in with the pattern of Old Testament religion, where divine grace can go hand in hand with divine justice. Samson is not the only such heroic model in the Hebrew Bible; King Solomon, who was "beloved of God," also took care to purge the realm of such enemies as Joab and Shimei. This kind of ethic appealed to many other writers of the seventeenth century. Grace* had to be reconciled with nature*. Milton's poem represents in this respect the culmination of a trend that can be discerned in Shakespeare's history plays and in the life and works of Sir Walter Ralegh* and many others. Samson's death at the end of the poem is salvation, triumph, and retribution all together.

With respect to Hebraic ideas, Milton displays, especially in his "heretical" *CD*, an unusually large number of religious*, moral, and philosophical* notions that may be attributed (and that he himself often attributes) to Hebraic sources. First among these is his anti-Trinitarianism.

Milton rejected the orthodox account of the Trinity, maintaining in contradiction to the Athanasian Creed that the Son is something less than God and is neither coeternal, coequal, nor coessential with the Father (*CD* 1:5). Although his argument has been related to the ancient Christian heresy of Arius* (third century), it is also explicitly derived from the Hebrew insistence on the unity of God (Deut. 6:4). Other writers of the time who were strongly influenced by Hebrew sources and doctrines, for example, Jeremy Taylor and Henry More, had similar difficulties with orthodox Trinitarianism. The question of the extent to which these views are reflected in *PL* has been much debated. But there can be no doubt that, though the Son plays a central part in the war in heaven* (Books 5–6) and as judge and intercessor on behalf of fallen mankind (Books 10–11), the basic concept of divinity in the poem is of a unitary, hierarchical structure derived from the Father.

Much of the angel* lore in *PL* is similarly Hebraic. Four angels figure prominently: Uriel, who confronts Satan and directs him unwittingly to Earth (Book 3); Gabriel, who challenges Satan after the latter has tempted Eve in her dream (Book 4); Raphael, who visits with Adam and Eve in Paradise (Books 5, 6, 7, and 8) and relates to them the happenings prior to their creation and other high matters; and Michael, who is sent to reveal the future to Adam and to escort him and Eve out of the forbidden zone of Paradise (Books 11 and 12). Michael and Gabriel are first named in the book of Daniel and the other two are first mentioned in the apocryphal Book of Enoch (probably 2d century B.C.). The connection with the Book of Enoch has been argued by Fletcher, McColley, and West. In Enoch, for instance, Uriel ("God is my light") is said to be appointed over the heavenly luminaries, and thus quite naturally becomes in *PL* (3.690) the "Regent of the Sun," who confronts

Satan on the orb of the Sun. But Milton's debt to the Book of Enoch has been exaggerated. Only fragments of it were available in printed form in Milton's day and he could hardly have learned his angel lore in detail from that source. It seems more likely that he knew of the angels from various intermediate sources, both Jewish and non-Jewish. The four archangels are succinctly listed in the prayer on retiring to rest in the standard Jewish order of service. There is a closer link with the Jewish tradition also. The angel Raphael who descends in Book 5 of *PL* to dine with Adam and Eve has his prototype in one of the visitors to Abraham in Genesis 18. Of the three angels mentioned in that chapter the Jewish tradition (see Rashi on Gen. 18 : 2) identifies one as Raphael. His job was to heal Abraham (from the wound of the circumcision) and later to rescue Lot from Sodom. The general setting of the visit to Abraham had suggested several features of Milton's account. Raphael comes to dine with Abraham and Sarah and does so at the heat of the day (Gen. 18 : 1). This explains both the pointed reference to the meal, and also to the excessive meridian heat in Milton's poem at this point (5. 300–307, 369–70).

But of more significance than these details is the general concept of the function of angels in Milton's poem. When Raphael first appears in Book 5 of *PL* he has all the grandeur of Hermes in the Greek epics*. He has "gorgeous wings" (line 250) in which the colors of blue and gold are prominent, and the reference to Hermes is explicit in the continuation :

> Like *Maia's* son he stood,
> And shook his Plumes, that Heav'nly fragrance filld
> The circuit wide.
>
> (5. 285–87)

Here is the Hellenic frame, the descent of Hermes being a common and repeated motif in the Greek epics. But the Hebraic role of Raphael suggests a different and humbler level, the point being that angels

in the Hebrew Bible and in the rabbinic literature are regarded as no more than messengers. Far from being gods, they are even less important in the drama of history and salvation than prophets and patriarchs. Jacob fights with an angel and overpowers him (Gen. 32 : 26) and the Rabbis tell of Moses' success in browbeating the ministering angels in order to prove how much worthier were the children of Israel and how much more deserving of the gift of the Torah. Something of this deflating or "demythologizing" tendency is evident in Milton also. He insists that Raphael comes to converse with Adam "as friend with friend" (5. 229). In the conversation between them which then develops there is a certain domestic realism. They sit at the supper table ("No fear lest Dinner cool," 5. 396) and converse of many matters high and low. The divine status of Raphael is not always evident. One may also note that Milton's distribution of the angelic functions in the poem between four different messengers is in keeping with a rabbinic dictum that "one angel does not carry out two missions" (Rashi on Gen. 18 : 2). No angel is allowed to have a dominant role in the poem. And indeed, it is during the extended conversation with Raphael that Adam's dramatic stature grows, until by the end of Book 8 he occupies the center of interest. Angels are but angels.

One Jewish type of heresy that has been noted by Denis Saurat in connection with the visit of Raphael to Adam is that of "materialism." Milton rather ostentatiously insists that Raphael ate the dinner Adam served "with keen dispatch/ Of real hunger" (5. 436–37), and Raphael proceeds to explain that the difference between his digestive system and that of Adam is one of degree, not kind :

> Wonder not then, what God for you saw good
> If I refuse not, but convert, as you,
> To proper substance, time may come when men
> With Angels may participate, and find
> No inconvenient Diet, nor too light Fare:
> And from these corporal nutriments perhaps
> Your bodies may at last turn all to Spirit . . .
>
> (5. 491–97)

Later on (at the end of Book 8) Raphael also acknowledges that the angels enjoy sexual relations with one another, though they are less encumbered with physical obstacles than are human beings (8. 618–29). It should not be thought that Milton is here degrading spirit to the level of matter. It is rather the other way round. For him sex and food were alike blameless and, when not misapplied, part of man's spiritual nature. In fact, the creation as a whole was a divine work and properly a part of the spiritual order until darkened by sin and the Fall. From this point of view *Mask* with its tendency to separate spirit from matter is less Hebraic and more Greek than *PL*. In *PL* we are made aware of the notion that this earthly sphere is the real arena of spiritual action. In *CD* this point of view is sharpened into the axiom that all material things originate in God ("omnia ex Deo"). The seed of the material universe is thus in itself spiritual and consequently good:

> For the original matter of which we speak, is not to be looked upon as an evil or trivial thing, but as intrinsically good, and the chief productive stock of every subsequent good. (1:7)

Saurat traces this and similar ideas in Milton to the Jewish Kabbalah. But there is no need to seek so far. They are part and parcel of biblical and Rabbinic Judaism, which recognized no absolute distinction between spirit and matter. He could have found the doctrine of *omnia ex deo* intimated in the *Pirke d'Rabbi Eleizer*, an eighth-century *Midrash*, translated by Vorstius in 1644, and quoted also by Maimonides in his *Guide* (Part 2, chap. 26). And on the material essence of souls he could have found considerable support in the *Fons Vitae* of the Jewish philosopher Solomon Ibn Gabirol (11th century; known in Milton's time as "Avicebron"). But the biblical basis of this should not be ignored. The material creation of the six days is constantly described in the Bible as "good" or "very good." The Hebrew language, as Milton

well knew, contains no special vocabulary to deal with spiritual or metaphysical states. "Heaven" is simply the blue expanse we see, and the "soul," as Milton points out, is merely the life of the body.

Linked with Milton's tendency to abolish the distinction between matter and spirit is his explicit enunciation of the heresy* of mortalism*. In the same chapter of *CD* in which he discusses the divine origin of matter, he denies the orthodox belief in the soul as an independent entity separable from the body. He bases himself here likewise on Hebraic-biblical categories. Quoting Genesis 2:7, "thus man became a living soul," he points out that the same Hebrew phrase is used of the animal creation (1:30) and thus it follows that

> man is a living being, intrinsically and properly one and individual, not compound or separable, not, according to the common opinion, made up and framed of two distinct and different natures, as of soul and body, but that the whole man is soul, and the soul man. (1:7)

Soul and body do not separate at death, but the whole man dies, soul and body alike descending into the grave, to rise again *together* at the resurrection. He is here reverting to a more strictly biblical view of man's fate, as in Ecclesiastes:

> For that which befalleth the sons of men befalleth beasts; even one thing befalleth them: as the one dieth so dieth the other; yea, they have all one breath; so that a man hath no preeminence over a beast: for all is vanity. (Eccles. 3:19)

This view may seem pessimistic, but it is also morally challenging, since it sees the earthly pilgrimage of man as the decisive moral test. If reward and punishment have any meaning, it is as a condition of human history, not as a way of squaring accounts after death. Milton's mortalist views may immediately derive from the Socinians and the Anabaptists of the sixteenth century and were shared by such contemporaries as Richard Overton (d. 1663), Thomas Browne (1605–1682), and Thomas Hobbes* (1588–1679).

Another aspect of Milton's humanist thinking that avowedly owes much to Hebraic sources is his "doctrine and discipline" of divorce. Milton's plea for freedom to dissolve an unhappy or unsuccessful marriage* looks back to the views of the German Protestant reformer Martin Bucer* (1491–1551) and of the liberal Dutch theologian Hugo Grotius* (1583–1645), but also to the Jewish rabbins whom he had read:

> Hence it is that the Rabbins, and *Maimonides,* famous among the rest, in a book of his set forth by *Buxtorfius,* tells us that *divorce was permitted by Moses to preserve peace in marriage, and quiet in the family (DDD,* 1:6)

The reference is to the twelfth-century codifier of Jewish law, Moses Maimonides and to his philosophical treatise *Guide of the Perplexed,* translated into Latin by Johannes Buxtorf, the younger, in 1629. Milton also finds support for his liberal view that divorce should be permitted on grounds other than adultery in the Hebrew biblical commentaries. But his liberal views are not limited to divorce. He also claims that, following the example of the Hebrew patriachs, polygamy* might be permitted for Christians.

It should not be thought that Milton was advocating a wholesale adoption of Mosaic law as such for a Christian commonwealth. On the contrary, he is at pains to square his irregular beliefs and proposals with the Gospels, proclaiming in a sound evangelical manner "our liberty also from the bondage of the Law" (*RCG* 1:3). He is thinking here in particular of the Protestant rejection of the priesthood and of the whole of the ceremonial law of the Old Testament. But if he rejects the Mosaic legislation in principle on the grounds that the gospel is the law of freedom, while the Law stands for captivity (*RCG* 1:3), he uses the same principle to urge in the divorce tracts the utter impossibility of Christ's binding where Moses had made free. The net result of such a two-edged argument is that liberal reforms in the

Christian canon law are urged on the example of Mosaic teaching as understood by the rabbis.

Behind Milton's thinking is the pervasive analogy between the moral destiny of Israel and that of England that one meets throughout the seventeenth century. If Charles I* in captivity compared himself to David betrayed by his enemies, his Puritan opponents likewise thought of themselves as the soldiers of David and sang his psalms when going into battle. In *Absalom and Achitophel* (1681) Dryden bases a political satire on an elaborate and meticulous parallelism between the history of the house of David and that of Charles II*. Milton's regicide tracts likewise lean heavily on arguments from the Talmud tending to prove that the kings of Israel were subject to the law. This analogy between the matter of Israel and that of England, which is part of the stock-in-trade of seventeenth-century theology, sermons, and political pamphlets, gains particular force for many from the feeling that the history of England, like that of Israel, is a *covenant* history. The term *covenant* is frequently found in Milton. For him it was a central concept, for it served to combine a radical sense of human freedom with a radical sense of divine obligation. Man chooses and is chosen. It is thus that Milton conceived the English to be a chosen people, commanded to be a light to the gentiles and elected for peculiar privileges and responsibilities. Theirs is a history of promise. England was a messiah nation, and the republic under Cromwell*, a divinely ordained commonwealth designed to point the way to the true fulfillment of the ends of the Reformation in Europe when all God's people would be prophets. This is the faith that shines through *Areop* in its most lyrical passages:

> Why else was this Nation chos'n before any other, that out of her as out of *Sion,* should be proclam'd and sounded forth the first tidings and trumpet of **Reformation** to all *Europ?*

Likewise he felt himself to be *personally* elected, his lips touched with holy fire (like the prophet Isaiah) in sign of his calling. His sense of dedication in the service of a great historical, revolutionary program (*RCG* 2, opening section) is precisely in accord with the covenant psychology that the Reformation had imbibed from Hebrew sources.

This will also explain the shattering nature of the disappointment and shock that Milton must have felt when later, with the Restoration of Charles II, the English clearly cast aside all messianic ambitions. They obviously did not share his Hebraic faith, nor did they see in him the appointed herald of change and revolution. In insisting on Samson's ultimate revival · and triumph, Milton witnesses to a still enduring Hebraic faith in the possibility of a this-worldly salvation to be achieved by human agency. [HF]

HEIMBACH, PETER. Milton was visited by the young scholar Peter Heimbach (dates unknown) in the summer of 1656; then or later, the poet presented him with a copy of the 1645 *Poems* inscribed in Latin : "John Milton, the author, to his friend the truly outstanding gentleman, elegant poet, flowery orator, keen philosopher, Peter von Heimbach, counsellor-at-law." When Heimbach embarked for the Continent, Milton requested that the young man inquire into the price of an atlas. In *Epistol* 20 (November 8, 1656), Milton wrote in answer to a letter from Heimbach that he could not afford the atlas he had desired. In 1657 Heimbach requested Milton to use his influence to help him obtain a position as secretary with the English minister to Holland, but in *Epistol* 27 Milton communicated that he could be of no help because of his lack of influence, being confined much of the time to his home, and that the position had already been filled. Heimbach's last known communication from Milton was written August 15, 1666 (*Epistol* 31), in answer to a very complimentary letter from Heimbach, then state-councillor to the Elector of Brandenburg. Milton re-

marked that he had indeed escaped the plague, and was glad that Heimbach had been raised to so honorable a position. [WM]

HEINSIUS, DANIEL (1580–1655), professor, poet, classicist, historian, theologian, literary critic, and editor of some thirty classical and patristic texts. As leaders in Protestant resistance to Spanish rule in the Southern Netherlands (i.e. Belgium), Heinsius's parents were forced into exile during the reconquest of Flanders during the 1580s. After brief stays in England and Holland, the family settled in Flushing, Zeeland, where Daniel began his studies. At sixteen he entered Franeker Academy as a student of law, but in 1598 he matriculated at Leiden and joined the coterie of brilliant young humanists surrounding the great Joseph J. Scaliger*. A gifted poet and scholar, Daniel quickly made his way in the realm of letters. At the university he rose from Professor of Poetry and Greek to Politics and History, the most prestigious chairs outside theology, and by 1610 to the sensitive posts of University Librarian and Secretary of the University Senate as well. Special honors later bestowed were Historiographer Royal to Gustavus Adolphus, Honorary Knight of San Marco (Venice), and Historiographer to the Province of Holland and West Friesland.

Several dimensions of his career are especially relevant to Milton. His editions of classical poets such as Horace*, Seneca, Ovid*, and Theocritus*; of ancient writers such as Aristotle*, Livy, or Silius Italicus; or of church fathers such as Clemens Alexandrinus enjoyed wide distribution under prestige imprints, including the Elzevir, Raphelengius, and Commelin presses, and a number of them were used in English schools and universities in Milton's youth. Heinsius was also managing editor for the famous Leiden printers Abraham and Bonaventura Elzevir at the height of their career during the 1630s and '40s.

At Leiden, Heinsius lived and worked in the very seat of strife within Calvinist* churches between the heterodox followers of Jacob Arminius* and the ultra-orthodox supporters of Franciscus Gomarus over the doctrine of predestination*, for both had been colleagues on the Leiden faculty. During the first decade and a half of the seventeenth century, moreover, Heinsius and Hugo Grotius* were fast friends, forming as it were a sort of Castor and Pollux of Neo-Latin belles-lettres in Holland. But in the climax of the religious struggles at the Synod of Dort in 1618–19, Grotius supported the Arminians, or Remonstrants as they were then called, suffering imprisonment and exile. Heinsius remained loyal to Reformed orthodoxy, however, and when the Synod convened, he was chosen Secretary of the Lay Commissioners controlling the gathering in the name of the States-General. After the synod ended, he was charged with putting the official Acta (to which orthodox Puritanism was to turn for authority in Milton's time) into their final form, and he later joined the official revisers of the "Staten" Bible, the official version of Dutch Scriptures commissioned by the Synod and authorized by the States-General. In later years, Heinsius turned to biblical criticism, publishing two notable works, *Aristarchus sacer* and *Exercitationes sacrae* in 1627 and 1639.

Though both books enjoyed considerable acclaim in England, the *Exercitationes* became a focal point of polemics directly connected with Milton. After the appointment of Salmasius* at Leiden in 1632, he and Heinsius clashed on various matters, especially Heinsius's view of the Koine (i.e., the popular Greek language of the Hellenistic period), and their antagonism spurred a dispute between Heinsius and J. L. Guez de Balzac regarding the use of classical mythology in Christian literature, one of the most famous literary quarrels of the century. Milton's exchange with Salmasius over the execution of Charles I* in a sense is essentially a closing skirmish in this old and bitter feud between rivals at Leiden, and in his responses to Milton, Salmasius attacked Heinsius and his son Nicolaas* for collu-

sion with the Parliamentary spokesman.

Heinsius was also one of the best Neo-Latin poets of Milton's time. Indeed, to Edward Phillips the most famed of "modern" Dutch poets was not Grotius, but Heinsius. His Latin lyrics ran some thirteen editions before his death, and together with Grotius's *Adamus exul*, Heinsius's *Auriacus* became a landmark in Neo-Latin tragedy at the turn of the seventeenth century. More important, Grotius and he turned their backs on their early tragedies, and with Heinsius's *De tragoediae constitutione* and his tragedy *Herodes infanticida*, the work that Balzac attacked, they launched around 1610 a new sort of tragedy that deliberately broke with the tradition of Buchanan* and Muretus (one in which tragedy was achieved by rhetoric rather than by emotion). Heinsius also was responsible for important innovations in Dutch poetry and in the continental baroque lyric generally, because his success in adapting Dutch to themes of national struggle and of love as well as of Calvinist religious sentiments provided models that Dutch, German, and Scandinavian poets thereafter followed. As the first poet to compose love emblems in organized sequences, he also initiated the international fashion of love *emblemata* that developed in the first decade of the seventeenth century.

Most significant in its time was Heinsius's criticism. The achievement of his *De tragoediae constitutione* (1610, 1643) was that, for a Renaissance text, it provided a remarkably successful attempt to interpret the theory of tragedy in Aristotle's *Poetics**. Probably the best critical work of the century, its approach pruned away much of the elaborate rhetorical* bias that colored Cinquecento interpretations of Aristotle and replaced it with a much simpler concern with tragedy* as a means of arousing the proper tragic emotions and the importance of plot in this process. Heinsius's ideas are evident in Milton's treatment of catharsis* and the ends of tragedy in the Preface to *SA*. What Heinsius's study of Aristotle did for the seventeenth century was to recover the "pathetic" in tragedy, an innovation observable in Vondel*, Milton, and, above all, Racine. [PRS]

HEINSIUS, NICOLAAS (1620–1681). Son of Daniel Heinsius*, Nicolaas was a Dutch philologist and Neo-Latin poet, highly admired by many illustrious contemporaries such as Grotius*, Chapelain, Gronovius*, Dati*, and Isaac Vossius*, a close friend. After travels in England, Belgium, France, and Italy during the 1640s, Heinsius entered the service of Christina* of Sweden at the instigation of Vossius. Besides the advantages of royal patronage, Nicolaas hoped to gain restitution of a huge debt owed by the Swedish crown to his father and his uncle, Janus Rutgers, for services to Gustavus Adolphus years earlier. As the queen had also invited Claudius Salmasius* to Stockholm at the same time as Nicolaas, the enmity between Nicolaas, who strongly supported his father against Salmasius, and the eminent Huguenot scholar was bound to erupt, and once at at court, Salmasius did his best to ruin Nicolaas's position. To avoid conflict, and also to secure access to the wealth of classical manuscripts and materials in Italy, Nicolaas journeyed south via Holland and France as the queen's personal agent charged with purchasing manuscripts, books, coins, and artifacts for her collections, often at his own expense. Even in Italy, however, Salmasius continued to plague him, especially after Milton's answer to Salmasius's *Defensio regia* in 1651, for Salmasius incorrectly assumed that the Heinsii had been in collusion with his English opponent and retaliated accordingly, as the attack on the Heinsii in the opening of his posthumous *Responsio* shows. Because Nicolaas was vitally concerned in matters affecting Salmasius, his correspondence with Vossius and others is filled with detail regarding Milton and Salmasius, and it is therefore a main source of evidence regarding the continental reaction to Milton's writings. Indeed, Nicolaas's quip that Salmasius defended a good cause badly, Milton a bad one well, is proverbial. The attitudes of Nicolaas and Vossius must not be regarded as typical of European views, however, since Nicolaas, as well as many of his friends, had vested material and personal interests in any injuries that Salmasius might suffer. Despite reports such as Phillips's that Milton's attack embarrassed Salmasius in Sweden and cost him the Queen's favor, the fact is that the latter's influence with Christina continued to prevail and, through his intriguing, even influential associates of Heinsius such as Vossius himself were tumbled from her grace thereafter. In 1652–53, Nicolaas was offered a chance for reconciliation with his Leiden foe, but since the price was the humiliation of praising Salmasius publicly, he refused, and with true stoic dignity resigned his post. [PRS]

HELL. Milton treats Hell in two ways: as a symbolic place and as a state of mind and soul. Yet, as Merritt Y. Hughes observes (*John Milton: Complete Poems and Major Prose*, p. 182), "Heaven and Hell could be imagined without limit as states of the spirit as long as their historical and local existence was not denied." Because Milton believed that the Bible* was "accommodated*" to man's understanding in concrete symbols perhaps not literally true, he uses traditional classical and Christian images to suggest an otherwise too abstract sense of the ultimate separateness of the soul from God.

Thus Hell is treated as a "local habitation," but, unlike Dante's Inferno, it is "located" in Chaos

As far remov'd from God and light of Heav'n
As from the Center thrice to th' utmost Pole.
(*PL* 1. 73–74)

Its physical qualities are described in three ways, apparently contradictory, but analogous to the state of mind of the fallen angels*. Since God created nothing evil*, the angels cannot be entirely evil as long as they exist. Their original nature inclines them to love Heaven* and loathe Hell, but they finally reach such depravity as to find Heaven unbearable and to need Hell.

Hell is therefore as paradoxical as Satan, who is doomed by his own choice to reject God's goodness and yet to find no goodness apart from Him. Thus Hell admits of such potential goodness as Elysium offers: music*, philosophy*, companionship. Its materials can be used to supply a golden palace, Pandemonium*, with artificial light. Yet all of this apparent good is derivative, counterfeit, and misused: partial song; vain philosophy; self-interest, rather than true concord; barbaric false magnificence; light from burning naptha, not from a sky.

The ugliness that the angels do not see in themselves is matched by their punishments and the landscape. As James Sims notes (*The Bible in Milton's Epics*, pp. 107–8), Milton first establishes Hell in biblical terms: disorder and darkness (as in Job 10 : 22); a pit with a lake of fire; and chains (Rev. 20 : 1–2, 20 : 15; 2 Pet. 2, 4; Jude, 6). Then he follows Plato*, Virgil*, and Dante* in describing infernal rivers, Furies, Gorgons, and Hydras, and realms of ice. Milton's Hell is characterized by paradoxical extremes: fire that burns with "darkness visible"; ice that "Burns frore"; baleful streams; a Lethe that can never be tasted; in short,

Perverse, all monstrous, all prodigious things,
Abominable, unutterable, and worse
Than Fables yet have feign'd, or fear con-
ceiv'd.
(*PL* 2. 625–27)

God's curse has created such a landscape. Although His Providence* leaves the fallen angels partly free to serve His purposes, He imposes certain external punishments. the angels are dragged from beds of fire to experience the ice of the frozen mountains, then exposed once more to fiery lakes or fiery mountains; and annually they suffer metamorphosis into serpents compelled to chew the bitter ashes of illusory fruits. Ultimately they will be sealed up in Hell forever.

Psychologically the most impressive treatment of Hell occurs in Satan's ironic recognition that his assertion that the "mind is its own place" is only partly true. He can create a Hell through his series of wrong choices, but eventually he becomes so committed to those choices that he has no escape from "Infinite wrauth and infinite despair." Worst of all, he must face the knowledge that "Which way I flie is Hell; my self am Hell . . ." (*PL* 4. 74–77). [AG]

HENRIETTA MARIA, QUEEN OF ENGLAND. Wife of Charles I*, and mother of Charles II* and James II, Henrietta Maria (1609–1669) was the center of a coterie of courtly poets and dramatists whose work was built around popular conceptions of "platonic love." She was indirectly attacked in William Prynne's* violent condemnation of masques and plays, *Histriomastix* (late 1632 or early 1633). In the prose, Milton mentions her many times, always disapprovingly. He feels that her control of Charles was an evil influence on him (*Eikon* 5 : 191; *2Def* 8 : 205), and that her Roman Catholic religion and French ancestry adversely influenced the king (*Eikon* 5 : 140). She "pawn'd" the Crown Jewels ("a crime heretofore counted as treasonable in kings") (*Eikon* 5 : 141), and bought ammunition in Holland to be used by the Royalists (*Eikon* 5 : 166). [WM]

HENRY OF HUNTINGDON (1084–1155), chronicler of Britain. Milton's *Brit* contains some sixty references to Henry of Huntingdon's chronicle; the story of King Canute's standing in the rising tide, also drawn from Henry, appears in *CB* (18 : 144). Henry began his chronicle after being appointed the first archdeacon of Huntingdon in 1139. The first draft brought the work down to 1129 and later it was extended to 1154; after 1127 the work is more original and, consequently, more valuable as a source. In spite of his being a cleric, his work shows "a surprising weakness in [its] treatment of ecclesiastical affairs" (*English Historical*

Documents, ed. D. C. Douglas, 2 : 305).

Milton condemned Henry's *Historia Anglorum,* along with other monkish works he cited, for its inaccuracies and fancies, while at the same time acknowledging he had nothing better (*Brit* 10 : 180). Often Milton used information not found in the other chronicles, although it is clear that he did not altogether trust his source (*Brit* 10 : 224). He did accept Henry's evidence for the massacre of the Danes by Aethelred (*Brit* 10 : 257). Fogle notes several conjectural details that Milton used (*Yale Prose* 5 : 162n). His textual source was Sir Henry Savile's* edition, *Rerum Anglicarum Scriptores post Bedam* (Frankfurt, 1601). [RMa]

HERBERSTEIN, BARON SIGISMOND VON, author of a *Commentaria Rerum Muscovitarum,* cited as an authority on Russian history by Thuanus* in his *Historia,* from which Milton cites a passage on divorce* in *CB.* His attention may have been drawn to this material by his reading for his own *Mosc,* but no mention of the book appears there. [WBH]

HERCULES: *see* MYTH AND MYTHOLOGY.

HERESIES, MILTON'S. Given the nature of Protestantism, the word *heresy* might be considered a misnomer for Milton's deviations from orthodox Calvinist* doctrines and traditional Christian belief, yet used in a loose sense it is helpful in describing some of the ideas and issues that continue to be of concern to students of his ideas.

Milton's own views of heresy are distinctively Protestant. In 1673 *TR* concluded a lifetime of religious polemics by defining heresy as "a Religion taken up and believ'd from the tradition of men and additions to the word of God" instead of from the word itself (6 : 167). *CivP* in 1659 had said virtually the same thing, and *CD,* composed about the same time, calls "unjust and foolish" those who "stamp with the invidious name of heretic

and heresy whatever appears to them to differ from the received opinions without trying the doctrine by a comparison with Scripture testimonies" (14 : 13).

According to *CD,* untried received opinions were themselves heretical : "I had not even read any of the works of heretics, so called, when the mistakes of those who are reckoned for orthodox, and their incautious handling of Scripture, first taught me to agree with their opponents whenever those opponents agreed with Scripture" (14 : 15). The early essay *Ref* in 1641 had accused such arch heretics as Arius* and Pelagius* of being "no true friends of *Christ*" (3 : 10), but the latest, *TR,* defended their followers who based belief in Scripture (6 : 168). These so-called heretics were more to be praised than those so-called orthodox who clouded over the word of God with such jargon as "Trinity, Triunity, Coessentiality, Tripersonality," the language of schoolmen rather than Scripture.

Milton based his own faith on Holy Scripture illuminated by the Spirit that resides in all men. When Scripture and Spirit appear to conflict, the Spirit is the more reliable, since the text of Scripture is subject to human corruption. Given this individualistic basis, his work could easily reflect "a unique combination of semi-Arian*, Arminian*, Anabaptist*, anti-Sabbatarian, Mortalist*, semi-Quaker*, 'Divorcer*,' and polygamist*" views (Parker). Yet among his contemporaries the only one of Milton's heresies widely discussed was that respecting divorce on grounds of incompatibility alone. For this he was publicly damned in Ephraim Pagitt's *Heresiographie* (1645) and, indirectly, in Thomas Edwards's* *Gangraena* (1646). Both accused him of leading the (nonexistent?) sect they called "Divorcers." In 1652 also there were dark hints abroad that Milton was a Socinian* because, as censor, he had passed favorably on publishing the Socinian manifesto called the *Racovian Catechism*.* But Milton assured the Government that his imprimatur was wholly consistent with his principles in *Areop,* to give heretical writings light enough to make their errors glaringly obvious.

As an artist Milton used heresies for dramatic purposes, most notably in having Satan proclaim the Manichaean heresy that angels* were coexistent with God, or assert that he owed his being to Fate*, his immortal being to his own power —and in this exhibit himself as the "father of lies" beneath the surface glitter of his "virtue." Milton's contemporaries would not have confused Satan's words with Milton's beliefs. In fact, his beliefs were considered orthodox enough to establish him for two centuries as England's great Protestant poet. Anglican and Dissenter alike praised his great religious power, while orthodox and heterodox Dissenters held *PL* second in importance only to the Bible.

Publication of *CD* in 1825 put Milton's orthodoxy in doubt, but only briefly. It made quite clear that he had abandoned the Calvinist doctrine of predestination* as well as the fundamental view of the Trinity*, with the Son* equal to the Father*, and the Spirit* equal to the Son. *CD* asserted an even more daring departure in ascribing materiality to God and refusing to distinguish between spirit and matter*. It spoke of creation* as from a prime matter that derived somehow from God's own substance and could never be annihilated; thus (as Raphael explains in *PL* 5. 469–90) "body" and "spirit" referred to different degrees of refinement of the same first matter. This would mean, for example, that both body and soul die at the same time, to await resurrection together (*see* MORTALISM). Still, despite such departures from received opinion, *CD* caused only two years of popular controversy. Its heresies disappointed the orthodox, but even the most orthodox could find comfort in Milton's restating most fundamental points of Christian doctrine. Complaints about heresy generally arose from his alleged inconsistencies from strict orthodoxy (Kelley, *Huntington Library Quarterly* 31:38), while commentators accepted

his deviations as errors that did not destroy their high regard for him as man or poet.

Masson's *Life* stirred interest in Milton's heresies again with publication of its sixth and final volume in 1880. Reserving discussion of *CD* for his final pages, Masson summarized the document concisely with due emphasis on the heretical passages, at the same time explaining (without apology) that these opinions were probably not consolidated until late in Milton's life; that Milton spoke for himself and for no sect or denomination; that he belonged "most truly and properly to the great Puritan body of his countrymen" (6 : 840). In the process, Masson singled out passages that reflected heresies he listed as anti-Trinitarianism, materialism, mortalism, pantheism, and anti-Sabbatarianism, as well as his polygamous, anabaptist, and millenarian* deviations. Though Masson's concern was chiefly biographical, he urged that *CD* could provide an aid to acute criticism, "an indispensable commentary to some obscure parts of [*PL*] by presenting in explicit and categorical prose what is here imaginatively assumed and even veiled" (p. 817).

Sixty years later in Maurice Kelley's *This Great Argument* (1941) *CD* received close scrutiny as a prose gloss on *PL.* Taking *CD* as synchronous with *PL,* Kelley tried to reestablish Masson's point that Milton's argument "is Christian, Protestant, and seventeenth century to the core" (p. 217). This restatement was necessary because many commentators had been spinning a legend about Milton as Leviathan swimming against the mainstream of his time. Inevitably, Kelley again singled out for reexamination those passages bespeaking Arminianism, Pelagianism, and especially Arianism.

For two decades thereafter, Kelley's discussion of these heresies attracted a host of commentators on Milton's religious thinking. One basic question making for controversy is whether *CD* is, as Kelley proposes, a faithful record of Milton's belief at the time he wrote *PL.* The opposite view insists that we have no way of dating at least the first fourteen chapters—including the alleged Arian fifth chapter—and they may just as easily be taken as having been written after *PL*.

Of chief concern, however, is Kelley's opinion that *CD* supports the notion that *PL* is an Arian, anti-Trinitarian document. In 1942, C. S. Lewis replied that generations of orthodox Christians well grounded in theology had read *PL* without being bothered by such heresy, so perhaps it was heretical only in modern eyes. And a decade later, Sister Miriam Joseph showed that *PL* could be read as a Trinitarian poem "in accord with Catholic dogma," thus supporting the position asserted in articles during the 1960s by William B. Hunter, Jr., and others. Hunter maintained that Milton's belief was not Arian but rather closer to that of early Church Fathers, who saw the Son as subordinate and in some respects inferior to the Father, deriving his being and divine gifts in some manner from the Father yet still in a sense coeternal and consubstantial with Him. This belief, which had been revived in Milton's time by the Cambridge Platonists*, was never specifically condemned in Church council and was probably not considered heretical by Milton or anyone else.

Barbara Lewalski, however, disagrees with Hunter, holding rather that Milton's anti-Trinitarian statements reflect his view that God's essence is incommunicable, its attributes of Unity and Infinity nontransferable. In accommodating* Himself to human understanding, He makes himself known only through the Son, who is His image and His word. "Milton cannot be exactly classified in terms of any of the common Christological positions," she says. "He has indeed constructed his own system as he claimed." At the same time, C. A. Patrides, working out the differences between Milton's and traditional Christian theology, has shown that he "used traditional ideas in such a way that they were transformed into seeming novelties," and Roland Mushat Frye has proposed that such transformation was Milton's

art of "accommodating" God's ways to man's understanding.

F. E. Hutchinson has tried to skirt the issues raised by *CD*, asking whether such passages in *PL* as those on the Trinity would seem orthodox to one who had never read *CD*. He points out that the Creed* itself asserts that the Son is "equal to the Father, as touching his Godhead, and inferior to the Father, as touching his manhood." The New Testament speaks of the Son existing before the world was created, but concludes nothing with respect to his generation from all eternity. Milton's early poems are orthodox enough : *Nat* speaks of "Trinal Unity" in 1629; *Ref* celebrates "one Tri-personal Godhead" in 1641—while at the same time criticizing Arianism (3 : 10, 23, 25). *PL,* however, reads ambiguously if not inconsistently. One crucial passage (3. 303) introduces the Son sharing the Father's "high collateral glorie," and when the Son offers to become man the Father assures him that he will not forfeit his divinity (ibid.). When the angels praise the Father and then the Son, they echo Paul's description of Christ as "the image of the invisible God, the first-born of all creation," terms familiar to orthodox contemporaries, who would not have found them heretical.

When the Son next appears (5. 716), the Father has just declared him Vice-Regent, and yet seems to associate the Son with Himself on equal terms. The crucial expression now becomes : "This day I have begot" (5. 603). Again, this echoes a familiar text, the Second Psalm quoted in the Epistle to the Hebrews (1 : 5) : "For unto which of the Angels said he at any time, Thou art my Son, this day have I begotten thee?" But the epistle refers to the Son's exaltation rather than to the beginning of the Son in time, while the psalm refers to the king's coronation. *PL* could be read as referring to the exaltation also—especially since Abdiel later speaks of the Son as having created the angels (5. 832).

With *CD* available we now know that Milton read the word *begotten* in a double sense, the one literal with reference to the production of the Son, the other metaphorical, referring to the exaltation. Thus, in citing the epistle and similar texts on the Son, Milton tells us that they "relate only to his metaphorical generation, that is, to his resuscitation from the dead, or to his unction to the mediatorial office" (14 : 81). When *PL* places the exaltation not at the Ascension (as in the New Testament) but before the fall of the angels, this is apparently dictated by the dramatic need to give Satan and his followers an excuse for resentment and rebellion, "fraught with envie against the Son of God" (5. 661–62). Such free handling of theological belief, then, seems less a heresy than a part of the process of transforming them into artistic expression.

Besides the problems resulting from such artistic transformation, however, some problems result from Milton's exceptionally literal reading of Scriptures. This is especially true of his materialism noted earlier. G. M. Conklin proposes that it derives from reading the opening lines of Genesis to mean "create out of matter," signifying that God produced everything out of Himself—"One Almightie is, from whom All things proceed, and up to him return" (*PL* 5. 469). Creation, then, consisted of God's imposing form on formlessness. Aside from its implications with respect to the Trinity, this materialism also accounts for such heresies in *PL* as the providing angels with food (5. 401–43, 461–503) and sexual behavior (8. 615–29)—heresies that, as R. H. West points out, were so far from Scripture that Milton excluded them from *CD,* using them as artistic rather than doctrinal materials. At the same time, the materiality of angels has serious ramifications, related not only to the nature of God but to the nature of His grace* —especially touching predestination.

When *PL* asserts that man's nature parallels angel's nature (5. 535–40), the suggestion is that both are subject to God's election. *CD* says it is "more agreeable to reason to suppose that the good angels are upheld by their own strength no less than man himself was before his fall; they are called elect in the sense of beloved or excellent" (1 : 9). This emphasis placed upon man's part in his own salvation is distinctively Miltonic, and there is also a characteristic emphasis on divine grace—the hero of *PR* is led to the wilderness "by some strong motion" (1. 290); the hero of *SA* wakes from despair by virtue of "Some rouzing motions" (1382). Contradicting the orthodox Calvinistic position that God's decrees are absolute, Milton asserts that they are conditional; His will is supreme and its supremacy is moral, so that He is not more bound to punish than forgive; He has elected to salvation or reprobation only those whose final faith or disbelief He foresaw, and such foreknowledge, even though certain, does not necessitate the event (*PL* 3. 112–23).

Milton departs further from orthodox Calvinism in asserting that atonement is universal rather than reserved for the elect alone. He holds that salvation is conditioned by faith that lies within the will of all, and controverts the doctrine that man is absolutely depraved, thus incapable of any spiritual good. Depravity is rather a bias or natural inclination. Man's will being free*, he can choose between faith* and unbelief and thereby weight his own destiny. This emphasis on the high degree of freedom left to the human will after the Fall is the same as that of the Arminians.

Milton's emphasis is so strong on moral freedom as to make it central to his thought. *Areop* complains that to deny Adam power of choice is to make him a "mere mechanical Adam." One of the choruses in *SA* directly attacks the idea that God's will is absolute rather than conditional (293ff.); and the whole thrust of *PL* is to show that the Fall* itself created the opportunity for a new exercise of moral choice and consequent atonement and salvation.

Exercise of such choice applies to belief as well. If a painstaking study of scripture leads to views contrary to orthodoxy, then Milton would cherish his heresies rather than accept untried truths. Nor would he run from others' heresies: "that which purifies us is triall, and triall is by what is contrary" (*Areop* 4 : 311). The final arbiter would be the Spirit, "that Holy Spirit promised to all believers" (*CD* 16 : 261) in order to enlighten all men "really spiritual" (p. 274). Then, if professed believers who are really spiritual still differ among themselves, "It is their duty to tolerate such differences in each other until God shall have revealed the truth to all" (p. 266). Such a position has no room for heresy, much less for the variety of heresies that commentators have leached out of Milton's own work—in alphabetical order: Anabaptism, Anti-Sabbatarianism, Anti-Trinitarianism, Arianism, Arminianism, Divorcism, Materialism, Millenarianism, Mortalism, Nestorianism, Pantheism, Pelagianism, Polygamism, Quakerism, and Socinianism. Rather, he would look upon heresy in the same spirit as Archbishop Laud* who, when asked what Arminians hold, replied, "The best bishoprics in England." [PMZ]

HERMETICISM was a gnostic, theosophical view of life based on texts attributed to Hermes Trismegistus—Hermes the thrice-great, that is, *very* great—a semi-divine figure allied to Thoth, from Egyptian mythology. The texts are in Greek and consist of individual tracts called, collectively, the *Pymander* (after the first tract), or the *Corpus Hermeticum*. Translated by Ficino in 1463 and published in 1471, the *Corpus Hermeticum* enjoyed great popularity in Renaissance intellectual circles until about 1625. Because the Hermetic vision of Creation and its views on the nature of man share images with scripture and Platonic works, the tracts were presumed to be the fountainhead from which Judeo-Christian theology and Greek philosophy flowed. The *Corpus Hermeticum* does not, however, set forth a systematic theosophy; different tracts depict man and matter negatively or positively. The Florentine

Academy exalted Hermeticism primarily for those passages which taught that matter is essentially spiritual and that man-as-*magus* can control the inherent virtues of matter.

The notions of *magus*-magic, along with belief in the religious authority of the Hermetic texts, prompted attacks by Christians throughout the fifteenth and sixteenth centuries. In 1614 Isaac Casaubon systematically analyzed the contents and style of the *Corpus Hermeticum* and announced the tracts to be post-Christian and therefore forgeries of anything that could be attributable to the now "alleged" Hermes. Casaubon's work greatly diminished their appeal, and by 1630 Hermeticism's once-vaunted tenets had been generalized into the working vocabulary of young artists who used its ideas and images to support general notions of Neoplatonic* transcendence, consciousness in nature, and *magus* potentialities of gifted men.

Milton was apparently familiar with the Hermetic tradition. In *Idea,* Hermes is called "glorious for his triple name" (line 33) and full of "esoteric knowledge." But the reference merely adds Hermes to a list of other pagan sources for Plato's* notion of a human archetype. In *IlP,* the persona seeks isolation "in some high lonely Towr, / Where I may oft outwatch the *Bear,* / With thrice great Hermes" (lines 86–88). This reference is primarily an aesthetic detail in the context of the persona's transcendental musing. In *Rous,* Milton speaks to his book of poems about to be placed on Bodleian shelves : "Now at last I bid you look forward to quiet rest . . . in the blessed retreats provided by kind Hermes and the alert protection of Rouse" (line 77). Here the reference is to Hermes-Thoth as the patron of learning.

On subjects allied to Hermeticism —Egypt, alchemy, and magic—Milton is sensibly guarded and generally orthodox. Egypt is a source of evil gods, *Baalim* and *Ashtaroth* (*PL* 1. 421); Egypt is also called "Fanatic" and seen as abused by gods in "brutish forms" (*PL* 1. 480–81). Alchemy in Milton's polemic works is synonymous with hypocrisy and deceit (*Ref* 3 : 56, and *Areop* 4 : 306), although in *PL* Milton grants alchemy qualified respect : "The Empiric Alchimist / Can turn, or holds it possible to turn, / Metals . . . to perfect Gold" (*PL* 5. 440–42). Milton views magic with similar ambivalence. As a phenomenon, magic exists; but its value is ultimately determined by the virtue of its possessor. Comus's magic dust deceived the Lady (*Mask* line 165); in the eyes of the Elder Brother, "unlaid ghost[s]" are associated with "magic chains" (*Mask* line 434). But the Lady has implicit magical potential to shatter Comus's "magick structures" with words prompted "by som superior power" (*Mask* line 800). In *SA*, Samson disavows any knowledge of black magic : "spells" and "forbidden Arts." But he calls his faith and new-found strength "Magic spells" from God (*SA* 1149, 1151).

Milton was influenced by Hermeticism insofar as it expressed positive views of man's ability to sympathize with the influences of the interlinked worlds of heaven and earth, and insofar as Hermeticism had prompted man to respect the sensuousness and integrity of God's Creation. From the discussion of angel's* love in Book 8 of *PL,* to the garden of Eden, to the healthy sexuality of Adam and Eve, to the banquet table in *Mask,* to the lusty springtime in *El* 5, Milton reveals his appreciation of the sensuous wholeness of Creation, although that value is never placed within specifically Hermetic contexts. Casaubon's scholarship and Milton's own faith in the essential supremacy of Christianity could never accord Hermeticism, by 1625, the same naive enthusiasm it had had in 1463 when it burst upon the Renaissance. [KK]

HERMOGENES of Tarsus, Greek rhetorician of the second century A.D. whose textbooks were influential for Byzantine and Renaissance rhetoric. In the opinion of Donald A. F. M. Russell (*Oxford Classical Dictionary*, 2d ed.), the *Progymnasmata* traditionally ascribed to

him is of doubtful authorship, and two of the four treatises in his *Ars Rhetorica* are spurious. Russell accepts *On Status* and *On Ideas* as genuine, but rejects *On Invention* and *On the Method of Gravity.* The recent study *Hermogenes and the Renaissance: Seven Ideas of Style* (Princeton, 1970) by Annabel M. Patterson lists significant editions and translations of the *Ars Rhetorica* between the Aldine edition in 1508 and the publication of Delminio's discourse on Hermogenes' *On Ideas,* along with translations and commentaries by Gaspar Laurentius for "all four parts" of the *Arts Rhetorica* in 1644.

The treatise *On Ideas* distinguishes seven principal "ideas" or virtues of style*, which Hermogenes finds exemplified in the work of Demosthenes. These are clarity, beauty, rapidity, *ethos,* grandeur, truth, and gravity. In *Educ* Milton includes Hermogenes along with other classical authorities (Plato* and Aristotle*, Demetrius and Cicero* and Longinus*) as teachers of the "rule" for a "gracefull and ornate Rhetorick*" (4: 286). In Milton's prose pamphlets Patterson detects a "frequent use of Hermogenic terms," as in the attack in *Apol* on ignorant clergymen who could not "distinguish the *ideas,* and various kinds of stile." [JMS]

HERODOTUS, Greek historian of the fifth century B.C., referred to as the "Father of History." His *History* has been faulted for not being accurate, and indeed he is often more interested in event and anecdote than in strict ordering of detail. Herodotus tends to be digressive and inclusive, providing summaries of popular knowledge and considerable information about the lives of great men, for he was writing history largely from a biographical point of view. He manages, however, to maintain a certain narrative continuity, and almost always to compel the interest of his reader. Milton considered him to be one of the ancient authors who could teach "what is suitable for the historian" (letter to Henry de Brass*, 12:103). Milton refers to him directly most often in *1Def,* and several parallels have been noted between Herodotus's *History* and passages in *PL.* Two are of special interest. Satan's flight through Hell to the throne of Chaos is like the gold-guarding griffins' pursuit of the one-eyed Arimaspi who steal from them *(PL* 2. 943–47). Milton retells the legend out of Herodotus (3. 116), implying that the griffin will be subdued by the sun god Apollo as Satan will be by Christ, a point made in Pierio Valeriano's *Hieroglyphica* (1613). Similarly, Milton's notion of winged serpents *(PL* 7. 484) goes back to Isaiah 30:6 and Herodotus (2. 75), and reflects the almost universal belief at the time in the existence of dragons and winged serpents. [JAR]

HEROIC VIRTUE is a technical term used by theologians to describe the practice of the natural and supernatural virtues to a degree of perfection that merits canonization. Pope Benedict XIV in his treatise on beatification and canonization defines it thus: the performance of "virtuous actions with uncommon promptitude, ease, and pleasure, from supernatural motives and without human reasoning, with self-abnegation and full control over natural inclinations." In a sense, it is an approach, through the victory of grace* over fallen nature, to the condition of Adam and Eve before the Fall*. There is no evidence that Milton had this technical definition in mind when he pictures Adam and Eve leaving the Garden of Eden hand in hand with all the battle of life before them. But his depiction of the new courage and the new heroic struggle of man against the power of Satan and sin* that his own disobedience* had released in the world has all the challenge of a new heroic ideal about it.

Aristotle* had previously defined *heroic virtue* as the practice of all the virtues to the degree that the practitioner becomes superhuman and godlike. And for Milton this notion of *heroic virtue* involved a practice of the natural and

supernatural virtues to such a degree of excellence that the practitioner becomes a true image of God. The Eternal Logos in the bosom of the Trinity* was, of course, for Milton the most perfect image of God. And Christ, the word-made-*man* was, therefore, the most perfect example of *heroic virtue.* In *PR,* Christ, active in time, especially in his repulse of the temptations of Satan, is shown practicing heroic virtue. In *PL* this concept of heroic virtue is revealed through a comparison and contrast of the three major characters. A good statement of how this works in *PL* is the following by John M. Steadman: "Since the Logos is the supreme exemplar of the godlike, Milton portrays in Messiah the divine archetype of heroic virtue. . . . In Satan, on the other hand, he discredits a conventional poetic conception of heroism by embodying it in a figure manifestly devoid of the 'essential distinction' of the hero; by this example he not only distinguishes genuine heroism from its counterfeit, but also defines true heroic virtue more clearly by describing its opposite. In Adam, finally, he delineates the original perfection of the divine image in man, its obscuration by sin, and its partial recovery through repentance and faith" (*Journal of the Warburg and Courtauld Institute* 22:105). [MBM]

HEROISM, CHRISTIAN AND PAGAN. The heroic in any age or culture is made up of the qualities for which the age or culture honors its great men. And what is considered as worthy of honor in great men shifts from age to age and culture to culture. Most cultures have embodied their ideal of human greatness concretely in their epic* heroes; and philosophers, from Aristotle* on, have attempted to define the qualities of human greatness, as their specific societies and cultures conceived them, in their definitions of the virtue of magnanimity*—the virtue* that is concerned with man's attitude toward his own honor and reputation. Hence a comparative study of epic* heroes and philosophical definitions of magnanimity provides an excellent index to the difference between the heroic ideals of one society or culture and another, and therefore, too, the difference between the ideals of a pagan and a Christian culture.

When such a study of epic heroes and philosophical definitions of magnanimity or human greatness in the chief cultures of the West is made, it becomes apparent that there is a great difference between what one or the other finds most distinctively worthy of honor in its great men. The Greek Achilles is not honored for the same thing that the Roman Aeneas is; and Beowulf, a Nordic hero in the Christian era, is honored for some qualities not found in either Achilles or Aeneas. There is an individualism and a self-centeredness in the Greek ideal that makes it possible for Achilles to insist on a redress of his honor from Agamemnon even at an exorbitant cost to the whole Greek army, and to be honored for his stand by gods and men precisely because, for the Greek, one's own reputation and fame were the highest goods in life. And hence, when Aristotle is discussing the qualities of the great-souled man (his magnanimous man), he remarks that, because he is preeminent in all the virtues, he cannot be excessive in his claims for recognition and honor. It is this unlimited egocentricity that constitutes the core of the pagan Greek heroic ideal.

The Romans looked at their hero somewhat differently. The state and ultimately the empire were too important to them to find untrammeled individualism the highest human good. Aeneas had to give up Dido to fulfill his mission of founding Rome. And Cicero's* analysis of magnanimity or greatness of soul in his *De Officiis* puts the concept of duty to the gods, to the state, and to one's fellow men at the heart of the matter. For the Christian the pursuit of honor, although for philosophers like St. Thomas Aquinas* a legitimate concern (St. Augustine* was less sure about it), had to be limited by a twofold recognition: first, that whatever one had that was deserving of honor he had from God and that therefore he had

to be *humble* enough to acknowledge that fact; and second, that he had been given what he had partly to use it for the benefit of others and not merely for his own self-aggrandizement and fame and that, therefore, he had to be *charitable* enough to use it in that way. The Christian precepts of humility and charity were definite limitations on the unlimited individualism of the pagan heroic ideal, especially in its Greek form.

When Milton came to write his heroic poem *PL,* he was well aware of the fact that he would have to reconceive and redefine the concept of the heroic if he was to write an epic with Adam and Eve as heroes. He sets about doing that explicitly at the beginning of Book 9 of *PL*. He admits that it is a "sad Task" to make heroes of Adam and Eve, who

brought into this World a world of woe Sinne and her shadow Death, and Miserie Deaths Harbinger.
(*PL* 9. 11–13)

But he goes on to say that this new epic theme is

Not less but more Heroic than the wrauth Of stern *Achilles* on his Foe pursu'd Thrice Fugitive about *Troy* Wall; or rage Of *Turnus* for *Lavinia* disespouse'd.
(9. 14–17)

It is worth noticing that he does not abrogate the Roman Aeneas but rather his opponent Turnus. Aeneas was fulfilling a duty to found a new Rome at some considerable sacrifice to himself, and, from Milton's point of view, he is close to his own personal and epical ideal. The positive new ideal of human greatness that evolves in the entire action of *PL* is an ideal built not out of the disobedience and the rebellious self-assertion of Satan but out of Adam and Eve's ultimate submission to the will of God, out of their humble and patient acceptance of the consequences of their own sin, and out of a new courage and hope based on the promise of a redeemer (12. 557–73, 581–605). But it is not only in the whole thematic development of *PL* that Milton redefines the concept of the heroic in Christian terms; he does so also explicitly in *CD* (2 : 9) where he defines magnanimity in almost the same terms as does St. Thomas Aquinas. In it he represents humility or the recognition of one's dependence upon God for everything one has as creating a necessary limitation on one's pursuit of honor and personal fame. And in *PR*, in which Christ's chief redemptive action is seen by Milton to reside in the example He gave of the new Christian virtues, Christ is represented, especially in His resistance to Satan's temptations to power and glory, as forthrightly questioning the unlimited pursuit of honor and glory as a rational and Christian ideal. (See *PR* 3. 21–38, 44–46, 60–64, 88–92, 121–48.) [MBM]

HESIOD. According to Edward Phillips and John Aubrey*, Milton taught the works of the Greek poet Hesiod (f. 850 B.C.) to his pupils; and Phillips's opinion that Hesiod was "a poet equal with Homer*" may reflect Milton's own high regard for Hesiod's most famous works, the *Theogony* and *Works and Days*.

Milton refers to Hesiod by name three times, twice in his academic *Prol* and once in *Educ*. In *Prol* 1 he quotes a line from the *Theogony*, "Of Chaos were Erebus and black Night born" (line 123); and in *Prol* 2 he speaks of "that divine sleep of Hesiod" which Milton conceived as the benefits of "intelligent and liberal leisure." As one of the pagan poets Milton recommends that students read in *Educ* (contrary to the prescriptions of two other prominent reformers, Vives and Comenius*), Hesiod will be easy and pleasant if read after sufficient practical experience in "natural knowledge," such as hunting, fishing, gardening, architecture, engineering, and anatomy.

In the *Works and Days*, Hesiod emphasized the practical pastoral life. His chief subject is farming and husbandry, though he occasionally describes the ancestry of those gods who helped influence the seasons and shape the geography* of the earth. Advice on farming

is mixed with gnomic commentary on life, and the last four hundred lines of the poem are devoted to a calendar recommending the best and worst days and seasons of the year in which to plant, plow, marry, or bear children, practical advice that Milton apparently thought valuable.

The *Theogony* is more interesting to a student of Milton's poetry. It is a genealogy of the principal Olympian gods and an account of the origins of the universe, the different wars between the gods before the creation of man and woman, the coming to power of Zeus, the wit combats of Zeus and the clever Prometheus*, the creation of Pandora, and the punishment of Prometheus and Epimetheus for Prometheus's theft of fire.

Milton may have borrowed from Hesiod's works a theory of divine poetic inspiration in sleep associated with the "great and holy mount of Helicon" (*Theogony*, Loeb ed., p. 79), the birth of Athena from the head of Zeus (p. 147), the laughter of Zeus (*Works and Days*, Loeb ed., p. 7), the idea of a Golden Age (p. 11), anti-military sentiment (*passim* in *Works and Days*), the name and stories of Pandora and Prometheus (*WD*, pp. 7–9; *Theogony*, pp. 117–25), Mnemosyne (p. 83), the Muses (pp. 83–88), Chaos and Night (p. 87), the Titans and Briareos (pp. 93–95), Atlas (p. 117), the Fates (p. 97), Echidna, half-woman and half-snake, who, like Milton's Sin, breeds many monsters (p. 101), Typhaon, the Chimaera, Cerberus, Hydra (p. 103), Leto, Hecate (p. 109), the wars between the Titans and the Olympian gods in which the Titans fall from Heaven for nine days (pp. 125–33), Tartarian chaos, the procession of Night and Day (p. 133), and the serpent-headed Typhaeus (pp. 139–43).

Many of these stories had been told by Homer* or were to be told again by Ovid*, Virgil* and others, but sometimes specific ascription is possible. Milton's extensive treatment of the war in heaven appears to owe much of its inspiration, apart from the Bible, to Hesiod's long episode describing the war of the Titans. And it seems probable that Milton had Hesiod's account of Prometheus, Epimetheus, and Pandora in mind when he compared Eve to Pandora (*PL* 4. 713–19; *DDD*) and Adam to Epimetheus (*DDD*).

The comparison of Adam with Epimetheus (whose name means "afterthought") is provocative, for it suggests that Adam did not fully understand the dangers that lay in Eve's "gifts." The comparison between Eve and Pandora can be pushed only so far, however, for unlike Hesiod's Pandora, Milton's Eve was not created as punishment for a prior offense and she is "more adorn'd, / More lovely then *Pandora*" (*PL* 4. 713–14).

Milton used Hesiod's long description of the war between the Olympian gods and the Titans in much the same way that he used the story of Pandora, as a classical story freely adapted to his own Christian purposes. Like other seventeenth-century writers, Milton appears to have been as familiar with Hesiod as he was with Homer, Virgil, and Ovid. But because much of what Milton could have read in Hesiod was also widespread mythological lore, it is difficult to know Milton's specific debt with any degree of certainty. [RCF]

HEXAMERAL TRADITION. Milton is the last great author in the hexameral tradition. The creation story in Book 7 of *PL* is a synthesis of elements readily found in the works of his predecessors when they elaborated upon the creation of the world depicted by Genesis 1 as occupying a six-day period (*hex*, six + *hemera*, day). The Old Testament and the New are singularly lacking in scientific information; Jahweh is an ethnic and ethical being rather than one who discloses facts about his universe. But the first chapter of the Bible* is "scientific" and it became for Christians the main repository of almost all scientific information transmitted directly by divine revelation. It was especially important furthermore in that John 1 had reinterpreted this information as the activity of the

Son, the creative Word, echoing the first phrase of Genesis : "In the beginning . . ." and asserting that without the Word "not anything was made that was made." Accordingly, early Christians annotated Genesis 1 extensively. The corpus of this literature is large; with almost every Father contributing to it, most topics were commonplace by the time of Augustine*. To elaborate and clarify the sketchy materials of Genesis, they drew upon cognate Greek traditions.

Almost all the hexameral writers are indebted to Plato*. Of special important is his *Timaeus*, in which he speaks of an omnipotent God whose goodness is the cause of the creation and whose agency is a Demiurge charged with bringing the world into actuality from patterns in the realm of the Ideal. Eternity*, as conceived by Plato, includes time*, which begins with the universe. The world, a single being, is bound together by a chain of love. Believing that Plato reflects Mosaic teachings (which he supposedly encountered while in Egypt), early Christians freely grant authority to his concepts. Augustine remarks that whether or not the teachings of Moses influenced Plato, of all the philosophers he was the closest to Christianity. Aristotle's primary contributions to hexameral literature are a simple geocentric descriptive astronomy, a physical system that proposes the generation of elements from primeval matter, and certain ideas about the animal and vegetable kingdoms. The Stoics introduce the theories that matter emanates from spirit and that the word or logos begins in the wisdom of the gods. Philo Judaeus* in *De opificio mundi* suggests that the creation was an instantaneous act and that all creatures throughout time derive from seminal *logoi* present from the moment of creation*. All of these ideas appear in the hexameral tradition, and readers of Milton will recognize in them some of the tenets basic to his theology.

Among the Christian Fathers in the hexameral tradition who have ideas with which Milton agrees (this is not, of course, to imply indebtedness) are Theophilus of Antioch, Origen*, Basil*, Gregory of Nazianzus, and Augustine. Thus, like Milton, Theophilus of Antioch thinks of the Logos as God's agent in the creation. He argues that the beasts became inimical only after and because of the Fall of Man*. Origen asserts that the logos is the invisible creator of the invisible Heaven, that the Son* is the logos manifested to the angels*, and that Christ is the Son incarnate among men, the *theanthropos,* God-man, a new being partaking of the natures of God and man. Basil, perhaps the most influential of early hexameralists, maintains that the angels were created before the world, that the sun is a body designed to absorb light, which had earlier been created, and that the purpose of the biblical "waters above the firmament" is to insulate the universe from fierce extremes of temperature in the surrounding Chaos. Gregory of Nazianzus dwells upon God as living in an eternal present; past and future are known certainly to Him because they are present in His Wisdom. Augustine preaches a transcendent God, who because of His Goodness creates the universe uninfluenced by necessity. The list of ideas and authorities is endless. Probably Basil's *Hexameron* is the most important for the modern student, though because of their traditional nature none really evinces true originality.

Prior to the rise of the modern scientific spirit, the Renaissance produced its own hexamera, some besides Milton's Book 7 also being essentially literary. Italy had Tasso's* *Le sette giornate del mondo creato* and France had Guillaume du Bartas's* *La Semaine,* translated into English couplets by Joshua Sylvester as the *Divine Weekes and Workes* to become one of the most popular and influential poems of the later Tudor and Stuart period. Milton certainly knew it; one line of *PL* is, in fact, a direct quotation from it. Rather typically, this long poem picked up in its turn an encyclopedic commentary by Simon Goulart, translated into English by Thomas Lodge. The earlier part of Ralegh's* *History of the World* offers yet another example. So, in a way, is Henry More's *Conjectura Cabbalistica.* Inasmuch as the hexameral literature is the stuff of early science*, it can be found in the work of such men as Gilbert, Dee, Swan, Maplet, and Fludd*. [HFR]

HEYLYN, PETER (1600–1662), Oxford B.A. and lecturer on geography*. Heylyn was ordained in 1624 and soon became a protégé of and spokesman for Laud* and the High Church position against the Puritans. With Laud he moved into power; with the Archbishop's collapse he too fell. He prepared the case against William Prynne* for having written *Histriomastix* and suffered at Prynne's hands as a result when the tables were turned. When war broke out he joined the king as a historian, chronicling current events in *Mercurius Aulicus.* The collapse of Charles* left him destitute, but he regained recognition and honor in 1660.

Heylyn was a bitter controversialist, academic in his attention to minutiae but well versed in church history and theological issues. Although Milton never mentions him or any of his writings (except possibly a translation of a collect for St. George's Day), the antiprelatical tracts show intimate knowledge at least of the tradition that Heylyn was arguing, and Heylyn was to some extent embroiled in the Smectymnuan* controversy in his defense of episcopacy. His *History of Episcopacie* was published in 1642. It seems probable that Milton did not consider him sufficiently important or representative to warrant a personal response. It has sometimes been thought that Milton is indebted to either of Heylyn's geographical works, *Microcosmus* or its enlarged version, *Cosmography* (1657), for details of some of his descriptive material, like his statement that Mount Amara is "A whole day's journey high" (*PL* 4. 284), though in view of the commonplace nature of most such information specific ascription may be doubtful. [WBH]

HICKMAN, SPENCER: *see* PUBLISHERS.

HISTORIOGRAPHY, MILTON AND SEVENTEENTH-CENTURY.

When Milton undertook some of his more important historical writings in the 1640s, England had experienced what has been called a revolution in the aims, methods, and materials of historiography. (See F. Smith Fussner, *The Historical Revolution: English Historical Writing and Thought 1580–1640* [1962].) The groundwork for that revolution had been laid in the sixteenth century through the work of an assorted group of antiquaries, historians, chroniclers, editors, and collectors who recovered many of the primary materials basic to a new study of England's past and developed new ways of sorting and shaping those materials.

The great medieval chronicle tradition had spent itself by the sixteenth century, being absorbed and transformed in the Tudor chronicles of Hall, Grafton, Lanquet-Cooper, Holinshed*, and Stow*. Although these chroniclers showed admirable devotion to the glory of England, industry in amassing historical materials, and eagerness to satisfy a growing popular appetite for history, they lacked a clear principle of selection by which the factual could be separated from the fabulous, the important from the unimportant. They exerted insufficient judgment in distinguishing among conflicting sources and authorities, too often leaving the responsibility for choice to the uninformed reader. In the main the chronicles displayed little sense of structure, little of the concept of anachronism, and a dangerous tendency to perpetuate legends and stories that could not meet the new standards of accuracy or probability emerging in English historiography under the influence of continental theory and practice in the writing of history. (See F. J. Levy, *Tudor Historical Thought* [1967].) John Stow's *Summarie of Englyshe Chronicles* (1565), and *The Chronicles of England* (1580), later called the *Annales* (1592; continued by Edmund Howes, 1615, 1631), represent a use of chronicle materials more discriminating and accurate than most of his predecessors, a tighter ordering of accounts, but his efforts did not contribute so much to an enlarged understanding of English history as did his *Survay of London* (1598), for all its emphasis on local history. John Speed's* *History of Great Britaine* (1611) makes use of some of William Camden's* antiquarian research in the *Britannia* (1586; expanded in each of 6 eds. to 1607) and of some fresh manuscript materials in Sir Robert Cotton's library, but even so Speed's work, though a clear advance in judgment and organization over previous chroniclers, represents a culmination of the chronicle tradition rather than a new departure in the direction of a "modern" historiography. The suggestions toward a new historical attitude and method contained in such works as Polydore Vergil's *Anglica Historia* (printed at Basle in part in 1534 and 1546, in full in 1555) and Sir Thomas More's *History of Richard III* (written ca. 1514–1518) had little effect on the chronicle tradition, and it never survived the century as a respectable form of historical writing. The new materials made available through the efforts of antiquaries and collectors called for new methods of evaluating and organizing the records of the past.

John Leland (1506?–1552), librarian and antiquary to Henry VIII, was among the first of the men who made serious efforts to find and preserve the documentary evidences of earlier days. Through his efforts many of the books and manuscripts set adrift at the dissolution of the monasteries were reclaimed and placed in safe keeping. He traveled widely to study the topography and archaeological remains of the country, carefully noting down his findings. He had ambitious plans for recording the development of England's government, her institutions, her degrees and dignities. Though his ambitions were never realized in his lifetime, his outlines of projects and the raw materials he assembled were later useful to Camden in forming the *Britannia*, the greatest monument of antiquarian research in the period.

John Bale (1495–1563), playwright, polemicist, and church historian, was another who made strenuous efforts to reclaim and protect the documents in danger of being lost with the monasteries, documents so necessary to the historiographical advances made by later antiquaries and historians. William Lambarde (1536–1601) assembled a collection of ancient laws going back to Saxon times, which he published as *Archaionomia* (1568), and in *Eirenarcha* (1581) produced a pioneer study of the office of justice of the peace. His *Archeion*, not published until 1635, attempted a history of the high courts of justice in England. His *Perambulation of Kent* (1576) not only presented new historical materials but also provided illustration of a method by which the materials could be converted to historical use.

Archbishop Matthew Parker (1504–1575) through his substantial wealth and great influence assembled a magnificent collection of books and manuscripts, enlisting the efforts of such scholars as Bale, Stow, and Lambarde. In 1568 the Privy Council directed a letter "to all and singular" Her Majesty's subjects who possessed monastic documents to make them available to Parker's deputies. Parker appears to have directed his main efforts to collecting significant materials relating to early English church history, especially works in Anglo-Saxon*, with a view to supporting the developing Elizabethan ecclesiastical establishment. He promoted the revival of Anglo-Saxon as an asset to historical studies, and he maintained a set of clerks at Lambeth Palace to transcribe documents and to assist in editing medieval texts. Another powerful figure in Elizabeth's government, William Cecil, Lord Burghley, was not only a notable collector of historical materials but also a great encourager of Anglo-Saxon studies and of such important projects as Camden's *Annales* of the reign of Elizabeth, not published until 1615. John Stow (1525?–1605) not only aided Archbishop Parker and formed his own chronicle but he also spent most of his life and resources collecting printed books, legal and literary documents and charters, and transcribing old manuscripts and inscriptions dealing with history, archaeology, and literature. Through his friendships with many of the leading antiquaries of the day, his materials became available to a wide circle of scholars.

But the greatest of all the collectors was undoubtedly Sir Robert Cotton (1571–1631), who may have discovered his antiquarian tastes during his days at Westminster School under Camden. Soon after Cambridge he settled in London and began a lifetime of collecting manuscripts, books, coins, archaeological remains, and nearly every kind of evidence of the past. His acquisitions came mainly through his own energy and the generous expenditure of his personal wealth, although some of them seem to have come by prolonged "borrowing." Whatever the means used, he managed to assemble a library that was "national," not only in scope but also in its availability to nearly every scholar of note in the period. Camden, Selden*, Speed, Spelman*, Bacon*, Ralegh*—all made use of the resources in the library, and there can be little question that the rapid advances in historical studies could not have been made without Cotton's assistance.

The work of the collectors was handsomely supplemented by the industry of the editors of the period. At the beginning of the sixteenth century the only English medieval "historical" texts available in print were versions of the *Brut* and Higden's *Polychronicon*. It remained to an Italian, Polydore Vergil, to produce the first critical edition of an early English source, his edition of Gildas* in 1525. In the latter half of the century a substantial number of important texts appeared. Archbishop Parker was instrumental in the publication of the *Flores Historiarum* of "Matthew of Westminster"* (1567), the chronicle of Matthew Paris* (1571), Asser's* life of Alfred* (1574), and Thomas Walsingham's chronicle (1574). On the Continent, Jerome

Commelin* issued his *Rerum Britannicarum* (Heidelberg, 1587), which contained texts of Geoffrey of Monmouth*, Gildas*, Bede*, and William of Newburgh*. An earlier edition of William of Newburgh had appeared at Antwerp in 1567. Florence of Worcester* had been edited by Lord William Howard (1592) and appeared again with the *Flores Historiarum* of "Matthew of Westminster" at Frankfurt in 1601. Sir Henry Savile* edited one of the very important collections of medieval chroniclers in his *Rerum Anglicarum Scriptores post Bedam* (London, 1596; rev. ed. Frankfurt, 1601), which contained texts of William of Malmesbury*, Henry of Huntingdon*, Roger of Hoveden*, Aethelweard, and pseudo-Ingulf*. By the end of the century a very impressive number of prime medieval sources were widely available in print, not, to be sure, in impeccable texts but substantially opening up new vistas on English medieval history.

As early as the reign of Henry VII, with the cessation of the Wars of the Roses, the need had been felt for a new history of England, not only to justify and consolidate the Tudor dynasty, but also to do justice to the heroic qualities of the English past and to establish a respectable position for England among the nations of Western Europe. Henry VII's choice of an Italian, Polydore Vergil, to rewrite that history was not altogether fortunate. Polydore's *Anglica Historia* represents a worthy attempt to re-examine the materials of English history, including a healthy skepticism about some of the more prized legendary stories of early Britain, like that of Arthur*, but his efforts were interpreted by some native writers as an attempt to impugn the dignity and reliability of English history, and he was attacked vigorously. Henry VIII's break with Rome added urgency to the felt need to discover the true role of England in the history of Western nations, especially now as she found herself set off from the rest of Catholic Europe. John Foxe* in his enormously popular and influential *Acts and Monuments* (1563, and many subsequent editions; see William Haller, *Foxe's Book of Martyrs and the Elect Nation* [1963]) proposed the view that English history, rightly perceived, was the record of God's providence* in preserving true Christian faith among the English and in choosing Englishmen as prime instruments in the restoration of that faith among nations corrupted by the growing tyranny of Rome. Influential as Foxe's work was, even into the seventeenth century and beyond, in supporting both popular and official positions on the reformation of religion, its acceptance of some of the legendary elements of English "story," which were being increasingly subjected to close and skeptical scrutiny, rendered it unsatisfactory as an answer to the demand for a new secular account of the growth of the nation.

There were those who aspired to meet the demand for a new kind of history based not on the chroniclers' principle of reporting all available evidence but on the principle of judging the evidence and presenting only the residue of the most reliable information in a unified, coherent, and appropriately expressed form. William Camden's early plans for writing the new complete history of England, now clearly called for, were thwarted by his own professed sense of inadequacy to the task and by his absorption in more specialized projects, such as his account of pre-Conquest Britain in the *Britannia* and his annals of the reign of Elizabeth. Sir Henry Savile had the learning and scholarly instincts to undertake the desired history, but his energies were directed toward editing his *Rerum Anglicarum*, in producing an elaborate edition of Chrysostom*, and in translating Tacitus*. Sir Francis Bacon* had ambitions to become the new official historian of England, but failing to gain royal encouragement he limited himself to an account of the reign of Henry VII (pub. in 1622, but planned much earlier), which though narrow in scope provided a model for the new approach to the study of history through an analysis of the human agents involved in the political events of a limited period. The increasing tendency to concentrate on single reigns and lives as subjects of historical study is to be seen in Sir John Hayward's studies of Henry IV (1599), his lives of the first three Norman Kings of England (1613), and his account of Edward VI (pub. posthumously in 1630). Lord Herbert of Cherbury's history of Henry VIII (begun in 1632 but not published until 1649) is another example of the closer focus that came to characterize historical writing. As the historical evidence accumulated and was sifted, and as new methods of analysis became requirements in the handling of that evidence, the more remote were the chances that any one scholar would have both the courage and the competence to undertake the huge task of writing the new, comprehensive history of the nation, no matter how deeply felt the need for such a history.

In the late years of the sixteenth century and the early years of the seventeenth a group of men appeared who were influential in changing the direction, order, and methods of historiography in England. New critical standards were developed for evaluating known historical documents; new materials were sought and found, especially local municipal and ecclesiastical registers; and new avenues to a knowledge of the past were followed—coins, archaeological materials of all sorts, geography*, and etymology. The Elizabethan College of Antiquaries (fl. 1586–1607), made up of lawyers, historians, chorographers, record keepers, and heralds, assiduously explored the origins of England's cultural past, her offices, her laws, her great families. (See Linda Van Norden, "The Elizabethan College of Antiquaries," diss. [University of California, Los Angeles, 1946].) Camden, Spelman, Cotton, and Stow were among the prominent members of the group who were devoted to an intensive search of original documents and records in an effort to establish the factual truth about the origins of English customs and institutions. Although their interests were too narrowly specific to allow for a comprehensive view of historical process, yet their insistence on original research and the authentication of documents foreshadowed the scholarly methods that would inform future secular historiography.

Allied to the antiquaries' efforts were the genealogical studies undertaken by the College of Heralds to establish the true lines of noble families. The more ancient houses were jealous to preserve their degrees and honors, while the families who had risen to more recent prominence were anxious to secure a lineage as distinguished as possible. Pedigrees had been complicated by the redistribution of lands following the dissolution of the monasteries, by the common practice of promoting profitable marriages between families, and by the eagerness of some to claim relationship with distinguished families on the basis of a mere similarity of names. In the process of establishing family descents, the Heralds assembled and digested a vast number of historical records that illuminated not only family histories but also the histories of the counties with which they were associated.

In the early years of the seventeenth century the growing political conflicts between Parliament and monarch stimulated historical research into public records for the origins of laws and institutions, for precedents by which parliamentary privileges and royal prerogatives could be substantiated, and for evidence as to the nature of the common law, the powers of the courts, and the rights of free citizens. The importance of the political issues tended to increase both the quantity and quality of the research. The authenticity of documents was more closely questioned, philology became an important means of extracting precise meanings from accepted records, and the utility of historical evidence came increasingly to be measured in terms of its political relevance. The moral value of the study of history was never seriously questioned, but its immediate effects were seen more and more in terms of its usefulness in the contemporary political situation. Historiography became more secular, more "scientific."

The publication of medieval texts continued into the seventeenth century. Camden edited a series of ancient documents in his *Anglica, Normannica, Hibernica, Cambrica, a Veteribus Scripta* (Frankfurt, 1603), including Asser's life of Alfred, Thomas Walsingham's chronicle, and Giraldus Cambrensis. John Selden edited Sir John Fortescue's "De Laudibus Legum Angliae" (1616), and Eadmer's *Historia Novorum* (1623), and assisted Sir Roger Twysden* in *Historiae Anglicanae Scriptores X* (1652), which included Simeon of Durham*, John Brompton, Henry Knighton, Aelred, and others. Of special importance was Abraham Wheloc's* edition of Bede's *Ecclesiastical History* and of the *Anglo-Saxon Chronicle,* with Latin translation, in 1643, reissued the following year with Lambarde's *Archaionomia.* Matthew Paris was newly edited by William Wats in 1640. In the first volume of his *Concilia* of 1639, Sir Henry Spelman published a collection of councils, decrees, laws, and constitutions of the English church that opened new possibilities for the study of ecclesiastical history. But Spelman's real importance lies not so much in his preservation of early documents as in his pioneering work in the field of philology, the recovery of the original meanings of key terms in those documents. He made possible a new understanding of the feudal structure of medieval society, he encouraged the Anglo-Saxon studies of such men as Wheloc and William Somner, and his comparative study of English and continental law, aided by the findings of French legal humanists, was a major contribution toward recovery of the meaning of early English constitutional and legal history.

John Selden was another figure whose importance went far beyond the editing of texts. He shared with Spelman the conviction that philology was essential to a proper understanding of the records of the past. He insisted that the facts of history could be ascertained only within specific historical contexts and that the principles of coherence and relevance must be applied to the search for the truths of history. To him history was an autonomous, "scientific" body of fact, which should not be influenced by preconceived ideas of what should or should not be true. Empirical evidence subjected to a process of thought supplied the matter of history. The prime example of his methodology is his *Historie of Tithes* (1618), in which he examines the evidence as to how and under what circumstances tithes had in actual fact been paid in the past, rather than whether or not they were justified by divine or ecclesiastical law. In thus separating history from divinity he may have invited trouble from the authorities, but he never wavered from his conviction that the facts of his *Historie* were justified by the evidence. What anyone wanted to make of those facts was not the concern of the historian. This essentially "modern" conception of the function of the historian was exemplified in Selden's other studies of Britain's original inhabitants and of her laws, customs, and titles of honor. He disdained the study of antiquity when it became mere affectation and an end in itself, but he was also aware of the importance of antiquarianism as a means of expanding our understanding of the problems of both past and present. Through his immense learning in languages and linguistics, his clear conception of the value of empirical evidence, and his intellectual sanity and balance in reaching conclusions, he represents a radical departure from an older historiography, which viewed history as mere accumulation of events, or as primarily moral instruction, or as propaganda in support of a current cause or institution.

Selden's exacting new standards for historiography led him to single out two contemporary works of history as approved models. Camden's *Annales* of the reign of Elizabeth, published in 1615, is a fine example of the new "politic" history which sought to understand the workings of the state through a deep knowledge of causation behind the events. Using a wide range of official and unofficial documents, Camden presents an objective account of the development of state policies in terms of the personalities of the chief actors and of the international political situation. He is wary of conjecture in the absence of absolute evidence, but he also recognizes its usefulness in arriving at the how and why of events. He is perhaps too deferential for modern taste in respecting the secret counsels of princes and the moral concerns of society, but his insistence on empirical evidence and his intelligent holding to an informing purpose in his account produced an outstanding example of the new secular history emerging in the period. The second work approved by Selden was Bacon's *History of the Reign of Henry VII* (1622), which presumes to explain Henry's rise to power and the consolidation of his position in terms of personalities and the principles of statecraft. Although modern scholars have questioned his failure to verify his sources and his apparent misuse of those sources, Bacon's method of arriving at conclusions by examination of individual instances and his firm ordering of material to achieve clear organization represent a major advance toward a modern, secular historiography.

James Ussher*, Archbishop of Armagh, stands as one of the great scholars of the century. His *Britannicarum Ecclesiarum Antiquitates* (Dublin, 1639), known briefly as *De Primordiis*, applies to ecclesiastical history the same high intellectual standards as those evidenced by Bacon and Camden in secular history. By his exhaustive examination of basic records, his discrimination in determining authenticity, and his fine judgment in separating legend from fact, he produced an account of the early British church more reliable than any previous history. His *Annals of the World* (1658) is one of the curiosities of historical literature, presuming to date precisely the beginning of Creation on the night preceding the 23rd of October, 4004 B.C., but it represents a serious attempt to clarify chronology, so essential to the work of the historian.

Along with these broader historical developments went a growing interest in local history. Lambarde's *Perambulation of Kent* (1576) and Stow's *Survay of London* (1589) provided models for many subsequent regional histories: Richard Carew's *Survey of Cornwall* (1602); Sampson Erdeswicke's *Survey of Staffordshire*, begun in the 1590s but not published until the eighteenth century; Sir John Doderidge's *History . . . of Wales* (1630); William Somner's *Antiquities of Canterbury* (1640); and above all, William Dugdale's *Antiquities of Warwickshire* (1656). Local studies were not all of uniform quality, but all involved the industrious sifting of county and municipal records that might not otherwise have become available to more general historians.

The great increase in available historical materials and the notable advances in technique and method did not of course bring about a complete revolution in historiography. Strong strains of classical, medieval, and humanistic thought continued to make themselves heard in the historical writings of the period. Ralegh's *History of the World* (1614), although giving some stress to secondary causes and utilizing the practical wisdom of an experienced man of the world in interpreting historical developments, emerges basically as a study of the workings of providence in the affairs of men and nations and as a guide to present conduct through lessons learned from the past. It was widely popular in the century for its literary qualities and for its stress on the moral function of history, but it did little to advance historiographical thought. Samuel Daniel's *Historie of England* (1612; enlarged 1618) reveals a strong sense of the classical idea of recurrence, an almost fatalistic acceptance of man's subservience to fortune, and a conviction of the unchanging qualities in human nature. Daniel shows little awareness of (or at least sympathy for) the new principles that were radically altering the practice of historical writing and research in the period. A survival from the old chronicle tradition was Sir Richard Baker's *Chronicle of the Kings of England* (1643), a purely derivative compilation that was nonetheless very popular, having gone through nine editions by 1696 with continuations by Edward Phillips, Milton's nephew.

The outlines of a fully modern historiography were not, of course, completely drawn by 1640. The Civil Wars, with their questioning of the principle of sovereignty and their questing for a principle of justice based on natural rights and the law of reason, obviously produced major changes in thinking about political theory and the value of historical precedent. (See J. G. A. Pocock, *The Ancient Constitution and the Feudal Law* [1957].) But the directions for the future had been clearly indicated by such men as Camden, Spelman, Bacon, and Selden. The new complete history of England had not appeared, partly because the very intensity of the new methodology made a work of such immense scope seem beyond the grasp of any one historian. But the lack of such a history was a matter of concern to scholars throughout the century. As late as 1695, Sir William Temple, in the preface to his *Introduction to the History of England*, could complain that the nation had not produced a single good general history of England. The new methods seemed to require such concentration on lives, reigns, and parcels of history that the whole design could not be attempted by a single writer.

When in the 1640s Milton set himself the task of writing the history of his own country, he intended to trace it from its origins down to his own day. Before he got to the formal writing of that history, however, he used his growing historical knowledge, gained from his research into original sources mainly in the period 1640 to 1644, to buttress his arguments in the antiprelatical tracts and to some extent in *Areop* and the divorce pamphlets. In *Ref.* his first published tract, he seems to regard history essentially as the record of God's ways and works among men, and the pattern he discerns in English history from its origins is a series of divine punishments in successive invasions by foreign powers, a period of intestine wars culminating in the Wars of the Roses, and finally a period of divine favor beginning with emancipation from Rome, confirmed by miraculous deliverances of England in the sixteenth century from threatened destruction, and climaxed by God's offered opportunity to the English to reform reformation itself and thereby fulfill their destiny to lead all nations to the recovery of truth and deliverance from the powers of darkness. Such a simplified pattern of the workings of providence in English affairs was not to survive Milton's intensive study both of England's past and of contemporary events.

When Milton began the writing of his *Brit* in the late 1640s his study had taken him beyond such chroniclers as Holinshed, Grafton, Speed, and Stow to the basic sources of English history—to Gildas, the *Anglo-Saxon Chronicle,* Bede, William of Malmesbury, and other writers made available in recent editions. He relied heavily on the work of the best of modern historians and antiquaries—Camden, Spelman, Selden, Ussher, Lambarde, Wheloc, and others. He was clearly well aware of the new materials available to an ambitious historian, although he may not have been fully aware of the new historiographical methods developed by the scholars who preceded him. He apparently felt no need to expand his knowledge of languages to Anglo-Saxon, since he quite clearly followed Abraham Wheloc's Latin translation of the *Anglo-Saxon Chronicle,* even in the mistakes Wheloc made. There is little evidence that he was concerned with philological problems in interpreting the texts he used. He does show a healthy skepticism toward some of the extravagances of Henry of Huntingdon, and he makes some effort to untangle the chronological difficulties in early records. He shows sound judgment in taking William of Malmesbury as the best of the medieval historians, and he displays respect for Bede and the *Anglo-Saxon Chronicle* as authorities on the pre-Conquest period. His caution in the use of sources has led Sir Charles Firth to sense something of the modern, skeptical temper in his attitude. (See *Proceedings of the British Academy* 3 [1907–08], rptd. in *Essays Historical and Literary* [1938], pp. 61–102.) Although he indicates a proper disdain for Geoffrey of Monmouth as an historian, he nonetheless uses mainly materials from Geoffrey for the first book of the *Brit,* wryly suggesting that at least rhetoricians and poets would know how to use them. He is properly skeptical of the Arthurian fables, as were most respectable historians by his time, although he can accept the fact of a historical Arthur. Finally, he exhibits little respect for the efforts of the antiquaries who in dealing with archaeological remains, ancient records, and place-names had provided quantities of material of great value to the historian trying to reconstruct the life of a past age. Milton seems to have had no awareness of the concept of anachronism, of the fact that language changes with the passage of time, that moral values may vary from age to age. To him, conditions in England in the fifth century on the withdrawal of the Romans could be seen as having close and meaningful correspondences to the situation during the Civil Wars of the 1640s; the qualities of Englishmen had not changed, the moral standards of judgment had not changed. Milton was conditioned to see history in terms of his humanist and classical upbringing.

Milton's conception of historiography was a characteristic blend of classical and Christian elements. From classical writers, notably Polybius and Sallust, he took his ideas and models for the manner and style of writing history; from his Christian background he derived the purpose of history, which was to show the workings of providence in human affairs; and from both sources he drew the notion that the prime end of history was instruction, whether in statecraft, in a knowledge of human motives in action, or in morality. As Milton undertook his history of Britain he saw his endeavor as "that which hitherto hath bin needed most, with plain, and lightsom brevity, to relate well and orderly things worth the noting, so as may best instruct and benefit them that read" (1670 ed., p. 3). The emphasis on brevity and on "things worth the noting" indicates his dependence on classical principles of historiography; the emphasis on instruction reflects Christian humanist views of the function of history.

Milton's essay in formal history in *Brit* may be seen, then, as a characteristic Miltonic blend of the traditional and the innovative. His views of the manner and matter of history were shaped by his devoted reading of the classical historians, Sallust primarily, but also Cicero*, Tacitus, Polybius, Lucian and others. For the function of history he drew on the long and honorable tradition, stemming from classical times and coming down through the Renaissance, that it was instructional both in public and private life. He could use the most advanced scholarship for the tools of historical endeavor, but he never wavered in his conviction that the uses of history were moral in the deepest sense. Whether he was dealing with the events of his own day or with the records of a thousand years ago, he had to view them with moral judgment, as parts of a larger pattern, not as curiosities for scientific observation. And yet for all his conservatism and despite the great advances in historical scholarship in the later seventeenth century, it is an interesting fact that his account of pre-Conquest Britain was the best that could be found for the period in the composite *Complete History of England* (1706), promoted by John Hughes.

Milton's *Brit* was first published in 1670 and had gone through four editions by the end of the century. It retained its appeal even in the face of major advances in historiographical studies during the period. Fussner says (p. 109) that "English historical and antiquarian scholarship reached maturity in the years between 1660 and 1730." Detailed study of the period is to be found in David C. Douglas, *English Scholars 1660–1730*, rev. ed. (1951), in which "a long succession of highly distinguished Englishmen" are seen to have "brought to its proper culmination the best sustained and the most prolific movement of historical scholarship which this country has ever seen" (p. 13). The story of the progress made in those years cannot be sketched here, but it is clear that without the earlier work of the pioneers in historiography —Camden, Selden, Spelman, Ussher, and others—the advance into the modern period of historical studies would not have been possible. For further consideration see the edition of *Brit* in Yale *Prose 5*. [FF]

HISTORY OF BRITAIN, THE. Sometime between 1643 and 1648 Milton began work on *Brit,* his only fulfillment of his recorded interest in King Arthur* and King Alfred as possible subjects for epic* poetry. His reading for it was remarkably wide and distinguished by its careful examination of original authorities. Much of this research was done in 1639–1641, though actual composition was probably not started for several years. Milton's original plan seems to have been to write a brief, readable history of his country from the beginnings to somewhat near his own time. He saw his purpose to be "the good of the British Nation" (10 : 3) and set forth on his new and demanding task with a clear sense of the public value in lessons from the past. But there is little agreement among scholars about the year in which Milton began to write. W. R. Parker places the composition in 1648 after the completion of *Mosc* (*Milton,* 1 : 325) while French Fogle thinks it was probably begun sometime between 1645 and 1647 (Yale *Prose* 5, pt. 1, xxviii–xliii). There is considerable evidence that the opening of the third

book was written early in 1648. The parallels between the chaos in Britain after the withdrawal of the Romans and the political and religious turmoil of his own day probably led Milton to compose the Digression, published posthumously in 1681 as *Mr. John Miltons Character of the Long Parliament and Assembly of Divines in 1641,* which Parker believes was completed by the fall of 1648 (1 : 337). Milton was diverted from his efforts to give some coherent shape and organization to early British history by the swirl of history in the making. The historian became orator. Parliament called upon his rhetorical* skills to still criticism of the trial and subsequent beheading of King Charles* on January 30, 1649. Within two weeks of the death of the King, Milton had published *Tenure*. Before he became Secretary for Foreign Tongues* in mid-March, Milton had completed Book 3 and most of 4, but he was not to return to the British past until the 1650s, when he employed in the last pages of Book 4 the chronicle of Simeon of Durham*, which was published in Twysden's* *Historiae* in 1652. Just when after this book appeared he returned to *Brit* to write or rewrite the conclusion to Book 4 and finish Books 5 and 6 is subject to speculation. Parker implies that Milton resumed his labors and completed it in 1655 (*Milton* 1 : 464–68); Fogle suggests that Milton may have continued to tinker with the manuscript up to the time of its printing in 1670 (Yale *Prose* 5 : xliii). The work in any case represents an extension and employment of the scholarship of contemporaries like Spelman* and Twysden.

The finished *Brit* is divided into six "books." Book 1 deals primarily with the legendary stories of British antiquity, covering the period from Noah's Flood to the sixth decade B.C. The second book starts with the Roman Conquest of Britain, which Milton dates in 53 B.C., and continues to the fall of the Empire, 409 A.D. in Milton's scheme. Book 3 deals with the chaos that befell Britain after the departure of the Romans, covers the romantic stories of Arthur, and concludes with the established Saxon kingdoms at the end of the sixth century. The fourth book describes the advent of Christianity and presents the gradual consolidation of rule by the time of Ecgbert's accession in 827. Book 5 presents the reign of the Anglo-Saxon* kings from Ecgbert through Edgar, with careful attention to the military accomplishments of Alfred and passing acknowledgment of his literary achievement. The last book begins with the reign of Alfred's great-grandson, Edward the Younger, and proceeds through the fall of the Anglo-Saxon kingdom with the defeat of Harold II at Hastings in 1066.

Milton's *History* is a remarkable compendium of learning, derived from many sources. Book 1 was largely drawn from Geoffrey of Monmouth's* *Historia Regum Britanniae,* particularly as this text appeared in Jerome Commelin's* compendium, *Rerum Britannicarum . . . Scriptores* (Heidelburg, 1587). The Roman matter of the second book had its source in Caesar's* *Commentaries,* but the specific edition that Milton used is not known. Milton continued beyond Caesar's narrative with information he assembled from Tacitus's *Annals,* Geoffrey's *Historia,* and Bede's* *Historia Ecclesiastica Gentis Anglorum.* The text of Bede was included by Commelin in his anthology, but Milton also used the text brought out by Abraham Wheloc* (Cambridge, 1643). In addition to Bede, Wheloc's edition contained a text of the *Anglo-Saxon Chronicle,* which became a major source for *Brit* in Book 3. Here Milton also relied heavily on Bede and on Gildas's* *De Excidio et Conquestu Britanniae,* which was also anthologized by Commelin. The *Chronicle* continued to be a major source throughout the rest of *Brit,* especially after the matter of Bede was exhausted in the middle of Book 4. Other early histories were heavily used: William of Malmesbury's* *Gesta Regum* (as it appeared in Sir Henry Savile's* *Rerum Anglicarum Scriptores* [Frankfurt, 1601]); Simeon of Durham's* *Historia Regum*

Anglorum et Danorum (as edited by Roger Twysden* in *Historiae Anglicaniae Scriptores X* in 1652); Matthew Westminster's* *Flores Historiarum* (as edited by Matthew Parker, and published in 1601). Milton supplemented the chronicle accounts of the age of Alfred with information from Asser's Life of Alfred (as it appeared in William Camden's* *Anglica* [Frankfurt, 1603]) and wisely examined the point of view of the Danish historian Johannes Pontanus (*Rerum Danicarum Historia* [Amsterdam, 1631]) when he described the Danish invasions. Milton also used other sources for particular pieces of information, among them: Henry of Huntingdon's* *Historia Anglorum,* Florence of Worcester's* *Chronicon ex Chronicis,* Orosius's* *Historiarum adversos Paganos,* and the history of Crowland, supposedly by Ingulf* the abbot (as printed by Savile in 1601).

Throughout his work Milton was deeply aware of the parallels between past events and problems of contemporary England. As he worked on Book 3, the problems of a disintegrated British society following the collapse of the Roman Empire seemed strikingly relevant to the bungling of the Long Parliament in a Britain suffering from the erosion of traditional authority. Milton digressed from the steady progress of his narrative to explore the nature of the 1641 Parliament and the 1643 Westminster Assembly* and to relate their shortcomings to a British failure to heed the lessons of their own past. This digression was removed, however, when *Brit* was published in 1670. Milton's reason for omitting the digression is cloaked in ambiguity. Whether the decision was reached solely to strengthen the narrative line of Book 3 or to avoid trouble in getting by the Licenser has been a matter for speculation ever since it was printed in the "Toland edition" of the prose in 1698. Fogle argues persuasively that Milton probably decided that the arguments written in the late forties had already been effectively made in work published long before 1670 (Yale *Prose* 5: 409–10).

The *History of Britain,* with a subtitle: *That part especially now call'd England. From the first Traditional Beginning, continu'd to the Norman Conquest. Collected out of the antientest and best Authours thereof,* was first published in 1670 in small quarto by J. M. for James Allestry at the Rose and Crown in St. Paul's Churchyard (Wing M2119). Some copies of this same edition were printed by J. M. for Spencer Hickman at the Rose in St. Paul's Churchyard and bear the date 1671 (Wing M2120). Modern scholarship is divided on the exact relationship of the various issues of this first edition but all evidence points to a continuous process of correction as the edition went through the press. From an examination of some sixty extant copies of the first edition, Fogle concludes that the random correction process renders no single state more "correct" than another (Yale *Prose* 5:lii–liii; Constance Nicholas, *Introduction and Notes to Milton's History of Britain* [1957] is an excellent source of information on the entire publication history).

An errata sheet that was made a part of the first edition was used as a guide for a second edition, published in 1677 and 1678 in octavo. The 1677 copies were printed by J. M. for John Martyn at the sign of the bell in St. Paul's Churchyard (Wing M2121); those bearing the 1678 date were printed by J. M. for Mark Pardoe for sale at the Black Raven, near Bedford House, in the Strand (Wing M2122).

Brit appeared next in a third edition in 1695. Although Harris Fletcher and Constance Nicholas have argued that this printing is but a reissue of the 1677–78 second edition (*CM* 18:646, and Constance Nicholas, p. 6 n12), Fogle has presented convincing evidence that it is a new edition (Yale *Prose* 5:1 n1). The title pages are clearly distinct from the first and second editions; some read: "Printed by *R. E.* for *R. Scot, R. Chiswell, R. Bentley, G. Sawbridge;* and are

to be Sold by *A. Swall,* and *T. Child,* in *St. Paul's* Church-yard (Wing M2124); others read "Printed for *Ri. Chiswell,* Sold by *Nath. Roles,* at his Auction-House in *Petty-Cannons*-Hall, near the North side of St. *Paul's* Church" (Wing M2123). But, more compelling, as Fogle reports, "there are differences in the running heads, in the spacing of many lines, in spellings, punctuation, marginal references, and substantial variants. . . . It is a different printing from a new set-up of type and is therefore a true third edition" (p. 1 n1).

The next edition of *Brit* to appear was in the 1698 *Works,* the "Toland edition," so-called because it contains John Toland's* biography of Milton. *Brit* (1 : 1–137) bears a separate title page dated 1694 with the notice "Published from a copy corrected by the author himself." This edition makes a substantial number of emendations and corrections, especially to amplify, in Book 2, the account of the Roman occupation of Britain. The substantive changes have generally been accepted by subsequent editors as Milton's and the "Toland" emendations and additions became the model for many subsequent editions. Notably, however, this edition was the last for some time to print "The Table" as a distinct index.

The strikingly original quality of Milton's *Brit* is his concern for sifting various historical records to grasp the final truth of an historical event. The early sections were particularly taxing in this regard, for much of the material could scarcely be considered more than legend. Milton was clearly sensitive to the value of myth and unflinchingly begins his narrative with the descent from Noah, as it is "generally beleev'd" (10 : 3), dismissing, however, "outlandish figments" (p. 4) that are not strictly concerned with the purported development of Britain. He openly states that he does not intend "to delay or interrupt the smooth course of History . . . with controversies and quotations . . . but shall endevor that which hitherto hath bin needed most, with plain, and lightsom brevity, to relate well and orderly things worth the noting, so as may best instruct and benefit them that read" (p. 3). The sense of the "smooth course of History" and the desire to tell what is "worth the noting" governs his entire work. Milton notes, for example, that the story of the Roman Conquest has been so well recorded by Caesar that it scarcely needs retelling; but, in order to keep the entire historical picture together, he retells it and the "many trivial discourses" of Roman military deeds are "best omitted" (p. 49). Although he labels the British descent from Brutus the "Trojan pretence" (p. 6), he still passes on this crucial story to his readers.

When the "smooth course" is difficult to perceive, however, Milton does not hesitate to share his doubts and problems with his audience. After outlining three years of King Alfred's wars against the Danes, he describes the original records as "set down so perplexly by the *Saxon* annalist, ill-guifted with utterance, as with much ado can be understood sometimes what is spok'n, whether meant of the *Danes,* or of the *Saxons*" (p. 220). Indeed, after his narrative of the events of 896, he openly states that "*Huntingdon* writes quite the contrary" (p. 219) but one record cannot prevail against a mass of evidence. More than once, the record must be confessed hazy. Milton manages to keep the flow of history valid and clear even when his sources on some points present a record "without coherence of sence or story" (p. 218).

Milton's sense of accuracy kept him from the usual narrative practice of inventing speeches that historical figures supposedly delivered at crucial moments. About halfway through Book 2 he states his policy quite clearly : "I affect not set speeches in a Historie, unless known for certain to have bin so spok'n in effect as they are writ'n, nor then, unless worth rehearsal" (p. 68). The imaginative construction of speeches in a history is "an abuse of posteritie, raising, in them that read, other conceptions of those times and persons then were true" (p. 68). When he found authentic utterances "worth reher-

sal," he did not hesitate to include them, as his presentation of the letter written to betray the sons of Queen Emma clearly shows (pp. 283–84). In spite of his loyalty and patriotism, he strenuously eschewed the historian's praise of nation "above truth," declaring such writers full of "inbred vanity" (p. 107). Milton's desire to discover the past and his unswerving devotion to the truth are also manifest in other stylistic features. As Parker has indicated (*Milton,* 1 : 340), Milton's model in *Brit* was Sallust*. The style is concise and relatively plain. While the normal syntactic patterns are often Latinate, the straightforward duty of historical exposition leads to a direct, occasionally simple expression. The author's delight seems to have come often from constructing vigorous descriptive phrases, not merely from orchestrating the rhythms of endless periodic sentences. Shortly after King Alfred's accession, the Danes forgot their oaths and returned, "dispeopleing the Countries round, dispossessing some, driving others beyond the Sea" (p. 213). The concept of slaughter is elsewhere described in close variation : London was "much ruind and unpeopl'd by the *Danes*" (p. 216); Canute's troops went into Mercia, "depopulating all places in thir way" (p. 269). The Saxon annalist cited above was pithily reduced as "ill-guifted with utterance" (p. 220). Parker judiciously cited (1 : 340) Milton's masterful description of the Britons who, to save their wives and children from the Roman advance, slew them "with a stern compassion" (p. 79).

Brit is clearly intended as a guide for national conduct. The last sentence admonishes the reader to remember the past in a more secure age but "to fear from like Vices without amendment the Revolution of like Calamities" (p. 316). This same idea is stated even more explicitly (though in a specific context) in the Digression : "For stories teach us that libertie sought out of season in a corrupt and degenerate age brought Rome it self into further slaverie" and that Britain, while full of courageous men, does not seem to be "over fertil of men able to govern justlie & prudently in peace" (p. 324). In the Digression Milton gave vent to his distress that the vital lessons of history for his own time had not been learned by Englishmen. Throughout the rest of *Brit* the same relationship between past and present is implied but specific applications are held in check. The devotion to historical truth, the careful evaluation of faulty and conflicting sources, the concern for a complete if brief record, and the efforts to achieve a concise descriptive style are all aspects of Milton's conviction that the narrative of national history has much to offer modern man, and detailed exempla are presented both to admonish and to inspire. Indeed, Milton's praise of Greek and Roman writers can be appropriately applied to his own accomplishment in *Brit* : "worthy deeds are not often destitute of worthy relaters : as by a certain Fate great Acts and great Eloquence have most commonly gon hand in hand, equalling and honouring each other" (p. 32). [RLC] [SHC]

CONTRIBUTORS TO VOLUME 3

AG	Ann Gossman. Texas Christian University, Fort Worth, Texas 76129.
ALS	Alice Lyle Scoufos. California State University, Fullerton, Calif. 92631.
AW	Austin Woolrych. University of Lancaster, Lancaster, England.
AWF	Albert W. Fields. University of Southwestern Louisiana, Lafayette, La. 70504.
BMB	Boyd M. Berry. Virginia Commonwealth University, Richmond, Va. 23220.
BW	Barry Wood. University of Houston, Houston, Texas 77004.
CAP	C. A. Patrides. University of York, Heslington, York, England.
DAR	Donald A. Roberts. Box 1077 Vineyard Haven, Mass. 02568.
DBC	David B. Carroll. California State University, Los Angeles, Calif. 90032.
DJD	Daniel J. Donno. Queens College, Flushing, N.Y. 11367.
EHD	Edgar H. Duncan. Vanderbilt University, Nashville, Tenn. 37235.
ERG	E. Richard Gregory. University of Toledo, Toledo, Ohio 43606.
FBY	Frank B. Young. University of Tennessee, Nashville, Tenn. 37203.
FF	French Fogle. Claremont Graduate School, Claremont, Calif. 91911.
FM	Frank Morrall. Carleton College, Northfield, Minn. 55057.
FRG	Frank R. Giordano. University of Houston, Houston, Texas 77004.
FSK	Frank S. Kastor. Wichita State University, Wichita, Kansas 67208.
GdeFL	George deForest Lord. Yale University, New Haven, Conn. 06520.
GHS	Gerald H. Snare, Tulane University, New Orleans, La. 70118.
GLM	George L. Musacchio. California Baptist College, Riverside, Calif. 92504.
HF	Harold Fisch. Bar-Ilan University, Ramat-Gan, Israel.
HFR	Harry F. Robins. University of Arizona, Tucson, Ariz. 85711.
JAR	James A. Riddell. California State College, Dominguez Hills, Calif. 90747.
JAW	Joseph A. Wittreich, Jr. University of Maryland, College Park, Md. 20742.
JMS	John M. Steadman. Huntington Library and Art Gallery, San Marino, Calif. 91108.
JHR	James H. Rieger. University of Rochester, Rochester, N.Y. 14627.
JTS	John T. Shawcross. City University of New York, New York, N.Y. 10031.

KK   Karl Kregor. Trinity University, San Antonio, Texas 78284.
MBM   Maurice B. McNamee, S.J. St. Louis University, St. Louis, Mo. 63103.
MM   Marian E. Musgrave. Miami University, Oxford, Ohio 45056.
NH   Nathaniel Henry. 200 East Horne Ave., Farmville, N.C. 27828.
PAF   Peter A. Fiore, O.F.M. Siena College, Loudonville, N.Y. 12211.
PMZ   Paul M. Zall. California State University, Los Angeles, Calif. 90032.
PRS   Paul R. Sellin. University of California, Los Angeles, Calif. 90024.
RC   Ralph Condee. Pennsylvania State University, University Park, Pa.
          16802.
RCF   Roy C. Flannagan. Ohio University, Athens, Ohio 45701.
RDE   Ronald D. Emma. Windham College, Putney, Vt. 05346.
RF   Robert Fox. St. Francis College, Brooklyn, N.Y. 11201.
RHW   Robert H. West. University of Georgia, Athens, Georgia 30602.
RLC   Rowland L. Collins. University of Rochester, Rochester, N.Y. 14627.
RMa   Rosemary Masek. University of Nevada, Las Vegas, Nev. 89109.
RMF   Roland Mushat Frye. University of Pennsylvania, Philadelphia, Pa.
          19104.
RRC   Robert R. Cawley. Late of Princeton University, Princeton, N.J. 08540.
SHC   Sarah H. Collins. Rochester Institute of Technology, Rochester, N.Y.
          14623.
SW   Susanne Woods. Brown University, Providence, R.I. 02911.
TAB   Thomas A. Brennan. University of South Alabama, Mobile, Ala. 36688.
TLH   Theodore L. Huguelet. Western Carolina University, Cullowhee, N.C.
          28723.
VRM   Virginia R. Mollenkott. William Paterson College, Wayne, N.J. 07470.
WAG   William A. Geiger, Jr. Whittier College, Whittier, Calif. 90608.
WBH   William B. Hunter, Jr. University of Houston, Houston, Texas 77004.
WM   Willis Monie. P.O. Box 105, Hartwick, N.Y. 13348.